The Global Financial Crises

Published by
ACADEMIC FOUNDATION
in association with

Institute of Public Enterprise

The Global Financial Crises

Challenges and Opportunities

Editors

R.K. Mishra and K. Trivikram

ACADEMIC FOUNDATION
NEW DELHI

www.academicfoundation.com

First published in 2013
by

ACADEMIC FOUNDATION
4772-73 / 23 Bharat Ram Road, (23 Ansari Road),
Darya Ganj, New Delhi - 110 002 (India).
Phones : 23245001 / 02 / 03 / 04.
Fax : +91-11-23245005.
E-mail : books@academicfoundation.com
www.academicfoundation.com

in association with

Institute of Public Enterprise, Hyderabad

Cataloging in Publication Data--DK
Courtesy: D.K. Agencies (P) Ltd. <docinfo@dkagencies.com>

The global financial crises : challenges and opportunities / editors, R.K. Mishra and K. Trivikram.
p. cm.
Contributed articles.
ISBN 9788171889846
ISBN 8171889840

1. Global Financial Crisis, 2008-2009. 2. Economic history--21st century. 3. International finance. 4. Financial crises--India. 5. India--Economic policy--1991- I. Mishra, R. K., 1948- II. Trivikram, K. III. Institute of Public Enterprise (Hyderabad, India)

DDC 330.90511 23

Typeset by Italics India, New Delhi.

Printed and bound by The Book Mint, New Delhi.
www.thebookmint.in

Contents

List of Tables and Figures

Tables

Figures

About the Editors/ Contributors

Editors:

R.K. Mishra, Senior Professor, Director and ONGC Subir Raha Chair Professor at the Institute of Public Enterprise (IPE), is a graduate of International Management Programme, SDA Bocconi, Milan, Italy. He has been a Fellow of British Council and Commonwealth Secretariat. He has had research stints at London Business School and Maison Des Sciences De L' Hommes, Paris. He has taught at the University of Bradford, United Kingdom and was a visiting Professor at Maison Des Sciences De L' Hommes, Paris. He is a member of the UN Task Force on International Task Force on Standards of Excellence in Public Administration and Education. He has been a management consultant to several organisations including Department for International Development (DFID), Deloitte, Adam Smith Institute, Asian Development Bank (ADB) and Centre for Good Governance. He has handled assignments for the Ministry of Finance, Ministry of Power, Ministry of Trade and Commerce, Ministry of Heavy Industry and Public Enterprises and Ministry of Finance (Department of Disinvestment). He is a member of editorial board of many international and national journals published. He has supervised doctoral research for several universities in public administration, management, economics, commerce. His current interests include: modernisation of state, civil service systems, financial administration, environmental administration, privatisation, state owned enterprises (SOE) reforms, restructuring, poverty management and good governance.

K. Trivikram (MA in Economics and PhD in Economics from Sri Venkateswara University) is a senior faculty member and programme coordinator of the PGDM as well as Executive PGDM at Institute of Public Enterprises, Hyderabad. He is also the Head of the School of Economics. He was formerly the Programme Director of MBA (PE) for the practising executives for nearly a decade. With more than two and a half decades of experience, he has conducted several consultancy and research assignments for Central and State Governments and international organisations such as World Bank, UNICEF and Department for International Development (DFID). He has designed and conducted a large number of management development programmes for Central and State level public enterprises for senior and middle-level executives, civil servants and corporate executives. He has published several research articles and working papers in national and international journals and books on skill development. He is the Editor of *Journal of Economic Policy and Research, IPE Journal of Management and the Journal of Institute of Public Enterprise* which is widely appreciated by distinguished scholars both from India and abroad. His areas of interest include: public enterprise policy, corporate governance, business environment and privatisation aspects.

Contributors:

Ray Barrell, Senior Research Fellow, National Institute of Economic and Social Research, London, United Kingdom.

Hans-H. Bleuel, Düsseldorf Universitätsstrasse, Düsseldorf, Germany.

Massimiliano Cali, Overseas Development Institute, London, United Kingdom.

Shaohua Chen, Senior Statistician, Development Economics Research Group, World Bank.

Adam Geršl, Czech National Bank and Institute of Economic Studies, Charles University, Prague.

Leo F. Goodstadt, Hong Kong Institute for Monetary Research, Trinity College, University of Dublin, The University of Hong Kong.

Dawn Holland, Senior Research Fellow, National Institute of Economic and Social Research, London, United Kingdom.

Srinivas Kolluru, Assistant Professor, IPE, Osmania University Campus, Hyderabad, India.

Zlatuše Komárková, Czech National Bank.

Isabella Massa, Overseas Development Institute, London, United Kingdom.

Ani Matei, Professor and Faculty of Public Administration, National School of Political Studies and Public Administration, Bucharest, Romania.

Lucica Matei, Professor and Faculty of Public Administration, National School of Political Studies and Public Administration, Bucharest, Romania.

Anna McCord, Research Fellow, Overseas Development Institute, London, United Kingdom.

Warwick J. McKibbin, Centre for Applied Macroeconomic Analysis (CAMA), Australian National University, The Brookings Institution and The Lowy Institute for International Policy.

Wayne M. Morrison, Specialist in Asian Trade and Finance Foreign Affairs, Defense and Trade Division, Congressional Research Division.

Maurice Odle, Economic Adviser to the Secretary-General, Caribbean Community.

Lucjan T. Orlowski, Department of Economics and Finance, John F. Welch College of Business, Sacred Heart University, USA.

Martin Ravallion, Director, Development Research Group, World Bank.

Andrew Stoeckel, Visiting Fellow, CAMA, Australian National University.

Milo Vandemoortele, Research Officer, Overseas Development Institute, London, United Kingdom.

Paul Vandenberg, International Labour Organization, Geneva.

Dirk Willem te Velde, Research Fellow and Programme Leader, Overseas Development Institute, London, United Kingdom.

Preface

The Great Depression of 1929 violently shook the entire world. The failure of banks in 1929 and the years that followed finally led to the collapse of the economies of several countries around the world. The economic philosophy of 'pump prime' was used as the palliative to cure the unhealing wound. The Asian economic crisis of 1997 reminded of the consequences of the 1929 Great Depression. However, temporary measures were taken to meet the crisis without putting in place a long-term perspective for a foreseeable global economic upheaval. The global financial crisis known as global meltdown came with a big bang in 2007 and continued to shake the world till 2009. The after effects of global meltdown are manifest in slow economic recovery, increase in the incidence of poverty, decline in public and private investment and more regulation.

The present volume makes an effort to analyse the causes of global meltdown, its specifics in various countries and the public policies adopted to tackle the global meltdown. The role of the central banks has been especially highlighted to examine the relevance of monetary and credit policies in such a situation. The various contributions in the book also deal with the fiscal policies adopted by the various governments to combat the global meltdown. Some case studies have been incorporated to show as to how the select countries formulated strategies and created a specialised institutional framework to deal with the global meltdown.

The authors are grateful to the individual contributors for their studies that have been included in this volume. The readers, researchers and policy makers may benefit from the conceptual framework and well-researched suggestions offered by the contributors to prevent the recurrence of such a crisis in future.

— R.K. Mishra & K. Trivikram

1 The Impact of Global Financial Meltdown on India's Macroeconomic Variables

R.K. Mishra, K. Trivikram and Srinivas Kolluru

Introduction

India's shift in macroeconomic policy framework during the 1990s with greater external and internal economic liberalisation laid a strong economic foundation and accelerated the growth. The reforms in fiscal policy, investment, trade, industrial, financial and banking sectors, helped the country to flee from the impact of Asian financial crisis in the late 1990s (Baru, 2009). The Indian economy has grown at an average annual growth rate of 3.6 per cent during 1960-1980, nearly 6 per cent during 1981-2003, and close to 9 per cent during 2003-04 to 2007-08. During 2003-04 to 2007-08, India has emerged as a significant player in the world economy by contributing substantially to both global output and growth. The period 2003-04 to 2007-08 witnessed the highest average growth rate ever achieved by India. Domestic savings and investment and lower average inflation rate contributed essentially to this dramatic growth (Reddy, 2010; World Bank, 2010). The further relaxation on foreign exchange restrictions in the capital account during the mid-1990s and investments from abroad made India's presence in the global economy. At the same time, the Indian financial sector was also strengthened by initiating reforms in the micro-structures, which promoted the operational efficiency of financial organisations and stability of financial markets (Reddy, 2010).

The collapse of Lehman Brothers and other 'Wall Street' investment bankers in September 2008 sent a wave of fear around world financial markets and the global financial meltdown affected the US, the European

Union (EU) and other emerging economies of the world including India (Govil and Singh, 2010; McKibbin and Stoeckel, 2009; Datt, 2009). The effect of the 2008 global financial meltdown has directly impacted upon some of the important macroeconomic variables and has been transmitted to the Indian economy through three diverse channels, such as the financial sector exports and foreign investment inflows. Though it did not have any impact on the Indian financial and banking sectors, since the sector was not overly exposed to the sub-prime crisis, subsequent global economic recession has had the effect of slowing down India's growth rate. The exports of goods and services constitute about 22 per cent of India's gross domestic product (GDP); the growth slumped quite sharply in the aftermath of the financial crisis. On the foreign investment inflows front, it has been observed that the foreign investment inflows have come down drastically.

Against this backdrop, the paper made an attempt to analyse the impact of the global financial crisis (GFC) on the Indian economy and the government's policy initiatives to position the economy back on the path of development. The paper is organised as follows: Section I looks into the background of the global financial meltdown and also delves into the reasons for the crisis. Section II focusses on the impact of the global financial crisis and resultant economic downturn have had on India. In this regard, the implications for the economic, social and development sectors will be examined. Section III studies the policy responses and recommendations of the central government and other apex regulatory institutions. The conclusions and main findings are summarised in Section IV.

I

GLOBAL FINANCIAL MELTDOWN: BRIEF BACKGROUND

The Concept of Financial Meltdown

The 19th and the early 20th centuries witnessed several financial crises linked with the banking sector and many recessions coincided with these meltdowns. The situations that are often called financial meltdowns include crashing of stock markets, bursting of other financial bubbles, currency crises and sovereign defaults (Kindleberger and Aliber, 2005;

Laeven and Valencia, 2008). In September and October 2008, as the world knows, the GFC intensified dramatically and affected the asset prices, credit availability and consumer and business confidence resulting in sharp declines in demand and production worldwide. The overview, nature and causes of the present financial crisis have been widely analysed and discussed by several researchers, economists and academicians across the world (Barth, 2008; Felton and Reinhart, 2008; Taylor, 2009). A group of both policy makers and research scholars, for instance, the de Larosiere Report (2009), the Turner Review (2009), the Geneva Report (2009), the Group of Thirty (2009) and the International Monetary Fund (IMF) (2009a), etc., are at work in analysing the causes of the crisis and finding both immediate and longer-term solutions (Mohan, 2009). It is also expected that many volumes and theses will also appear over the coming years explaining why the crisis was actually inevitable and why it should have been foreseen, had the world only taken note of these prior warnings (Naude, 2009).

Avgouleas (2008) averred that the global financial meltdown began in the US and the UK when the global credit market came to decline in July 2007 and started to show its effects in the middle of 2008. With the beginning of the crisis, the stock markets around the world have fallen; large financial institutions and bankers have collapsed. The governments in both the developed as well as the developing nations have had to come up with rescue packages to bail out their financial systems and institutions (Adamu, 2009). Adamu (2009) described that the financial markets have stumbled and slumped the world over: from London to Tokyo, Seoul to Sydney, Sao Paulo to Moscow, Bombay to Frankfurt etc. As Greenspan (2008) refers to this as 'once-in-a-century credit tsunami' and no economy in the world whether developed, emerging or developing is, so far, insulated from this debacle.

Nature and Causes

When the financial system creates bubbles, it drives up the cost of assets far beyond their true value in producing or storing wealth. When the bubbles burst, the value of the assets plummets. Those with ready cash then buy them up on the cheap. As Cook (2009) rightly asserted that when the dust settles more wealth gets concentrated in fewer hands and the rich get richer and ordinary people are left in a deeper condition of indebtedness, poverty and pressure to perform according to the liking of the financial majors. He also highlights that the same thing has happened in 2008 as the financial system has seemingly gone belly-up and is coming back only through massive government bailouts.

The financial crisis is the outcome of several diverse and multifaceted reasons, but largely can be attributed to a number of factors in both the housing and the credit markets, which developed over an extended period of time. Some of these include: unregulated environment, mortgage lending to subprime borrowers, inability to make their mortgage payments, speculation and overbuilding during the boom period, risky mortgage products, high personal and corporate debt levels, financial innovation (Stiglitz, 2008). Avgouleas (2008) also listed the reasons of the crisis as: breakdown in underwriting standards for sub-prime mortgages, flaws in credit rating agencies' assessments of sub-prime residential mortgage-backed securities (RMBS) and other complex structured credit products especially collateralised debt obligations (CDOs) and other asset-backed securities (ABS), risk management weaknesses of some large US and European financial institutions and regulatory policies, that failed to mitigate risk management weaknesses. Portes (2009) described that 'global macroeconomic imbalances were the major underlying cause of the crisis. These saving-investment imbalances and consequent huge cross-border financial flows put great stress on the financial intermediation process. The global imbalances interacted with the flaws in financial markets and instruments to generate the specific features of the crisis'.

In addition, speculations played an important role in causing the crisis. Traditionally, homes were not treated as investment like stocks, but this behaviour changed during the housing boom as it attracted speculative buyers. This makes speculation in real estate a contributing factor. During 2006, 22 per cent of homes purchased (1.65 million units) were for investment purposes, it means that nearly 40 per cent of home purchases were not primary residences (Wikipedia, 2008).

This speculative buying made housing prices to fall drastically. According to Crotty (2008), new financial architecture (NFA) is 'a globally integrated system of giant bank conglomerates and the so-called "shadow banking system" of investment banks, hedge funds and bank-created special investment vehicles (SIVs). This makes excessive risk to build up in giant banks during the boom; and the NFA generated high leverage and high systemic risk, with channels of contagion that transmitted problems in the US subprime mortgage market around the world.' The poor credit rating due to securitisation practices, credit rating agencies have the tendency to assign investment-grade credit rating to mortgage-backed securities (MBS), and this makes loans with high default rate to originate, packaged and transferred to others. Above all, the unregulated government policies fuelled by the US government mortgage policies which encouraged trends towards issuing risky loans caused the crisis.

The Model of the Crisis

Sen (2008) identified the roots of the financial crisis as the dominant force of uncertainty in financial markets (usually, which is ignored in mainstream economics) and the use of financial derivatives (largely with deregulation of financial markets). Figure 1.1 explains that the current financial crisis, which led to a global economic slowdown, is the product of several factors. Such are: irresponsible lending coupled with unregulated, risky financial and investment packaging and corporate greed. Roughly, this is how it started starting in the mid-to late 90s and, thereafter, collapsing in the years 2006-2008 of this millennium (NRBSL, 2008).

Sen (2008) described the approach to this crash as: (i) drop in property prices, which led to house owners failure to service debt, announce foreclosure of the mortgage deal; (ii) investment banks face losses due to non-payment by borrowers and losses are aggravated by sharp declines in ABS prices in the market and (iii) losses for other foreign investors who hold such assets. According to Sen (2008), the crash is captured by the following equation:

$$q = f(A, r) \qquad (1)$$

Where q is average return on ABS, A is average market value of ABS and r is the initial rate of average down payments on mortgaged houses. Where f'A and f'r are positive as long as ∂A and ∂r are both positive. Thus :

$$dq = r.\ f'A + A.\ f'r < 0 \text{ when } \partial A \text{ and } \partial r \text{ are both negative} \qquad (2)$$

Figure 1.1

Possible Links in the Sub-prime Crisis

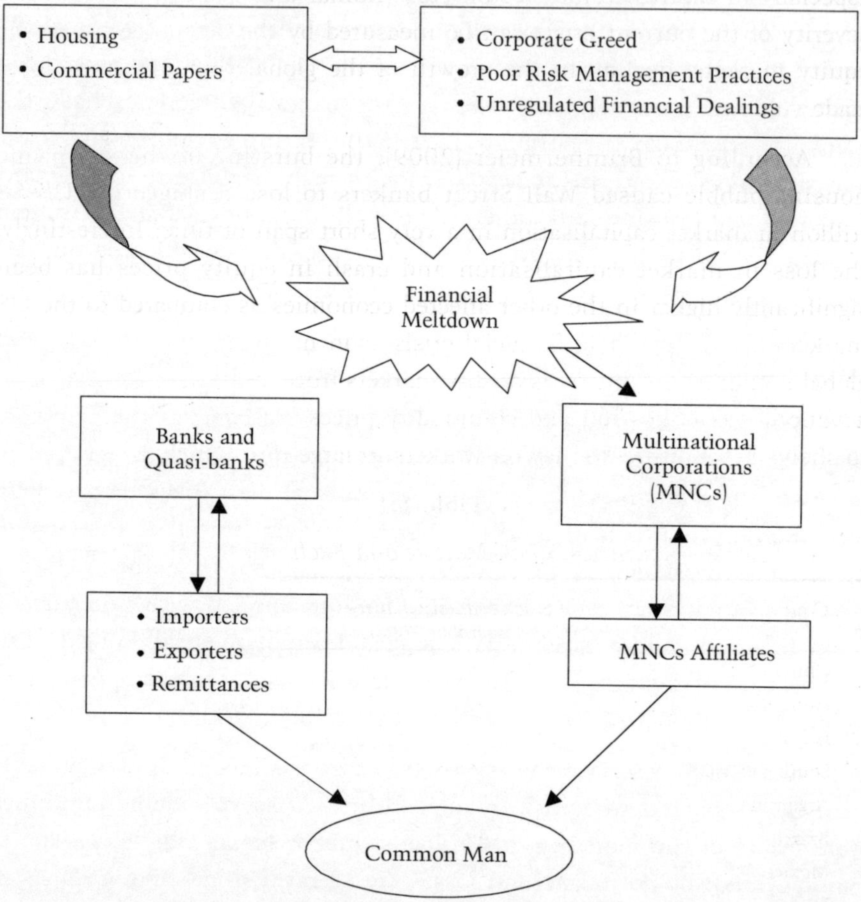

Source: Modified from NRBSL (2008).

As a whole, the crisis reflects a scene of systemic disaster with greed and miscalculation as is typical when it ends with an unreliable investment.

Severity of the Crisis Worldwide: A Brief Note

The recent financial sector crisis shares the most important features like search for increasingly higher yields in financial markets, a careless regulatory regime by the regulators, mismatching in appetite for risk and the capacity for bearing the risk, consequent buildup of asset bubbles especially in the real estate sector, etc., (Kumar and Vashisht, 2009). The severity of the current crisis can be measured by the steep decline in the equity markets, decline in the growth of the global economy and global trade volumes.

According to Brunnermeier (2009), the bursting of the sub-prime housing bubble caused Wall Street bankers to lose a staggering US $8 trillion in market capitalisation in a very short span of time. Interestingly, the loss in market capitalisation and crash in equity prices has been significantly higher in the other affected economies as compared to the US markets (Table 1.1). The financial crisis soon morphed into a full-fledged global economic downturn as credits markets froze, aggregate demand in all advanced economies fell and commodity prices crashed, forcing exporters to shelve expenditure and lay off workers in large numbers.

Table 1.1

Selected Countries Stock Market and Exchange Rate Changes

Countries	*% of Stock Market Changes (June-December 2008)*	*% of Exchange Rate Changes (June-December 2008)*
China	-48	1
Hong Kong	-40	1
India	-41	-13
South Korea	-36	-20
Argentina	-51	-13
Brazil	-49	-31
Mexico	-29	-26
Japan	-36	18
Euro Zone	-37	-11
The US	-36	–

Sources: Loser (2009); Asian Development Bank (2009).

The impact of the crisis can also be assessed from the IMF's forecast for the world economy. The IMF has revised its forecasts about four times from July 2008 to April 2009. In July 2008, IMF projected the growth rate for the global economy at 3.9 per cent for 2009, but in November 2008, it reduced to 2.2 per cent and further to 0.5 per cent in January 2009. Finally in April 2009, for the first time in 60 years, the Fund predicted a global recession with negative growth of 1.3 per cent for world GDP in 2009 (Table 1.2).

Table 1.2

Growth Projections by IMF

Countries	*GDP Estimates for 2009*				*GDP Estimates for 2010*	
	July 2008	*November 2008*	*January 2009*	*April 2009*	*January 2009*	*April 2009*
The US	0.8	-0.7	-1.6	-2.7	1.1	-0.04
The UK	1.7	-1.3	-2.8	-4	0.2	-0.4
Germany	1	-0.8	-2.5	-5	0.1	-1
Japan	1.5	-0.2	-2.6	-6.1	0.6	0.5
France	1.4	-0.5	-1.9	-2.9	0.7	0.4
Canada	1.9	0.3	-1.2	-2.5	1.6	1.1
Italy	0.5	-0.6	-2.1	-4.4	-0.1	-0.4
Russia	7.3	3.5	-0.7	-5.9	1.3	0.5
China	9.8	8.5	6.7	6.5	8	7.5
India	8	6.3	5.1	4.5	6.5	5.6
World	3.9	2.2	0.5	-1.3	3	1.8

Source: International Monetary Fund (2008, 2009).

Initially, the IMF projected a positive growth rate of 1.8 per cent for 2010 indicating a somewhat weak V-shape recovery. But by July 2009, this had changed and the possible recovery in 2010 was forecast to be much stronger. Because the recession in developed countries is expected to continue, developing countries are anticipated to lead the global turnaround (Kumar and Vashisht, 2009). Another worrying issue is the decline in the global trade (value of total merchandise exports plus value of total merchandise imports), which has experienced a historical collapse in 2009 (Figure 1.2).

World Trade Organization's (WTO) *International Trade Statistics 2010* highlights that the growth rate of global trade was 0 per cent in 2008 over 2007 (the same 15% growth registered in these two years). Furthermore, the WTO noticed a decline of world trade by 23 per cent in 2009, which would make it the biggest contraction in global trade.

Figure 1.2

Annual Growth (in Per cent) of Global Trade in Value

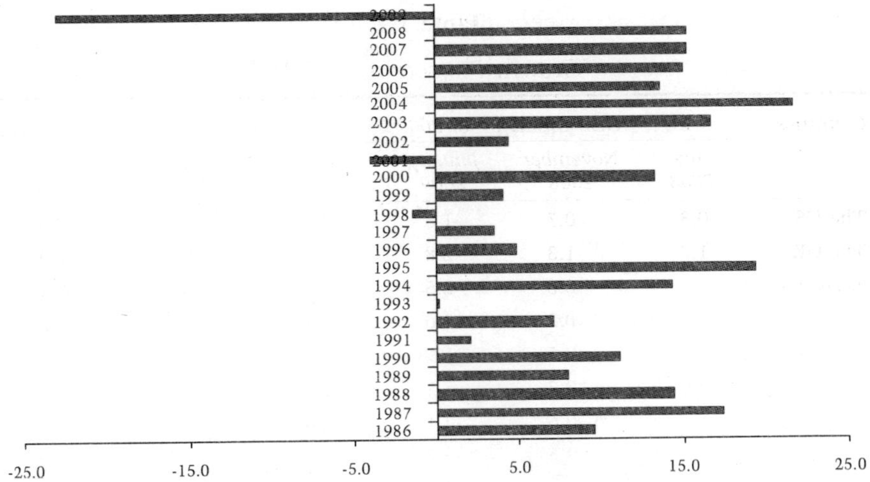

Sources: World Trade Organization, *International Trade Statistics 2010*.

Global Financial Crisis and Asia

Conceivably, globalisation is the key happening in the world economy over the last two decades, which led to develop a new structure of the world economy and has also some important implications for business cycles around the world. The increasing trade shares of two emerging countries in Asia, especially China and India, have led to faster global growth. Researchers like Kose *et al.* (2008), Akin and Kose (2008), He *et al.* (2007) described that despite the globalisation trend, business cycles in developed and industrial countries and emerging Asian economies have so far remained largely independent of each other, which they termed as decoupling of business cycles. IMF (2008) argues that the 2008 financial slowdown could have a larger impact on Asian economies than earlier global meltdowns due to the extensive trade and financial integration of Asian economies, especially with the USA. In addition to this, Hong *et al.* (2009) historically analysed that earlier worldwide financial crises often had overwhelming impacts on the Asian economies.

Asia has accounted for more than one-third of the world's economic growth, raising its share of GDP from 28 per cent to 32 per cent in 2007. China and India, which together account for almost 40 per cent of the world's population, have seen real per capita incomes rise more than 10-fold and three-fold, respectively, since 1980. It is widely agreed that a key source of Asia's rapid advancement has been the openness of countries in the region to global trade and finance (Bernanke, 2009). Owing to the 2008 financial meltdown and the worsening economic climate, Asian GDP growth slowed in the second half of 2008. For the region as a whole, the economic contraction in the fourth quarter of 2008 was pronounced, with activity falling at an annual rate of nearly 7 per cent. The declines were especially dramatic in Taiwan and Thailand (more than 20 per cent at an annual rate) and in South Korea and Singapore (more than 15 per cent at an annual rate) (Chhibber *et al.*, 2009). The World Bank data on exports of goods and services clearly brings out how exports growth slumped quite sharply in the aftermath of the financial crisis, turning negative across the region, especially in South and Southeast Asia (Figure 1.3).

Figure 1.3

Exports of Goods and Services from Asia (Annual Per cent Growth)

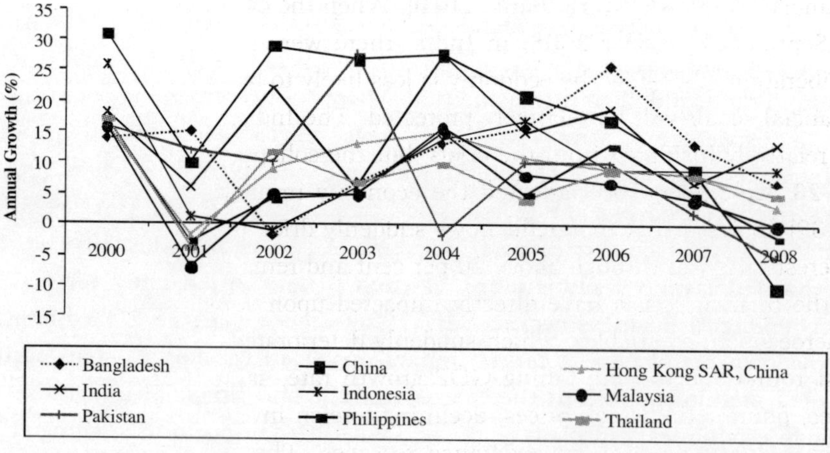

Source: The World Bank, *World Development Indicators 2010*.

Although the initial impact appeared limited, the global financial meltdown severely impacted Asian economies from late 2008 to early 2009. The region was directly hit when the crisis spread to the real sector and caused the volume of trade to collapse. According to the data from the World Bank (2010) and the IMF (2009b), the real GDP growth has declined in industrial Asia (Japan, Australia and New Zealand) from 3.2 per cent in 2007 to -2.3 per cent in 2009. In the case of Asia's newly industrialised economies (Hong Kong, Republic of Korea, Singapore) it declined from 5.7 per cent to -2.4 per cent. Even China and India were severely affected, with growth in those countries fall from 13 per cent to 8.5 per cent and from 9 per cent to 6.7 per cent, respectively. This is due to their openness, which made them vulnerable to the sudden collapse of global trade (Takagi, 2009).

II

IMPLICATIONS FOR INDIA

The Crisis and the Impact on Indian Economy

India, one of the South Asia's largest economies, has been facing critical challenges in the economic and the social fronts owing to the global financial meltdown (World Bank, 2010). When the crisis first broke globally in September-October 2008, in India, there were much discussions and deliberations that how the economy is less likely to be affected and how the financial sector will be relatively protected. The Indian economy looked to be relatively insulated from the crisis, but the collapse of Lehman Brothers on 23 September, 2008 affected the economy immediately. Kumar *et al.* (2009) analysed that the credit flows suddenly dried up and money market interest rates ran through above 20 per cent and remained high. The effects of the financial crisis have directly impacted upon some of the important macroeconomic variables, which suddenly deteriorated (Ghosh, 2009). The first round effects were falling GDP growth rate, savings and investment rates, plummeting stock prices, declining foreign investment inflows and a large reduction in foreign exchange reserves. The second round effects emerged from the slowdown in domestic demand and exports of goods and services. The domestic demand effects have been particularly severe in housing, construction, consumer durables and the information technology (IT) sectors. Exports of goods and services declined drastically during 2008.

Impact on the Basic Macroeconomic Variables

Economic Growth

India's growth picked up in 1992-93 and then moved to a higher trajectory of around 8.5 per cent from 2003-04 (see Figure 1.4). Debroy (2009) describes that this growth occurred due to the external environment on the one hand and increased consumption, investment and exports on the other.

Figure 1.4

Trends in India's GDP Growth Rate

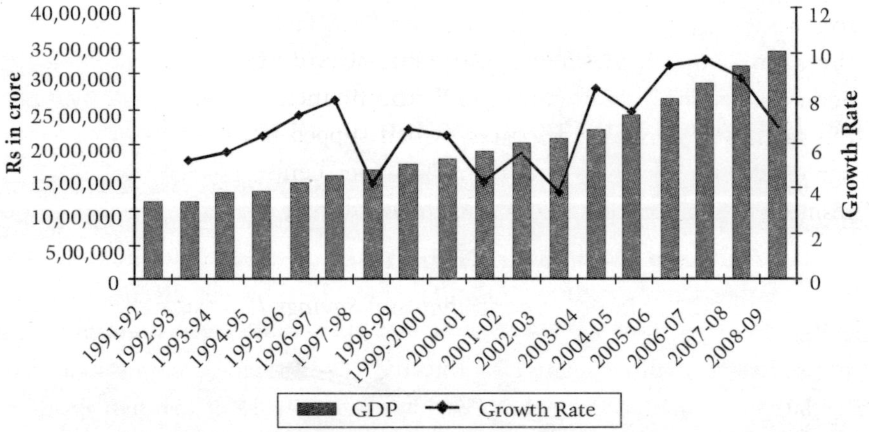

Source: Reserve Bank of India, *Handbook of Statistics on Indian Economy 2008-09*.

The impact of the recent financial meltdown on the Indian economy became evident when the economy grew by 5.8 per cent during the second half of 2008-09, which is significantly below the 9 per cent, recorded in the same period of 2007-08. In the financial year ending March 2009, the economic growth has slipped to 6.7 per cent from 9 per cent in the year ending March 2008 (Figure 1.4). At the sectoral level, the secondary sector in general and the manufacturing sector in particular performed extremely poor owing to the decline in the domestic and export demand. The manufacturing sector contracted by 0.3 per cent, while growth in construction slowed down significantly from 8.3 per cent to 5.5 per cent in 2008-09.

Another indication of the slowdown has come from the index of industrial production (IIP). According to the data from the Ministry of Statistics and Programme Implementation (2009), the IIP grew by 4.8 per cent in September 2008 as against 7 per cent in the corresponding period of 2007. The cumulative growth during April-September 2008 was only 4.9 per cent as against 9.5 per cent during the corresponding period in 2007.

Investment and Savings Rates

In India, during the pre-reform period, growth process was constrained by the 'two gaps'—a domestic savings gap and an external financing gap. After the liberalisation of the Indian economy in the 1990s, the economy caught up and the increasing domestic savings and investment rate have helped in bridging these gaps, thus contributing to higher economic growth (Figure 1.5). Generally economists believe that the recent increase in economic growth has been facilitated by a sharp rise in the savings and investment rates. But according to the data from the Economic Advisory Council (2009), the financial meltdown has affected the savings and investment rates, which slipped to 35.9 per cent from 38 per cent and 35.5 per cent from 37.4 per cent, respectively. This has resulted in the declining economic growth during 2008-09.

Figure 1.5

India's Investment and Savings Rates

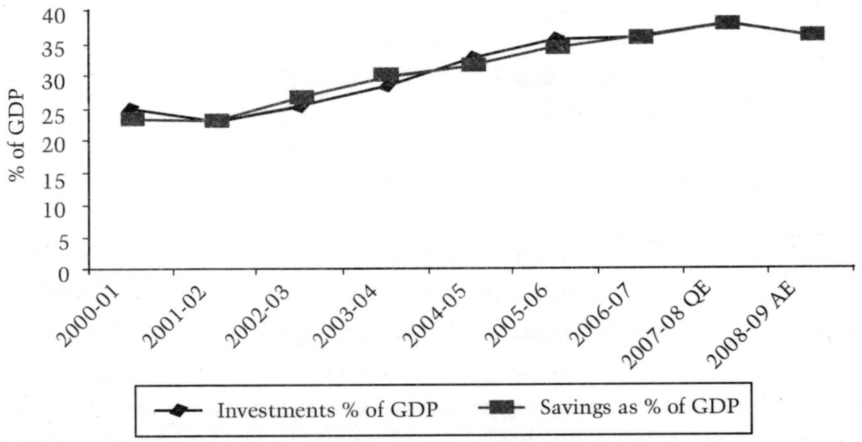

Note: QE indicates quick estimate and AE indicates an advance estimate.

Source: Economic Advisory Council to the Prime Minister, Government of India, 2009.

Stock Market Indicators

The stock markets across the globe panicked. India's stock markets witnessed a major collapse during October-November 2008. The impact of the crisis on Indian stock markets is evident from the falling business confidence expressed in the stock market indicators (Ghosh, 2009). The Sensex, shown in Figure 1.6, had reached historically high levels in the early part of 2008, capping an almost hysterical rise over the previous three years in which it more than tripled in value from about 7,000 points to approximately 21,000 points. But it has plummeted since then, with high volatility around an overall declining trend, such that its levels in early March were below the levels attained in December 2005.

Figure 1.6

Movements in the Stock Market

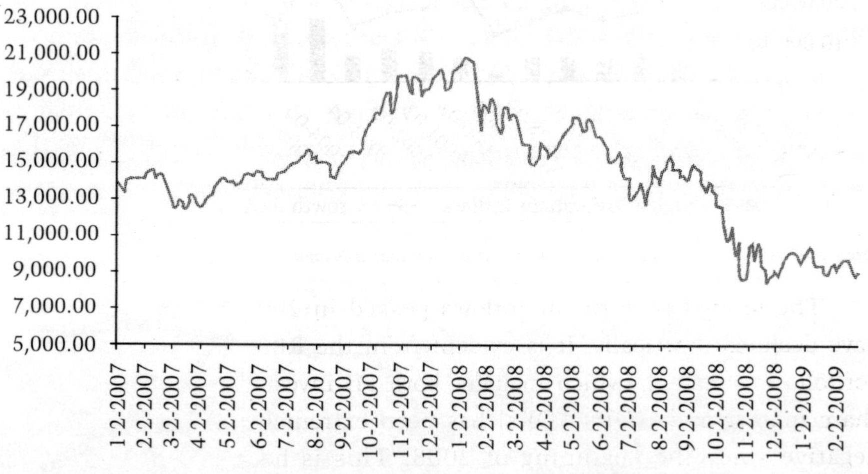

Source: Ghosh (2009).

Foreign Investment Inflows

Over the years, India emerged as one of the highly attractive destinations for foreign institutional investors, but due to the recent crisis, investors are eschewing investment opportunities in the emerging markets like India (Thomas, 2009). From 2003-04 onwards, the share of foreign investment in India's GDP has gone up and foreign capital inflows have increased drastically. One of the reasons for this growth could be higher remittances from overseas Indians. Figure 1.7 describes the changes in total foreign investment inflows (direct investment plus portfolio investment) and its growth rates over the period since 1992-93. A trend of increase followed by decline could be observed from Figure 1.7. The Reserve Bank of India (RBI) (2009) analysed that the direct investment has been more stable with relatively moderate fluctuations.

Figure 1.7

Foreign Investment Inflows, India

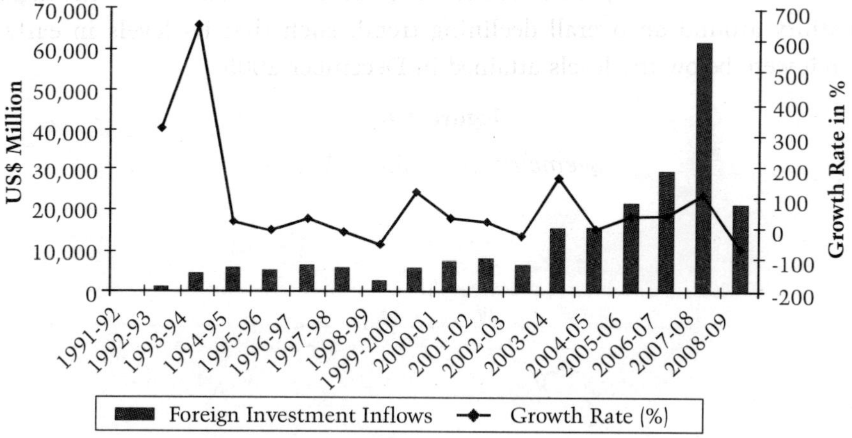

Source: Reserve Bank of India, *Handbook of Statistics on Indian Economy 2008-09.*

The foreign investment inflows peaked in 2007-08 and, thereafter, have declined drastically. It is evident from the RBI (2009) data that the portfolio investment (which includes both FII investment in the domestic share market and GDRs/ADRs) has been extremely volatile and largely negative since the beginning of 2008. This is because of the lack of confidence of investors worldwide on the markets and the negative trend in the portfolio investment dominated the overall foreign investment trend.

Foreign Exchange Reserves

India has been accumulating foreign exchange reserves since 2007. As a result of the domestic macroeconomic policies combined with the measures to prevent exchange rate appreciation to prevent the increasing domestic absorption, largely increased the reserves (Ghosh, 2009). The crisis also affected the country's foreign exchange reserves market. Figure

1.8 shows the steadily increasing of foreign exchange reserves since January 2007, which started declining after June 2008. The reasons for this decline could be attributed to: (i) a 20 per cent fall of rupee from end-April 2008 to November 2008, (ii) the RBI's intervention in selling dollars to smoothen the fall of Indian Rupee and (iii) the heavy selling, which led to massive decrease in the stock of reserves from US$ 315 billion in May 2008 to US$ 246 billion in November 2008.

Figure 1.8

India's Foreign Exchange Reserves

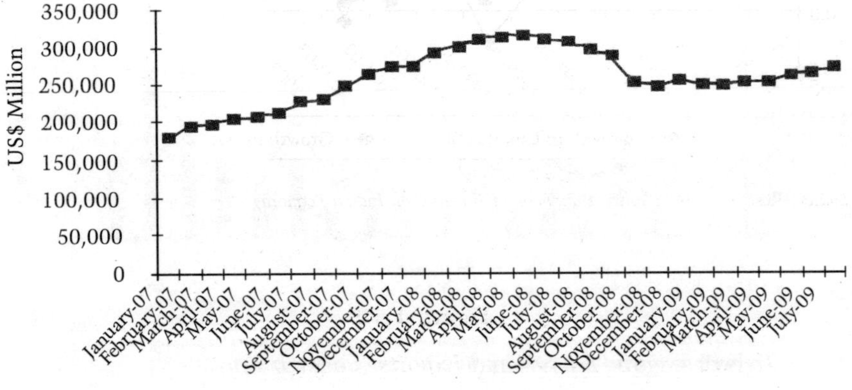

Source: Reserve Bank of India, *Handbook of Statistics on Indian Economy 2008-09*.

Exports Growth

The contribution of exports to GDP has risen progressively over the past 10 years from about 10.8 per cent of GDP in 1999-2000 to 29 per cent by 2007-08. But the financial slowdown in the developed world affected the demand for India's exports in their major markets. The current account of India's balance of payments had shown strong growth during the first half of 2008-09: merchandise exports grew by 35 per cent, imports by 45 per cent. But in the second half, the story has changed dramatically: merchandise exports declined by 18 per cent, imports by 11 per cent (Figure 1.9).

It has also been observed that there is positive correlation (0.46) between growth in exports and the country's GDP (Figure 1.10). For example, when between 1995-96 and 2002-03 the average growth rate in exports was less than 10 per cent, i.e., 9.5 per cent, then the GDP growth also averaged below 6 per cent.

Figure 1.9

Growth of Exports and Imports, India

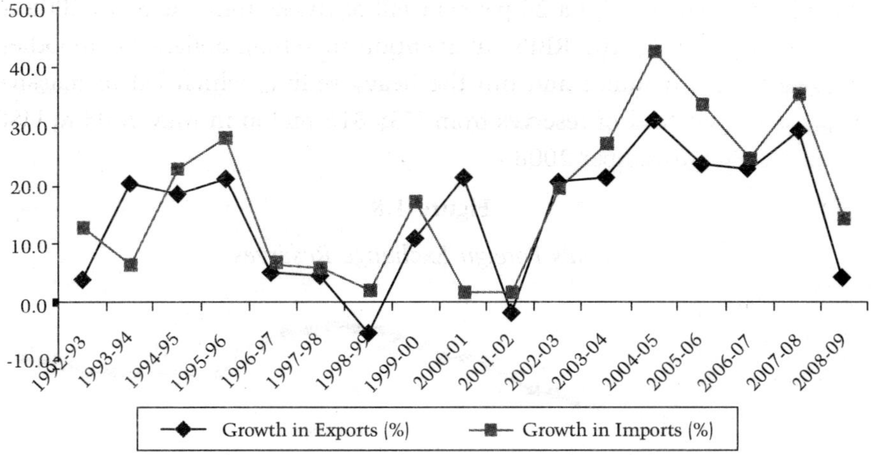

Source: Reserve Bank of India, *Handbook of Statistics on Indian Economy 2008-09*.

Figure 1.10

Trends in India's GDP and Exports (Growth Rate in Per cent)

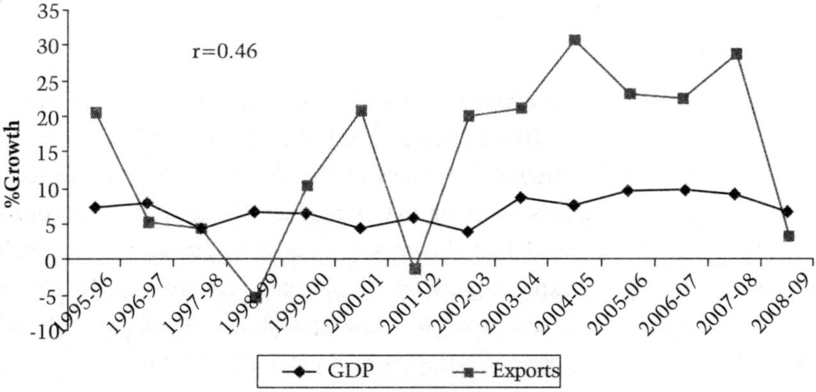

Source: Reserve Bank of India, *Handbook of Statistics on Indian Economy 2008-09*.

The Crisis and Social Impact on India

Impact on Employment

The financial meltdown and the deceleration in export growth have impacted the social development sectors in India. In this regard, the impact on employment was immediate. Since, close to 40-45 per cent of India's exports such as textiles, garments, gems and jewellery, leather, etc., originate from the labour-intensive small and medium enterprises. A quick fall in export growth could mean job losses in these sectors. Word Bank (2009) estimated job losses to the tune of 0.5-1 million between October and December 2008 in India, especially in the construction and small-scale export manufacturing sectors. Chhibber *et al.* (2009) pointed out that the crisis hardly impacted on the youth and older workers. The low-skilled immigrants in the sectors like construction and tourism were among the first to be laid off. Open unemployment and increasing underemployment initially affected the urban areas which were the major areas of factory employment.

The crisis also affected the cultivators, migrant workers and home-based workers severely (Ghosh, 2009a). The producers in the small-scale and medium enterprises in all sectors are being affected by the falling demand and credit crunch. The investments in the projects are being curtailed due to greater uncertainty.

III

POLICY RESPONSES AND CONCLUSION

After recognising the severity of the crisis by late 2008, the governments in both advanced and the emerging economies engaged in some fiscal expansions and announced various fiscal stimulus packages. Table 1.3 provides a schematic survey of the response policy packages in major countries and regions of the world. The countries like South Africa and China have announced mega-stimulus packages which account for about 24.0 per cent and 12 per cent of their respective GDPs. On the other hand, the US has announced a bailout-cum-stimulus package of worth US$ 8.1 trillion in absolute terms (Kumar and Vashisht, 2009). Kumar and Vashisht (2009) and Chibber *et al.* (2009) analysed that the stimulus packages of selected nine countries, such as the US, Japan, the EU, Australia, China, Korea, Chile, Mexico and India, combined comes to about US$ 10 trillion, which is roughly 20 per cent of the global GDP.

Table 1.3

Fiscal Stimulus and Support to the Financial System in Selected Countries and Regions (Per cent of GDP)

Country/Region	*2009*	*2010*	*2012*	*2013*	*Cumulative*
The US	2.07	1.55	1.04	0.52	5.2
Japan	1.46	1.1	0.73	0.37	3.7
The UK	1.32	0.99	0.66	0.33	3.3
Germany	1.38	1.04	0.69	0.35	3.5
The Euro Area	1.3	0.98	0.65	0.33	3.3
Canada	1.68	1.26	0.84	0.42	4.2
Australia	2.48	1.86	1.24	0.62	6.2
Rest of OECD	1	0.75	0.5	0.25	2.5
China	4.8	3.6	2.4	1.2	12.0
India	0.5	0.38	0.25	0.13	1.3
Other Asia	2	1.5	1	0.5	5.0
Latin America	0.5	0.38	0.25	0.13	1.3
Other LDC	0.5	0.38	0.25	0.13	1.3

Source: UNCTAD (2009).

Chhibber *et al.* (2009) interestingly pointed out that both the size of the fiscal stimulus and its composition are important in determining the output growth and the human development effects of the package. Chhibber *et al.* (2009) also highlighted that 'fiscal policy that provides more wage income directly to unskilled workers and in rural areas is likely to be much more effective in increasing aggregate incomes than other forms of public spending, because of the higher value of the multiplier in such expenditure'.

As a response to the financial crisis, the Government of India has taken highly proactive measures to stabilise the financial sector, ensure adequate liquidity, and stimulate domestic demand. Rapidly deteriorating economic situation of the country shifted the policy focus to monetary and fiscal measures. According to the RBI (2009), the government had announced fiscal stimulus packages by December 2008 to increase the aggregate demand. It is also estimated that India's two fiscal packages

Table 1.4

Policy Response of Indian Government

Particulars	*Responses*
Monetary policy responses	• Reductions in repo rates. • Reduction in cash reserve ratio. • Sale of foreign exchange (US dollar) through agent banks to augment supply in the domestic foreign exchange market.
Fiscal policy responses	• Economic stimulus package that includes additional government spending worth 200 billion rupees (US$ 4 billion), a cut on value-added tax, credit support for textile, leather, handlooms and other labour-intensive sectors and infrastructure financing.
Fiscal stimulus package	• Increase in planned expenditure and tax cuts (INR 200 billion) plus amount provided in the budget for 2008 but mostly unspent (INR 2,800 billion) (Total INR 3,000 billion, US$ 60 billion).
Proposed initiatives announced on 7 December, 2008	• Support to exports, textile sector, infrastructure, housing and SMEs. • Increase expenditure on public projects to create employment and public assets. • Interest rate cuts on loans for infrastructure and exports. • Cut of 4 per cent in excise duties across the board on all manufactured goods (except petroleum products).
Package to help realty and infrastructure sector announced on 2 January, 2009	• India Infrastructure Finance Company Ltd. permitted to raise funds to provide refinancing to public sector banks in the infrastructure sector. • External Commercial Borrowings policy liberalised to increase lending to borrowers in the infrastructure sector. • Countervailing duty and special countervailing duty reimposed on cement imports.
Tax cuts announced on 25 February, 2009	• Service tax cut across the board from 12 per cent to 10 per cent • Excise duty reduced by 2 per cent for items currently attracting 10 per cent.

Source: Chhibber *et al.* (2009).

together accounted for US$ 8.1 billion, which represent 0.7 per cent share of the country's GDP in 2008. The monetary and fiscal stimulus package placed greater emphasis on supporting the labour-intensive and export-oriented industries, ensured liquidity in the financial system, and encouraged investments in the infrastructure sector (Table 1.4). With all these policy initiatives of the government, it can be expected that there is a good basis for recovery of Indian economy in 2010.

Nevertheless, as was seen in the analysis of this paper, although the GFC originated in the US and spread to the EU, India could not escape from its adverse consequences too. This means that the unsustainable global imbalances played a significant role in bringing about the crisis. Long before the burst of the crisis, the economists, researchers, and academic scholars and observers suggested that India would benefit significantly from a more balanced growth strategy with a greater reliance on domestic demand, which enable towards meeting developmental goals.

References

Adamu, Abdul (2009). "The Effects of Global Financial Crisis on Nigerian Economy". (Available at SSRN: *http://ssrn.com/abstract=1397232*)

Akin, C. and M.A. Kose (2008). "Changing Nature of North-South Linkages: Stylized Facts and Explanations", *Journal of Asian Economics* 19(1): 1-28.

Asian Development Bank (2009). *Key Indicators for Asia and the Pacific 2009*. Manila: ADB.

Avgouleas, E. (2008). "Financial Regulation, Behavior Finance, and the Financial Credit Crisis in Search of a New Regulatory Model". (Available at SSRN: *http;//papers.ssrn.com)*

Barth, J.R. (2008). "US Subprime Mortgage Meltdown", Paper presented at the *14th Dubrovnik Economic Conference*, June 25. Dubrovnik, Hungary (Available at: *www.hnb.hr/dub-konf/14-konferencija/barth.ppt*).

Baru, Sanjay (2009). "The Global Economic Slowdown: Geopolitical Implications for India", *ASCI Journal of Management* 38(2): 1-34.

Bernanke, Ben S. (2009). "Asia and the Global Financial Crisis", Speech delivered at the Federal Reserve Bank of San Francisco's Conference on *Asia and the Global Financial Crisis*. Santa Barbara, California. October 19.

Brunnermeier, M.K. (2009). "Deciphering the Liquidity and Credit Crunch 2007-2008", *Journal of Economic Perspectives* 23 (1): 77-100.

Chhibber, Ajay, Jayati Ghosh and Thangavel Palanivel (2009). *The Global Financial Crisis and the Asia-Pacific Region*. Colombo, Sri Lanka: UNDP Regional Centre for Asia and the Pacific.

———. (2009). *Asia Rebounds But Lasting Recovery Needs New Paradigm: A Synthesis Study Incorporating Evidence from Country Case Studies*. UNDP Regional Centre for Asia and the Pacific. November.

Cook, Richard C. (2009). "The Nature of the Current Financial Crisis: The System is Designed to Exert Total Control over the Lives of Individuals", *Global Research*, May Issue. Canada: Centre for Research on Globalization (Available at: *http://www.globalresearch.ca/index.php?context=va&aid=13551)*.

Crotty, J. (2008). "Structural Causes of the Global Financial Crisis: A Critical Assessment of the 'New Financial Architecture'", *Working Paper No.* 180. Amherst: Political Economy Research Institute (PERI), University of Massachusetts.

Datt, Gaurav (2009). "Has India's Economic Growth become more Pro-Poor in the Wake of Economic Reforms?", *Policy Research Working Paper* 5103. World Bank.

Debroy, Bibek (2009). "Growth Downturn and its Effects", in Rajiv Kumar, Bibek Debroy, Jayati Ghosh, Vijay Mahajan and Seeta K. Prabhu (eds.), *Global Financial Crisis: Impact on India's Poor*. India: United Nations Development Programme. pp.14-24.

de Larosiere Report (2009). *Report of the High-Level Group on Financial Supervision in the EU* (Chairman: Jacques de Larosiere). Brussels.

Economic Advisory Council (2009). *Review of the Economy 2008-09*. New Delhi: Prime Minister's Economic Advisory Council, Government of India.

Felton, A. and K. Reinhart (2008). *The First Global Financial Crisis of the 21st Century*. A VoxEU.org Publication (Available at *www.voxeu.org/index.php?q=node/1352*)

Geneva Report (2009). "The Fundamental Principles of Financial Regulation", *Geneva Reports on the World Economy 11* (by Markus Brunnermeier, Andrew Crocket, Charles Goodhart, Avinash D. Persaud and Hyun Shin).

Ghosh, Jayati (2009). "The Global Financial Crisis, Developing Countries and India". (Available at: *http://www.networkideas.org/ideasact/jan09/PDF/Jayati.pdf)*

———. (2009a), "Global Crisis and the Indian Economy", in Rajiv Kumar, Bibek Debroy, Jayati Ghosh, Vijay Mahajan and Seeta K. Prabhu (eds.), *Global Financial Crisis: Impact on India's Poor.* India: United Nations Development Programme. pp.25-35.

Govil, Mani and Satyendra Kumar Singh (2010). "The Financial Tsunami and the Indian Banking Sector", *Journal of International Economics* 1(1): 83-94. Institute of Public Enterprise.

Greenspan, Alan (2008). "Greenspan: Economy in 'Once-in-a-Century' Crisis". Available at: *http://money.cnn.com/2008/09/14/news/economy/greenspan/*

Group of Thirty (2009). *Financial Reform: A Framework for Financial Stability* (Chairman: Paul A. Volcker). Washington D.C.

He, D., L. Cheung and J. Chang (2007). "Sense and Nonsense on Asia's Export Dependency and the Decoupling Thesis", *Working Paper* 03. Hong Kong: Hong Kong Monetary Authority.

Hong, K., J.-W. Lee and H.C. Tang (2009). "Crises in Asia: Historical Perspectives and Implications", *Journal of Asian Economies* 21(3): 265-79.

International Monetary Fund (2008). "Can Asia Decouple? Investigating spillovers from the United States to Asia", Chapter II, in *World Economic and Financial Surveys, Regional Economic Outlook: Asia and Pacific*. Washington, USA: International Monetary Fund. pp.27-41.

———. (2009). *World Economic Outlook*. Washington, USA: International Monetary Fund.

———. (2009a). "Initial Lessons of the Crisis", *IMF Lessons Paper*. Washington D.C.

———. (2009b). *Global Economic Outlook 2009*. Washington, D.C.

Kindleberger, C.P., and R. Aliber (2005). *Manias, Panics, and Crashes: A History of Financial Crises*. 5th Edition. Wiley.

Kose, M.A., C. Otrok and E. Prasad (2008). "Global Business Cycles: Convergence or Decoupling?", *Working Papers No.* 14292. National Bureau of Economic Research, Cambridge (Available at: *http://www.nber.org/papers/w14292*).

Kumar, Rajiv and Pankaj Vashisht (2009). "The Global Economic Crisis: Impact on India and Policy Responses", *ADBI Working Paper Series* No. 164. Tokyo, Japan: Asian Development Bank Institute.

Kumar, Rajiv, Mathew Joseph, Dony Alex, Pankaj Vashisht and Debosree Banerjee (2009). "Indian Economic Outlook 2008-09 and 2009-10", *Working Paper* No. 234. New Delhi: Indian Council for Research on International Economic Relations.

Laeven, L. and F. Valencia, (2008). "Systemic Banking Crises: A New Database", *International Monetary Fund Working Paper* 224. USA: International Monetary Fund.

Loser, C.M. (2009). "Global Financial Turmoil and Emerging Market Economies: Major Contagion and a Shocking Loss of Wealth?", *Discussion Paper*. Manila: Asian Development Bank (Available at: *http://www.adb.org/media/Articles/2009/12818-global-financial-crisis/MajorContagion-and-a-shocking-loss-of-wealth.pdf)*.

McKibbin, Warwick J. and Andrew Stoeckel (2009). "The Global Financial Crisis: Causes and Consequences", *Working Papers in International Economics* (November). Lowy Institute for International Policy.

Ministry of Statistics and Programme Implementation (2009). *Statistical Year Book India 2009*. New Delhi: Government of India.

Mohan, Rakesh (2009). "Global Financial Crisis—Causes, Impact, Policy Responses and Lessons", Speech delivered at the *7th Annual India Business Forum Conference*, London Business School, London, April 23.

Naudé, W.A. (2009). "The Financial Crisis of 2008 and the Developing Countries", *UNU-WIDER Discussion Paper* 2009/01.

NRBSL (2008). "The Global Financial Meltdown, Economic Crisis and Implications to Bank Operations", *NRBSL Business and Economic Briefer* (Available at: *http://www.nrbsl.com/archives/beb20081210.pdf)*.

Portes, Richard (2009). "Global Imbalances", in Mathias Dewatripont, Xavier Freixas and Richard Portes (eds.), *Macroeconomic Stability and Financial Regulation: Key Issues for the G20*. London: Centre for Economic Policy Research.

RBI (2009). *Handbook of Statistics on Indian Economy 2008-09*. Mumbai: Reserve Bank of India.

Reddy, Y. V. (2010). *India and the Global Financial Crisis: Managing Money and Finance*. London, UK.: Anthem Press.

Sen, Sunanda (2008). "Global Financial Crisis: A Classic 'Ponzi' Affair?", *Working Paper No:* 2008/12. New Delhi: Institute for Studies in Industrial Development.

Stiglitz, Joseph (2008). "How to Prevent the Next Wall Street Crisis", Special to CNN. (Available at: *http://edition.cnn.com/2008/POLITICS/09/17/stiglitz.crisis/index.html)*

Subbarao, Duvvuri (2009). "Impact of the Global Financial Crisis on India—Collateral Damage and Response", Delivered at the Symposium on *The Global Economic Crisis and Challenges for the Asian Economy in a Changing World*. Tokyo: Institute for International Monetary Affairs. February 18.

Takagi, Shinji. (2009). "The Global Financial Crisis and Macroeconomic Policy Issues in Asia", *Research Policy Brief* 32. Japan: ADB Institute.

Taylor, J.B. (2009). "The Financial Crisis and the Policy Responses: An Empirical Analysis of What Went Wrong", *NBER Working Paper* 14631. Cambridge, MA: USA. National Bureau of Economic Research.

Thomas, Jayan Jose (2009). "India and the Global Financial Crisis: Some Lessons and the Way Forward", Presented in *Annual Money and Finance Conference 2009.* Mumbai: Indira Gandhi Institute of Development Research. January 23-24.

Turner Review (2009). *The Turner Review: A Regulatory Response to the Global Banking Crisis* (Chairman: Lord Turner). UK: Financial Services Authority.

UNCTAD (2009). *World Investment Report 2009*. Geneva: United Nations Conference on Trade and Development.

Wikipedia (2008). "Subprime Mortgage Crisis", (Available at: *http://en.wikipedia.org/wiki/subprimemortgage.crisis*).

World Bank (2010). *World Development Indicators 2010*. Washington, USA: The World Bank.

2 The Global Financial Crisis

How Did We Get Here and How Do We Move Forward

Maurice Odle

Introduction

The financial sector of the developed countries and emerging market economies have been severely traumatised since the beginning of the last quarter of 2008 with what began as a United States of America (USA) mortgage-backed securities (MBS) crisis (triggered by the burst of a housing bubble). This evolved into a full-fledged financial crisis impacting the investment and commercial banking sectors and the insurance industry, with international transmission of the crisis to Europe and Japan and, eventually, to mainly the larger and more advanced developing countries. The financial crisis then took on the peculiar characteristic of a credit crisis, with the banks not wanting to lend (even after receiving bailout resources) because of a lack of confidence. This led to a real sector economic crisis. The decline in real sector production activity and growing unemployment worsened the crisis for the financial sector (e.g., increased foreclosure in the USA) with a spiralling downwards effect on the global economy.

We are, therefore, in the midst of a deepening recession that has not been equalled since the 1930s and, which, many economists feel will not bottom-out before the end of 2009. Tens of millions are being thrown out of job and millions are slipping back into poverty being denied the very basic needs. It is, therefore, appropriate for us to ask the question: 'How did we get here and how do we move forward?'.

How Did We Get Here?

In trying to answer this question, we shall refer to the significance of the following issues:

(a) Systemic weakness in the global financial system;
(b) Financial sector weakness as a product of an extremist market philosophy;
(c) Diminished role of the state and
(d) Globalisation and the paradigm of free trade.

Systemic Weakness in the Global Financial System

Foreign exchange crises have not been an infrequent occurrence in the world's post-war economy. In fact, according to the International Monetary Fund (IMF), there have been over 120 international, regional or national financial crises since the 1970s, when the USA came off the gold standard and the avalanche of dollars commenced. For example, in the USA, major financial crises included the 'Savings and Loans Crisis' of the 1980s and the hedge fund related Long-Term Management Fund Crisis of the 1990s and, in the 1980s, Britain had to be bailed out by the IMF.

However, most of the financial crises occurred in the developing countries, particularly in the larger and more industrialised ones that are known as emerging market economies, such as Mexico in 1982, Chile in 1985, Turkey in 1994 (and again in 2000), Mexico again in 1995, South-east Asia in 1997-98 (starting with Thailand and spreading to Indonesia, Korea, Malaysia and the Philippines, *inter alia*), Russia in 1998 and Argentina in 2001-02.

The crises in these emerging market economies that started in the financial sector and the impact on the real sector, almost invariably resulted from some unfavourable economic development indicators resulting in a loss of confidence and a sudden withdrawal of foreign portfolio capital in the context of a failure to impose adequate capital controls, except in the case of Malaysia.

The Caribbean has also experienced its own essentially home-grown financial crises due to weak regulatory systems, rather than the flight of portfolio capital. For example, Trinidad and Tobago experienced problems in the financial system in the 1980s and, again, in the 1989-1993 period, when three financial houses became insolvent and were placed under central bank supervision. In Jamaica, a significant part of the country's financial sector collapsed during the 1990s and besides instituting financial reforms, a Financial Sector Adjustment Company (FINSAC) was established by the government in 1997 to honour depositors' liabilities and this resulted in a near doubling of the public debt. Also in Guyana, there was failure of an investment bank, Globe Trust and Investment Company Ltd. (GTICL) in the late 1990s and in the case of Antigua and Barbuda, a financial house had to be rescued by the Antigua-Barbuda investment bank.

It is because of the international nature of many financial transactions and the pivotal role of the USA economy that weakness in that country's regulatory structure was able to result in a global financial meltdown. The weakness was primarily of a systemic nature, in that, financial regulation was too limited in scope and did not effectively include a US$ 10 trillion interconnected network of non-commercial bank type institutions such as investment banks, hedge funds, mortgage originators and the like, who were engaged in extreme forms of risk-taking via various derivative instruments and inspired by mathematical model builders. In this regard, there were a number of related weaknesses of a structural nature, including the absence of a strong corporate governance role by stakeholders and complicit and co-opted behaviour at times on the part of the gatekeepers—lawyers, accountants and auditors; and interlocking/cronyism relationships between corporate managers and regulators. In addition, the United Kingdom's (UK's) financial regulator is reported in the *Financial Times* of 10 February, 2009, as saying that 'attempts by the IMF to warn off risks posed by large countries' financial systems have been frustrated by governments watering down the criticism'.

In order to address the issue of regulatory gaps and lack of market discipline in the financial system of the administration of USA, President Obama unveiled on 26 March, 2009, proposals for a major reform of the system, including:

- Imposing tougher standards on financial institutions judged 'too big to fail';
- Regulation of financial derivatives, especially credit default swaps;

- Requiring large hedge funds and other private pools of capital, including private equity funds and venture capital funds to register with the Securities and Exchange Commission; and
- Creating a systemic regulator role.

Weak Financial Regulation as a Product of the Neoliberal Paradigm

Weak financial regulation in the USA (and other developed countries) is not an accident of history. It is a product of a neoliberal philosophy that took off in the 1980s and which took the *Laissez-faire* market tenets of Adam Smith to new heights that are reflected in the Washington Consensus that had strong institutional (including international financial institutions, IFIs) academic and media support. The notion was propounded that the market was not only an efficient allocator of resources but also, that it had certain self-correcting properties, a significant advance on the Adam Smith's 'invisible hand' notion. This blind faith in the market or market fundamentalism actually led to a certain amount of financial deregulation during the 1980s and 1990s. In fact, President Clinton in the late 1990s declined the opportunity to introduce hedge fund regulations.

Diminished Role of the State

The corollary of market fundamentalism is a diminished role for the state. Ex-president Reagan of the USA and prime minister Thatcher of Britain had their followers in both developed and developing countries who executed privatisation programmes with gusto and delighted in the downsizing of other areas of government, including the regulatory arms and the demonising of government intervention in general.

The IFIs for their part, imposed various conditionalities in their lending to developing countries including expenditure limitations on education, health, subsidies and other transfers of benefit to the most vulnerable that impacted negatively on social safety nets and tended to be inconsistent with their proclaimed poverty alleviation policies and targets. Maximisation of employment became a secondary objective of government, despite the fact that a system of well-paid jobs constitutes the most effective safety net and medium for social stability. Similarly, the state became less concerned with the ever-widening disparities in the distribution of income or with the falling incidence of unionisation. It is this lack of concern, coupled with an exaggerated view of the worth of capital *vis-à-vis* labour, that contributed to the exponential growth of compensation for managers and the latter's resultant penchant for taking excessive risk in the hope of generating huge short-term gain for themselves and the shareholders. The system has struggled to find the happy mean between economic efficiency and social justice.

Globalisation and the Paradigm of Free Trade

The significantly increased internationalisation of trade, finance and investment has served to make the financial crisis and economic recession a truly global phenomenon in which not only the USA, Europe and Japan, but also, China, India and the other developing countries are very much affected. During the boom years of the last two decades, it was argued that the increased integration of the world economy benefitted all participating countries, even though some commentators strongly argued that the developing countries were benefitting from a mere trickle down effect. Thus the slogan, 'a rising tide lifts all boats'. However, globalisation has its downside, in the sense that a financial and economic bust is like a tsunami sweeping away all in its path.

Similarly, in a regional integration situation, an economic shock experienced by a member state as a result of events in the developed world could have adverse effects on other member state(s). Thus, the adverse impact on the CL Financial Group (Colonial Life Insurance Company, CLICO) headquartered in Trinidad and Tobago, as a result of a fall in the price of methanol and real estate in the USA, has had an unwelcome impact (direct and indirect) on CLICO subsidiaries in the Bahamas, Barbados, Belize, Guyana, Suriname and Turks and Caicos, *inter alia*.

But globalisation involves more than finance. While sound finance is necessary rather than speculative finance, fair trade is required rather than mere free trade for a just and stable global economic environment. Unfortunately, free trade agreements do not allow for much economic policy space within which to employ adjustment strategies in the event of a crisis. For example, the 2008 Economic Partnership Agreement (EPA) between Caribbean Forum (CARIFORUM) and the European Union (EU) allows the employing of capital controls for a period of only six months during serious balance of payments crises. At the larger level, there is the 'global imbalance' view of certain luminaries, including economist Paul Krugman and ex-US treasury secretary Hank Paulson, that a glut of money from countries with high savings rates and huge foreign exchange reserves (including China, Japan, Korea and the Middle East) flowed into the USA and saturated the credit market, thus fuelling a boom in the price of houses and equity whose collapse precipitated the financial crisis.

What is at stake is, therefore, more than just an appropriate international financial architecture. What is perhaps required is nothing less than an acceptable model of sustainable and equitable global economic and social development.

Impact of the Crisis on the Caribbean and Measures to Arrest Movement Backwards

As in other parts of the world, the Caribbean's financial and real sectors have been adversely affected, to a greater or lesser degree and, in response, there has been employed counter-cyclical fiscal and monetary policies whose success rate is uncertain given the evolving and deepening nature of the crisis.

Financial Sector Impact

Within the last couple of months, it has become apparent that the region has not been spared the financial sector trauma, with varying degrees of primary, secondary and tertiary effects being felt.

Primary Effects

In the early stages of the global crisis, it was reported that countries in the region were insulated from the fallout being experienced by certain other developed countries. This assessment was based on a number of factors. First, except for Citibank, there were no subsidiaries of foreign banks from the USA and European countries which were the most impacted by the crisis. In fact, almost all the banks from outside the region were wholly or partially owned by firms headquartered in Canada, which happened to be among the least adversely impacted of the developed countries. Moreover, the Canadian and the USA banks in the Caribbean operated as standalone subsidiaries rather than as branches. Second, because the countries of the region were not considered to be emerging market economies, with large markets making for economies of scale in transactions costs, they were not sold any of the toxic MBS that precipitated the financial crisis. Third, in terms of ownership, there has been a decoupling of the Caribbean insurance sector from that of North America and Europe. Today, except for American Insurance Group (AIG) agencies in Trinidad and Jamaica, the region's insurance industry is dominated by three indigeneous firms that are Pan- Caribbean in nature, with cross-border operations in a number of territories.

However, adverse effects are not entirely absent. Any portfolio assets held by Caribbean financial entities (and real sector firms and individuals) in Europe or North America would be depreciating quite significantly. This may particularly be the case for insurance companies that do not adhere to the statutory fund-related local asset ratio requirements.

Secondary Effects (and Mitigating Measures)

The CL Financial Group's Meltdown

The depreciation of the value of vast real estate assets held in Florida by a major Pan-Caribbean company (CL Financial Group) that had extensive transnational links and the dramatic fall in the price of methanol products, triggered a major financial upheaval in the country in which it is headquartered (Trinidad and Tobago). A major reason is the particular nature of the group's conglomerate operations (made up of 28 companies) and risky business model in which four of the financial companies are used to provide investment funds for its vast array of real sector companies. When liquidity problems arose, exacerbated by withdrawal of funds by nervous customers from the group's investment banking arm (CLICO Investment Bank (CIB) and Caribbean Money Market Brokers (CMMB) and by surrender of policies held in its insurance operations CLICO and British American Insurance Company (BAICO), a genuine crisis developed and the corporate strategy related to the vast empire (see Table 2.1) was found to be unsustainable.

Table 2.1

CL Financial Group's Major Member Companies and the Companies Major Marketing Attributes

Republic Bank Ltd.	Colonial Life Insurance Co.
CMMB	CLICO Holdings (Barbados) Ltd.
CLICO Investment Bank	CLICO Fire and General Insurance
CLICO Balance Fund	CLICO International Life
CL Permanent	British American Insurance
CL Capital Markets Inc.	Angostura
Central American Money Market Brokers	CL World Brands Ltd.
CLF Latin America	Tru Value Supermarket Ltd.
IBIS Asset Management Ltd.	Health Net
CLICO Energy Company Ltd.	CLICO Property Development, Inc.
Methanol Holdings	HCL Group
Primeral Oil and Gas Ltd.	
Highlighted Strengths and Achievements	
Owner of 14 financial institutions.	Winner of several real estate awards in Florida.
Significant oil and gas operations.	Owner of the largest conglomerate in Jamaica.
The largest real estate developer in the Caribbean with significant projects in Jamaica.	Owner of the largest wine auctioning website in France.
Significant operations in Europe.	Asset base of US $17 billion.
The largest methanol plant in the world.	Owner of the largest spirits distillery in the US.

Source: Partly based on CL Financial Group's discussion brochure, April 2008.

As the Trinidad and Tobago central bank governor remarked to the media on 30 January, 2009, the CL Financial Group had three basic weaknesses. First, there were excessive related party transactions and the transactions' concentration carried significant contagion risks. Second, the group employed an aggressive high risk interest rate resource mobilisation strategy to finance equally high risk investments much of which were in illiquid assets. Third, there was resort to a very high leveraging of the Group's assets which constrained the potential amount of cash that could be raised from asset sales.

The Government of Trinidad and Tobago has transferred the third party assets and liabilities on the books of CIB and CMMB to First Citizens

Bank, in which it already has substantial ownership and has revoked CIB's licence. The government also committed itself to provide resources so as to complement CLICO's divestment of assets efforts in order to make up for the TT$ 10 billion shortfall in the company's statutory fund requirement. These actions are designed to safeguard the interest of over 1,00,000 persons who may be policyholders or depositors.

There also occurred a regional transmission of the CLICO crisis as a result of the existence of a number of subsidiaries and a similar corporate strategy of interlocking and hierarchical transactions that endangered all concerned. The parent company of CLICO Belize, CLICO Turks and Caicos is CLICO Bahamas which, in turn, is parented by CLICO Barbados (and the latter is indirectly partly owned by CLICO Trinidad and Tobago). Thus when CLICO Bahamas, which had invested 59 per cent of its assets in a related company CLICO Enterprises, was petitioned into liquidation because its liabilities were estimated to exceed its assets by at least $9 million, it found that it could not pay claims of US$ 2.6 million in the Turks and Caicos; CLICO Belize was also forced to go under judicial management. A few days before, CLICO Guyana too was forced into judicial management since 53 per cent of its assets had been held by CLICO Bahamas.

In the case of CLICO Barbados, the government has guaranteed $10 million in case assistance is needed, since the deficit in the insurance company's statutory fund at the end of 2007, was US$ 46.5 million. Thought is now being given to selling the life insurance operations of CLICO Barbados while retaining the general insurance, mortgage and property development activities. A dilemma faced by CLICO Barbados is that CLICO Trinidad and Tobago owns 51 per cent of Republic Bank which, in turn, owns 63 per cent of CLICO Barbados's shares.

The Stanford Group Debacle

Reminded of the US$ 20,000 fine that the Stanford Group (including Stanford International Bank (SIB) and Stanford Trust received in 2007 for failing to adequately state the risks involved in the sales of certificates of deposits issued by the Antigua-based affiliate (SIB) of the Houston-based investment firm and stung by accusations that its investigators were asleep during Bernard Madoff's decades long US$ 50 billion Ponzi scheme, the US

Securities Exchange Commission (SEC) had sprung into action and charged billionaire Allen Stanford for carrying out a 'massive Ponzi Scheme 2 (via offers that were much higher than average market interest rates) and misappropriating at least $1.6 billion of investors' money. The Antigua-based SIB had over $8 billion in assets and over 30,000 clients.

The SEC's action immediately resulted in a run on the Antigua bank (and on other Stanford-owned banks in Latin America) and the ensuing panic prompted a takeover by the government. The SIB has been replaced by a new entity called the Eastern Caribbean Amalgamated Financial Co., in which Antigua holds 40 per cent interest (25 per cent government and 15 per cent held by the Antigua Commercial Bank) and the remaining 60 per cent has been allocated in equal proportions among four Organization of Eastern Caribbean States (OECS) banks (St. Kitts-Nevis-Anguilla National Bank Ltd., Eastern Caribbean Financial Holding Co. Ltd. (ECFH), National Commercial Bank of St. Vincent and the Grenadines and National Bank of Dominica).

As in the case of the action taken by the Government of Trinidad and Tobago where CLICO is headquartered, the action taken by the Government of Antigua and Barbuda is not very transparent as to whether other national and/or related party interests are being taken care of. For example, the Hand-in-Hand Trust Corporation of Guyana has a current exposure, in the form of certificates of deposits to the Stanford Group of US$ 4 million, in addition to US$ 1.5 million invested on behalf of pension funds. Also, the respective powers of the Antiguan and USA (SEC) authorities are not clear. These block assets could be tied up almost interminably in litigation, since the Stanford receiver in the USA is only seeking release of accounts that contain US$ 1,99,999 or less. Moreover, the receiver has stated in court that there is a liquidity crisis in the Stanford Group Co., and that only hundreds of millions of Stanford assets are likely to be recovered for investors instead of billions.

Similarly, recovery is not guaranteed for CLICO Guyana, CLICO Belize and CLICO Turks and Caicos policyholders, *inter alia* and certain national compensatory and social safety arrangements might be in order. This is particularly so in Guyana, since the National Insurance Scheme (NIS) has about US$ 30 million invested in CLICO Guyana.

Tertiary Effects

The Caribbean financial fallout from the global crisis is still emerging and there may be more surprises in store for the financial authorities. For example, there may be contagion effects by way of firms and individuals withdrawing foreign currency denominated funds from reasonably sound institutions and hoarding same or making deposits in foreign jurisdictions (that ironically were the source of the crisis) where the deposit insurance limits are significantly higher. Thus on 2 March, 2009, the Central Bank of Trinidad and Tobago announced that it had pumped as much as US$ 280 million into the banking system in the past two months to satisfy the need for the US cash despite the large amounts of foreign exchange that the 40-50,000 visitors to Carnival would have brought in. Governments themselves are not averse to taking defensive action, however, unwarranted. For example, the Barbados Government has announced a desire to re-purchase the 65.13 per cent of the shares of Barbados National Bank that is held by Republic Bank (in which the latter bank, CLICO owns 51 per cent of the shares). Regional financial integration apparently has its downsides.

The ultimately tragic effect of the global crisis would be one in which the recession had deepened to such an extent that plummeting real sector activity and employment in the region, along with drying up of remittance flows, caused a significant rise in non-performing loans and non-payment of insurance premiums (including surrenders) as to pose a systemic threat to the banking and non-banking systems.

Real Sector Impact

The impact of the global economic and financial crisis on the real sector in the Caribbean has been quite sharp and swift, given the Caribbean's structural dependence on external trade and investment flows and traditional susceptibility and vulnerability to external economic shocks.

The tourism sector has been severely impacted because consumers of their sun, sand and sea product are from the two regions most adversely affected by the crisis—Europe and North America. There has been a dramatic fall off in tourist arrivals and by as much as two-thirds in some locations. The low occupancy rate persists despite a reduction of hotel room rates and other incentives.

Adverse economic effects are also being felt in tourism-related entertainment industries (night clubs, restaurants, beach sports, handicraft sales) and complementary input activities (airline and taxi transportation, fresh fruit and vegetables suppliers, etc.). Similarly, there has been a major decline in (and postponement of) hotel construction activity and 'second home' building activity, due to the falloff in foreign direct investment (FDI), with adverse effects on firms providing construction and building materials and furnishings, *inter alia*.

In the non-food commodities sector, the impact has been equally severe. For example, declining global demand and related fall in petroleum and petrochemical products have forced Trinidad and Tobago producers of ammonia, methanol and urea to shut down operations or bring forward maintenance work. (In addition, state-owned oil producer, Petrotrin, reported a loss in 2008 of TT$ 200 million, after making a profit in 2007 of TT$ 2 billion). The country's steel plant has also been closed since last October. In the Jamaica bauxite/alumina industry, all the major expansion projects have been halted, as foreign investments from both Alcoa and Rusal have dried up and the plants are threatening closure. The Jamaican-Brazilian sugar divestment project has also fallen apart, as the Brazilian purchases have been unable to source the funds in the USA to close the deal. In Guyana, the bauxite and timber/woodworking industries have also reported a slowdown in activities.

The decline in the economic activity in the Caribbean has resulted in major actual and potential employment and social effects. The hotel owners have laid off many workers (e.g., in the Bahamas 1,200 in 2008 and 300 so far in 2009) and the numbers are likely to increase during the spring and summer seasons of 2009. The shutdown or slowdown of primary sector operations in some countries also involves the lay off of some workers; such shedding of high wage earning labour is likely to have an employment multiplier effect downwards on other sectors as a result of the fall in aggregate demand. The overall economic impact is the likelihood of either negative or very low growth in Caribbean economies in 2009, especially since foreign investment, now dried up, normally accounted for a very high proportion of total capital formation.

A major concern is a worsening security fallout, since social safety nets are rather weak. If the global crisis persists for another 18 months, as is the worse case scenario, hundreds of thousands will slip back into poverty and the region will be hard pressed to contain the crime situation, which is already grim as a result of the drugs and related guns trade.

Counter-cyclical and Other Mitigating Measures

There have been a number of counter-cyclical and other mitigating factors that have been announced over the last few months by the Caribbean governments. With respect to the adverse impact on the financial sector in the Caribbean, reference has already been made to the CL Financial Group meltdown and the interventions by various national governments, including the Government of Trinidad and Tobago assuming control over the investment banking and insurance arms; precautionary measures taken by Barbados; liquidation in the Bahamas and the placing of the subsidiaries under judicial management in Belize and Guyana. In the case of the Stanford debacle, decisive action was taken by the government of Antigua and Barbuda, assisted by other countries in the OECS sub-region. At the regional level, the governments have set up a college of negotiators for effective cross-border regulation and supervision. With respect to the real sector, there have been efforts to increase government expenditure and waive tourism-related taxes. But a problem of fiscal policy space exists since the Caribbean countries are already highly indebted and are currently faced with declining tax revenues, owing partly to the decline in demand for exported products, including tourism. The limited capacity for stimulus creating fiscal policy (including concern for the most vulnerable elements of the population) has been buttressed by expansionary monetary policy via inducing lower interest rates on lending in most Caribbean countries.

However, modification and finetuning have been found to be necessary. Jamaica has been forced to employ a policy mix involving combining a policy of fiscal stimulus and contractionary monetary policy. Contractionary monetary policy (including higher interest rates) was necessary in order to protect foreign exchange reserves and the Jamaican dollar, which depreciated to almost J$ 90 to purchase a US$ 1. Also, Trinidad and Tobago was forced to announce a $5.3 billion downsizing in the increases in expenditure planned for 2008-09, as a result of the fall in crude oil prices below the original US$ 70 threshold price, on which government expenditure projections were based.

Examples of announced national and regional stimulus packages by member states include the following:

(i) *Antigua and Barbuda:* Securing of a $81.5 facility from the Caribbean Development Bank (CDB), part of which is to be used to assist the tourism sector in exchange for the latter, minimising the shedding of labour and to create an Unemployment Benefit Fund. Reduction of taxes include the common external tariff and the customs service charge, increase in the number of items enjoying zero-rated taxes, including flour and flour-based products and expansion of the list of vehicle parts granted tax and duty concessions.

(ii) *The Bahamas:* Securing of funds (including a $200 million banks consortia loan) for construction expenditure related to roads, schools and government buildings, a multipurpose stadium with mainly Chinese resources, ports and airports, enhanced marketing of tourism, a temporary unemployment assistance programme, a food and rent assistance programme and provider of last resort assistance to mortgage holders.

(iii) *Barbados:* Setting up of a Council of Economic Advisors and creation of a 'short- and medium-term action plan' of between $80 to $120 million (equivalent to 1 per cent to 1.5 per cent of GDP) focussing on employment stimulating road improvements and Tourism Industry Relief Fund support. In addition, US$ 150 million is being sought in the Trinidad and Tobago market to support the foreign exchange reserves position.

(iv) *Belize:* Providing $200 million (US$ 100 million) economic stimulus package to be funded by regional and international institutions.

(v) *Grenada:* Providing cost of living-related tax relief on interest charges, national reconstruction levy, fuel prices and barrels of goods from diaspora sources. Proposals made for increased expenditure on rural roads and rural credit and on tourism development and for the creation of a social pact/protocol.

(vi) *Jamaica:* Providing US$ 168 million in liquidity support to the financial system and securing US$ 350 million from multilateral agencies with promise of a further US$ 600 million. At the real sector level, hotel taxes have been reduced. A J$ 500 million loan has been provided to those experiencing cash flow problems, the manufacturing sector has been granted relief via removal of customs user fees, enhanced depreciating allowance and preferred procurement access and the small business sector has been provided with onlending funds and the tax on dividends paid by all locally-owned companies has been abolished. At the personal or individual level, the income tax threshold has been increased, a special training programme has been introduced for workers who have been laid off, the length of period, before which a mortgage loan is deemed a non-performing loan by the authorities, has been extended, property transfer taxes have been reduced and the import duty charges on barrels and packages below a US$ 3,000 value have been removed.

(vii) *Montserrat:* Seeking of three or four million pounds additional budgetary support from the UK Government for stimulus activities.

(viii) *OECS:* Strategy to stimulate expenditure in the construction, tourism and fisheries sector as well as arranging bulk procurement of essential goods and introducing appropriate tax incentives. (For example, St. Kitts and Nevis introduced an incentives package for small hotels involving the waiving of import duty and consumption tax on fixtures, furniture, appliances and equipment imported for use in refurbishment projects, in exchange for a requirement of the hotels to train all employees for a minimum of 12 hours per year and to purchase local agricultural commodities.

(ix) *Saint Lucia:* Implementation in train of a $26 million stimulus package directed at mainly creating short-term employment in targetted communities and including $7 million for tourism marketing activities. In addition, measures were implemented to reduce the retail prices of some basic food and non-food items by removing import duties and consumption taxes on these items and the setting up of a Tripartite Committee (similar to that in Barbados of representatives of government, the private sector and labour unions) is being contemplated.

(x) *St. Vincent and the Grenadines:* Conferring lower tax rates on yachts and hotels, including hotel electricity rates and making an EC$ 25 million loan facility available to hoteliers and reducing the corporate tax rate.

(xi) *Trinidad and Tobago:* Assurance despite cutbacks in new construction projects, that there would be no reductions in wages and salaries, social programmes, pensions, disability grants, Unemployment Relief Programme (URP) and Community-based Environmental Protection and Enhancement Programme (CEPEP), and programmes dealing with crime and training. Increased foreign exchange reserves were made available to the banking system.

Policy Implications for Regulation, Supervision and Oversight

Recent economic developments in the region resulting from the global crisis, have shown there to be a number of systemic weaknesses at the financial/economic and social levels which require the taking of appropriate policy action.

Financial/Economic Weaknesses

First, the pursuit of greater firm size and related 'bulking-up' so as to achieve economies of scale and scope (along with sectoral and geographical diversification) does not constitute an unmixed blessing. A conglomerate, like the CL Group, that includes both financial and real sector activities, could experience wide deviation from original core competence, in addition to an overstretching of managerial resources. Most importantly, it is possible for a conglomerate's financial arm to be used as a captive source of financing for real sector activities, some of which may not even deserve to be undertaken. This is a systemic risk management-related problem of corporate governance and the relationship between parent and subsidiaries. The role of the gatekeepers (lawyers, accountants and auditors) is also relevant. (It should be noted that most conglomerates in the region have a financial arm).

Second, a conglomerate that provides a variety of financial services (financial supermarket) can also present a regulatory challenge if there is blurring of the distinction between commercial banking and investment banking and, also, between banking, on the one hand and insurance on the other. Similarly, challenging is a situation of rapid financial innovation, whether it involves an exotic product or a process that is billed as a 'unique investment strategy'. The authorities would need to improve their surveillance capabilities.

Third, while greater size could confer increased competitiveness and efficiency to firms in small economies, mergers and acquisitions should be carefully monitored and the Regional Competition Commission would need to be proactive. Other corporate operational practices require equal attention. For example, a few years ago, there was quite a bit of controversy when a conglomerate attempted to use its vastly superior bidding power in order to gain monopoly control over the supply of molasses originating from Guyana. The Trinidad and Tobago Government's assumption of control over certain CLICO companies, rather than the mere provision of credit, suggests the need for a new enhanced role of the state.

Fourth, there is a danger of a conglomerate (especially a financial enterprise) becoming 'too big to fail' (because of the economic and social repercussions) thus requiring a typically cash strapped state to engage in bailing out activities. High risk brings with it both high rewards and large failures. In this regard, vigilance and active monitoring are important.

Fifth, there is need for a greater degree of transparency and disclosure on the part of firms that operate in the free market place. In this regard, providing incentives for firms to go public, rather than remain a family firm (or private equity firm) should be encouraged. For example, if CLICO were a public company, more information would have been available on its various activities. In fact, CLICO might have resorted to raising capital on the open market rather than the clandestine strategy of tapping related party firms.

Sixth, the national financial authorities need to strengthen their surveillance and oversight. The claim, by a firm like Stanford Group, of making a 10-14 per cent return over the last decade should have aroused the suspicion of it being 'too good to be true'. The need is even greater with respect to non-bank sector activities like insurance and pension funds. In this regard, giving the Ministry of Finance or a commissioner of insurance this responsibility, has not proven to be very successful, although either the central bank or a universal type financial services authority would not do much better unless a special investigative effort is made. For example, it is quite revealing that for certain insurance firms in Barbados, Trinidad and Tobago, of fiscal policy space there was a significant shortfall in the statutory fund requirement and that in Guyana, the local asset ratio requirement was honoured more in the breach. (The Caribbean should also deal with the issue of 'suitcase traders' in which agents of foreign-based companies visit the region and sign contracts for the insurance of large property without either a local physical presence or without any assets being deposited locally to cover the local liabilities).

Seventh, greater cross-border supervision, requiring close collaboration, cooperation and exchange of information between national financial jurisdictions, is a *sine qua non* in an era of free and seamless cross-border movement of capital within the region (and, as has been shown to be frequently the case outside the region). What is really required is a greater commitment to the notion of a single economy. The current regional financial crisis requires a regional policy solution.

Eighth, there is need for the other Caribbean Community (CARICOM) countries to join the Bahamas, Barbados, Jamaica and Trinidad and Tobago in instituting a system of deposit insurance in their territories, increased operational costs and moral hazard notwithstanding. Distortion and risk arbitrage can occur in a single economy situation in which the parent firm and/or some of the subsidiaries of a Pan-Caribbean bank operate in certain locations where there is a deposit insurance requirement while other subsidiaries operate where there is no such requirement. In fact, in a panic situation, savers may flee to those jurisdictions that employ deposit insurance.

Ninth, given the current regional financial crisis, the 'opportunity' should be seized to have a thorough review of the system, including such practices as capital adequacy ratios, liquidity ratios, lending practices, financial innovation, risk management, etc. In this regard, the draft CARICOM Financial Services Agreement should be quickly made ready for signature, taking into account any modification or strengthening that is required as a result of the experiences gained from the present crisis.

Tenth, at the macro level, consideration should be given to renewing the effort (suspended in 2003) of setting up a Regional Stabilisation Fund, given the region's vulnerability to external economic shocks and the frequency and intensity of international and regional financial crises. An alternative approach is a significant increase in foreign exchange reserves for import cover in boom times as a hedge against contingency needs in bust conditions.

Social Weaknesses

Identifiable social policy weaknesses and gaps in the social safety net might be reflected in the following:

- The bailout policy of, for example, the Government of Trinidad and Tobago amounts to a 'privatisation of profits but socialisation of losses'. This protection of capital needs to be balanced with an effective programme of unemployment insurance;
- In a situation where compensation of managers has been growing exponentially, a meaningful minimum wage policy and also, support for unionisation should be encouraged in the interests of a better distribution of income and greater capacity for survival in a crisis;
- Workers and 'flexible labour policy' should not bear the sole burden of adjustment;
- Alleviation of poverty and the attainment of Millennium Development Goals (MDGs) should be an integral and proactive part of the policy spectrum;
- Massive real estate investments in developed countries (e.g., in the USA by CL Financial Group) when needs in the Caribbean are so palpable, constitute a socially questionable geographical allocation of capital;
- Subsidies, transfer mechanisms and fiscal relief should not be a policy consideration only in recession conditions if a more equitable society is a national objective;
- The private sector operation of pension schemes, management of life and non-like and medical insurance policies and investments of

national insurance schemes need to be more closely monitored in order to protect the interests of the more vulnerable; and

- Tripartite partnerships (involving government, private sector and trade unions) should become the norm in the Caribbean.

Reform of the International Financial Architecture of Particular Interest to the Caribbean Economies

While member states are, as would be expected, focussed on devising measures to mitigate the effects of the crisis and exploring means of strengthening their financial regulatory frameworks at a national level and also at a consolidated supervisory level to deal with the cross-border effects of the operations of Pan-Caribbean financial intermediaries, the region should not lose sight of the origins of the global crisis and the need for a reform of the international financial architecture that serves the interest of both developed and developing countries. It would be well for the G-20 meeting that is scheduled for 2 April 2009, to take on board the recommendations for International Finance Architecture reforms which included the following that resulted from the UN dialogue of 25th-27th March 2009:

- A new global reserve system;
- Reforms of the governance of the international financial institutions;
- A global economic coordination council;
- Better and more balanced surveillance;
- Reform of central bank policies to promote development;
- Reform of financial market policies (in relation to: (a) financial product safety; (b) comprehensive application of financial regulation; (c) regulation of derivatives trading; (d) regulation of credit rating agencies; (e) global financial regulation and competition; (f) host country regulation of foreign subsidiaries and (g) regulatory institutions);
- Support for financial innovations to enhance risk mitigation;
- Mechanisms for financial innovations to enhance risk mitigation;

- Mechanisms for handling sovereign debt restructuring and cross-border investment disputes;
- Completion of a truly-development oriented trade round and
- More stable and sustainable development finance.

Among the reforms of particular interest to Caribbean countries (see Box 2.1) there are two that deserve special mention:

Box 2.1

Types of Reforms of the International Financial Architecture of Particular Interest to Caribbean Economies

- IFIs lending to be more counter-cyclical (rather than procyclical)
  - need for adjustment (non-deflationary) to be achieved at a higher level of income;
  - in a crisis, conditionalities for economic assistance should not at the same time require higher interest rates or a reduction in social expenditure.
- Concurrence with proposed Zoellick Stabilisation Fund
  - 0.7 per cent of current stimulus packages in the developed countries to be made available to developing countries;
  - any loan should be at zero rates of interest since developing countries did not create the crisis;
  - achievement of 0.7 per cent of GDP aid targets to be mandatory.
- Greater policy space with respect to capital account controls during crises
  - freedom to employ capital account controls in times of balance of payment crises;

...contd...

  - no limitation on duration of capital account controls during the life of a crisis.
- Graduation from access to concessionary loans (to loans on commercial terms) to be based on factors other than mere GDP per capita
  - special treatment to be accorded to highly indebted middle income countries (HIMICs) that are vulnerable to external economic shocks;

contd...

...contd...

- added consideration for countries susceptible to natural hazards (e.g., hurricanes);
- per capita income is a poor index of economic sustainability.

• More sympathetic international credit rating system
- international credit rating agencies cease to have an exaggerated view of risk in the developing countries;
- lower risk assessment to result in lower borrowing rates on the international capital market.

• A more level playing field with respect to the financial stability treatment of small offshore jurisdictions
- reduce targetting of small offshore jurisdictions;
- require all jurisdictions in both developed and emerging market economies to adhere to the same requirements of transparency and effective exchange of information demanded of the smaller jurisdictions.

• Democratisation of the decision-making process in IFIs
- greater role for G-20 and the United Nations;
- non-automaticity in choice of leader of world bank and the IMF;
- abolition of veto powers over loan disbursements, *inter alia*;
- enlargement of IMF resources (via more use of special drawing rights) and increase of country quotas;
- need for a genuine international reserve system rather than dependence on national currencies in which to hold country reserves.

One is the need for special treatment to be accorded to highly indebted middle income countries (HIMICs) who find it difficult to grow out of their debt without special assistance from the international community, because of a number of structural vulnerabilities, including:

i. Diseconomies of scale of government expenditure in small economies; for example, a small economy has to set up virtually the same number of ministries and public sector agencies as the larger economies;

ii. Susceptibility and vulnerability to exogeneous shocks owing to the very open nature of the economies and requiring government counter-cyclical expenditure. In addition, these economies are dependent on exports of a limited number of commodities, some for which the market is either shrinking or preferential market access is continually being eroded;

iii. Exposure to natural disasters, in particular, hurricanes of increasing frequency and intensity, requiring repeated government reconstruction of infrastructure and other recovery-related expenditure;

iv. Physically difficult terrain of small island economies and the lack of close proximity to each other, requiring additional government expenditure, especially in relation to road networks, sea and airport facilities and other transport-related needs;

v. Structurally weak private sectors, necessitating significant government intervention to fill investment gaps; and

vi. A high brain-drain requiring government expenditure for replacement training.

As a result of the above, the CARICOM countries should not be graduated out of access to concessionary loans on the basis of mere per capita income, particularly since such a level of income may not be sustainable.

A second reform relates to the need for a more level playing field with respect to the treatment of the offshore jurisdictions in small developing countries. This is important because of the limited scope for structurally dependent economies to diversify their economies. Moreover, the countries in CARICOM were encouraged to diversify into services not only by local advisors but also, by the international community who suggested that services were the best alternative to real sector production.

In addition, the CARICOM countries had expended considerable human and financial resources to reform their offshore sector in the early 2000s, according to the principle of transparency and effective exchange of information, as a result of being blacklisted by the Organisation for

Economic Co-operation and Development (OECD) and the Financial Action Task Force (FATF). Alternatives to the sector appear to be very limited, as a generator of high wage employment and government revenue.

Acknowledgement: This paper was prepared for presentation at the ILO Carribbean Tripartite Conference on "Promoting Human Prosperity Beyond Global Financial Crisis", April 1-2, 2009, Kingston, Jamaica.

3 The Global Crisis: Fatal Decisions

Four Case Studies in Financial Regulation

Leo F. Goodstadt*

Introduction

In the forums that seek to apportion blame for the turmoil that has overtaken the world's financial markets since 2007, the officials entrusted with responsibility for the stability of monetary systems and financial institutions have largely escaped retribution. To some extent, they owe this immunity to the exceptional nature of the disaster. The global crisis has proved so protracted and so intractable that informed public discussion has focussed on day-to-day crisis management. The urgent issues have been the financing of business survival—the availability and cost of bank credit, in particular—and executive emoluments. In debates about the appropriate response to the continuing crisis, the sharpest divide has been 'ideological': the merits or otherwise of fiscal rather than monetary remedies.[1]

Nevertheless, central bankers and financial regulators have their accusers who are determined to hold them to account for the destruction of institutional assets and personal wealth on a scale unmatched since the Great Depression, 80 years earlier. The most serious charge made against these officials who presided over monetary affairs is that they were warned of the threats to market stability but failed to intervene, regardless of their legal powers or their public duty.

---

* The views expressed in this paper are those of the author, and do not necessarily reflect those of the Hong Kong Institute for Monetary Research, its Council of Advisers, or the Board of Directors.

> The financial crisis...[was] rooted in the refusal of regulators, lawmakers and executive-branch officials to heed warnings about risks in the system and to use their powers to head them off. It is the result of anti-regulatory bias and deregulatory zeal—ascendant over the last three decades, but especially prevalent in the last 10 years—that eclipsed not only rules and regulations, but the very will to regulate (New York Times, 2009).

Under indictment here is the Anglo-American regulatory 'culture' which reflected a wider political consensus that extended well beyond the officials themselves. Markets were regarded as capable of regulating their own affairs, and there was a conviction that government intervention would inevitably hinder economic progress.

This 'culture' is reviewed in the companion working paper: 'The Global Crisis: Why Regulators Resist Reforms' (HKIMR No. 35/2009). Its analysis suggests that the 'culture' emerged from the response of American and British regulators to a shift by financial institutions from New York to London during the early 1970s in search of a less interventionist environment. For the United States (US), the exodus was a serious economic loss. For the United Kingdom (UK), the influx was a mixed blessing. The expansion of its financial markets had brought with it a potential liability for the stability and solvency of these newcomers. As the paper explains, the two countries quickly saw the advantages of regulatory consultation and coordination.

A longer-term incentive came with the worldwide trend towards de-regulation and globalisation in that decade and the 1980s which was accompanied by widespread financial instability. Badly hit was the Third World, which 'experienced a continuous history of severe banking crises'.[2] As the two largest financial markets, New York and London were heavily exposed, which provided the two countries with a powerful motive to join forces in persuading governments to promote financial stability while pursuing market liberalisation. The companion working paper traces how these joint American and British efforts led to the Basel endeavours and the construction of an international framework within which to improve and harmonise national standards of financial regulation. Basel itself became a forum in which the Anglo-American 'culture' could spread. The foundations of this 'culture' were the shared economic assumptions which became the dominant intellectual force driving economic reforms and market liberalisation worldwide. The Anglo-American 'culture' retains its dominance, the paper explains, thanks to a political consensus that has remained intact despite the global crisis and which allows American and British central bankers and financial regulators to retain their leading role in policymaking.[3]

The starting point for this paper is whether complaints about the adverse consequences of this Anglo-American 'culture' are valid. This limited focus seems justified by the International Monetary Fund (IMF) data. These statistics indicate that the damage sustained by the American and British banking systems exceeds that suffered by the rest of the world during the global crisis. According to the IMF, the two countries account for 58 per cent of total write-downs by the world's banks for 2007-2010. Cumulative losses on loans and securities are estimated at 8.2 per cent for the US and 7.2 per cent for the UK, compared with a global average of 5 per cent. Losses appear to decrease considerably with 'distance' from the New York and London markets.[4]

The analysis that follows will focus on four areas in which major malfunctions of the financial markets occurred. It will ask how aware were central bankers and financial regulators of these problems as they were emerging and what rationale these officials offered, both before and after the onset of the global crisis in 2007, for not taking remedial action. As far as possible (and unless otherwise indicated), information about regulatory policies and their implementation is derived from public statements made by the officials responsible.

The Regulators' Role

In the current debate over what changes should be made to regulatory policies and practices to take account of the global crisis, central bankers and financial regulators insist that their intervention in business affairs should continue to be as minimalist as possible. They claim that regulation increases moral hazard and encourages investors and executives to act less prudently and efficiently because they will assume that the government will rescue firms from the consequences of their own mismanagement. The case studies presented below will suggest that the regulators' respect for moral hazard before 2007 facilitated the self-destructive business practices which led to the extensive market scandals and corporate collapses of the global crisis.

A strong case can be made that all regulatory activities have an effect on business behaviour because they create an environment in which investors and executives identify what sort of conduct the legal authorities will condone and what they will penalise. This process goes beyond the threat of criminal penalties or civil liabilities. William J. Baumol has argued that it is 'the rules of the game that determine the relative payoffs to different entrepreneurial activities' and that 'at times the entrepreneur may even lead a parasitical existence that is actually damaging the economy'. These 'rules' are set by a variety of pressures including government policy, statutory and regulatory requirements and their enforcement (Baumol, 1990: 895, 899, 917). When regulators are reluctant to use their legal powers to prevent such abuses and they disregard business innovations that create products harmful to their purchasers, investors and executives have a clear indication of how nominal the penalties for misconduct will be in practice.

In the contemporary world, the behaviour of entrepreneurs and executives is not the only cause for regulatory concern. Corporate structures have become 'flatter, rely more on teamwork and less on hard rules and narrow job descriptions'. Supervision of the average employee's day-to-day operations, whether by senior management or by official regulators, often seems remote. Currency traders working for international banks, for example, have been depicted in one academic study as operating 'in a domain that is not subject to national or international legal regulation' and having a 'part-employee/part-entrepreneur pay structure'. The result is that 'traders keep track of their profit and loss balance with practically every trade', the authors report and 'their worth is explicit not only to themselves but also to their supervisors, at every moment in time'. The clear impression left by this research is that apart from the individual's profitability, oversight of employees' conduct has to be random rather than regular and they are shown to be free to develop patterns of behaviour which are in breach of such rules of conduct as have been prescribed for them (Cetina & Bruegger, 2002: 906, 910-1, 939, 942-4).

The Anglo-American 'culture' has not adjusted to this radical change in business practice. In their response to the lessons of the global crisis, American and British officials cannot reject entirely the case for improved oversight of individual financial institutions. But they insist that the regulatory priority must be '"the financial system as a whole... not just its individual components" and that the aim should be to control "systemic" risk' (Bernanke, 2009a). The distinction being made here is 'between the regulation of structure and the regulation of conduct'. That is: 'Regulators may be concerned with the way the market is organised (structural regulation), or with behaviour within the market (conduct regulation)' (Kay *et al.*, 1988). In the events that led up to the global crisis, this paper will show, the major damage was caused by 'behaviour within the market'—the imprudence of mortgage institutions in the subprime market, for example and the incompetence of ratings agencies. The structure of the market has been a lesser problem and most 'structural' problems, the official record indicates, could have been remedied by the regulators.

Asia's Early Warning

The regulators' preference for non-interventionism seemed to be vindicated by the robustness of the global financial system and the sustained momentum of world economic growth in the wake of the Asian financial crisis of 1997-98. Its consequences were truly catastrophic for the region. Asian economies suffered 'far more dramatic falls in output and employment than the major developed countries have faced' since 2007 (Turner, 2009b). This event was, in fact, the first unambiguous signal that the markets could not be trusted to generate global prosperity with minimal financial volatility.[5] The implications of that painful episode for global stability were largely ignored, however.[6]

Several sources of instability that contributed to the downturn in Asia's fortunes at the end of the previous century were to reappear as prominent features of the global crisis. In the 1990s, financial institutions took a highly optimistic view of the new Asian opportunities, and the region was hailed as an 'economic miracle' (World Bank, 1993: 1-2). Its glittering performance seemed to promise large profits and attracted substantial inflows of foreign investment.[7] International banks showed a considerable appetite for assets throughout Southeast and East Asia with little regard for the risks involved. The profits proved fragile and often illusory, as a World Bank survey of 5,550 publicly-listed corporations in nine East Asian economies covering the period 1988-1996 was to demonstrate.

> *Ex-post*, it has become clear that the operational performance of East Asian corporates was indeed not as stellar as many had thought and in fact involved investment with high risks. This poor performance and risky financing structures of East Asian corporates were, however, not notably featured among observers writing on East Asia prior to the financial crisis. Quite the opposite, East Asian corporates were considered an important contributing part of the East Asian miracle and were generally viewed upon as very competitive and adept at exploiting new market opportunities and, consequently, attracted considerable amounts of foreign capital (Claessens and Djankov, 1999).

Reckless disregard for Asian business realities persisted. 'Even the most sophisticated operators in global financial markets' were prepared to go on lending 'well after the increased risks in the region were generally apparent', a prominent economist warned. He identified the increasing use of structured derivatives by global banks as contributing to this perverse behaviour. In the aftermath of the Asian financial crisis, these products were described as a serious threat to financial stability in terms that foreshadowed their subsequent contribution to the making of the current global crisis.[8]

> It is the role of most derivative packages to mask the actual risk involved in an investment and to increase the difficulty in assessing the final return on funds provided for the primary lenders and for market regulators. The incentives motivating such [products] provide little support for the common belief in the self-regulating nature of private capital markets in terms of risk assessment or of their ability to allocate capital efficiently.

Asia's 'Revenge'

The disregard for reality was especially evident in the case of China. Here an economic liberalisation programme was making the country the Third World's most attractive location for foreign direct investment (FDI) even though state controls and national and provincial five-year plans remained prominent features of the business landscape.[9] Foreign bankers preferred to dispense with the costs and complexities of undertaking rigorous due diligence. The temptation to cut corners was particularly strong when investing via International Trust and Investment Corporations (ITICs) and similar bodies. These had been established with special exemptions from normal state controls so that they could help to accelerate economic development.[10] Foreign financial institutions assumed that since the ITICs were entities established and owned directly by Central and local governments, they would have the status of government borrowers, which would relieve their foreign partners from the burdensome regulations usually imposed on foreign investments. This assumption was to prove painfully misconceived.[11]

In late 1998, the Guangdong International Trust and Investment Corporation (GITIC) was discovered to be virtually insolvent with liabilities estimated at over US$ 4 billion. The Chinese government declined to authorise its rescue. (Financial Times, 1999). Foreign bankers now learnt that insolvent ITICs were not regarded as state entities under Chinese Law. Loans to ITICs which had not been made in full compliance with state exchange control regulations were at risk of being categorised as unlawful and, therefore, unrecoverable (Keenan, 1999). In response to overseas lobbying on behalf of the foreign investors, Chinese officials insisted on strict respect for legalities, a message underlined by the then Prime Minister:

> If Chinese companies cannot afford to pay their debts, they must apply to the People's Bank of China and court to be made bankrupt," Zhu [Rongji] said. "The Chinese Government will protect the rights and interests of foreign creditors according to the law (Zhu, 2000).

GITIC's insolvency was followed by the collapse of similar vehicles in many other parts of the country and by defaults on the samurai and other foreign bonds issued by a dozen or so ITICs (Bloomberg News, 2000). The government decided on a radical overhaul of these institutions, purging firms engaged in unauthorised activities and arresting corrupt officials. By 2004, only 59 of the 240 ITICs originally established were still in business (Xiao, 2001; Xia, 2004).

These financial scandals did not hinder China's breakneck growth. The continued expansion of the global economy led to massive trade surpluses for China and other emerging economies. The flow of capital was now reversed, with Asian funds flooding into Western assets. Ironically, Asia's economic success later came to be viewed as a significant factor in the financial woes of the United States and Europe. American and British officials claimed that the 'growth of significant global imbalances over the last decade'– particularly from 'newly emerging countries, like China'–was a major cause of financial instability[12] (Darling, 2009: EV366). This allegation was tantamount to self-incrimination as it was an acknowledgment that the much vaunted American and British financial markets could not absorb these inflows efficiently.

Officials from both countries attributed the breakdown in the good sense expected of the markets to 'the *ex-ante* excess supply of global savings over investment, which pushed real interest rates on safe assets to historically low levels, reinforced by loose monetary policy'.

> This 'savings glut', as Chairman Ben Bernanke christened it, was in part the result of high national savings rates in some Asian emerging economies, especially China, which despite high investment rates, chose to export capital rather than import it, as standard theory would lead one to expect. One factor behind the high level of savings by the emerging market economies was their experience during the 1997-98 Asian crisis, when several countries were forced to tighten policy sharply in the face of a 'sudden stop' of capital inflows from abroad. Thereafter, a strategy of relying on domestic savings to finance investment and the accumulation of a substantial war chest of foreign reserves looked more appealing (Bean, 2008: 2-3).

But this shared American and British version of Asia's involvement in the global crisis will not do. Unexplained is the most striking market failure in the prelude to the global crisis: the inability of the American financial system in particular to accommodate free flows of capital from overseas.

The net volume of foreign savings received by the US quadrupled as a share of gross domestic product (GDP) from 1995 to reach around 6 per cent of GDP in 2006. Properly invested, these inflows would have been highly beneficial, the Chairman of the Federal Reserve Board has stated.

> Unfortunately, that was not always the case in the US. Financial institutions reacted to the surplus of available funds by competing aggressively for borrowers and, in the years leading up to the crisis, credit to both households and businesses became relatively cheap and easy to obtain. One important consequence was a housing boom in the US, a boom that was fuelled in large part by a rapid expansion of mortgage lending. Unfortunately, much of this lending was poorly done, involving, for example, little or no down payment by the borrower or insufficient consideration by the lender of the borrower's ability to make the monthly payments (Bernanke, 2009b).

Regulatory intervention could have corrected this mismanagement, the Chairman added in conclusion, but the American regulatory system was not up to the task. The market, left to its own devices, was unwilling to halt the imprudent lending.

On the Federal Reserve Board's own analysis, incompetent bank lending and defective regulation in the US combined to transform a benign inflow from overseas into toxic assets through which contagion was exported to world markets. But there was another regulatory failure. 'The global imbalances were the joint responsibility of the US and our trading partners' America's chief central banker has stated, but not enough effort was made to resolve the situation 'although the topic was a perennial one at international conferences' (Bernanke, 2009a). His British counterpart has made an almost identical confession (King, 2009: 15). A serious threat had been identified well in advance of the global crisis, but the world's central bankers and financial regulators had failed to give it the priority which it deserved.

Mismatched Insurance

By the start of the current century, the Bank of England had identified the potential dangers created by the growing popularity of derivatives and of credit default swaps in particular. The main source of these products was a handful of the larger international banks. Their principal purchasers were insurance companies and credit derivatives (notably collateralised debt obligations) were being transformed into products close to insurance contracts. A British official warned that the market suffered from a lack of transparency and considerable uncertainty about what the fate of these products might be in a crisis. More serious still was the growing interdependence of the banking and insurance industries, whose basic businesses were radically different.[13]

> ...the credit transfer business is bridging the lending, securities and insurance markets. Contracts in banking, on the one hand and insurance markets, on the other, are in some respects different animals. An insurance contract, for example, is not typically a commitment to timely payment; whilst timing is of the essence in securities markets.

British officials realised how this mismatch between the two industries' models for managing risk 'can give rise to cash flow and liquidity implications which, for bankers and others in the financial markets, are potentially highly disruptive'. There was also a mismatch in regulatory régimes which allowed banks to evade official supervision through 'using credit risk transfers to insurance subsidiaries, or asset securitisation sales to third party insurers or credit insurance and derivatives sold by insurers'. The case for the regulators to become involved was convincing. But British officials resisted intervention. They were more worried about the damage that could be caused by 'a call for harmonisation of regulation or a blind assertion of the need for a completely level playing field'. Instead of urging preventive action, the official recommendation was confined to a call for re-examination of the issue (Large, 2003: 4-5).

American central bankers were even more complacent about allowing banking institutions to become dependent on the insurance industry through its role in the development of the derivatives market and credit default swaps. An official review in 2002 identified 'the increasingly active portfolio management of credit risk, by both banks and insurance companies' as the driving force behind the credit derivatives market, but played down fears of the influence of 'regulatory capital arbitrage'. American officials were convinced that credit derivatives were proving a force for stability. The evidence in support of this reassuring conclusion was based on market perceptions during major corporate collapses earlier in the new century. These products appeared to have 'spread the credit risk associated with these large borrowers' who had defaulted. Officials argued that this was now a mature market, whose participants had 'understood the risks and been willing and able to bear them'.

This official review offered the recommendation that 'the regulators should continue to insist that banks manage their counterparty credit risk prudently, [which] includes paying attention to potential concentrations of counterparty credit risk'. But this reassurance was not meant to lead to any concrete measures because, it was claimed, the regulatory process itself was more of a peril to progress than a protection for the public.[14]

> However, just as important is ensuring that regulators keep enough distance from the markets to give financial innovations such as credit derivatives a chance to succeed. The new market for credit derivatives has grown largely outside of traditional regulatory oversight and as I have described, evidence to date suggests that it has made an important contribution to financial stability in the most recent credit cycle.

The Anglo-American consensus could not have been more explicit on the merits of keeping regulation away from the banking-insurance relationship. An unintended but foreseeable consequence was the catastrophic collapse in 2008 of the American International Group (AIG), the world's biggest insurance corporation.

Misleading Ratings

Among the parties on whom central bankers and financial regulators wish to place a large share of the blame for the global crisis and its market disasters are the rating agencies (which became subject to the US regulation only in 2006). 'The Big Three credit-rating agencies have failed investors', a senior American regulator has declared, 'The largest rating agencies awarded their highest ratings to complex debt instruments that were undeserving of investment grade status'. But the misinformation, which played such a calamitous role in the prelude to the global crisis, was not a new phenomenon. This official described the rating errors that have come to light in the current crisis as one more installment in a long line of flawed assessments that he traced back to the Orange County scandal in the 1990s. His list included the investment grade status which 'Enron, WorldCom, Parmalat, and many other companies earlier this decade' retained right up to their bankruptcies (Casey, 2008).

In 1999, the Basel Committee had endorsed the use of credit-rating agencies as a way of standardising the treatment of risk and an effective strategy for dealing with the proliferation of the 'special purpose vehicle (SPV) issuing paper secured on a pool of assets' earlier in that decade. At the same time, the Committee drew attention to 'concerns about the incentive and consequential effects of a more extensive use of external assessments... on the agencies themselves'. It emphasised that both the regulators and the individual banks should accept responsibility for 'the quality of the assessment source and methodology' (Basel, 1999: 13, 26, 36). But this caution was ignored in practice. The rating agencies were widely assumed to be capable of setting the standards with which financial institutions would have to conform in order to defend their market reputations; and the regulators were expected to undertake their own rating exercises (Redak, 2006: 199-200). It quickly became apparent that reliance on rating agencies would aggravate rather than reduce the bond markets' difficulties in assessing risk.[15]

Officials had been aware of the growing threat posed by reliance on unregulated ratings agencies well before the start of the global crisis. A British central banker, for example, had analysed how the growing dependence on the agencies' assessments could increase instability especially 'in the case of collateralised debt obligations [where] whole categories of assets are dependent on their rating'. He stated that the agencies' 'increasingly public significance raises calls for them to be regulated'. Once again, however, the official preference was not to intervene out of fear that 'attempts to do so could actually create additional moral hazard, particularly in today's compensation orientated society'. 'If rating agencies were regulated', he asked, 'who would you blame if mistakes are made: the rating agency, the regulator, or both?' (Large, 2004: 14-5).

The obvious question is why this state of affairs was tolerated for so long. Plainly, the markets themselves were at fault. They were not performing with the wisdom that the Anglo-American regulatory 'culture' took for granted. Regulatory officials now point out that whatever the shortcomings of the agencies and their analytical techniques, their assessments were never intended to replace the investor's own due diligence (Bair, 2008a). Financial institutions holding derivatives and similar products ought to have carried out their own credit reviews. However, in a world of increasingly esoteric products, officials also explain, financial institutions were tempted by the apparent efficiency of contracting out this responsibility to specialists employed by professional rating agencies, especially as in-house expertise to investigate the financial engineering was expensive to hire. In the event, the agencies proved no more successful than the individual corporation in overcoming 'the highly complex information problems underlying some securities'. Their recommendations had disastrous consequences for investors in the global crisis (Jenkinson *et al.*, 2008: 10-11).

The professional misjudgments were compounded by mismanagement and misconduct within the agencies. The Securities and Exchange Commission (SEC) has reviewed the past record of the three largest agencies, which issue 98 per cent of all ratings and receive 90 per cent of the industry's revenue. This investigation uncovered extensive evidence of serious malpractice and gross conflicts of interest (Casey, 2008).

Property Bubbles

The immediate shock that started the collapse in market sentiment and the financial crisis that followed in 2007 came from the US property market and its high-growth, subprime mortgage products. The SEC has declared that the rating agencies' failures were particularly culpable in this affair.

> ...the CEO of Moody's, told a meeting of the firm's managing directors that the subprime market 'was a slippery slope'. He said that what happened in 2004 and 2005 with respect to subordinated tranches was that firms in the credit rating industry 'went nuts' and that 'everything was investment grade. It didn't really matter' (Cox, 2008).

The Commission has described the origins of the subprime debacle as excessive enthusiasm for 'the noble goal of broader home ownership' that led 'to a range of bad policies and dangerous lending practices'. The most notorious were 'the "no-doc" loans in which borrowers not only did not have to disclose income or assets, but even employment was not verified' (Cox, 2008).

Initially, it seemed that a downturn in the American property sector would be manageable. In 2006, total mortgage-backed assets had accounted for only 7.4 per cent of the aggregate value of assets issued on the world's securities markets, while non-agency, subprime mortgages accounted for less than 1 per cent of the total (House of Commons Treasury Committee, 2008b: 17). A British regulatory official felt able that year to issue what amounted to an unconditional assurance that the economic and financial indicators were robust not only for the American and British economies but for global markets as well, with no danger of financial instability (Gieve, 2007: 7-8).

This optimism was shattered when American mortgage defaults became an international issue on August 9, 2007 after the French bank, BNP Paribas, revealed that 'three of its investment funds were no longer able to value a series of complex financial instruments backed by so called 'subprime' residential mortgages in the US (House of Commons Treasury

Committee, 2008b: 5). Overnight, the collapse of institutional as well as depositor confidence had been transformed from a regional American disaster into a worldwide calamity.

A British regulatory agency's post-mortem on the global crisis has provided what is perhaps the best summary of how the collapse of subprime mortgagcs and other securitised products came to wreak such global havoc.

> ...the new model of securitised credit intermediation was not one of 'originate and distribute'... [but] 'acquire and arbitrage' [which] resulted in the majority of incurred losses falling not on investors outside the banking system, but on banks and investment banks themselves...with financial sector assets and liabilities in the UK and the US growing far more rapidly as a proportion of gross domestic product than those of corporates and households (FSA, 2009: EV 457).

As with so much of the global crisis, this market downturn had been a disaster waiting to happen. The US subprime mortgage crisis began as a typical property bubble in which bank loans financed increased competition for real estate. The new (higher) property prices allowed the banks to expand their lending on these property assets in line with their new valuations. As with most bubble markets, monetary policies were facilitating lower real interest rates, which further stimulated bank lending while loan quality deteriorated as the property market boomed (Demyanyk and Van Hemert, 2008: 5).

Evidence was already accumulating at the turn of the century that American real estate had 'taken on some of the characteristics of a commodity market'. An important factor was a change in investment management fashions that dated back to the 1980s. Portfolio theory had begun to raise the weighting of real estate because of the opportunities it provided for pension funds and investment companies in particular to diversify their asset allocations. By 2000, the mortgage market was described by careful academic researchers as 'much more sophisticated in managing and pricing interest rate risk, pre-payment risk and credit risk'. However, the high-growth subprime sector was identified as an obvious source of instability, leading the academics to forecast that 'default rates will rise sharply' if house prices dropped. Nevertheless, its overall finding was that 'the industry is better positioned than it was a decade ago to withstand a substantial national downturn' (Case, 2000: 132-3, 136, 144).

American officials, in their inquest into how the good intentions behind the drive to finance an expansion of home ownership could go so disastrously wrong, have been candid about their own culpability. In 2002, the regulators now point out, the capital weighting for triple and double-A rated asset and mortgage-backed securities was substantially reduced. As a result, 'the same dollar of capital could now support as much as five times the volume of these triple-A securities'. 'In retrospect', the Federal Deposit Insurance Corporation (FDIC) has admitted, 'regulators may have unintentionally, encouraged banks to bet heavily on a new class of non-transparent securities' (Bair, 2008b).

While the American subprime market was able to expand at a spectacular rate, the comprehensive data available on its performance meant that the market's professionals and its regulators had ample warning of the rising risks from mortgage-based securities well before 2007. In 1995, its volume had totalled US$ 65 billion of which 30 per cent was securitised. In 2005, market volume reached US$ 500 billion, with a securitisation rate of over 80 per cent. But business growth now depended on lending to new cohorts of retail customers of diminishing creditworthiness. In the next two years, delinquencies in this market increased by 50 per cent, ruining many mortgage institutions and triggering global panic in 2007.[16] Much of the rise in delinquencies can be attributed to a decline in the standards of screening for loan applicants that, in turn, was linked to the increasing ease with which mortgages could be sold down to third parties. In short, a deterioration in due diligence among purchasers of securitised subprime mortgages encouraged a rise in the volume of lending to higher-risk customers for mortgages (Keys *et al.*, 2008: 1, 5, 28).

The dangers created by property bubbles had been reviewed by British regulators well ahead of the subprime disaster. A Bank of England official had claimed in 2002 that real estate collapses in the 1970s and 1990s had made his colleagues particularly alert to property markets as 'barometers of economic conditions and potentially also the source of financial risks; and even, in extreme cases, financial crises'. His analysis, however, took a benign view of the American trend towards greater securitisation of mortgages. His general conclusion was that 'new instruments and structures have the potential to deliver a better match between borrowers' and lenders' preferences'. He acknowledged, nevertheless, that 'new financing techniques give rise to new risks—for borrowers, lenders and policy-makers'. His response to this uncertain situation was to do little more than 'seek to identify potential problems' (Clementi, 2002: 2-3, 4-5).

As things turned out, there was a heavy price to pay for the lack of concern among British regulators about the property market. The UK's banking system suffered its own property meltdown in 2007 after the collapse of Northern Rock. This bank's unsustainable business model relied on short-term market funding to finance mortgages which went to increasingly unqualified and undocumented applicants, in much the same way as American subprime mortgages did. A 2008 parliamentary inquiry reported that while the directors of Northern Rock 'pursued a reckless business model which was excessively reliant on wholesale funding', 'the regulatory authority systematically failed in its regulatory duty'.

> The [Financial Services Authority] did not supervise Northern Rock properly. It did not allocate sufficient resources or time to monitoring a bank whose business model was so clearly an outlier...the FSA appears to have systematically failed in its duty as a regulator to ensure Northern Rock would not pose such a systemic risk, and this failure contributed significantly to the difficulties, and risks to the public purse, that have followed (House of Commons Treasury Committee, 2008a: 35).

Protecting the Public

In their response to the global crisis, a persistent theme of the policy-makers is a warning that this crisis will lead to campaigns for more stringent regulation, which would cripple the future growth of the vital financial services sector (Gieve, 2009: 70). The regulators' rearguard action has been made necessary by what may prove a lasting legacy of the global crisis: the community's disillusionment with the market's ethics and the public's mistrust of appeals to moral hazard.

When the SEC's former Chief Accountant testified at a Congressional hearing on the failure of AIG, he declared that, 'if honest lending practices had been followed, much of this crisis quite simply would not have occurred' (Cox, 2008). The range and value of the illegal and improper practices that had flourished with the rapid expansion of the derivatives market was remarkable. Involved were many of the most respected names in the international financial community. For example, after the failure of the US$ 330 billion auction rate securities (ARS) market in 2008, UBS, Citigroup, Merrill Lynch and Bank of America, among others, were forced to reach settlements with their investors worth US$ 67 billion—'the largest settlement sums in the history of the SEC' (Walter, 2009).

The financial markets' collapse slashed personal wealth drastically in 2008. In the United States, household net worth dropped by some 18 per cent, the largest annual fall ever recorded. Household net worth relative to disposable income fell from a ratio of some 6:1 to less than 5:1, 'erasing about a full year's worth of income in wealth'. The public no longer felt able to entrust its financial fortunes to the markets and the prevailing mood of helplessness was movingly summed up by a central banker.

> Traditional rules of income and asset diversification appear to offer scarcer protection than generally advertised. As a result, households are questioning the route to financial security. Homeownership is no longer perceived to ensure low-risk capital appreciation. And assurances by investment managers to invest in "stocks for the long haul" are being subjected to intense scrutiny (Warsh, 2009).

The impoverishment of American families through the catastrophic decline in the value of their homes and personal savings has highlighted 'the link between protecting consumers from abusive products and practices and the safety and soundness of the financial system'. A leading regulator has called for 'a new independent financial product safety commission' on the grounds that 'products and practices that strip individual and family wealth undermine the foundation of the economy' (Bair, 2009).

The commitment to unfettered market freedom in the Anglo-American regulatory 'culture' meant that this proposal would encounter considerable opposition. The Chairman of the Federal Reserve Board defined the battle lines. He noted the public's mistrust of financial innovation and he acknowledged that regulators ought 'to strive for the highest standards of consumer protection'. But he expressed alarm that 'innovation, once held up as the solution, is now more often than not perceived as the problem'. Regulators, in his opinion, must find a balance that protects the freedom of 'responsible innovation' despite public resentment at the havoc wreaked by 'subprime mortgage loans, credit default swaps, structured investment vehicles, which have become emblematic of our present financial crisis' (Bernanke, 2009c).

Calls for consumer protection create a potentially large political challenge to the 'culture' that has dominated the American and British regulatory environment for the last three decades. Public indignation has compelled other industries to accept regulatory intervention, most notably pharmaceuticals whose case against government oversight is at least as strong as that of financial services. The bulk of the pharmaceutical products that could cause concern are subject to strict testing before being marketed. They are prescribed and administered by trained professionals so that at every stage of their use, the purchaser of the product has access to expert advice and monitoring. Firms in this industry face severe reputational costs if their products prove unsafe and the penalties for adverse results from their use can be punitive, especially at the hands of American courts. There is, in addition, the risk that over-cautious regulators could inhibit the development of new or improved products. Yet, the Food and Drug Administration (FDA) cannot be abolished so long as successful litigation involving even the largest and most reputable manufacturers continues to reveal how they suppress unfavourable test results, suborn expert opinion and deliberately mis-sell products in order to maximise their profits.[17]

The debate in the US about financial services and the proper balance between the pursuit of profits and the public's protection has been complex, with most regulatory officials resisting radical initiatives. 'The essence of our financial system is to let people take chances with their money', a senior official declared in 2009, 'and to enjoy most of the benefits and to endure most of the pain associated with taking those risks'. This assertion was strikingly frank, given the acute pain the public had suffered in the global crisis. 'From a policy perspective', she went on, the goal must be 'to let financial entities fail if they make bad decisions.'[18]

The Federal Reserve Board has fought back vigorously against demands for better protection for the public, claiming that its programme to defend the consumer is already very extensive (Duke, 2009). The American central bank's strategy seems to be to make the issue a postscript to its larger plans for regulatory initiatives dealing with the 'systemic' weaknesses that contemporary banking brings.[19] In the UK, too, regulatory officials do not want to be distracted from the task of controlling 'systemic' risk.[20] An important factor in the British government's cautious approach to reforms is the perceived loss of business opportunities for financial services that would follow increased regulation (HMG, 2009: 140).

Conclusions

The analysis presented above (and also in the companion paper) indicates that not only were the potential financial shocks foreseeable but that they could have been prevented though appropriate intervention by the regulators. Indeed, central bankers and financial regulators themselves have identified the major areas in which they had the powers needed to halt what, in retrospect, can be labelled a process of self-destruction by financial markets and their participants. The Governor of the Bank of England has pledged to preserve 'an institutional memory...so that the lessons from the crisis are not forgotten and those impediments to excessive risk-taking are not swept away once memories of the crisis recede' (King, 2009: 6). There are few signs, however, that official or their political masters will be more proactive when faced with similarly perilous situations in the future.

Reluctance to intervene prior to the global crisis owed a great deal to 'cultural' preconceptions which convinced regulators that markets were best left to remedy their own deficiencies and that regulation actually did more harm than good. (The companion paper reviews this phenomenon in detail.) That 'culture' still commands political credibility in Washington and London, as well as widespread business support. Thus, there is little likelihood of dramatic regulatory initiatives to match, for example, the radical change in the mindset of central bankers that followed the crisis caused by the Herstatt Bank collapse in 1974 (Bond, 2006). Two years after the start of the worst global crisis in modern financial history, the best that could be said in 2009 about prospects for reform was that 'an overhaul of international standards of bank regulation remains a clear but highly uncertain goal'[21] (Cohen, 2009).

Notes

1. A notable example of the polemic is Krugman (2009).
2. The liberalisation agenda often included steps like removal of administrative controls on interest rates, bank by bank credit ceilings, rules for the allocation of credit to preferred sectors or borrowers, limits on new entry and even opening the capital account. The enthusiasm with which liberalisation was adopted in many countries in the absence of necessary institutional underpinnings left financial systems facing largely uncharted territory. In the period 1976-1996, 'developing countries' suffered 59 banking crises for which 'the average cost was over 9 per cent of GDP' (Carpio and Honohan, 1999: 44, 49).
3. For example, the good standing of both the Chairman of the Federal Reserve Board and the Governor of the Bank of England has received formal affirmation despite the global crisis. See US Treasury (2009) and House of Commons Treasury Committee (2008c: 4).
4. Estimated write-offs are: 5.1 per cent for 'other mature Europe' banks; 3.6 per cent for Euro Zone banks and only 2.1 per cent for Asia's banks. It should be noted that there is a considerable difference in the incidence of the losses among specific sectors of American and British banking, with London's overseas portfolio hit particularly hard (IMF, 2009: 10, 60).
5. For a belated acknowledgment of the parallels with the current global crisis, see Bernanke (2009a).
6. Among the regulators' challenges during the Asian financial crisis, which were to prove no less menacing in the current global crisis, were the poor quality of corporate information and the severe pressure on bank credit triggered by sharp falls in share prices. (Clark, 2000 and Clementi, 2001)
7. This topic is analysed in some depth in World Bank (1995). See also Guitián (1998).
8. The analysis in this paragraph, together with the accompanying quotation, is drawn from Kregel (1998: 678, 679, 690).
9. An excellent analysis of China's domestic and international financial situations in this period is provided by Lardy (2003).
10. A good summary of the ITICs, their history, role and problems can be found in Salomon Smith Barney (1998).
11. The legal situation had changed in 1995, a fact ignored by foreign bankers. See Taube (2002: 103).
12. It should be noted that there is a less compressed and more objective listing of the external factors: 'Large current account surpluses accumulated in the oil-exporting countries, Japan and some other East Asian developing nations, while fiscal and current account deficits grew in the US, UK and some members of the Eurozone' (FSA, 2009: EV 456).
13. The analysis in this paragraph, together with the quotation, is drawn from Clementi (2000).
14. The analysis of the American outlook, together with the quotations, is drawn from Ferguson and Roger (2002).
15. 'Just as Basel-I created incentives for behaviour in the financial markets which undermined the intent of the initial Capital Adequacy Accord, the political economy of bond rating may be the weakest link in the Basel-II proposals'. This comment is from a useful summary of the ratings agencies' historical role in American and other

financial markets, together with a prescient review of the dangers inherent in the expanded role which the Basel arrangements conferred on them (King and Sinclair, 2003: 346-9, 351-4, 358).

16. Data on the declining quality of these mortgages and their market impact are from Bair (2008c).
17. For details of the most important recent litigation (relating to anti-arthritic drugs, pain-killers and anti-depressants), see Saul (2008), Meier (2007) and Meier and Carey (2009).
18. A saving clause was added: 'If we cannot afford to have them fail, then they should be regulated so as to prevent imposing systemic risk' (Tafara, 2009).
19. Consumer protection was presented literally as 'a word' in concluding the Chairman's congressional testimony (Bernanke, 2009d).
20. Indeed the British consumer's concerns have been parodied, a notable example being the reference to 'a nostalgic elegy for a past age of innocence and stability: with Captain Mainwaring's back behind the desk in the branch at Walmington-on-Sea casting a censorious eye over any householder or small-business man silly enough to want to take on too much credit, while the wide boys of the City and Wall Street are free to speculate but well away from sober middle England' (Turner, 2009a).
21. Dismay about the slow pace of reform has been voiced, *albeit* diplomatically, by the IMF Managing Director (Strauss-Kahn, 2009).

References

Bair, Sheila C. (2008a). *Bear Stearns Mortgage and Structured Product Conference* (17 January 2008). URL: *http://www.fdic.gov/news/news/speeches/archives/2008/chairman/spjan1708.html*

———. (2008b). *Global Association of Risk Professionals* (25 February, 2008). URL: *http://www.fdic.gov/news/news/speeches/archives/2008/chairman/spfeb2508.html*

———. (2008c). *Testimony on the State of the Banking Industry before the Senate Committee on Banking, Housing and Urban Affairs* (4 March, 2008). URL: *http://www.fdic.gov/news/news/speeches/archives/2008/chairman/spmar0408.html*

———. (2009). *Testimony on Modernising Bank Supervision and Regulation before the Senate Committee on Banking, Housing and Urban Affairs* (19 March, 2009). URL: *http://www.fdic.gov/news/news/speeches/chairman/spmar0319.html*

Basel Committee on Banking Supervision (1999). "A New Capital Adequacy Framework", *Consultative Paper.* (Basel, June). URL: *http://www.fsa.gov.uk/pubs/additional/cp030699.pdf*

Baumol, William J. (1990). "Entrepreneurship: Productive, Unproductive and Destructive", *Journal of Political Economy* 98(5).

Bean, Charles (2008). "Some Lessons for Monetary Policy from the Recent Financial Turmoil", Conference on *Globalisation, Inflation and Monetary Policy* (22 November). URL: *http://www.bankofengland.co.uk/publications/speeches/2009/speech368.pdf*

Bernanke, Ben S. (2009a). *Financial Reform to Address Systemic Risk*. Council on Foreign Relations (10 March). URL: *http://www.federalreserve.gov/newsevents/speech/bernanke20090310a.htm*

———. (2009b). *Four Questions about the Financial Crisis*, (14 April). URL: *http://www.federalreserve.gov/newsevents/speech/bernanke20090414a.htm*

———. (2009c). *Financial Innovation and Consumer Protection*, Sixth Biennial Community Affairs Research Conference (17 April). URL: *http://www.federalreserve.gov/newsevents/speech/bernanke20090417a.htm*

———. (2009d). "Regulatory Restructuring", Testimony before the House of Representatives Committee on Financial Services (24 July). URL: *http://www.federalreserve.gov/newsevents/testimony/bernanke20090724a.htm*

Bloomberg News (2000). *International Herald Tribune*. 8 August.

Bond, Ian (2006). "Managing a Bank-specific Crisis: A UK Perspective", *BBA Workshop on Managing a Bank-specific Crisis* (26 October) URL: *http://www.bankofengland.co.uk/publications/speeches/2006/presentation061026.pdf*

Carpio, Gerard and Patrick Honohan (1999). "Restoring Banking Stability: Beyond Supervised Capital Requirements", *Journal of Economic Perspectives* 13(4): 43-64.

Case, Karl E. (2000). "Real Estate and the Macroeconomy", *Brookings Papers on Economic Activity* 2000(2): 119-62.

Casey, Kathleen L. (2008). Remarks at the Commission Open Meeting (3 December). URL : *http://www.sec.gov/news/speech/2008/spch120308klc.htm*

Cetina, Karin Knorr and Urs Bruegger (2002). "Global Microstructures: The Virtual Societies of Financial Markets", *American Journal of Sociology* 107(4): 905-50, January.

Claessens, Stijin and Simeon Djankov (1999). "Publicly-Listed East Asian Corporates: Growth, Financing and Risks", Paper Presented to Regional Conference on *Asian Corporate Recovery: Corporate Governance, Government Policy.* World Bank. March 15.

Clark, Alastair (2000). *Accounting Standards and International Financial Markets*. Institute of Chartered Accountants in Banking, Dublin (3 May). URL: *http://www.bankofengland.co.uk/publications/speeches/2000/speech84.htm*

Clementi, David (2000). *Crisis Prevention and Resolution—Two Aspects of Financial Stability*. South Bank University Centre for Monetary and Financial Economics (6 September). URL: *http://www.bankofengland.co.uk/publications/speeches/2000/speech97.htm*

———. (2001). "Banks and Systemic Risk—Theory and Evidence, Bank of England Conference (23 May). URL: *http://www.bankofengland.co.uk/publications/speeches/2001/speech130.htm*

———. (2002). *Property and the Economy*. Chartered Surveyors Livery Company International Dinner (29 April). URL: *http://www.bankofengland.co.uk/publications/speeches/2002/speech170.htm*

Cohen, Norma (2009). "Regulation: Doubts over Political Resolve for Reform", *Financial Times.* October 5.

Cox, Christopher (2008). *Joint Meeting of the Exchequer Club and Women in Housing and Finance* (4 December). URL: *http://www.sec.gov/news/speech/2008/spch120408cc.htm*

Darling, Alistair (2009). *Banking Crisis*, Vol. I Oral evidence (HMSO: HC 144–I, March 2009). URL: *http://www.publications.parliament.uk/pa/cm200809/cmselect/cmtreasy/144/144i.pdf.*

Demyanyk, Yuliya S. and Otto Van Hemert (2008). "Understanding the Subprime Mortgage Crisis" (5 December). URL: *SSRN-id1020396[1].pdf*

Duke, Elizabeth A. (2009). "Consumer Protection", Testimony before the House of Representatives Subcommittee on *Domestic Monetary Policy and Technology*,

Committee on Financial Services (16 July). URL: *http://www.federalreserve.gov/newsevents/testimony/duke20090716a.htm*

Ferguson, Jr. and W. Roger (2002). "Financial Engineering and Financial Stability", Annual Conference on the *Securities Industry*, American Institute of Certified Public Accountants and the Financial Management Division of the Securities Industry Association (20 November). URL: *http://www.federalreserve.gov/boarddocs/speeches/2002/20021120/default.htm*

Financial Times (1999). *Financial Times*. 28 January and 22 April.

FSA (2009). Memorandum from the Financial Services Authority (FSA). House of Commons Treasury Committee, *Banking Crisis*, Vol. II Written evidence (HMSO: HC 144–II, March 2009). URL: *http://www.publications.parliament.uk/pa/cm200809/cmselect/cmtreasy/144/144ii.pdf*

Gieve, John (2007). "Uncertainty, Policy and Financial Markets", Barbican Centre (24 July). URL: *http://www.bankofengland.co.uk/publications/speeches/2007/speech321.htm*

———. (2009). "Seven Lessons from the Last Three Years" (19 February). URL: *http://www.bankofengland.co.uk/publications/speeches/2009/speech377.pdf Working Pap33/*

Guitián, Manuel (1998). "The Challenge of Managing Global Capital Flows, Finance and Development", June. HMG (2009), *Reforming Financial Markets* (Cm 7667/ 2009). URL: *http://www.hm-treasury.gov.uk/d/reforming_financial_markets080709.pdf*

House of Commons Treasury Committee (2008a). *The Run on the Rock Fifth Report of Session 2007-08*. Vol. I (London: HMSO, HC56-I, January 2008). URL: *http://www.publications.parliament.uk/pa/cm200708/cmselect/cmtreasy/56/56i.pdf*

———. (2008b). *Financial Stability and Transparency Sixth Report of Session 2007–08* (London: HMSO HC 371, March 2008). URL: *http://www.publications.parliament.uk/pa/cm200708/cmselect/cmtreasy/371/371.pdf*

———. (2008c). *Re-appointment of Mervyn King as Governor of the Bank of England, Tenth Report of Session 2007-08*. Vol. I (London: HMSO HC 524-I, June 2008). URL: *http://www.publications.parliament.uk/pa/cm200708/cmselect/cmtreasy/524/524.pdf*

IMF (2009). *Global Financial Stability Report: Navigating the Financial Challenges Ahead.* Washington: International Monetary Fund. October. URL *http://www.imf.org/external/pubs/ft/gfsr/2009/02/pdf/text.pdf*

Jenkinson, Nigel, Adrian Penalver and Nicholas Vause (2008). "Financial Innovation: What Have We Learnt?", Reserve Bank of Australia Conference on *Lessons from the Financial Turmoil of 2007 and 2008*, (14-15 July). URL: *http://www.bankofengland.co.uk/publications/speeches/2007/speech321.htm*

Kay, John, John Vickers, Colin Mayer and David Ulph (1988). "Regulatory Reform in Britain", *Economic Policy* 3(7): 285-351.

Keenan, Faith (1999). "Finance: Picking up the Pieces", *Far Eastern Economic Review.* May 6.

Keys, Benjamin, Tanmoy K. Mukherjee, Amit Seru and Vikrant Vig (2008). *Did Securitisation Lead to Lax Screening? Evidence from Subprime Loans 2001-2006*, (December), EFA 2008 Athens Meetings Paper. URL: SSRN-id1093137[1]

King, Mervyn, (2009). "Finance: A Return from Risk" (17 March). URL: *http://www.bankofengland.co.uk/publications/speeches/2009/speech381.pdf*

King, M.R. and T.J. Sinclair (2003). "Private Actors and Public Policy: A Requiem for the New Basel Capital Accord", *International Political Science Review*: 345-62 (July).

Kregel, J.A. (1998). "Derivatives and Global Capital Flows: Applications to Asia", *Cambridge Journal of Economics* 22(6): 677-92.

Krugman, Paul (2009). "Fighting off Depression", *New York Times*. January 5.

Lardy, Nicholas and R. Lardy (2003). "The Case of China", in Chung H. Lee (ed.), *Financial Liberalisation and the Economic Crisis in Asia*. London: Routledge Curzon.

Large, Andrew (2003). "Convergence in Insurance and Banking: Some Financial Stability Issues," Mandarin Oriental Hotel (12 June). URL: *http://www.bankofengland.co.uk/publications/speeches/2003/speech196.htm*

———. (2004). *Financial Stability Oversight, Past & Present*. London School of Economics (22 January). URL: *http://www.bankofengland.co.uk/publications/speeches/2004/speech212.htm*

Meier, Barry (2007). "3 Executives Spared Prison in OxyContin Case", *New York Times*. July 21.

Meier, Barry and Benedict Carey (2009). "Drug Maker is Accused of Fraud", *New York Times*. February 26.

New York Times (2009). "It's the Regulations, Not the Regulator", *New York Times*. March 18.

Redak, Vanessa (2006). "Risks, Ratings and Regulation: Toward a Reorganisation of Credit *via* Basel II?", in Peter Mooslechner, Helene Schuberth and Beat Weber (eds.), *The Political Economy of Financial Market Regulation: The Dynamics of Inclusion and Exclusion*. Cheltenham: Edward Elgar Publishing Ltd.

Saul, Stephanie (2008). "Merck Wrote Drug Studies for Doctors", *New York Times*. April 16.

Solomon Smith Barney (1998). *Fixed Income—Local Government ITIC Credits*. November 26.

Strauss-Kahn, Dominique, (2009). "Beyond the Crisis: Sustainable Growth and a Stable International Monetary System", *Sixth Annual Bundesbank Lecture* (4 September). URL: *http://www.imf.org/external/np/speeches/2009/090409.htm*

Tafara, Ethiopis (2009). *A Few Observations Based on International Regulatory Conversations*, CESR Conference (23 February). URL: *http://www.sec.gov/news/speech/2009/spch022309et.htm*

Taube, Markus (2002). "Economic Relations between the PRC and the States of Europe", *China Quarterly* 169: 78-107.

Turner, Adair (2009a). *The Financial Crisis and the Future of Financial Regulation*. The Economist's Inaugural City Lecture (21 January). URL: *http://www.fsa.gov.uk/pages/Library/Communication/Speeches/2009/0121_at.shtml)*

———. (2009b). "Priorities for the Reform of Global Regulation: Challenging Past Assumptions", Speech at *IOSCO 2009*, Tel Aviv (11 June 2009). URL: *http://www.fsa.gov.uk/pages/Library/Communication/Speeches/2009/0611_at.shtml; URL: http://www.fdic.gov/news/news/speeches/archives/2008/chairman/spjan1708.html*

US Treasury (2009). *The Role of the Federal Reserve in Preserving Financial and Monetary Stability*. Joint Statement by the Department of the Treasury and the Federal Reserve, (23 March, 2009). URL: *http://www.treas.gov/press/releases/tg66.htm*

Walter, Elisse B. (2009). *Testimony before the House of Representatives Committee on Financial Services*. March 20. URL: *http://www.sec.gov/news/testimony/2009/ts032009ebw.htm*

Warsh, Kevin (2009). *The Panic of 2008*. Council of Institutional Investors (6 April). URL: *http://www.federalreserve.gov/newsevents/speech/warsh20090406a.htm*

World Bank (1993). *The East Asian Miracle. Economic Growth and Public Policy*. New York: Oxford University Press.

———. (1995). *Managing Capital Inflows in East Asia*. Washington: World Bank.

Xia, Bin (2004). *Renmin Ribao*. July 27.

Xiao, Xu (2001). *China* Daily. October 20.

Zhu, Rongji (2000). *China Daily*. October 17.

4 The Global Financial Crisis

Financial Flows to Developing Countries Set to Fall by One Quarter

Massimiliano Cali, Isabella Massa and Dirk Willem te Velde

Introduction

The global financial crisis that has spread around the world has caused a considerable slowdown in most developed countries and has already affected financial markets and growth prospects in the developing countries. Governments around the world are trying to contain the crisis, but some suggest the worst is yet to come. House prices in the United States of America (USA) have collapsed with losses of up to $2.4 trillion in the eight months to July 2008 (Lin, 2008), hitting the balance sheets of banks exposed to the housing sector which affected the entire US financial sector and, then, in turn, other developed and developing countries. Leading indicators of global economic activities, such as shipping rates, have declined at alarming rates. Asian markets are also slowing down, while orders for Chinese exports are falling.

Global financial contagion is already upon us. Stock markets in both the developed and the developing countries are down to 50-75 per cent from their recent peaks. The USA has lost equities worth $16.2 trillion this year. Investment banks have collapsed and high street banks have been rescued, with government sponsored packages worth more than one trillion US dollars. The International Monetary Fund (IMF) has begun to support countries such as Hungary, Iceland and Ukraine. On 8th October, interest rates were cut around the world in what looks like a coordinated response and have fallen further in a number of countries.

much quicker than through real channels. For example, a shock in income growth in a developed country may have a gradual impact on a developing country through trade channels, but could have a much quicker effect on economic activity of that country through correlations in stock market fluctuations.

There are two main financial channels through which the recent turmoil, triggered by the sub-prime crisis in the USA since mid-2007, has spread to developing countries:

- *Net private equity flows*: This includes FDI aimed at acquiring a long lasting stake in developing country entities and portfolio equity inflows.
- *Net private debt flows*: This includes short, medium and long-term debt flows.

The developed country financial crisis affects private capital flows to developing countries in a number of ways:

- *Solvency effect:* During the current financial crisis, several financial institutions in the developed countries experienced a strong deterioration in their balance sheets due to huge losses in sub-prime mortgages. This deterioration caused a substantial fall in the amount of bank capital and because of risk-based capital requirements, banks have restricted asset growth by cutting back on lending. As a consequence, cross-border syndicated loans to developing countries and intra-bank lending have been curtailed.
- *Liquidity effect:* The financial crisis increased the pressure of liquidity constraints on bank and non-bank intermediaries (i.e., institutional investors like mutual funds and hedge fund) in developed economies with adverse consequences for developing countries. Indeed, the increased uncertainty about counterparty risk in the banking sector caused a surge in demand for short-term financing thus putting banks' liquidity under pressure and making fewer resources available for cross-border bank lending. Moreover, hedge fund investors in mature economies, who had faced margin calls and redemption orders at home, have been forced to liquidate some of their foreign equity positions thus intensifying the sell-off of risky assets in the developing world.

- *Investor perceptions:* The uncertainties on the global economic outlook created by the current financial turmoil have reduced investors' appetite for risk, thus causing a flight to quality. International investors have become more risk averse and have preferred to flee to high quality assets (e.g., government bonds) from large economies like Europe and ironically the USA, rather than continuing to invest in risky emerging markets' assets. This phenomenon has been exacerbated by investors' concerns about the existence of some overvaluation in the emerging markets and about the risk of a sudden slowdown in their economic growth. Consequently, bond issuance and net private equity flows in the developing countries have declined. In particular, the lack of investors' confidence has led to a reduction in the number of initial public offerings (IPOs), as foreign investors have become less willing to invest in equities issued by companies going public in developing countries.
- *Asymmetric information and herding:* Because of the opacity of the structured products market, the sub-prime mortgages crisis has led to a high degree of asymmetric information among banks about the distribution of losses and counterparty risk. Banks have, therefore, become reluctant to lend even to developing countries and have increased the cost of borrowing. The presence of information asymmetries among investors have also led to the herding phenomena, where uninformed investors decide to sell off risky assets in developing countries just following the behaviour of perceived informed investors.
- *Real economy effects:* Given the strong links between global growth and net private capital flows to the developing economies, the projected reduction in global growth mainly driven by the developed countries may lead to a further reduction in net private capital flows to developing countries.
- *Liability management effect:* The absence of a prudent liability management by financial institutions may have additional negative effects on capital flows to the developing countries, because of increasing uncertainty of whether the developing countries will be able to roll over short-term debt as well as medium and long-term

debt. According to the Institute of International Finance (IIF, 2008), which has looked at 30 developing countries, short-term debt flows have increased in the last two years from an average value of $25 billion in 1997-2006 to $253 billion in 2007 and $141 billion in 2008. On the other hand, the overall amortisation payments of debt due by private sector borrowers are expected to amount to $90 billion in the last quarter of 2008 and to $130 billion in the first half of 2009. Brazil and Russia are among the countries with the largest debt close to be due in the next months.

The magnitude of these effects on net private capital flows to the developing countries will differ country-by-country depending on a number of factors:

- *The composition of international financial flows:* Bank lending and to a lesser extent, portfolio flows are substantially more volatile than FDI, especially in times of turbulence (World Bank, 2003 and 2004). This implies that developing countries that have, in the past, relied heavily on borrowing from foreign banks to finance the growth of their domestic market are expected to suffer more from the current financial crisis. Figure 4.1 suggests that the financial turmoil will have a strong impact on the European and Central Asian developing countries where gross cross-border bank lending has increased from about $37 billion in 2000 to a value of $252 billion in 2007.
- The maturity structure of external debt may affect the incidence and the severity of the financial crisis. In particular, evidence exists suggesting that countries where external debt has a short maturity are more exposed to the risk of being hit by financial crises. Figure 4.2 highlights that the financial turmoil is more likely to spread to the developing countries in Europe and Central Asia.
- *The current account balance and the reserve holdings of each developing country:* Indeed, large current account surpluses and reserve holdings may provide insurance against a sudden shift in private capital flows reducing the adverse shocks of the financial turmoil. For this reason, emerging Asia and the Gulf Cooperation Council (GCC) countries that have huge current account surpluses are expected to suffer less from a sudden reversal in foreign financing than Latin American countries, where the current account

Figure 4.1

Gross Cross-Border Bank Lending to Developing Countries by Region (2000-2007)

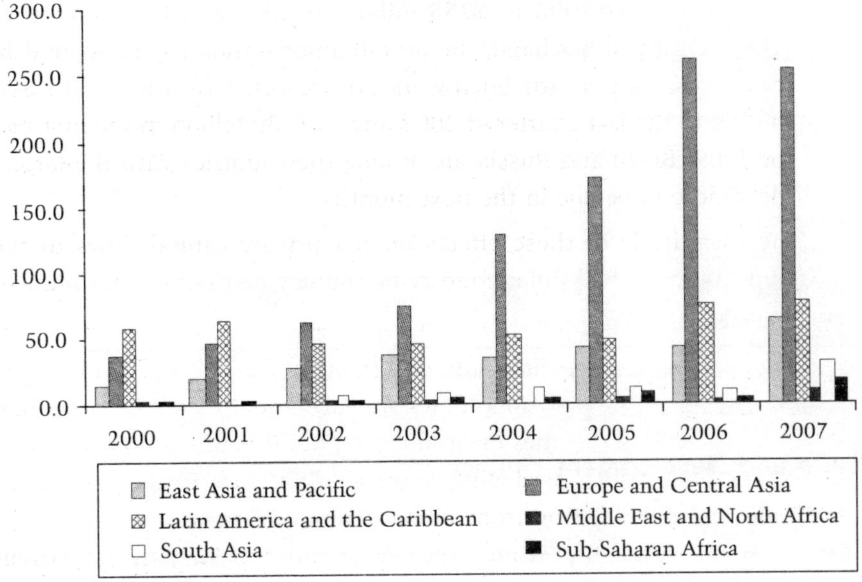

Note: Amounts in billions of US$.

Source: World Bank (2008).

Figure 4.2

Net Short-Term Debt Flows to Developing Countries by Region (2000-2007)

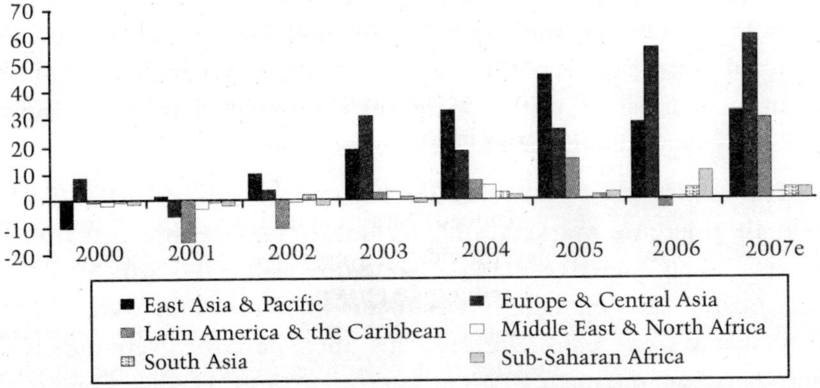

Note: Amounts in billions of US$; e = estimate.

Source: World Bank (2008).

surplus is contracting, or even worse Emerging Europe countries, where the current account deficit is high and increasing (see Table 4.1).

Table 4.1

Current Account Balance in Emerging Market Economies by Region (2006-2008)

Region	*2006*	*2007*	*2008e*
Emerging Europe	21.50	-23.60	-34.60
Emerging Asia	289.30	421.80	365.90
Latin America	54.00	26.60	14.00
Africa/Middle East	14.90	11.00	33.00
GCC countries	210.60	206.10	377.40

Note: Amounts in billions of US$; e = estimate.
Source: IIF (2008).

Trade and Development Finance

Trade and development finance are important sources of external finance for the developing countries. Export credit is short-term finance that enables trade to take place. Recently, developing country firms have funded themselves in the developed countries by issuing bonds and arranging loans which means that the financial crisis affects such firms. These effects are also felt through the lack of export credits as these are important for countries heavily dependent on exports.

The family of multilateral and bilateral DFIs has substantial resources backed by guarantees and capital endowments from governments in developed countries. In 2005, total commitments to loans, equity, guarantees and debt securities of the main regional, multilateral and bilateral DFIs totalled $45 billion (Table 4.2).

The mandates of DFIs require them to leverage such liquidity to invest in emerging markets and, for some, low-income and frontier markets. When emerging markets are doing well, DFIs will be able to obtain high returns on equity investments and developing country firms will be able to repay loans. Until recently, there have been very high levels of income across the main DFIs. At the International Finance Corporation (IFC), in 2006/07 total capital (capital stock plus designated and undesignated retained earnings) was close to total commitments of loans, equity and debt securities (see Figure 4.3), and the institution's capital adequacy ratio has risen from 45 per cent in 2002/03 to 57 per cent for 2006/07. The FMO's (Dutch DFI) capital adequacy has increased from 38.4 per cent in 2000 to 50.5 per cent in 2005. CDC's (UK DFID) rate of return outpaced emerging markets stock market indices.

Table 4.2

Annual Commitments by DFIs

(US$ million)

DFIs	*2005*	*2004*	*2003*
IFC	6,703.00	5,370.00	4,750.00
EBRD	5,328.07	5,138.56	4,207.82
EIB (FEMIP, ALA, IF)	6,842.41	6,063.57	5,543.33
IADB	7,147.50	6,019.90	6,810.00
ADB	7,432.40	5,712.90	6,295.70
AfDB	3,279.89	4,319.39	2,631.80
FMO	870.78	752.20	621.96
DEG	837.14	699.98	572.20
OPIC	2,612.00	3,217.00	2,000.00
NIB	1,308.04	840.47	837.95
PROPARCO	461.05	269.17	
CDC	283.92	366.00	425.43
MIGA	1,300.00	1,200.00	1,100.00
Total	44,406.20	39,969.14	35,796.18

Note: IFC: International Finance Corporation.

EBRD: European Bank for Reconstruction and Development.

EIB (FEMIP, ALA, IF): European Investment Bank (Facility for Euro-Mediterranean Investment and Partnership, Asia and Latin America, IF).

IADB: Inter-American Development Bank.

ADB: Asian Development Bank.

AfDB: African Development Bank.

FMO: Dutch Development Bank.

DEG: German Investment Corporation.

OPIC: Overseas Private Investment Corporation (US).

NIB: Nordic Investment Bank.

PROPARCO: French DFI.

CDC: Commonwealth Development Corporation.

MIGA: Multilateral Investment Guarantee Agency.

Source: Dellacha and te Velde (2007).

Figure 4.3

Ratio of Portfolio Commitments to Total Capital, IFC

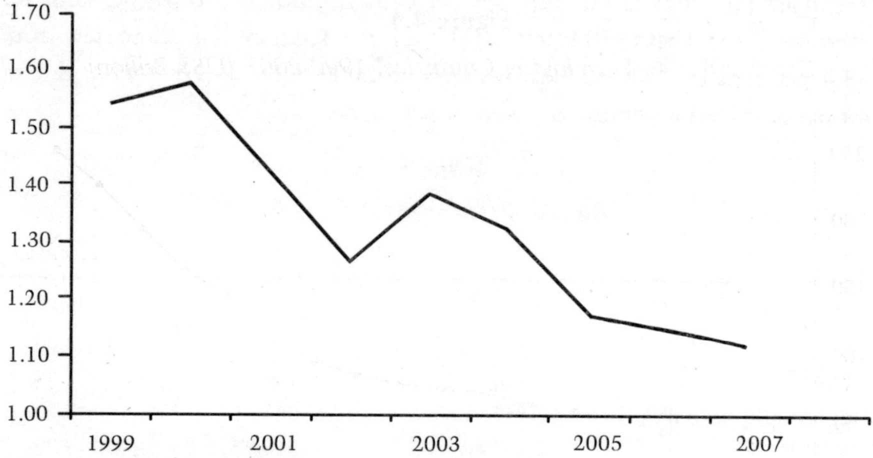

Note: Commitments include loans, equity invesments and debt securities. Capital includes stock plus designated and undesignated retained earnings.

Source: International Finance Corporation.

Remittances

Remittances sent home by migrants represent the largest source of external capital in many developing countries. This source is now being affected by the current financial crisis. Remittances were estimated at $251 billion worldwide in 2007 (World Bank, 2008), which represents more than twice the level of international aid. Adding remittances through informal channels, the number is higher by 50 per cent (World Bank, 2006). The level of remittances has been increasing for many years (Figure 4.4), but if the predictions are confirmed, 2008 risks being the first year of decreasing levels of remittances in several decades. This would set back developing countries as remittances have a poverty reducing impact on both the sending households and the country of origin. Remittances are much less concentrated in certain countries than foreign direct investment, which tends to flow to certain countries.

Aid

The 22 member countries of the OECD Development Assistance Committee, the world's major donors, provided $103.7 billion in aid in

2007 (see Figure 4.5). Though it is not clear how the crisis might affect aid flows (apart from exchange rate effects).

Figure 4.4

Remittances to Developing Countries, 1990-2007 (US$ Billion)

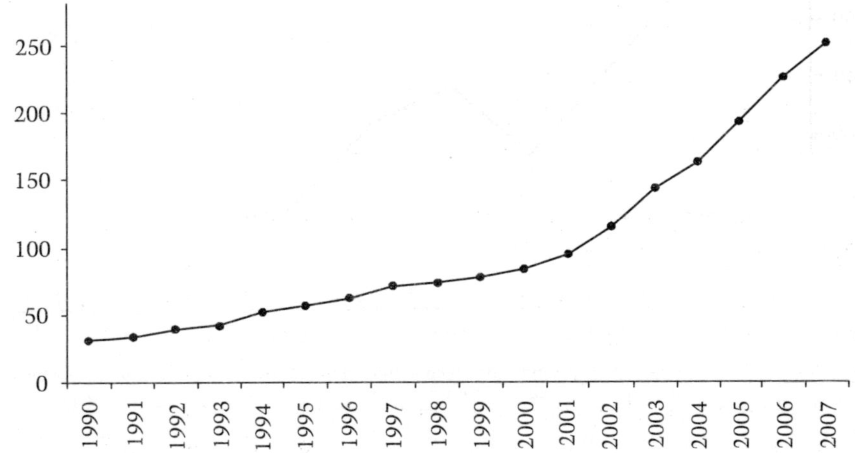

Source: World Bank (2008).

Figure 4.5

OECD DAC Aid (US$ Million)

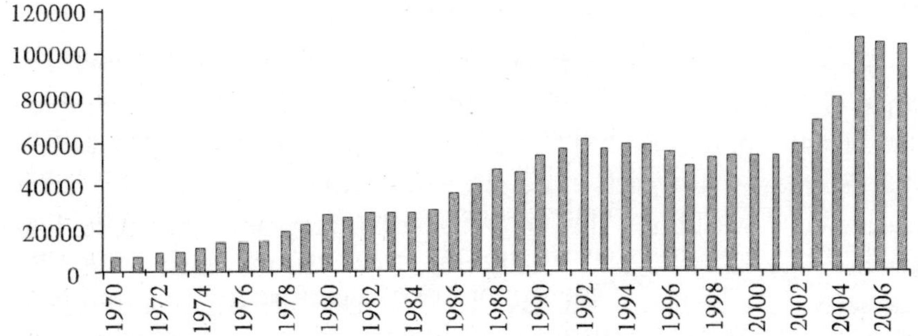

Source: Development Assistance Committee (*www.oecd.org/doc*).

Domestic Finance

While the focus of this Section is on international capital flows, domestic resources is also discussed. Exports to crisis affected states will be affected and this will be particularly in sectors such as tourism and mining.

The private sector will struggle more to raise finance in the current climate with falling stock markets. Lower growth will also put government spending under pressure.

The Evidence So Far

This section discusses the potential effects of the current financial crisis on developing countries, organised by type of flow. Inevitably, this is based on a number of assumptions and, therefore, any forecast or forward thinking will need to be treated with caution.

Foreign Direct Investment, Portfolio Flows and International Bank Lending

There is already significant evidence of financial contagion across the developing world. For example, Figure 4.6 shows how emerging equity markets after an initial period of admirable resilience against the financial turbulence, in October 2008, had started to fall. Notably, on 6 October, 2008, these markets have suffered the worst fall since the Black Monday crash in October 1987, with the Morgan Stanley Capital International (MSCI) Emerging Markets Index dropping 11 per cent.

Figure 4.7 shows how net private capital flows have fallen in Emerging Europe, Emerging Asia, Latin Amrica as well as in the Middle East and Africa alike.

According to the Institute of International Finance (IIF, 2008), in a sample of 30 developing countries, net bank lending has declined from a value of $401 billion in 2007 to a much lower value of $245 billion in 2008. Similarly, net portfolio equity flows that in 2007 have turned negative to $-5.8 billion due to increased investment abroad by local investors have fallen to $-68.9 billion in 2008. On the other hand, FDIs have been more resilient and have faced a relatively small decline from $302 billion in 2007 to $288 billion in 2008. Nevertheless, some countries have been hit harder than others. For example, Turkey has experienced a reduction of 40 per cent in FDI which has a significant effect on prospects for economic growth (see Figure 4.8). FDI in India dropped by 40 per cent from 2008 Q1 to Q2, FDI in China was $6 billion in September 2008, 20 per cent down from the monthly average in 2008 and mining investments in South Africa have been put on hold. Previous downturns in world growth

Figure 4.6

Emerging Equity Markets (2001=100, National Currency) (January 1, 2002-October 3, 2008)

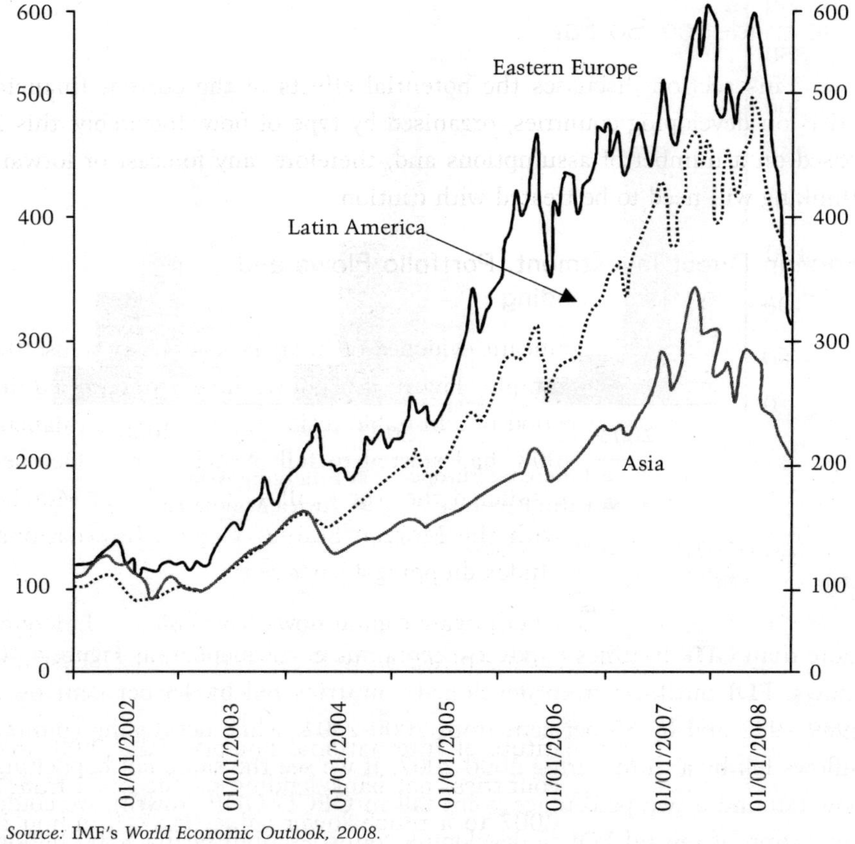

Source: IMF's *World Economic Outlook, 2008.*

in the range of 2 per cent led to fall in FDI to developing countries of around 25 per cent. A similar drop would imply a fall in FDI of $150 billion to 2009.

A complementary way to understand the possible future impact of the current financial crisis on FDI is to examine what happened in past downturns. The current downturn has slowed developed country growth by around two percentage points (see Introduction). Such a slowdown has already occurred twice in the past three decades, i.e., from 1989-1992 and from 2000-2002 (see Figure 4.9). These slowdowns coincided with substantial declines in absolute FDI flows. FDI has tended to decline by

Figure 4.7

Net Private Flows

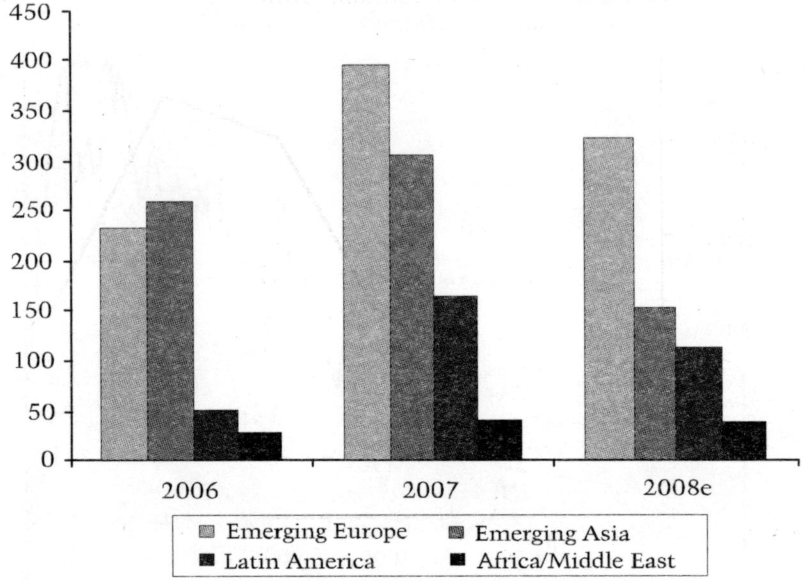

Note: Amounts in billions of US$; e = estimate.

Source: IIF (2008).

more than GDP in times of adverse economic consequences, as Figure 4.10 shows. FDI outflows from developed countries fell by 15 per cent over 1989-1992 and by 55 per cent from 2000-2002, while developing country inflows fell by a third during 2000-2002. If we see the same fall happening now (around a two percentage point fall in OECD GDP growth), we could see a drop of inward FDI to developing countries from nearly $500 billion to around $350 billion.

Emerging Europe and in particular Hungary, is a recent example of the solvency effect. Like many other developing countries, Hungary sold its banks to foreigners, aiming to stabilise and reinvigorate its financial system. This choice worked during the past years. Investors and banks were confident regarding the future of the economy and lent fearlessly without demanding enough securities (Austria's loan books amounted to 43 per cent of GDP). Now that the financial system has become so volatile, foreign banks are beginning to scale back lending to their Hungarian subsidiaries, resulting in problems in rolling over their loans. When local

Figure 4.8

Net Foreign Direct Investment, Turkey (2003-2008)

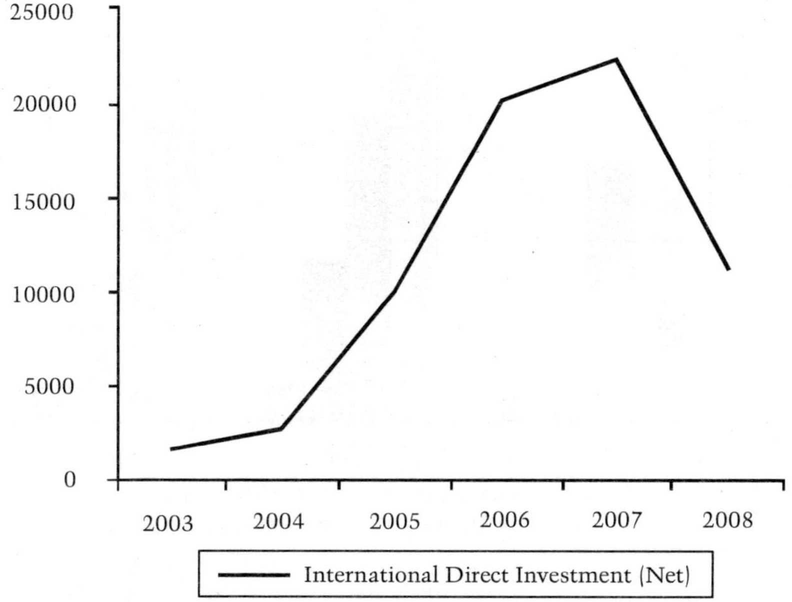

Note: Provisional data. Figure in 2008 was recorded until August. Amounts in millions of US$.
Source: TURKSTAT, Central Bank of the Republic of Turkey.

banks or subsidiaries start running out of money due to bad loans (Hungarian firms and households took out hard currency loans, accounting for 90 per cent of all new mortgages and 20 per cent of GDP), parent banks in the Euro area may refuse to send them more cash, increasing the chances for bankruptcy and financial collapse. The European Central Bank (ECB) granted Hungary a short-term credit line of $8.1 billion, while the IMF provided a $15.7 billion loan, and the World Bank made available $1.3 billion, hoping to isolate Hungary and prevent the further spread of the crisis to other emerging countries.

Investors' risk aversion has increased sharply as shown in Figure 4.11 and is above levels seen for two decades.

The drop in bond and equity issuances and the sell-off of risky assets in the developing countries embodies an additional piece of evidence helping to understand the severity of the current financial situation.

Figure 4.9

GDP Growth Rate in Advanced Countries (1980-2007)

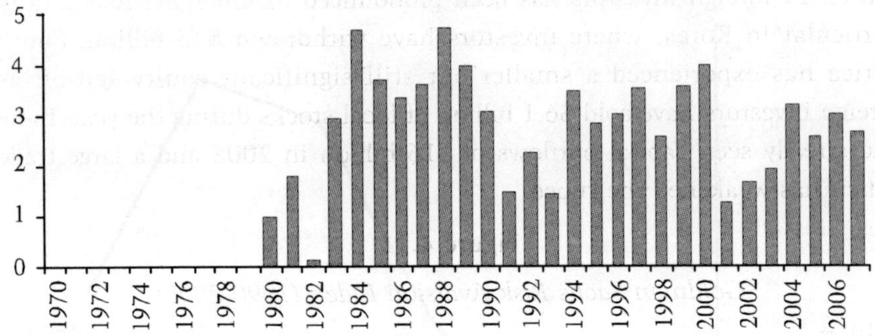

Source: IMF. *World Economic Outlook*.

Figure 4.10

Foreign Direct Investment Flows, US$ Million as Per cent of GDP (1970-2008)

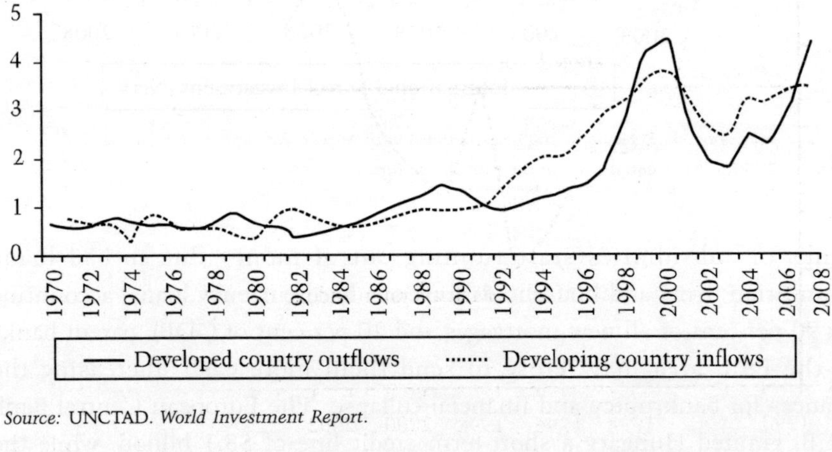

Source: UNCTAD. *World Investment Report*.

According to the World Bank (2008), the average volume of bond issuance by developing countries between July 2007 and March 2008 has been only $6 billion, compared to an average of $15 billion over the same period in 2006. Moreover, between January and March 2008, equity issuance by developing countries has reached its lowest level in the last five years reaching only $5 billion. This directly resulted in a considerable decrease in IPOs. The World Bank (2008) reported that 91 IPOs have been withdrawn or postponed in the first term of 2008. In the United Arab Emirates (UAE), for example, Abu Dhabi-based Al Qudra Holding in March has delayed what would have been the UAE's second largest IPO. Moreover, the equity sell-off by foreign investors has been pronounced in Emerging Asia and in particular in Korea, where investors have withdrawn $45 billion. South Africa has experienced a smaller but still significant equity sell-off as foreign investors have sold $6.1 billion of local stocks during the year. India had already seen capital outflows of $16 billion in 2008 and a large trade deficit has weakened the rupee.

Figure 4.11

Goldman Sachs Risk Aversion Index (1990-2008)

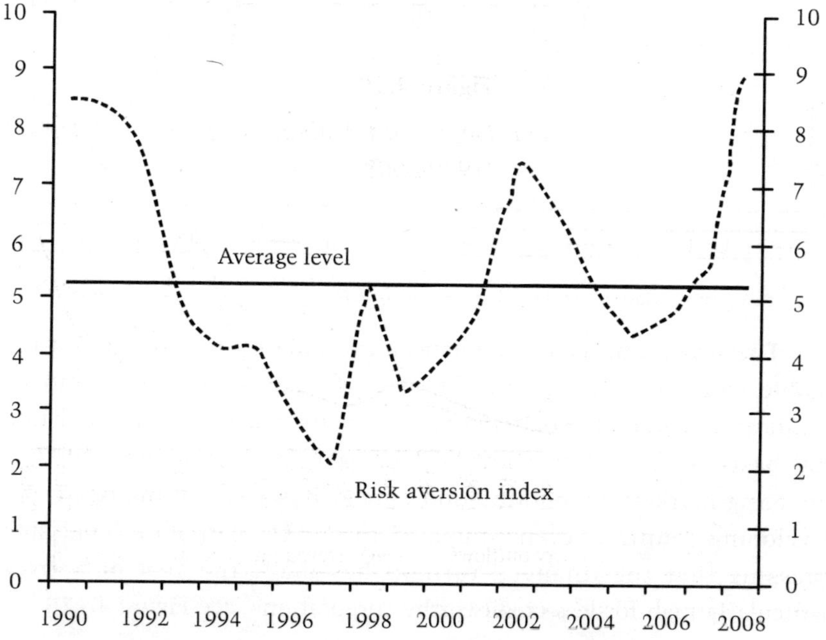

Note: Index annual averages. The average for 2008 ends in May.

Source: IMF. *Global Financial Stability Report*, October 2008 and Authors' calulations.

The increase in the cost of borrowing provides evidence of the liquidity effect and the spread of information asymmetries in the banking sector. Given that banks do not trust each other, they must protect themselves by reducing lending to other banks otherwise known as raising the cost of credit. This is precisely what has happened. There has been a dramatic surge in the spreads between interbank borrowing rates and yields on government securities. Figure 4.12 shows the spread between the US

Treasury Bills and the Euro and US LIBOR, a proxy for interbank lending. Liquidity constraints have also put pressure on international mutual funds, which, according to AMG Data Services, have suffered $31 billion of redemptions in the third quarter of 2008.

Figure 4.12

US Treasury Bill and Euro and US LIBOR in Per cent (2007-08)

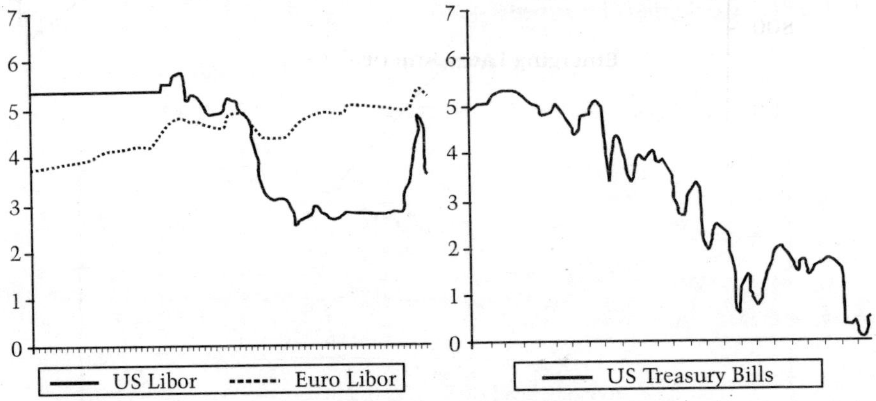

Source: US Board of Governor of the Federal Reserve System.

The strong impact of the financial turmoil on the cost of credit is also visible from the emerging-markets sovereign bond spread and more significantly corporate bond spread. The bond spread has widened to over 300 basis points, after a low of 150 basis points in June 2007. The emerging-markets corporate bond spread has risen dramatically in all developing countries even compared to the US corporate bond spread, stressing that the financial turmoil has made the cost of borrowing particularly high for less creditworthy corporations (see Figure 4.13).

A recent report by the IIF (2008) suggested that a projected 0.7 percentage point change reduction in global growth would lead to a $60 billion decline in net private flows to developing countries by the end of 2009.

Aid, Development Finance and Domestic Resources

At the Gleneagles (UK) G8 summit in 2005, donors committed to increase their aid to $130 billion in 2010 (at constant 2004 prices). While a few countries have slightly reduced their targets since 2005, the majority of

Figure 4.13

Emerging Markets External and US High Grade Corporate Spreads in Basis Points (January 2007-October 2008)

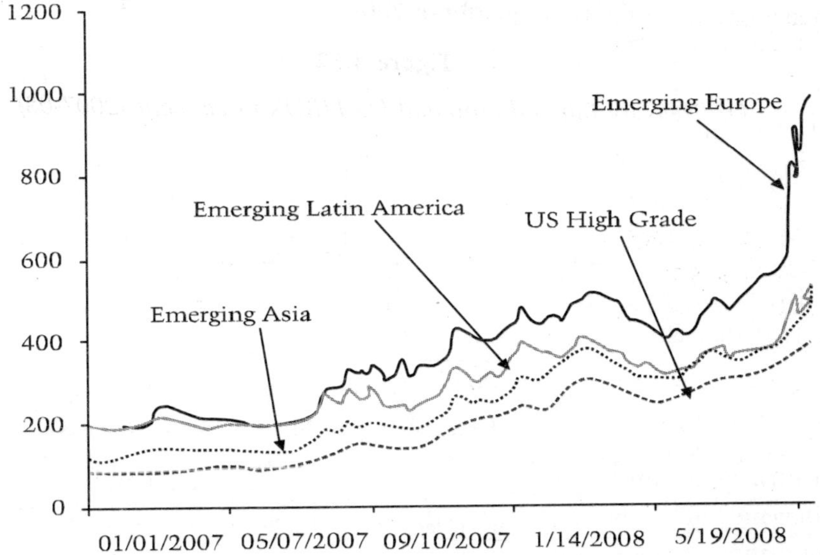

Source: J.P. Morgan & Co. and Merrill Lynch.

these commitments remain in force. According to OECD (2008), most donors were not on track to meet their stated commitments to scale up aid by April 2008; they will need to make unprecedented increases to meet their 2010 targets. Financial resources will be under pressure because developed countries will face a deep and long recession.

However, there is no simple relationship between downturns and changes in aid. For example, there was no decline in aid in the period 2000-2002 in absolute terms (of course this came after long decline in aid/GDP ratios).

Development finance operations will be affected by the crisis. Whether DFIs are operating at an optimum level of risk taking (i.e., exposure to risky projects) might be indicated by past experience, for example, by looking at the Asian financial crisis of the late 1990s. During this period, DFI portfolios were riskier, loan losses for some higher and returns lower than they are at present. And, yet, this poorer financial performance did not seem to adversely affect institutional credit ratings or their credibility as investment institutions. The EBRD argued in 2007 that it was able to withstand the impact of a major shock with an impact equivalent to about 3.5 times the magnitude of the financial crisis of 1998, without a need to call capital, although a large share of its accumulated reserves are projected to be consumed. Thus, we assume that many DFIs have sufficient capital: indeed, until recently, they had lost the battle of liquidity, having difficulty finding suitable projects.

DFIs are reacting to the financial crisis by establishing new mechanisms. IFC, the private sector arm of the World Bank group, approved a $500 million increase to the IFC Global Trade Finance Programme, bringing the programme's ceiling to $1.5 billion. The expansion enhances IFC's counter-cyclical role and its ability to respond to the global credit crisis by supporting trade with emerging markets. The IFC argues that during a liquidity crisis, banks typically reduce their exposure as a defensive measure, often resulting in a decrease in short-term trade lines. Through the Global Trade Finance Programme, IFC can guarantee the payment risk of issuing banks up to the full value of a transaction. This enables the continued flow of trade credit into the market at a time when imports may be critical and the country's exports can generate the much-needed foreign exchange.

The IMF has established a new facility for short-term finance. This would create a new short-term lending facility to channel funds quickly to emerging markets that have a strong track record but need rapid help during the current financial crisis to recover from temporary liquidity problems. The IMF has also made $200 billion available for immediate lending to emerging markets and can draw on an additional $50 billion in additional resources if necessary. So far, only few countries have drawn on it: Ukraine ($16.5 billion), Hungary ($12.5 billion) and possibly Pakistan.

Remittances

The current crisis is likely to reduce the growth (and possibly the size) of total remittances substantially as it would (negatively) affect both the size of the migrants' population and the amount remitted per capita. Economic theory suggests that migration is driven by the difference between the expected wage obtained in the destination country and the actual wage earned in the source country. The current crisis would reduce wages in developed countries, squeezing the difference in wages and reducing the level of migrant flows. But the migration stock may also be affected as some migrants may lose their jobs, thus increasing the rate of return migration or the level of unemployed migrants. Moreover, the downturn may force even those who maintain their job to reduce the amounts remitted, due for instance to a reduction in real wages (if these are linked to firms' profitability) and to a depreciation in the exchange rate of the country of destination. For instance a currency depreciation (*vis-à-vis* that of many developing countries) is currently occurring in the UK.

A large enough reduction in growth in remittances could turn into a reduction in the absolute level of remittances. Recent evidence suggests that the decrease in remittances can be substantial for certain countries. For example, in the first eight months of 2008, remittances to Mexico (which rely almost exclusively on the US market) have decreased by 4.2 per cent (at annual level). And the drop has been the strongest in the last two months of data: remittances fell by 12.2 per cent in August and by 9.6 per cent in the July-August period. Remittances to Kenya (which depend on the US economy) have been hit even harder, with the central bank estimating a 38 per cent year-to-year drop in August.

Not all countries and sectors are likely to be affected in the same way. First, certain sectors may be less affected than others. The health sector for instance, is likely to be among those less affected. As a primary need, the demand for health services has a low elasticity with respect to income. Therefore, health expenditures may remain fairly stable even in a period of deep crisis. According to the Philippines' central bank, this seems to be the case of Philippines, whose inflow of remittances is expected to experience a less drastic drop than other countries in the aftermath of the current crisis. Second, to the extent that the crisis is localised to certain regions, the more concentrated a country's migrant population is in those regions, the more adverse the potential consequences of the crisis on remittances. Third, the more reliant a country is on remittances to fund its imports or its public budget, the more exposed it is to the potential reduction in remittances. Table 4.3 presents a list of remittance-dependent developing countries with a ratio of remittances inflows to the size of their economy (measured in 2006) larger than 10 per cent.

In the absence of recent experiences of global financial crises, lack of data limits the ability to formally test for the impact of such past crises (especially in the developed countries) on remittances to developing countries. However, there have been relatively recent episodes of localised crises, which may be useful for that purpose. Based on an IMF paper by Laeven and Valencia (2008), it is possible to identify a few examples of countries hit by large systemic banking crises (along with the relative starting year). Figure 4.14 plots the evolution in remittance outflows in the sample countries which have experienced systemic banking crises. As is evident from the figure, most episodes seem to have a substantially negative effect on the subsequent level of remittances. While in the

Table 4.3

Remittance-Dependent Countries, Remittances

(in US$ million)

	Region	*2003*	*2004*	*2005*	*2006*	*2007*	*Share in GDP (%)*
Tajikistan	ECA	146	252	467	1,019	1,250	36.2
Moldova	ECA	487	705	920	1,182	1,498	35.2
Tonga	EAP	56	68	66	72	77	32.2
Honduras	LAC	867	1,151	1,796	2,367	2,675	25.6
Guyana	LAC	99	153	201	218	218	24.3
Lesotho	SSA	287	355	327	361	371	24.2
Lebanon	MNA	4,743	5,591	4,924	5,202	5,769	22.9
Haiti	LAC	811	932	985	1,070	1,184	21.5
Jordan	MNA	2,201	2,330	2,500	2,883	2,934	20.4
Jamaica	LAC	1,399	1,623	1,784	1,946	2,021	19.4
El Salvador	LAC	2,122	2,564	2,843	3,471	3,695	18.6
Armenia	ECA	686	813	940	1,175	1,273	18.4
Bonia & Herzegovina	ECA	1,749	2,072	2,052	2,157	2,514	17.6
Kyrgyz Republic	ECA	78	189	322	481	715	17.1
Nepal	SAS	771	823	1,212	1,453	1,734	16.3
Albania	ECA	889	1,161	1,290	1,359	1,359	14.9
West Bank & Gaza	MNA	472	455	598	598	598	14.7
Serbia & Montenegro	ECA	2,661	4,129	4,650	4,703	4,910	13.65
Phillppines, The	EAP	10,243	11,471	13,566	15,251	17,217	13.0
Gambia, The	SSA	65	62	57	64	64	12.5
Nicaragua	LAC	439	519	600	656	990	12.4
Cape Verde	SSA	109	113	137	137	143	11.9
Guatemala	LAC	2,147	2,591	3,032	3,626	4,130	10.3

Source: World Bank (2008) based on IMF Balance of Payment Statistics.

majority of the cases this effect is short-lived and remittances quickly returned to their pre-crisis level, in the case of Sweden and Japan this has not yet been the case.

Rough estimates based on Figure 4.14 suggest a 20 per cent drop in the value of remittances in the aftermath of the crisis. On the basis of this figure, it is possible to speculate about the costs of the crisis in terms of the

Figure 4.14

Remittance Outflows in Selected Countries (1972-2006)

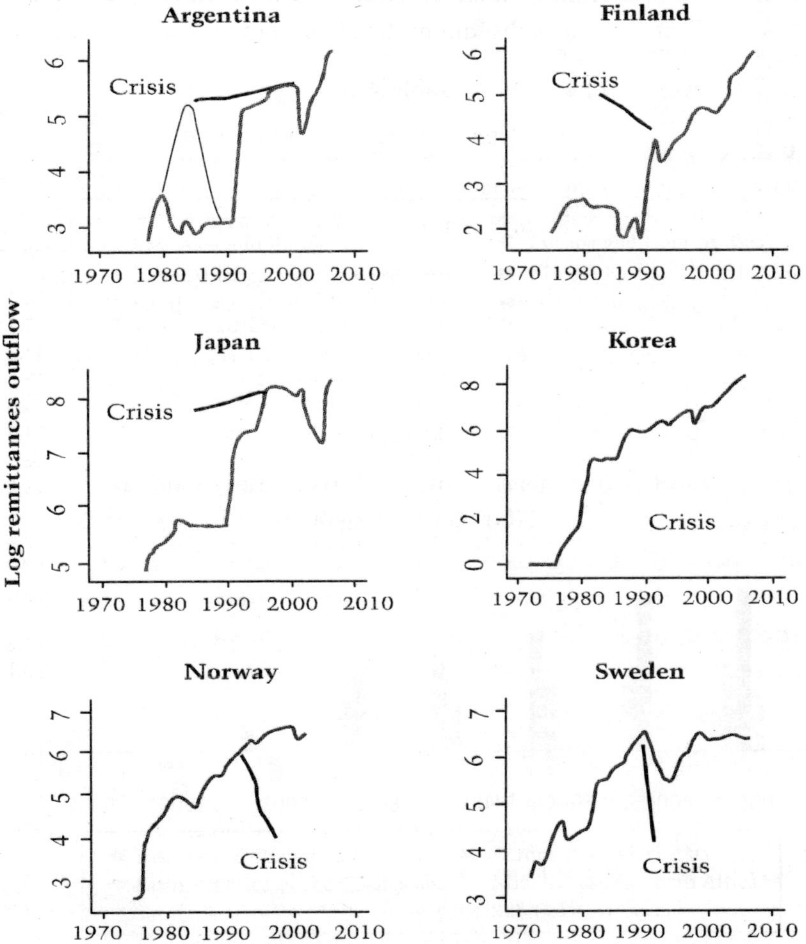

Source: Authors' elaboration on World Bank (2008) and Laeven and Valencia (2008).

level of remittances towards developing countries. In order to do that, let us assume that only remittances from high income countries are affected by the crisis (as full decoupling takes place); and let us also assume that 80 per cent of total remittances towards developing countries come from high income countries (based on estimations by Ratha and Shaw, 2007). This implies that remittances to developing countries would drop by around $40 billion following the current crisis. Although significant (the average estimate is around one-third of the total yearly external development assistance), this drop is likely to be short-term, with remittances likely to return on their long-term growth path once the crisis is over. While these estimates may provide some idea of the scale of the direct losses for one of the largest sources of external capital for developing countries, they are based on a number of specific assumptions.

Summary Table

Table 4.4 provides a summary overview of the type of flows we discussed in this Section, the baseline flows in 2007 and the expected drop during the current financial crisis. We suggest it is possible that international financial resources to developing countries fall by some $300 billion or experienced a drop by a quarter.

Policy Implications

Efforts are needed to restore international financial flows and the developing and the developed countries need to respond to the financial crisis depending on how they are affected. Looking ahead, the developed and the developing countries will need a number of appropriate arrangements to promote finance for development (for supplementary views by eminent economists see Annexure Table A-4.1) in addition to dealing with the consequences of the crisis:

- Developed countries must act to contain the global financial crisis by slashing interest rates further, coordinating their capital market responses (some is already policy) and designing fiscal packages to stimulate the economy. Some fiscal stimulus may well come in the form of aid to other countries.

Table 4.4

Gross Financial Resources to Developing Countries, Latest Year Available

(US$ billion)

	Baseline Financial Flows in 2007	*Possible New Estimate for 2008/09 (Assuming a 2% Drop in GDP over 2008-09 due to the Crisis)*	*Expected Fall*	*Examples*
Foreign direct investment (gross)	US$ 499 billion (UNCTAD)	US$ 350 billion (own estimate)	A third	Xstrata Pulled out of a US$ billion in deal South Africa, drop of net FDI by 40% in Turkey.
International bank lending (net)	US$ 400 billion (IIF)	US$ 250 billion (estimate for 2008 by IIF)	A third to two-fifths	International bank cross-border claims worldwide fell by US $862 billion in the second quarter of 2008.
Portfolio equity flows (net)	US$ 6 billion	Zero or negative net flows		Investors in Korea have withdrawn US $45 billion, US $6.1 billion during the year in South Africa and US $16 billion in India in 2008.
Remittances (gross)	US$ 251 billion	US $210 billion	A fifth	Annual decreases of 12% in Mexico and 38% in Kenya.
Aid (gross)	US$ 100 billion	US $100 billion	No change (assumption, but acknowledge pressures on aid and other budgets)	Governments in France, Italy and Spain could be planning to freeze or cut aid may budgets. Joe Biden said that foreign aid may have to be re-examined as the US looks for places to cut spending.
Development finance institutions (gross)	US $50 billion (2005/6), not including IMF	US $75 billion (in 2008 assuming trend growth	Increase (assumption)	New facilities (IFC, IMF US $200-250 billion); IMF deals with Ukraine (US $16.5 billion); Hungary (US $12.5 billion), and possibly Pakistan.
Sum of above	Around US $1.3 trillion	Around US $1000 billion	Decrease of US $300 billion (fall by 25%)	

- Developed countries need to help to prevent the emerging markets from sliding further into global turmoil through the use of loans and other support.
- Suggestions that aid 'will decline' may risk becoming a self-fulfilling prophecy. Now is the time for increased aid to poor countries (e.g., economic growth in Africa will barely be enough to keep pace with population growth next year). Smarter aid towards managing economic shocks and to those that suffer from shocks through safety nets will become more important. Maintaining aid budgets in the face of the impact of the crisis in donor countries will be a real challenge. Increased aid would lead to increased exports (around a $6: $1 ratio) and, hence, home country economic growth while a fiscal stimulus at home would anyway involve significant leakages abroad (around half).
- More emphasis on procyclical development finance (e.g., by IFC and bilateral DFIs) should promote short-term trade finance as well as long-term capital towards economically viable projects that currently face credit constraints. A current review of the UK DFID (CDC) suggests CDC could do more in the crisis affected countries. IFC has already announced it would do so.
- Encourage an enhanced, reformed and independent role for the IMF to monitor and prevent financial crises and intervene in credit constrained countries.
- Broaden G8 discussions to promote good governance of public goods and foster coordination amongst developed and key emerging countries (e.g., cross-border monitoring, rules and incentives, establish and independent regulator rating agencies).
- Reinforce the need for quantity and quality resources. Business needs to continue to improve its development impact; remittances and diaspora investment must be facilitated; the domestic tax and resource base need to be enhanced; aid quality needs to be improved; and domestic institutions need to ensure maximum benefits from decreasing financial resources.

References

Dellacha, G. and D.W. te Velde (2007). *Analysis of Development Finance Institutions Financial Accounts.*

Institute of International Finance (2008). *Capital Flows to Emerging Market Economies.* Washington D.C. October 12.

International Monetary Fund (2008a). *Global Financial Stability Report.* Washington D.C. October 12.

———. (2008b). *World Economic Outlook.* Washington D.C. October.

Laeven, L., and F. Valencia (2008). "Systemic Banking Crises: A New Database", *IMF WP/08/224.* Washington D.C.

Lin, J. (2008). "The Impact of the Financial Crisis on Developing Countries", *World Bank Draft.* Washington D.C.

OECD (2008). *Debt Relief is Down: Other ODA Rises Slightly.* Development Co-operation Directorate, OECD.

Ratha, D., and W. Shaw (2007). "South-South Migration and Remittances", *World Bank Working Paper No.* 102. Washington D.C.

World Bank (2008). Remittances Data. Online Database available at: *http://siteresources.worldbank.org/INTPROSPECTS/Resources/334934110315015165/RemittancesData_Jul08(Release).xls*

———. (2003). *Global Development Finance.* Washington D.C.

———. (2004). *Global Development Finance.* Washington D.C.

———. (2006). *Global Economic Prospects—Economic Implications Remittances and Migration.* Washington D.C.

———. (2007). *World Development Report.* Washington D.C.

———. (2008). *Global Development Finance.* Washington D.C.

Acknowledgement: © Overseas Development Institute, 2008.

Annexure Table A-4.1

What G20 Leaders must do to Stabilise Our Economy and Fix the Financial System

Author	*Key Policy Recommendations*	*Other Suggestions*
Alberto Alesina, Guido Tabellini	Cut interest rates are as low as possible without disrupting financial markets. In the US, a combination of tax relief for the lower middle class and spending on public infrastructure.	Southern Europe should make unemployment insurance more available. Also tax changes that reduce wedge between gross and net wages would sustain employment and aggregate demand.
Refet Gurkaynak	IMF should be able to 'name and shame' countries; call attention to countries that increase stimulus-linked government expenditures in a manner that leaves them deeper in debt but no better off in terms of their deep problems.	Avoid wasting time on a unified global framework to deal with crisis. Establish common levels of government guarantees for deposits.
Michael Spence	Well-targetted fiscal stimulus programmes needed; should combine with credible plans to restore fiscal balance and healthy public sector balance sheets over a period of time.	Mortgages need to be removed from damaged balance sheets, terms reset and foreclosures limited. Collateralised and structured assets, not trading and with uncertain values, similarly need to be evaluated, purchased and dismantled.
Dani Rodrik	Expand funding of the new short-term liquidity facility (SLF) at the IMF and support the Federal Reserve's new swap facilities. Access to SLF available to all developing countries is adversely affected by the financial turbulence emanating from the sub-prime fallout. Ministers of finance to establish a high-level working group that will convene as soon as practically feasible to seek wider input.	Countries with large account surpluses will adopt policies that boost domestic demand. Chinese government to make available part of its foreign currency reserve assets towards expanded swap facility in support of global financial stability. Ensure protectionist barriers are not not raised by asking the secretariat of the World Trade Organisation to monitor and report unilateral changes in trade policy, 'naming and shaming' of G20 members.
Willem H. Buiter	Institutional reform: Increase financial resources of the IMF - additional $750 billion minimum, $1.75 trillion required to act in systemic emerging markets crisis. Reform the G7/8 to include the US, the EU, Japan, China, India, Brazil, Saudi Arabia, and possibly Russia or South Africa. Change IMF	Fire-fighting measures: Treasury guarantees for cross-border inter-bank lending. Mandatory recapitalisation of banks to a uniform international standard. Coordinated global fiscal expansion, modulated by

contd...

...contd...

	quotas and voting rights in line with shares of world GDP at PPP exchange rates. Turn IMF into permanent secretariat for the new G7/8. Agree to adhere rigorously to mark-to-market accounting. Steps toward a single global regulator for large highly leveraged institutions that have significant border-crossing activities. Permit capital controls and barriers to entry for foreign entities. Create a uniform global regulatory framework for rating agencies. Do not bother with multilateral surveillance.	'ability to borrow.' Fiscal bail-outs of advanced industrial countries whose systematically important banks have a solvency gap that exceeds the government's fiscal capacity. Avoid moral hazard race to the bottom through binding international agreements on the kind of guarantees extended by governments to financial institutions and creditors in their jurisdictions. Agree common access rules and common methods for valuing illiquid assets in different national TARP-like structures.
Raghuram Rajan	G20 leaders should focus on global governance; boost the IMF's financial firepower. Facilitate better international economic dialogue by creating a group of all major countries (G-20+) with a single seat for the EU and a reformed IMF as secretariat. IMF lending capacity should be increased.	IMF must broaden mandate beyond exchange rate surveillance; become self-financing; eliminate any country's official veto power; choice of management transparent and nationality-neutral. Expand IMF's arrangements to borrow from countries with large reserves or from financial markets.
Barry Eichengreen	Create a new entity, the 'World Financial Organisation' (analogous to WTO) that would blend national sovereignty with globally agreed rules on obligations for supervision and regulation. Boost IMF lending capacity in exchange for revamping old G7/8 group into a new group.	Increase funding to IMF. New G7 composed of the US, the EU, Japan, China, Saudi Arabia, South Africa and Brazil
Stijn Claessens	Creation of an 'International Bank Charter' for the world's largest, most international banks with accompanying regulation and supervision, liquidity support, remedial actions and post-insolvency recapitalisation fund in case things go wrong.	
Daniel Gros	G20 members should boost IMF independence so it may act as a 'whistle-blower' to warn off the next crisis. representation.	Bring reach of banking Supervisors more in line with the reach of banks. Creation of the the unified EuroArea IMF

contd...

...contd...

Paul De Grauwe	Restrict banks to traditional, narrow banking with traditional oversight and guarantees while requiring only commercial banks may attract deposits from the public and from other commercial banks; firms operating in financial markets to more closely match the average maturities of their assets and liabilities. Financial institutions forced to choose between status as commercial bank or investment bank.	Commercial banks benefit from the lender of last resort facility and deposit insurance; other financial institutions not allowed to finance illiquid assets by short-term credit lines from commercial banks. New international agreement needed to remodel the banking system and separate commercial banks from investment banking activities.
Takatoshi Ito	Improved surveillance mechanisms to avoid future crises; reinforced liquidity support for small nations hit by shocks originating from other nations; better coordination of national financial supervisory and regulatory frameworks; international agreement on bankruptcy procedures for large banks with extensive transnational involvement.	Changes: IMF management and staff should be 'independent' of large shareholders; new lending facility calibrated to the size of the capital flows necessary to fill the gap; financial sector assessment programme should be strengthened; establishment of an international bankruptcy court.
Wendy Dobson		Leaders should agree on a coherent international framework for regulating financial institutions and markets that encourages strong and appropriate oversight within countries. Speed up IMF restructuring. High priority on real economy. Replace G-7 with G-20 as leaders' forum.
Yung Chul Park	Regional funding arrangements could complement IMF in enhancing efficiency and stability. G-20 nations should collaborate to make the SRPA a credible regional lender by enlarging the SRPA's reserve pool, ensuring policy conditions are no more stringent than the IMF's SLF.	
Guillermo Calvo		New Bretton Woods institutions should focus first on global macroeconomic and financial stability issues to generate conditions for sustainable growth. Create institutions at country level to

contd...

...contd...

		help offset credit market distortions. Multilateral development banks should be prepared to increase lending. Public-private partnerships supported by G7 could sustain growth in the South. Credit lines should be accompanied by foreign exchange and banking regulations that limit the extent of capital flight.
Vijay Joshi and David Vines	New system with three objectives; control of inflation, preservation of financial stability and avoidance of excessive international imbalances through policy instruments; monetary policy, regulatory supervision and fiscal policy. With IMF enforcement. IMF to determine appropriate exchange rate values—'fundamental equilibrium exchange rates' and new system of IMF issuance of SDRs.	
Erik Berglof and Jeromin Zetteleyer	IMF budget should be increased with funding from large emerging economies.	To prevent discriminatory practices, the IMF or Basel Committee should be given broader jurisdiction. Redraft the articles of the IMF to bring closer in line with more constraining spirit of the text signed at Bretton Woods, or more realistically emulate the EU's enhanced cooperation solution at the global level, with the IMF ensuring that the rules are respected.
Ernesto Zedillo		Countries should not fall into the protectionist temptation. G20 countries should commit substantial resources toward promised 'aid for trade fund' to support poor countries with adjustment costs of implementing Doha round. Rich countries should pledge to reinforce respective social compacts to make enhanced trade integration more palatable to their people.

Source: Barry Eichengreen and Richard Baldwin, A VoxEU.org Publication, 2009.

5 The Impact of the Global Financial Crisis on the World's Poorest

Shaohua Chen and Martin Ravallion

Prior to the crisis, the incidence of poverty in the developing world had been on a trend decline. Figure 5.1 shows our estimates of the poverty rate for the developing world as a whole over 1981-2005 using two poverty lines, $1.25 and $2.00 a day, at 2005 purchasing power parity (PPP) for consumption; the former line is the average of the national poverty lines found in the poorest 15 countries and the latter line is the average for the developing world as a whole. The trend rate of decline in the $1.25 a day poverty rate over 1981-2005 was 1 per cent point per year and only slightly lower (about 0.8 per cent points per year) for the $2 a day line.

This trend would have almost certainly continued in the absence of the crisis, given the expected growth rates prior to the crisis (World Bank, 2008). To assess what impact the crisis is likely to have on aggregate poverty, we need to estimate the difference between the expected level of poverty, given the crisis and what we would have expected based on the pre-crisis trajectories. This paper provides our estimates of that impact for 2009 and 2010.

Growth Impacts of the Crisis

The poverty impact of the crisis in a given country will depend on how it affects both average consumption and the distribution of consumption relative to the mean. The World Bank has made projections for average consumption at country level, which can be compared to the bank's pre-crisis projections to assess the expected impact of the crisis. We use the World Bank's latest growth projections for 2009 and 2010 (as of mid-April 2009) as the 'post-crisis' growth rates while the counterfactual (pre-crisis) projections for those done by the bank in December 2007 for 2009 and 2010. We have used the growth projections for private consumption per capita. Consumption is more appropriate than gross domestic product (GDP) for predicting the short-term impacts on poverty, since the shock to GDP is unlikely to be passed on fully to consumption in the short-term.

Figure 5.1

Headcount Indices for the Developing World, 1981-2005

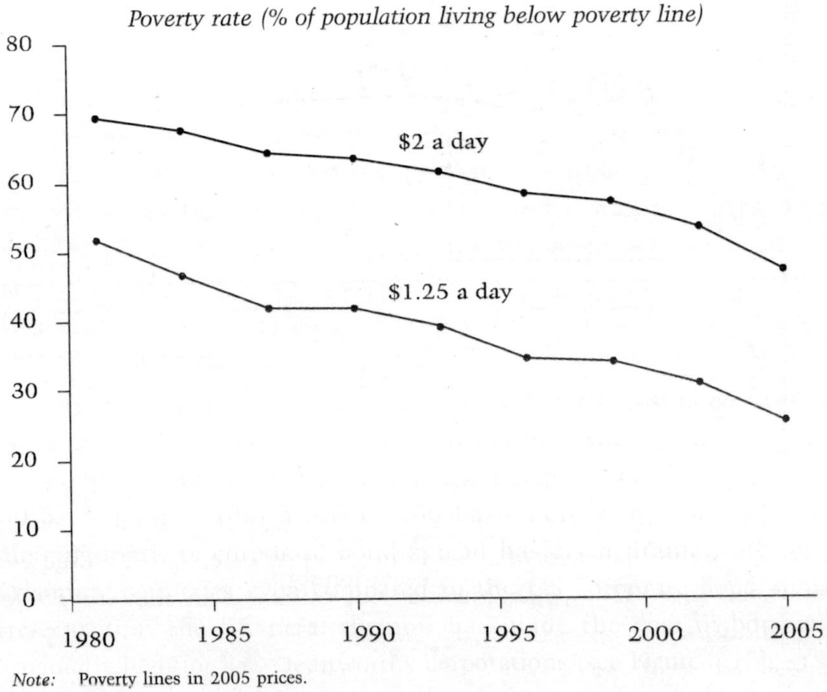

Note: Poverty lines in 2005 prices.
Source: Chen and Ravallion (2008).

The crisis is expected to sharply reduce growth in 2009. In December 2007, the bank forecast a growth rate of consumption per capita of 5.1 per cent for 2009. (This is an expenditure-weighted mean for the same set of countries for which we measure poverty using household surveys.) At the time of writing (mid-April 2009), the expected growth rate in consumption per capita for 2009 is 0.7 per cent. The expected growth is lower in 2010, with a pre-crisis rate (as projected in December 2007) of 4.4 per cent *versus* 2.6 per cent post-crisis.

Figure 5.2 plots the impacts on growth rates in 2009 across countries against the pre-crisis poverty rate using the $1.25 line. It can be seen that growth impacts tend to be higher in less poor countries. (Eastern Europe and Central Asia figure prominently in this group.) This pattern will undoubtedly help dampen the overall impact on poverty of the crisis.

Figure 5.2

The Expected Growth Impacts of the Crisis Tend to be Smaller in Poorer Countries

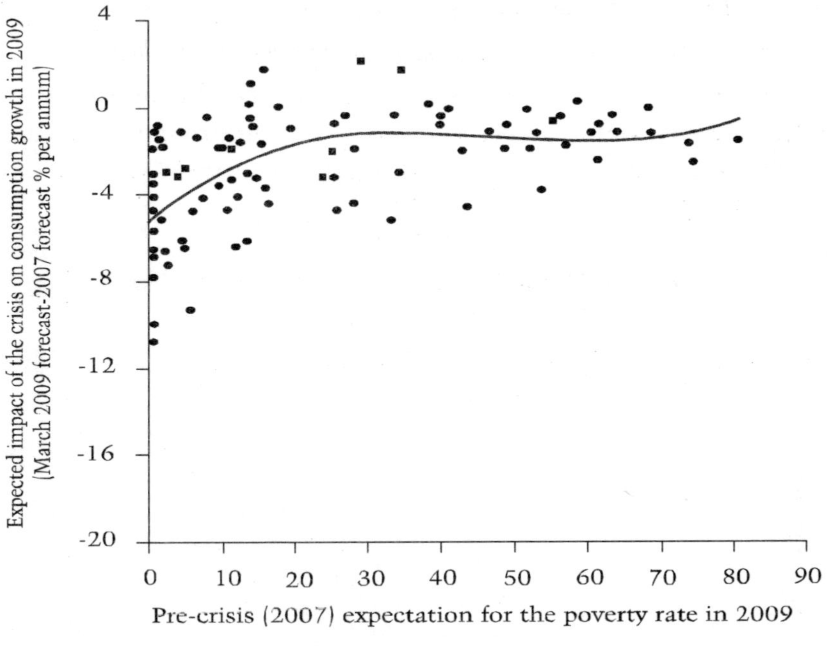

Note: The fitted values are based on a cubic polynomial.

Source: Authors' calculations.

Distributional Impacts within Countries

Past experience suggests that relative inequality falls about as often as it rises during aggregate economic contractions, with zero change on average. This is in keeping with one of the stylised facts to emerge from research on growth and distributional change, namely that economic growth tends to be distribution neutral on average (Ferreira and Ravallion, 2009). So the most defensible assumption for the present purpose is that the burden of the crisis will be more or less proportional to initial income leaving relative inequality unchanged within a given country.

To test this assumption, we have estimated the poverty rates across countries at each available survey using the most recent prior survey and assuming distribution neutrality over the intervening period. In other words, we compare the 'actual' poverty rate calculated for a given country at a given survey date t, with a prediction based on the most recent available survey, for date $t-\varepsilon$, say; the prediction is obtained using the mean for date t but the distribution of incomes normalised by the mean for date $t-\varepsilon$.

Figure 5.3 gives the results of this test. (The figure uses all the available surveys, with multiple observations for some countries.) It can be seen that the predictions accord fairly closely with the actual values on

Figure 5.3

Testing the Distribution-Neutrality Assumption Using Past Changes in Poverty

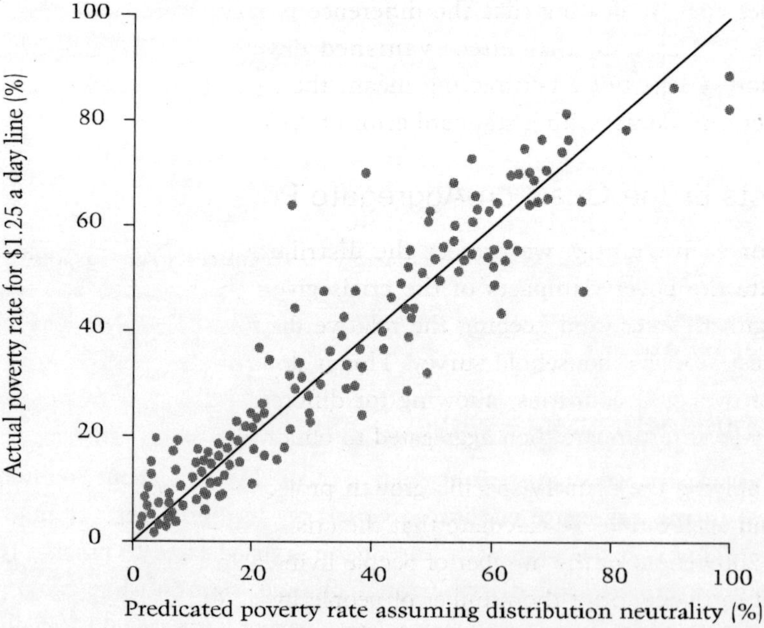

Source: Authors' calculations.

average at each level of poverty. (There is a sign of underestimation at very high levels, though there are only a few observations involved.) There is no significant difference in the means (the difference in means is 0.05 per cent points with a standard error of 0.28 per cent). Statistically, one cannot reject the null hypothesis that the predictions based on distribution neutrality are unbiased estimates of the actual changes.

It is of interest to see how well the assumption performs if we concentrate solely on cases in which the mean was falling over the period. Then we find a slight tendency for the distribution neutrality assumption to underestimate poverty on average, suggesting that the actual changes in distribution were poverty increasing in contracting economies. However, the underestimation is not statistically significant; the mean difference is 0.43 per cent points, with a standard error of 0.54 per cent.

On applying the same tests to the $2 a day measures, we again find that the distribution-neutrality assumption tends to underestimate poverty on average, again suggesting a distributional shift against the poor. For the full sample, the difference was 1.07 per cent points with a standard error of 0.35 per cent, indicating that the difference is statistically significant in this case. However, this effect vanished entirely when we confined attention to cases of a contracting mean; then the difference dropped to 0.18 per cent points with a standard error of 0.55 per cent.

Impacts of the Crisis on Aggregate Poverty

For each country, we project the distribution in levels forward to estimate the poverty impacts of the crisis given the pre-crisis and post-crisis growth rates, and keeping the relative distribution unchanged from the latest available household survey. This is done at the country level, for each of over 100 countries, allowing for different initial conditions. The country-level results are then aggregated to obtain the overall impact.

Applying the country-specific growth projections to our survey-based data and aggregating, we calculate that the crisis will add 53 million people to the 2009 count of the number of people living below $1.25 a day and 64 million to the count of the number of people living under $2 a day. Given current growth projections for 2010, there will be a further impact on poverty in that year, with the cumulative impacts rising to an extra 73 million people living under $1.25 a day and 91 million more under $2 a day by 2010.

Given current growth projections, the aggregate poverty rate is still expected to fall over time, *albeit* at a slower pace. The same (post-crisis) growth projections imply that the aggregate $1.25 a day poverty rate will fall from 21 per cent in the 'pre-crisis' year of 2008 to 18 per cent (1,040 million people) in 2009; the pre-crisis growth rate for 2009 would have instead brought the poverty rate down to 17 per cent (987 million). Using the $2 a day line, the poverty rate falls from 42 per cent in 2008 to 39 per cent (2,232 million) in 2009 under the lower expected growth rate, while the pre-crisis trajectory would have brought the poverty rate down to 38 per cent (2,169 million).

Caveats

There are three main caveats on these calculations. First, our impact estimates rely on aggregation to eliminate the distributional effect; the estimates for any individual country could be widely off the mark in some cases, as suggested by Figure 5.3. While distribution-neutrality is plausible on average, there will be some countries where the poverty impact of the crisis is greater than these calculations suggest and somewhere it will be smaller. Country-specific analysis would be needed to determine which countries might have above-average impacts.

Second, an aggregate poverty measure cannot tell the whole story. Even an economy-wide crisis can have diverse, heterogeneous, impacts at household level, which warn against generalisations based on aggregate poverty counts and also Point to the need for a flexible social policy response (Ravallion, 2009). In the (relatively rare) cases in which longitudinal survey data were available spanning a crisis—tracking the same households before and after the crisis—one finds evidence of both losses and gains during a crisis. An aggregate measure may hide considerable suffering.

Third, impacts on non-income dimensions of poverty can also be anticipated based on research on past crises (Development Research Group, 2008). When poor families are compelled to cut short their kids' schooling in response to a shock, this creates a lasting impact on poverty since school dropouts tend to earn less as adults. Declining wages during a crisis make child labour relatively less attractive and schooling more so, but (at the same time) lower parental incomes increase the value of the extra money that children can bring to the family budget if they work. The balance of these forces will vary from place to place. There is evidence that in low-income countries schooling tends to decline in a macroeconomic or agro-climatic crisis, while schooling rates actually increase in some middle-income countries (Ferreira and Schady, 2008).

Impacts on the nutrition and health of young children in poor families are of special concern. A number of research findings suggest that poor nutrition in the early years of life retards child growth, cognitive and learning ability, schooling attainments and (in all likelihood) earnings in adulthood. The balance of the evidence suggests that crises have a negative effect on child's health (and mortality) in most poor and middle-income countries (Development Research Group, 2008).

References

Chen, Shaohua and Martin Ravallion (2008). "The Developing World is Poorer than we Thought, but no less Successful in the Fight against Poverty", *Policy Research Working Paper* 4703. World Bank.

Development Research Group (2008). "Lessons from World Bank Research on Financial Crises", *Policy Research Working Paper* 4779. World Bank.

Ferreira, Francisco H.G. and Martin Ravallion (2009). "Poverty and Inequality: The Global Context", in Wiemer Salverda, Brian Nolan and Tim Smeeding (eds.), *The Oxford Handbook of Economic Inequality*. Oxford: Oxford University Press.

Ferreira, Francisco and Norbert Schady (2008). "Aggregate Economic Shocks, Child Schooling and Child Health", *Policy Research Working Paper* 4701. World Bank.

Ravallion, Martin (2009). "Bailing Out the World's Poorest", Challenge 52(2): 55-80.

World Bank (2008). *Global Economic Prospects*. Washington DC: World Bank.

Disclaimer: These are the views of the authors and should not be attributed to the World Bank or any affiliated organisation.

Acknowledgement: This article first appeared on *www.VoxEU.org*. Reproduced with permission.

6 The Global Financial Crisis

Poverty and Social Protection: Evidence from 10 Country Case Studies

Anna McCord and
Milo Vandemoortele*

While the repercussions of the financial crisis on poverty in the developing world are severe and likely to worsen, the response to date by governments and donors has been marginal. The World Bank estimates that the 'triple F' crisis: financial collapse, combined with the food and fuel price crises will increase the number of poor by between 53 and 64 million people in 2009 based on estimates of those on less than $2 a day and $1.25 respectively (Chen and Ravallion, 2009). The UK Department for International Development (2010), meanwhile, estimates that an additional 90 million people will be living on less than $1.25 a day by the end of 2010.

What we are seeing, however, is a minimal social protection response to the crisis. Even the rollout of the existing social protection commitments is being threatened by the reduction in public resources.

The combined effects of worsening poverty as a result of the financial crisis and a weak social protection response set the scene, not only for severe and growing poverty and inequality in the medium and long-term, but also for stifled growth when the upturn comes—undermining progress towards the Millennium Development Goals (MDGs).

Working with national researchers, the Overseas Development Institute (ODI) has conducted an assessment of the impact of the financial crisis in 10 countries—Bangladesh, Benin, Bolivia, Cambodia, Ghana,

* Research funded by the UK Department for International Development and the Government of the Netherlands.

Kenya, Nigeria, Indonesia, Uganda and Zambia. An ODI Working Paper discusses the macroeconomic, poverty and social protection impacts by te Velde *et al.* (2009). This paper highlights social protection, underscoring its importance to stop people falling into poverty; stop the poor and vulnerable falling deeper into poverty and promote the livelihoods of poor people so they can catch the upturn when it comes. It examines social protection policy responses to date.

The Poverty Impact of the Crisis

While the overall poverty impact of the 'triple F' crisis has been estimated, the specifics of that impact becomes less clear when one begins to drill down. Timely, relevant and disaggregated data is hard to find. The impact has not yet been fully felt. Nor can poverty implications be attributed to the global financial crisis alone. Poverty, in the broadest sense, is transferred through five key transmission channels that link macro-level shocks to poor people (see also Lustig and Walton, 2009): employment, prices, public and private transfers, assets and access to goods and services (Figure 6.1). How shocks are transmitted through these channels determines who is affected, how deeply and for how long.

Figure 6.1

Impact of Global Financial Crisis on Poverty

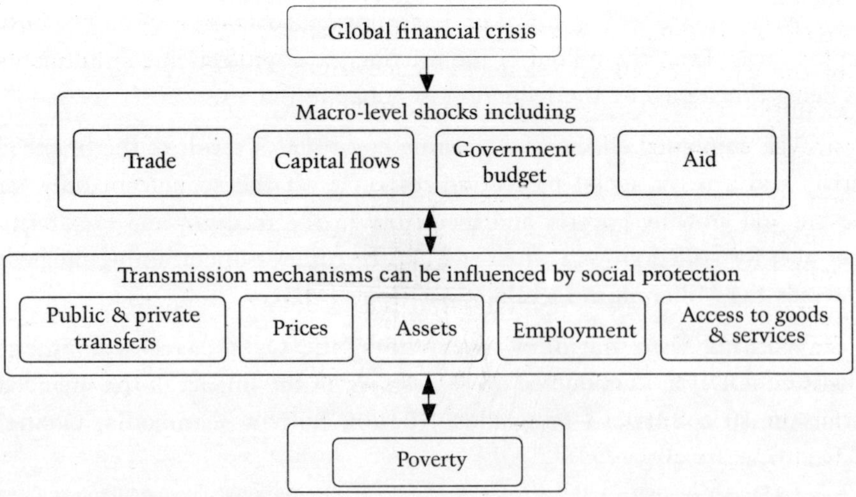

Source: World Bank/Bou Sarouen.

Employment

Loss of jobs has been a feature across the 10 countries. In Zambia, for example, the mining sector lost 27 per cent of its jobs in 2008. By mid-2008, Cambodia's construction sector had lost around 5 per cent of its jobs, leading to some de-urbanisation, as affected workers return to rural areas. The garment industry has been hard hit, with around 4 per cent of workers (51,000) laid off (many of them women) between September 2008 and March 2009. There is bound to be a fallout for the wider economy. In Zambia, for example, each job in the formal sector is reported to support another 20 jobs in services and the wider informal economy (Green, 2009). The potential implications for poverty are staggering.

Loss of income in a poor household is a serious shock. Obviously, it increases poverty in that household. It also makes it more likely that the wider community will become poor. It undermines a household's ability to buy basic supplies and can lead to ways of coping that will derail family well-being in the longer term, such as pulling children out of school or cutting back on food. These strategies undermine the younger generation's chances of moving out of poverty or contributing to economic growth. It may push vulnerable households into a vicious cycle of chronic inter-generational poverty.

The ability of a household to cope is linked to assets which may be social, physical, natural or financial. Following the food and fuel price crises, poor people may be exceptionally vulnerable to the additional shock of the global financial crisis. Evidence from Zambia's copper belt, for example, suggests an increase in commercial sex work as households struggle to cope.

Not only are people losing their jobs, employment conditions are also worsening. In Cambodia's garment industry, workers are being forced to work fewer hours. On the other hand, some people are being asked to work more hours, with less remuneration (i.e., Cambodia's tourism sector). A female head of household who has to increase her working hours will have less time to spend running her household, feeding her children, and caring for the sick. She will also have less time to rest, undermining her own health and well-being.

The immediate poverty impacts of this crisis are likely to be concentrated in regions supplying the export sectors. In Indonesia, for example, the plantations supplying international markets are concentrated in five provinces, each of which depends on revenue from a small range of crops or even just one. Zambia's export sector, for example, is almost entirely dependent on the copper belt in the north, which is, therefore, more likely to feel the pressure. In 2008, copper represented approximately 70 per cent of total exports from Zambia.

Prices

Poor people will also be affected by changes in prices as a result of the financial crisis. Changes in both consumption and production prices affect net consumers and net producers in different ways.

Lower global market demand for commodities is pushing prices down, reducing the profits of firms and the incomes of producers. In Cambodia for example, reduced demand for cassava has resulted in a steep drop in profits. Some farmers are reacting by letting their once valued crop rot in the fields. Others, who took loans to grow cassava or expand production, are seeing those loans turn into debts that they are now struggling to repay.

A drop in prices is good for net consumers. However, the fall in world food prices has not yet reached poor consumers (Blas, 2009). Evidence from Bangladesh shows that since November 2008, food-price inflation has been higher than aggregate inflation, particularly in rural areas. Poor people spend a large proportion of their household budgets on food, so food-price inflation hits them particularly hard.

In countries that distinguish between aggregate and food-price inflation, the latter tends to be higher. Persistently high inflation, in particular in food prices, will challenge food security and reduce the resources poor consumers can spend on non-food items such as education and investment.

Private and Public Transfers

The World Bank (2006) estimates that remittances to Kenya reduce the number of people living in absolute poverty by 8.5 per cent. Yet Kenya has seen a fall in international remittances of over 10 per cent; declining from $316.6 million in the second half of 2007 to $281.7 million in the second half of 2008. Between January 2008 and 2009, MoneyGram (a bank that transfers remittances) in Ghana reported a fall in remittances of 10-13 per cent. Based on a study in Uganda, as much as one quarter of remittance income is spent on school fees. So a drop in revenue from remittances may induce families to remove children from school, damaging their future ability to seize economic opportunities.

Reduced public revenue and an expanding debt (resulting from currency depreciation) are increasing the pressure on government budgets. How governments reprioritise public spending (both including and beyond social protection spending) across regions, vulnerable groups and over time will shape the short and long-run impacts of the financial crisis on growth and poverty.

Assets and Goods and Services

The provision of goods and services by governments, non-governmental organisations (NGOs) and the private sector may be waning as a result of falling revenue. In Uganda, for example, NGO revenues are reported to have fallen by over 5 per cent in the space of a year with the decline more pronounced since October 2008. Reductions in both service provision and uptake are likely to deepen as the impact of the crisis works its way through the economy.

The Social Protection Response

Social protection plays an integral role in mitigating against the impact of poverty in an economic crisis and, is therefore, an important counter-cyclical social policy. However, the social protection response to the global financial crisis has been minimal and increases in coverage have been marginal.

Countries have adopted a range of different responses to the poverty impacts of the crisis, with some struggling to meet pre-existing social protection commitments (Kenya and Uganda). Others try to extend the coverage (Ghana), even at the cost of a widening fiscal deficit (Cambodia). Still others have put social protection aside and now focus on addressing macroeconomic stabilisation (Indonesia) or promote fiscal stimulus packages while controlling a widening deficit by reducing social sector expenditure (Nigeria).

What Determines the Response?

Resources to address the poverty impacts of the financial crisis are limited. Actual and anticipated falls in public revenues are constraining the social protection budget and existing funds have already been subjected to additional demands to cope with the fuel and food crises. Developing country governments face tough decisions on what to prioritise in terms of public expenditure as deficits rise, including the provision of social protection. Developing country responses, therefore, depend not only on their budgets, but also on the relative priority they give to social protection and whether they can access alternative sources of income to address the fiscal deficit (e.g., official development assistance).

Social Protection Provision

Social protection coverage is low in all the 10 countries. The distribution of programmes is inequitable and they help only a small percentage of the poor, offering disproportionate support to those in formal employment, particularly, government employees. There is little evidence of any major increase in coverage, in response to the crisis, with only Bangladesh and Cambodia reporting significant expansion during 2008 and 2009. In the case of Bangladesh, however, much of this expansion was planned before the onset of the financial crisis (rather than in response to it). Some countries, such as Indonesia, are prioritising spending to stimulate the economy, rather than social protection, with social protection investment still based on plans drawn up in 2006.

While the financial crisis has not yet resulted in major policy reform or the large-scale expansion of social protection in most countries, a number of pre-existing programmes have been extended and new programmes introduced, *albeit* on a modest scale and largely in response to the food and fuel price crises. The major interventions to date are food subsidies and rationing (Bangladesh and Indonesia), food distributions for vulnerable groups, including school feeding programmes (Bangladesh, Cambodia, Ghana, Indonesia, Kenya and Nigeria), in-kind transfers offering fertilisers to promote agricultural production (Kenya), cash transfers (Ghana), education scholarships and subsidies (Cambodia and Ghana) and public works programmes (Bangladesh, Cambodia and Indonesia).

Across the 10 countries, social protection provision is piecemeal and fragmented. Some countries are struggling to protect funding for existing commitments, while others are trying to extend coverage. Cambodia has initiated new programmes and Ghana is trying to expand its existing programmes with support from the World Bank. However, these may be unsustainable, institutionally and financially. Kenya is developing national programmes, but there is little prospect of these being realised on a significant scale in the short-term, given the reduction in available funding.

This weak social protection response is, in part, because large-scale impoverishment arising from the crisis is not yet visible. Without data on the scale and depth of the problem, policymakers may be reluctant to allocate additional resources to poverty alleviation and food security, particularly, when it is not clear who is affected or where.

Resource Availability

The financial effects of the crisis were not recognised fully in most 2008-09 budgets, which underestimated the likely impact on government revenue. The budgets of the 10 countries were based on more optimistic growth scenarios than those currently forecast by the International Monetary Fund (IMF), leading most budgets to indicate only modest reductions in the real value of social protection allocations. The medium-term effects on social protection allocations are more likely to be significant and the extension of social protection to those affected by the crisis is likely to be compromised by lack of resources. Even the extension of existing programmes, planned prior to the financial crisis, will be limited by falling revenues and concerns regarding the control of budget deficits.

The Role of Donors

Evidence suggests that most donors have held firm on their funding allocations and commitments for social protection. Several countries will face a growing dependence on donor funding in the wake of the crisis, if they are to meet their commitments to health and education and continue rolling out social protection. Timely emergency funding by the World Bank and Asian Development Bank has supported one-off responses in countries such as Ghana and Cambodia. But large-scale, long-term funding from donors is needed if social protection is to reach those impoverished by the crisis, particularly, given the governments' reluctance to take on medium- or long-term financial liabilities in the context of a volatile economic climate.

Given the paradox of greater need for social protection at a time of dwindling resources, there is a need for more efficiency in social protection spending and the rationalisation of resource allocation which is fragmented at the present, in terms of programming and objectives in each of the case study countries.

Policy Priorities

The extent to which expenditure on social protection and social sector generally is protected, is informed by both political priorities and perceived need. In Kenya, for example, the needs of internally displaced people following the civil unrest in 2008 and the national food shortage mean that 15 per cent of the total government budget is allocated to food security. Where components of social sector expenditure are funded from conditional Highly Indebted Poor Country (HIPC) debt relief funds, these allocations are ring-fenced and enjoy some protection even when other areas of social sector expenditure are cut (as with Universal Primary Education in Nigeria and Uganda). In Zambia, ring-fencing has been less positive, with spending on pensions for government employees—accounting for 75 per cent of government social protection expenditure—being protected, while provision for others has decreased.

Elsewhere, stimulus packages and growth-oriented initiatives are being prioritised over the provision of direct social protection for the poor. Governments are trying to respond to the needs of the poor indirectly through the anticipated employment effects of increased infrastructure investment (Indonesia) and labour market initiatives to stimulate formal and informal sector employment.

Conclusion

The impact of the global financial crisis on poverty is likely to be mediated and felt in different ways across different countries, sectors, social groups, locations, time and according to the level of integration into the global economy. The immediate impacts appear to be transmitted most strongly through employment, private transfers and prices and these impacts are likely to worsen over the medium-term without direct measures to dampen them. The second and third wave effects are yet to be fully experienced in many developing countries.

Social protection responses to the crisis have, in general, taken the form of marginal increases to already limited programmes and countries are struggling to maintain existing commitments. The rollout of new initiatives developed before the crisis is threatened by the fiscal contraction caused by the crisis. There is little evidence of interventions to address its poverty consequences on any significant scale.

Social protection is essential to stop more people falling into poverty, to stop those who are already poor falling further into destitution and to support inclusive growth when the upturn comes, with all groups able to contribute to and benefit from growth.

Recommendations for National Governments

- Monitor the poverty impact of the crisis: identify who is affected and where and what other groups will be affected in the medium- and long-term;
- Rationalise and target social protection interventions and expenditure spending to address priority needs;

- Ensure that responses mitigate against the immediate poverty impacts of the financial crisis as well as promoting macroeconomic stability and growth in the medium-term.

Recommendations for Donors

- Support the development and implementation of nationally-owned social protection strategies providing high levels of coverage among the poorest, rather than continuing to promote multiple small-scale or pilot initiatives with patchy and inequitable coverage;
- Commit to medium- to long-term social protection funding at national level (5 to 10 years), to facilitate developing country government planning in response to the crisis;
- Safeguard existing ODA allocations for the health, education and social protection sectors.

References

Blas, J. (2009). "Poor still Hit by High Food Prices, says UN", *Financial Times*, Global Economy Section. March 19.

Chen, S. and M. Ravallion (2009). *The Impact of the Global Financial Crisis on the World's Poorest. (http://tinyurl.com/ccagl8)*

DFID (2010). *DFID in 2009–10: Response to the International Development (Reporting and Transparency) Act 2006.* London, UK: DFID.

Green, D. (2009). *A Copper-Bottomed Crisis? The Impact of the Global Economic Meltdown on Zambia*. Oxford: Oxfam *(http://tinyurl.com/llouna)*.

Lustig, N. and M. Walton (2009). *Crises and the Poor: A Template for Action*. Washington, DC: World Bank *(http://tinyurl.com/mvu68w)*.

te Velde, D.W. *et al.* (2009). "The Global Financial Crisis and Developing Countries: Synthesis of the Findings of 10 Country Case Studies", *Working Paper* 306. London: ODI.

World Bank (2006). *Global Economic Prospects: Economic Implications of Remittances and Migration*. Washington DC: World Bank (as cited in Kenya's report).

Acknowledgement: © Overseas Development Institute, 2009.

7

The Global Financial Crisis and Developing Countries

Which Countries are at Risk and what can be Done?

Dirk Willem te Velde

The global financial crisis is already causing a considerable slowdown in most developed countries. Governments around the world are trying to contain the crisis, but many suggest the worst is not yet over. Stock markets are down more than 40 per cent from their recent highs. Investment banks have collapsed, rescue packages are drawn up involving more than a trillion US dollars and interest rates have been cut around the world in what looks like a coordinated response. Leading indicators of global economic activity, such as shipping rates, are declining at alarming rates.

What does the turmoil mean for developing countries? Many developing country economies are still growing strongly, but forecasts have been downgraded substantially in the space of a few months. And for how much longer can growth persist? What are the channels through which the crisis could spread to developing countries and how are the effects being felt in developing countries? Which developing countries will be able to withstand the international macroeconomic challenges created by the downturn in developed economies and which are most at risk? What is the role for development policy and what do developing country policymakers need to know?

This paper discusses recent growth performance in developed and developing countries, the channels through which the global crisis affects developing countries, which countries might be most at risk and possible policy responses.

Growth in Developed and Developing Countries: Decoupling or Delayed Coupling?

With a recession already underway in the United Kingdom (UK), Germany, France, the United States of America (USA) and other developed countries, it is quite startling to hear the Malawian finance minister argue that Malawi's economy is projected to grow by more than 8 per cent this year. Yet this is today's stark reality. The USA is going through the greatest financial crisis since the 1930s, but as the *Financial Times* has reported, 'Lagos is not Lehman'. Nigeria, held back by decades of economic mismanagement, is growing at nearly 9 per cent. Leaders in China suggest that they can help the world by offering growth rates of up to 10 per cent and many African countries still gain significantly from this (they are growing at 6-7 per cent).

Growth performances vary substantially among developed and developing countries. African growth exceeds OECD growth by margins not seen for 25 years. East Asia's growth is diverging as much as it did during the last significant global economic downturn in the early 1990s (see Figure 7.1).

The relationship between Organisation for Economic Co-operation and Development's (OECD) gross domestic product (GDP) and Africa's GDP has weakened as a result of the emergence of countries such as China as well as structural changes in African economies. According to the International Monetary Fund's (IMF) *World Economic Outlook* report in April 2008, a decline in the world growth of one percentage point would lead to a 0.5 percentage point drop in Africa's GDP, so the effects of global turmoil on Africa (via trade, foreign direct investment (FDI), aid) would be quite high. The correlation between African GDP and world GDP since 1980 is 0.5, but between 2000 and 2007, it was only 0.2. As there have been significant structural changes (and a move into services that were able to withstand competition much better) as well as the rise of China, African growth has temporarily decoupled from OECD GDP.

Several Asian countries have built up healthy government reserves, and solid export performance has helped their strong current account position. Latin American countries are currently in a much better fiscal and

Figure 7.1

Growth Rates have been Diverging, but for how long?

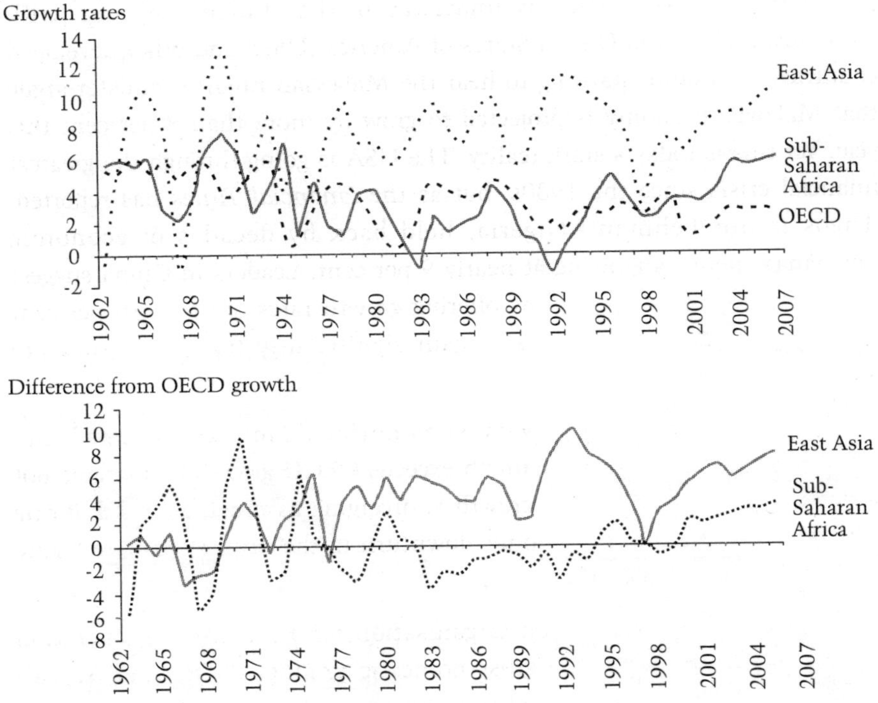

Source: World Development Indicators.

external position compared to the 1990s, the decade in which several financial crises struck.

However, there are also several worrying signs. The combination of high food prices and high oil prices has meant that while the current account of oil and food importers was in balance by 2003, it was in deficit by 4 per cent in 2007. Inflation has also doubled. Many developing and especially small and African countries are, therefore, in a bad position to face yet another crisis. The terms of trade shock tend to be the highest in small importing countries such as Fiji, Dominica, Swaziland. However, African countries such as Kenya, Malawi, Tanzania are projected to have faced terms of trade shocks of greater than 5 per cent of GDP (World Bank, 2008).

Table 7.1

World Economic Outlook Projections

	Projections				*Difference from July 2008 WEO Projections*	
World	*2006*	*2007*	*2008*	*2009*	*2008*	*2009*
USA	5.1	5.0	3.9	3.9	-0.2	-0.9
Euro Area	2.8	2.0	1.6	0.1	0.3	-0.7
UK	2.8	2.6	1.3	0.2	-0.4	-0.1
Brazil	2.8	3.0	1.0	-0.1	-0.8	-1.8
Russia	3.8	5.4	5.2	3.5	0.3	-0.5
China	7.4	8.1	7.0	5.5	-0.7	-1.8
India	11.6	11.9	9.7	9.3	-	-0.5
Sub-Saharan Africa	9.8	9.3	7.9	6.9	-0.1	-1.1
Middle East	6.6	6.9	6.1	6.3	-0.5	-0.5
ASEAN-5	5.7	5.9	6.4	5.9	0.2	-0.1
World trade volume	5.7	6.3	5.5	4.9	-0.1	-1.0
APF/MRE	9.3	7.2	4.9	4.1	-1.2	-1.9

Source: International Monetary Fund.

And there are also signs of a slowdown in Asia, the engine of recent world growth. In the space of a couple of months, the Asian Development Bank has revised its forecast for Asian countries downwards by 1-2 percentage points. The IMF growth forecasts have been revised significantly, especially for the United Kingdom (UK) (-1.8 percentage points down from the last forecast for 2009), but also India (-1.1 percentage points down to 6.9 per cent real GDP growth) and China and Africa (both down by -0.5 percentage points to 9.3 per cent and 6.3 per cent respectively).

The magnitude of the crisis will depend on the response of the USA and the EU. Trillion dollar rescue packages are launched around the world, but while the markets may eventually respond, the UK is already in a recession. Its magnitude will depend, in part, on how accommodative monetary policy can be, with the recent interest rate cut, a sure sign the authorities are concerned more about the financial crisis than recent inflationary pressures. There is less scope for expansionary fiscal policy—in fact, these rescue measures have increased public debt.

Impact of the Current Financial Crisis on Developing Countries

The current financial crisis affects developing countries in two possible ways:

First, there could be financial contagion and spillovers for stock markets in emerging markets. The Russian stock market had to stop trading twice; the Indian stock market dropped by 8 per cent in one day at the same time, as stock markets in the USA and Brazil plunged. Stock markets across the world—developed and developing—have all dropped substantially since May 2008. We have seen share prices tumble between 12 and 19 per cent in the USA, the UK and Japan in just one week, while the MSCI emerging market index fell down by 23 per cent. This includes stock markets in Brazil, South Africa, India and China. We need to better understand the nature of the financial linkages, how they occur (as they do appear to occur) and whether anything can be done to minimise contagion.

Second, the economic downturn in developed countries may also have significant impact on the developing countries. The channels of impact on developing countries include:

- *Trade and trade prices*: Growth in China and India has increased imports and pushed up the demand for copper, oil and other natural resources, which has led to greater exports and higher prices, including from African countries. Eventually, growth in China and India is likely to slow down, which will have a knock-on effect on other poorer countries.
- *Remittances*: Remittances to the developing countries will decline. There will be a fewer economic migrants coming to developed countries when they are in a recession, so fewer remittances and also probably lower volumes of remittances per migrant.
- *Foreign direct investment (FDI) and equity investment*: These will come under pressure. While 2007 was a record year for FDI to the developing countries, equity finance is under pressure and corporate and project finance is already weakening. The proposed Xstrata takeover of a South African mining conglomerate was put on hold as

the financing was harder due to the credit crunch. There are several other examples e.g. in India.

- *Commercial lending*: Banks under pressure in the developed countries may not be able to lend as much as they have done in the past. Investors are increasingly factoring in the risk of some emerging market countries defaulting on their debt, following the financial collapse of Iceland. This would limit investment in such countries as Argentina, Iceland, Pakistan and Ukraine.
- *Aid*: Aid budgets are under pressure because of debt problems and weak fiscal positions, e.g., in the UK and other European countries and in the USA. While the promises of increased aid at the Gleneagles summit in 2005 were already off track, just three years later, aid budgets are now likely to be under increased pressure.
- *Other official flows*: Capital adequacy ratios of development finance institutions will be under pressure. However, these have been relatively high recently, so there is scope for taking on more risks.

Each of these channels needs to be monitored, as changes in these variables have direct consequences for growth and development (see e.g., te Velde, 2008, on pro-poor globalisation). Those countries that have done well by participating in the global economy may also lose out most, depending on policy responses and this is not the time to reject globalisation but to better understand how to regulate and manage the globalisation processes for the benefit of developing countries. The impact on developing countries will vary. It will depend on the response in developed countries to the financial crisis and the slowdown and the economic characteristics and policy responses in developing countries.

Which Countries are at Risk and how?

The list of channels above suggest that the following types of countries are most likely to be at risk (this is a selection of indicators):

- Countries with significant exports to crisis affected countries such as the USA and EU countries (either directly or indirectly). Mexico is a good example;

- Countries exporting products whose prices are affected or products with high income elasticities. Zambia would eventually be hit by lower copper prices and the tourism sector in the Caribbean and African countries will be hit;
- Countries dependent on remittances: With fewer bonuses, Indian workers in the city of London, for example, will have less to remit. There will be fewer migrants coming into the UK and other developed countries, where attitudes might harden and job opportunities become more scarce;
- Countries heavily dependent on FDI, portfolio and DFI finance to address their current account problems (e.g., South Africa cannot afford to reduce its interest rate and it has already missed some important FDI deals);
- Countries with sophisticated stock markets and banking sectors with weakly regulated markets for securities;
- Countries with a high current account deficit with pressures on exchange rates and inflation rates. South Africa cannot afford to reduce interest rates as it needs to attract investment to address its current account deficit. India has seen a devaluation as well as high inflation. Import values in other countries have already weakened the current account;
- Countries with high government deficits. For example, India has a weak fiscal position which means that they cannot put schemes in place;
- Countries dependent on aid.

While the effects will vary from country to country, the economic impacts could include:

- Weaker export revenues;
- Further pressures on current accounts and balance of payment;
- Lower investment and growth rates;
- Lost employment.

There could also be social effects:

- Lower growth translating into higher poverty;
- More crime, weaker health systems and even more difficulties meeting the Millennium Development Goals (MDGs).

Possible Policy Responses

The current macroeconomic and social challenges posed by the global financial crisis require a much better understanding of appropriate policy responses.

- There needs to be a better understanding of what can provide financial stability, how cross-border cooperation can help to provide the public good of international financial rules and systems and what the most appropriate rules are with respect to development;
- There needs to be an understanding of whether and how developing countries can minimise financial contagion;
- Developing countries will also need to manage the implications of the current economic slowdown—after a period of strong and continued growth in developing countries, which has promoted interest in structural factors of growth, international macroeconomic management will now move up the policy agenda. Do countries have room to use fiscal and monetary polices?
- Developing countries need to understand the social outcomes and provide appropriate social protection schemes;
- There will also be implications for development policy:
  - There will be limits to financial solutions if the problems lie in the real economy, but developing finance institutions (DFIs) may be able to take some risks and support investment flows to developing countries, counteracting reductions in other financial flows. Whether DFIs can take higher risks might be informed by past experience, for example, by looking at what happened during the Asian financial crisis of the late 1990s. During this period, DFI portfolios were riskier, loan losses higher and returns lower than they are at present. And, yet, this poorer financial performance has not had an adverse affect on

institutional credit ratings. The European Bank for Reconstruction and Development (EBRD) argued in 2007 that it is able to withstand the impact of a major shock with an impact equivalent to 3.5 times the magnitude of the financial crisis in 1998, without a need to call capital;

- Aid volumes will come under pressure[1] but there may also be implications for the composition of aid. Should aid be provided to countries with high risks and how should this be channelled? Are existing IMF and World Bank schemes sufficient for this, as they already have to address balance of payment problems in countries due to high food and oil prices?

Note

1. There are several reasons why developed countries provide aid during a downturn to promote development in developing countries. This includes the need to reduce poverty in developing countries (the traditional case for doing development), the desire to promote global public goods (see ODI Opinion 5 by Dirk Willem te Velde (2002) on aid financing of global public goods) and self-interest to promote the interests of the UK (see ODI Opinion 104 by Simon Maxwell (2008) on a poll indicating the interest of UK nationals in providing aid).

References

Maxwell, Simon (2008). "Doing Development in a Downturn", *Opinions* 104. UK: Overseas Development Institute.

te Velde, Dirk Willem (2002). "Aid Financing for International Public Goods?", *Opinions* 5. UK: Overseas Development Institute.

———. (2008). "The Global Financial Crisis and Developing Countries", *ODI Background Note*. UK: The Overseas Development Institute.

World Bank (2008). "Civil Society Statement on the Implications of High Food and Energy Prices for Economic Management", Paper for the Commonwealth Secretariat. Commonwealth Finance Ministers Meeting. St. Lucia. October 6-8.

Acknowledgement: © Overseas Development Institute, 2008.

8 China and the Global Financial Crisis

Implications for the United States

Wayne M. Morrison

China's Stake in the Current Crisis

China's economy is heavily dependent on global trade and investment flows. In 2007, China overtook the United States (US) to become the world's second largest merchandise exporter after the European Union (EU). China's net exports (exports minus imports) contributed to one-third of its gross domestic product (GDP) growth in 2007. The Chinese government estimates that the foreign trade sector employs more than 80 million people, of which 28 million work in foreign-invested enterprises.[1] Foreign direct investment (FDI) flows to China have been a major factor behind its productivity gains and rapid economic growth. FDI flows to China in 2007 totalled $75 billion, making it the largest FDI recipient among the developing countries and the third largest overall, after the EU and the US. A global economic slowdown (especially, among its major export markets—the US, the EU and Japan) could have a significant negative impact on China's export sector and industries that depend on FDI flows. There are indications that the Chinese economy is already slowing down. Chinese real GDP growth for January through September 2008 was 9.9 per cent, which was 2.3 percentage points lower than growth in the same period in 2007.[2] Global Insight, an international forecasting firm, projected in October 2008, that China's GDP growth would slow from 11.9 per cent in 2007 to 9.8 per cent in 2008 and to 8.4 per cent in 2009.[3] Some analysts contend that annual economic growth of less than 8 per cent could lead to social unrest, given that every year there are 20 million new job-seekers in China.[4] According to the International

Monetary Fund (IMF), China was the single most important contributor to world economic growth in 2007.[5] Thus, a Chinese economic slowdown could also have global implications.

China's Exposure to the Global Financial Crisis

The extent of China's exposure to the current global financial crisis, in particular, from the fallout of the US sub-prime mortgage problem, is unclear. On the one hand, China places numerous restrictions on capital flows, particularly outflows, in part so that it can maintain its managed float currency policy.[6] These restrictions limit the ability of Chinese citizens and many firms to invest their savings overseas, compelling them to invest those savings domestically, (such as in banks, the stock markets, real estate and business ventures), although, some Chinese attempt to shift funds overseas illegally. Thus, the exposure of Chinese private sector firms and individual Chinese investors to sub-prime US mortgages is likely to be small.

On the other hand, Chinese government entities, such as the state Administration of Foreign Exchange, the China Investment Corporation (a $200 billion sovereign wealth fund created in 2007),[7] state banks and state-owned enterprises (SOEs), may have been more exposed to the troubled US mortgage securities. Chinese government entities account for the lion's share of China's (legal) capital outflows, much of which is derived from China's large and growing foreign exchange reserves. These reserves rose from $403 billion in 2003 (year end) to $1.9 trillion as of September 2008.[8] In order to earn interest on these holdings, the Chinese government invests in overseas assets. A large portion of China's reserves are believed to be invested in US securities, such as long-term Treasury debt (used to finance the federal deficit), long-term US agency debt (such as Freddie Mac and Fannie Mae mortgage-backed securities), long-term US corporate debt, long-term US equities and short-term debt.[9] The Treasury department estimates that as of June 2007, China's holdings of US securities totalled $922 billion, making China the second largest foreign holder of such securities (after Japan).[10] Of this total, $467 billion were in long-term Treasury securities, $364 billion were in long-term US agency securities,[11] $29 billion in long-term equities, $28 billion in long-term corporate securities and $23 billion in short-term debt.

If China held troubled sub-prime mortgage-backed securities, they would likely be included in the corporate securities category and certain US equities (which include investment company share funds, such as open-end funds, closed-end funds, money market mutual funds and hedge funds) which may have been invested in real estate. However, these were a relatively small share of China's total US securities holdings.[12] China's holdings of Fannie Mae and Freddie Mac securities (though not their stock) were likely to have been more substantial, but less risky (compared to other mortgage-backed securities), especially, after these two institutions were placed in conservatorship by the Federal government in September 2008 and, thus, have government backing.

The Chinese government generally does not release detailed information on the holdings of its financial entities, although some of its banks have reported on their level of exposure to sub-prime US mortgages.[13] Such entities have generally reported that their exposure to troubled sub-prime US mortgages has been minor, relative to their total investments, that they have liquidated such assets and/or have written off losses and that they (the banks) continue to earn high profit margins.[14] For example, the Bank of China (one of China's largest state-owned commercial banks) reported in March 2008 that its investment in asset-backed securities supported by US sub-prime mortgages totalled $10.6 billion in 2006 (accounting for 3.5 per cent of its investment securities portfolio). In October 2008, it reported that it had reduced holdings of such securities to $3.3 billion (1.4 per cent of its total securities investments) by the end of September 2008, while its holdings of debt securities issued or backed by Freddie Mac and Fannie Mae were at $10 billion. Fitch Ratings service reported that the Bank of China's exposure to US sub-prime-related investments was the largest among Asian financial institutions and that further losses from these investments were likely, but went on to state that the bank of China would be able to absorb any related losses 'without undue strain'.[15]

However, Chinese banks are not immune to financial problems.[16] There are several indicators that China's economy is slowing, which could present difficult challenges for the banking system in the years ahead, such as a sharp increase in non-performing loans. For example, the real estate market in several Chinese cities has exhibited signs of a bursting bubble, including a slowdown in construction, falling prices and growing levels of unoccupied buildings. This has increased pressure on the banks to lower interest rates further to stabilise the market, but has raised concerns that doing so could result in higher inflation (which, until recently, has been a major problem for the economy).[17] In addition, the value of China's largest stock market, the Shanghai Stock Exchange Composite Index, fell by 67 per cent from January 1 to October 27, 2008. China's media reports that export orders in 2008 have declined sharply. From January to August 2008, toy exports were 20.8 per cent lower than they were during the same period in 2007 and from January to July, more than half of China's toy exporters shut down.[18] The Federation of Hong Kong industries recently estimated that 2.5 million Chinese workers employed by Hong Kong firms in the Pearl River Delta region could soon lose their jobs.[19] On November 3, 2008, Wen Jiabao warned that 2008 would be the 'worst in recent times' for China's economy.[20]

China's Response to the Crisis

China has taken a number of steps to respond to the global financial crisis. On September 27, 2008, Chinese Premier Wen Jiabao reportedly stated that, 'What we can do now is to maintain the steady and fast growth of the national economy and ensure that no major fluctuations will happen. That will be our greatest contribution to the world economy under the current circumstances'.[21] On October 25, a Chinese Foreign Affairs official was reported by China's media as saying that, 'China supported "effective and comprehensive reforms" of the global financial system.' On October 30, another official stated: 'In the future we are also willing, within the ambit of our abilities, to continue positively, considering participating in a range of rescue plans'. China has agreed to participate and play an active role in a summit meeting of the Group of 20 countries (G- 20) in Washington, D.C., on November 15, 2008, to discuss financial markets and the global economy.

On October 8, 2008, China's central bank announced a cut (50 basis points) on its benchmark interest rate (and the reserve-requirement ratio), which coincided with rate cuts by the US Federal Reserve and several other major central banks. China cut its rates again (by 27 basis points) on October 29 following the Federal Reserve's cut (by 50 basis points). China has also indicated plans to make greater efforts to shore up its own economy to promote greater domestic demand, boost living standards in the poorer sections of the country, achieve more balanced economic growth (e.g. lowering dependency on exports) and address a number of economic and social issues, such as boosting energy efficiency, lowering pollution, narrowing income disparities and improving the social safety net (such as health care, education, pensions and social security). A number of initiatives were announced by the government in October 2008, including plans to: implement a new economic stimulus package, including an acceleration of construction projects, new export tax rebates; tax and interest rate cuts on housing transactions; increased agriculture subsidies and new loans for small and medium-sized enterprises; and elimination of taxes on interest income from stocks and savings.[22] On November 9, the Chinese government announced it would implement a two-year $586 billion stimulus package, mainly dedicated to infrastructure projects.

China's Potential Role and Implications for the United States

Analysts debate about what role China might play in responding to the global financial crisis, given its huge foreign exchange reserves but its relative reluctance to become a major player in global economic affairs and its tendency to be cautious with its reserves. Some have speculated that China would, in order to help stabilise its most important trading partner (the US), boost purchases of US securities (especially Treasury securities) in order to help fund the hundreds of billions of dollars that are expected to be spent by the US government to purchase troubled assets and stimulate the economy.[23] Additionally, China might try to shore up the US economy by buying US stocks. On September 21, 2008, the White House indicated that President Bush had called Chinese President Hu Jintao about the financial crisis and steps the administration was planning to take. An unnamed Chinese trade official was reported as stating that, 'the purpose of that call was to ask for China's help to deal with this financial crisis by urging China to hold even more US Treasury bonds and US assets'. The official was further quoted as saying that China recognised that it, '"has a stake" in the health of the US economy, both as a major market for Chinese exports and in terms of preserving the value of US-based assets held by China and

15. Fitch Ratings, Press Release, January 24, 2008.

16. Although Chinese banks have claimed to have earned large profits in recent years, many analysts contend the banking system may be weaker than reflected in their reported data. A large share of bank loans go to state-owned firms and risk management remains relatively weak. A slowing Chinese economy could produce a new wave of non-performing loans.

17. New York Times, October 23, 2008.

18. China Xinhua News Agency, October 14, 2008.

19. South China Morning Post, October 24, 2008.

20. China Xinhua News Agency, November 4, 2008.

21. Chinaview, September 27, 2008.

22. China Xinhua News Agency, Special Report, Financial Crisis.

23. Such a move could help keep US interest rates relatively low. If China chooses not to boost its holdings of US securities and other investors (domestic and foreign) did not increase their holdings, US interest rates could go up.

24. *Inside US Trade, China Trade Extra*, September 24, 2008.

25. For example, in June 2007, China's sovereign wealth fund bought $3 billion worth of shares from Blackstone LP (a US private equity firm) at $31 each, but the value of those shares fell below $8 as of October 2008.

26. For additional information, see Morrison and Labonte (2011). China's Holdings of US Securities: Implications for the US Economy, by Wayne M. Morrison and Marc Labonte.

27. China's currency has appreciated by about 19 per cent to the dollar since reforms were made in July 2005, but many US policymakers contend that it remains significantly undervalued.

28. Most Chinese firms that have been allowed to invest overseas are state-owned enterprises.

29. For example, efforts by a Chinese state-owned oil company (CNOOC) in 2005 to purchase a US energy company (Unocal) was widely opposed in Congress and eventually led the Chinese company to drop its bid. In 2007, a Chinese firm (Huawei) attempted to buy a stake in a US technology company (3Com), but dropped its bid after a number of national security concerns were raised in a review by the US Committee on foreign investment in the US.

References

Martin, Michael F. (2008). "China's Sovereign Wealth Fund", *CRS Report* RL34337. January 22.

Morrison, Wayne M. and Marc Labonte (2008). "China's Currency: Economic Issues and Options for U.S. Trade Policy", *CRS Report* RL32165. January 9.

———. (2011). "China's Holdings of US Securities: Implications for the US Economy", *CRS Report* RL34314. September 26.

9 French Banks Amid the Global Financial Crisis

Yingbin Xiao*

Introduction

The ongoing global financial crisis has posed great challenges to financial systems and governments around the globe, including in France. The unprecedented nature of the crisis and government bailouts highlight the importance of having a sound system and an appropriate policy response. It also points to the value of having a good grasp of financial sector performance and government support measures of systemic importance.

This paper attempts to analyse the performance of French banks and the financial support measures taken by the French government. France has a large and sophisticated financial system, which accounts for 10 per cent of the global banking system and five per cent of the global capital markets. Besides, it hosts the second largest mutual fund industry. The impact of the crisis on the French financial system, especially the banks, and the policies adopted, matter for the global economy and financial stability.

The rest of the paper is organised as follows. Section II presents an overview of the French banking and supervision structure. Section III conducts international comparative analyses of profitability, asset quality,

* The author thanks Erik De Vrijer, Ann-Marie Gulde-Wolf, Danièle Nouy, Muriel Tiesset, and seminar participants at the Ministry of Economy, Industry and Employment in Paris for helpful comments and suggestions. He also thanks Anastasia Guscina and Judith Rey for their assistance. All remaining errors are his own.

capital adequacy, leverage, quality of capital, funding profile and liquidity of banks. Section IV analyses business lines, potential spillovers, write-downs and losses, new capital raised and market perceptions of risk. Section V analyses the government support plan of banks and carries out an event study of the market impact of the measures. Section VI provides the conclusion.

Banking and Supervisory Structure

The French banking system features a small number of large universal banks spanning a wide range of business functions. The banks are largely organised along commercial, mutual and cooperative lines. Private commercial banks dominate the system with an asset value of about five times that of mutual and cooperative banks. The close ties among banks, life insurance companies and asset management companies, sometimes underpinned by cross-shareholding, tend to blur divisions among different types of institutions.

The French banking sector is an integral part of the European and international banking system. Home banks' external claims well exceed host banks' external claims. Foreign banks have made few inroads into French mainstream banking, except for Hong Kong and Shanghai Banking Corporation (HSBC). Although domestic banks dominate retail banking, foreign banks are free to compete and have gained a strong market presence in wholesale banking and securities trading. However, cross-border mergers and acquisitions (M&As) may blur the line between domestic and foreign banks as leading French banks become partly foreign-owned, as in the case of the Belgian government's ownership of BNP Paribas after its recent acquisition of Fortis bank.

French banking is highly consolidated. The nine largest banks account for 75 per cent of the total banking assets. The top five banks represent half of total deposits and more than a half of total lending. Banking concentration has largely stabilised over the last three years, but will rise with the merger between Groupe Caisse d'Epargne (GCE) and Groupe Banque Populaire (GBP) this year.

The financial supervision structure is based on a functional approach with some twin peaks elements. The oversight of financial services was reformed in 2003 with a view to enhancing regulatory efficiency. Hence, the financial supervisory framework was reorganised and substantially simplified. The French Monetary and Financial Code does not distinguish between commercial banks and investment banks. The prudential supervision of both banks and investment firms falls under the Commission Bancaire (CB), which ensures consistent coverage of all credit institutions. The proximity between the Banque de France (BdF) and CB facilitates timely information sharing as the Governor of the BdF serves as the chairman of the CB and BdF provides budget, human resources and other support to the CB. The board of financial sector authorities offers a domestic coordination framework.

International Comparative Analyses

The analyses employ select soundness indicators of French banks and comparators during 2006-2008. The period covers the pre-crisis period, the beginning and the middle of the global financial crisis. Given the financial integration and the global nature of banking business, a bank-based, rather than country-based, comparison group is constructed. It consists of 48 large banks in advanced Europe. To ensure comparability, only banks adopting the International Financial Reporting Systems (IFRSs) are included. Bank data come from Bankscope and Thomson Financial. Composite indicators weighted by size for the comparison group and nine major French banks respectively are constructed to facilitate aggregate comparisons.

Select soundness indicators focus on bank profitability, asset quality, capital adequacy, leverage, capital quality, funding profile and liquidity. Profitability is measured by operating income on return on average assets (RoAA) and return on average equity (RoAE), gauging both the operating performance and the bottom line. Asset quality is measured by the non-performing loans (NPLs) ratio and coverage ratio, gauging NPL and the sufficiency of provisions, respectively. Capital adequacy is measured by the Tier-I ratio, a widely used regulatory indicator. Leverage is defined as assets over shareholders' equity. Capital quality is measured by the share of Tier-II capital in total capital and the core Tier-I ratio in view of investors' recent focus. The banks' funding profile is measured by the share of wholesale funding in total funding and the share of short-term wholesale funding in short-term funding, gauging the banks' dependence on capital market funding. Liquidity is measured by the deposit-to-loan ratio and liquid ratio defined by liquid assets over liquid liabilities, examining liquidity from an asset-liability management (ALM) perspective.

Profitability

French banks were less profitable than their European peers before the crisis, but were pounded less hard by the crisis. The operating RoAA and RoAE were below those of peers in 2006, reflecting narrower interest margins and less exposure to profitable, but risky non-traditional banking activities. With the intense competition among banks, the net interest margin of French banks eroded to a level below their peers. Both French banks and their European peers registered plummeting operating performance and net income in 2008, with the profitability of European banks turning negative while that of French banks overall remained slightly positive. This is largely due to the fact that the majority of French banks still earned modest profits in 2008.

Figure 9.1

Profitability

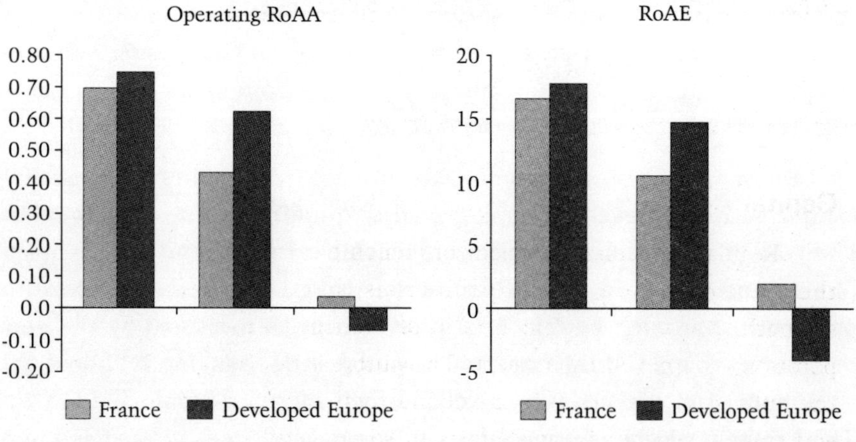

Source: Bankscope, Thomson Financial and Fund Staff estimates.

Asset Quality

The quality of French banks' loan portfolios was almost on par with that of their European peers, but the fall of provisions was less pronounced during the crisis. Both French banks and their European peers saw a declining NPL ratio in 2007, but a reversal in 2008, reflecting the turn of the economic and credit cycle, as well as the ensuing rise in defaults. The coverage ratio of both French banks and European peers dropped appreciably in 2008, suggesting less provision to cover more problem loans. French banks had less coverage than their European peers initially, but with a less marked deterioration ended up with a higher coverage ratio in 2007-2008.

Figure 9.2

Asset Quality

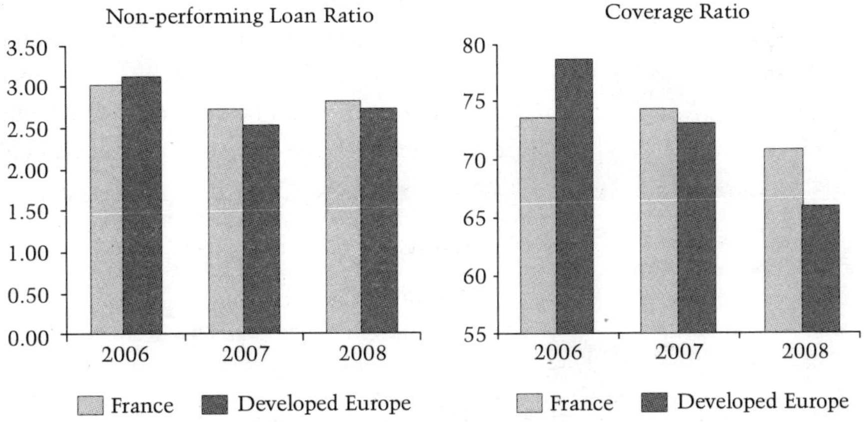

Source: Bankscope, Thomson Financial and Fund Staff estimates.

Capital Adequacy

Regulatory capital adequacy of French banks was stronger than that of their European peers before the crisis, but gradually lost its relative strength. In 2006, the Tier-I ratio of French banks was about 100 basis points above that of their peers. The outbreak of the crisis in 2007 eroded the buffers for both French banks and their European peers. With massive government recapitalisation efforts in some countries in 2008, the edge of the capital positions of the French banks shrank and converged with the others.

Figure 9.3

Capital Adequacy

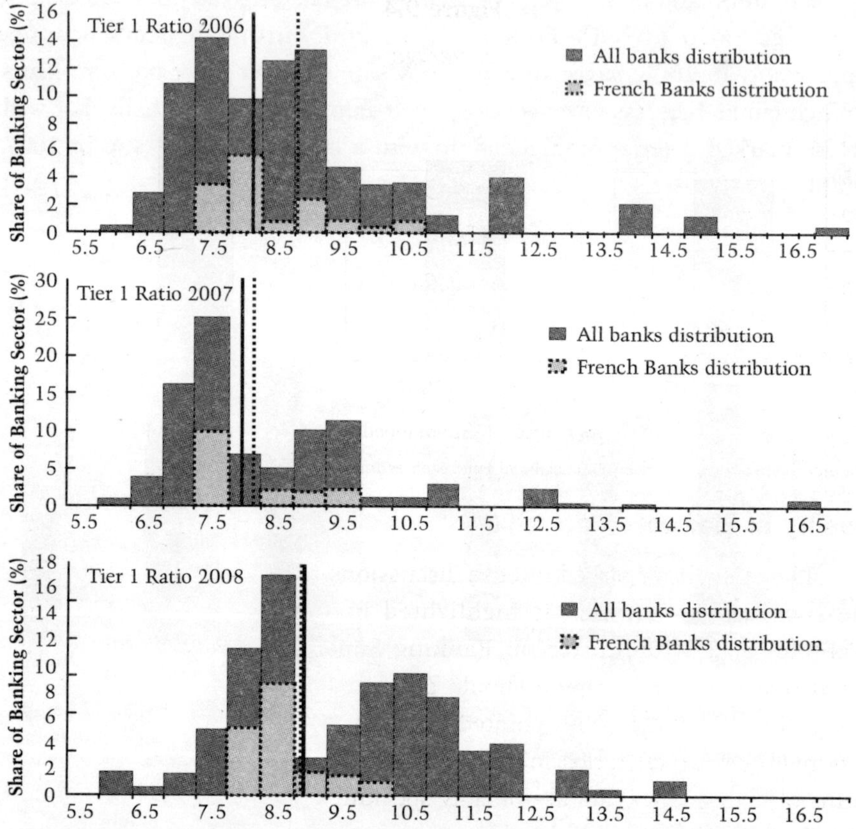

Source: Bankscope, Thomson Financial and Fund Staff estimates.

Leverage

The level and evolution of the leverage of French banks mirrored those of their European peers. Both groups showed no signs of deleveraging from their pre-crisis levels, an interesting phenomenon that contradicts the conventional perception that banks would be forced or inclined to reduce leverage because of the crisis. The CB's 2008 annual report noted that the banks continued to expand their intermediation business, although at a slower pace. The report examined leverage as measured by the ratio of loan volume over equity and loan volume weighted by asset quality over equity. It concluded that leverage stabilised and French banks did not appear to choose an aggressive strategy of reducing outstanding loans or restricting the distribution of riskier loans.

Figure 9.4

Leverage

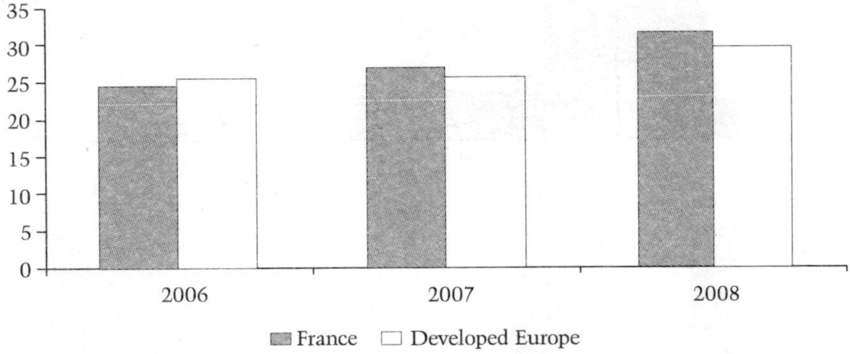

Source: Bankscope, Thomson Financial and Fund Staff estimates.

Quality of Capital

The crisis has sparked intense discussions about the quality of capital, the significance of which is highlighted in supervisory guidelines. For example, Basel Committee on Banking Supervision (BCBS) Guidelines noted that core Tier-I capital should be a predominant part of Tier-I. The Turner Review (FSA, 2009) pointed out that 'The FSA, therefore, believes that required capital ratios for such banks should be expressed entirely in terms of high quality capital—broadly speaking the current Core Tier 1 and Tier 1 definitions—and should not count dated subordinated debt as providing relevant support. This is in line with the direction of Basel Committee deliberations'. The United States (US) Supervisory Capital Assessment Program (SCAP) argued that 'Supervisors have long indicated that common equity should be the dominant component of Tier 1 capital...'

French banks had a higher capital quality initially, but their lead was eroded following the raft of global recapitalisations across the industry. Both French banks and their European peers increased the share of Tier-II capital in the capital structure in 2008, although the increase was somewhat smaller for French banks. With investors putting less emphasis on Tier-II capital, several European banks, including some French banks, have considered or conducted liability management operations to buy back their lower Tier-II capital to improve the quantity and quality of capital. The core Tier-I ratio of French banks was about 15 basis points above that of others in 2007 and stood on par with their peers after the wave of government recapitalisations in 2008.

Figure 9.5

Capital Quality

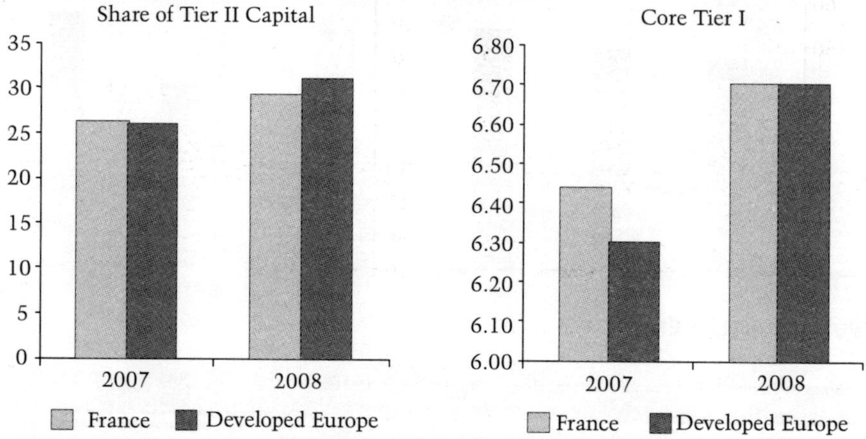

Source: Bankscope, Thomson Financial and Fund Staff estimates.

Funding

French banks appear to have a rising and higher-than-average reliance on wholesale funding. A bank's funding strategy at different maturities tends to affect the banks' fragility and its sensitivity to a liquidity dry-up. Deposit funding and wholesale funding may carry different risks in causing a potential liquidity crisis and bringing about changes in funding costs. French banks have increased their recourse to wholesale funding with the rapid expansion of their activities and a shift to high fee generating products for funding. An examination of French banks' average funding profile during 2006-2008 reveals that wholesale funding represents 58 per cent of total funding and short-term (ST) wholesale funding accounts for about 35 per cent of ST funding in the case of French banks, but 47 per cent and 28 per cent, respectively, in the case of their European peers. Though at first appearance it seems at odds with the high savings ratio of

France, this reflects the role of the money market funds and life insurance products in diversified bank funding.

Figure 9.6

Funding

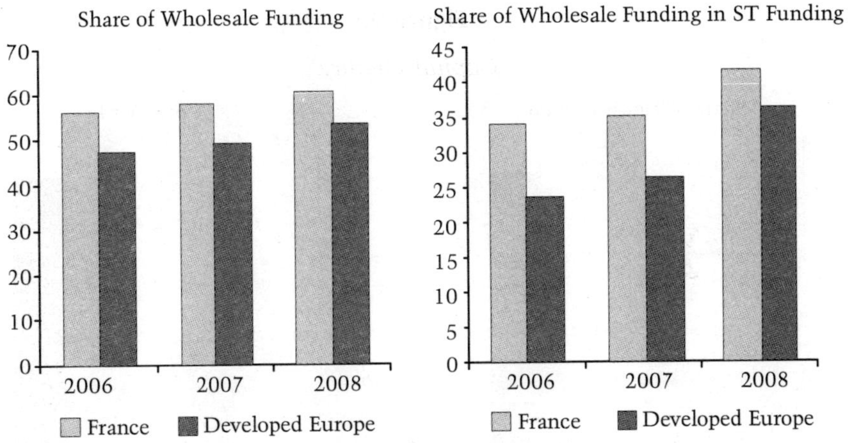

Source: Bankscope, Thomson Financial and Fund Staff estimates.

The liquidity profile of French banks from the ALM perspective appears to be slightly more favourable than that of their European peers, although this is becoming less so over time. While the funding profile focusses on the liability side, the ALM perspective focusses on liquidity matching from both assets and liabilities. The deposit-to-loan ratio shows the extent to which domestic credit is funded by banks' deposit liabilities. Any shortfall, as reflected in a ratio of less than 100 per cent, has to be funded by bank borrowing from the non-bank private sector or from overseas, both of which have become constrained in the crisis. Banks with a high coverage ratio of customer loans by deposits are less vulnerable and more resilient in the face of increased tension in liquidity markets. The deposit-to-loan ratio of French banks rose to 75 per cent in 2007, but slid in 2008, although still remained above the level of European peers. The liquid ratio of French banks declined by half to reach a similar level as their peers in 2008. However, the liquidity profiles of French banks may improve with the generalisation of *Livret A* and *Livret Bleu* (special saving accounts in France) at the beginning of 2009, which has encouraged banks to attract more deposits.

Figure 9.7

Liquidity

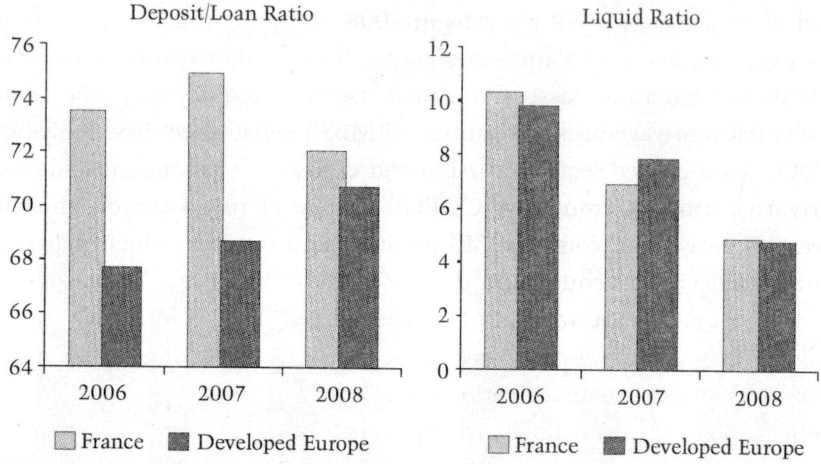

Source: Bankscope, Thomson Financial and Fund Staff estimates.

Analyses of Business and Exposures

The analyses of business and exposures supplement the above soundness check to gain more insights about the relative performance of French banks. Specifically, this Section analyses business lines, international exposures, write-downs and losses, new capital raised and market perceptions of risk. Financial data come from Bloomberg, the BIS, Datastream, Thomson Financial and financial statements of banks.

Domestic and international retail banking activities contributed to the financial results of French banks. French banks have adopted a domestic retail dominated universal banking model. An analysis of business lines shows that retail banking activities, especially international banking, continued their brisk growth throughout the crisis. The share of domestic business climbed modestly to 46 per cent, reflecting the low risk and high saturation of domestic markets. The contribution of international banking to operating income rose significantly from 18 per cent in 2006 to 27 per cent in 2008, reflecting the French banks' geographic diversification and brisk expansion to fast-growing countries.

However, Corporate and Investment Banking (CIB) and asset management activities detracted from the financial strength of French banks. CIB business, the key profit driver in the past, was hit the hardest by the crisis. Its contribution to operating income fell from the pre-crisis level of 24 per cent to 10 per cent in 2008, reflecting plummeting revenue and even sizeable losses for some banks. They suffered from impairment charges and fair value losses from toxic assets including sub-prime related residential mortgage-backed securities (RMBS), collaterised debt obligations (CDO), asset-backed securities (ABS) and exposures to monoline and credit derivative product company (CDPC). Increased risk aversion shunned investors away from complex CIB products and services, which materially compressed CIB revenues and depressed its profitability. The economic downturn and market volatility also weighed on other structured products such as commercial mortgage-backed securities (CMBS), leveraged buyouts (LBO), collaterised loan obligations (CLO) as well as trading and advisory services. Significant outflows arising from volatility, a loss of confidence associated with a 'breaking of the buck' in the US money market funds, problems with the 'dynamic' money market funds and poor performances of hedge funds dealt a blow to profits from asset management activities,

Figure 9.8

Business Lines

(Evolution of Business Line)

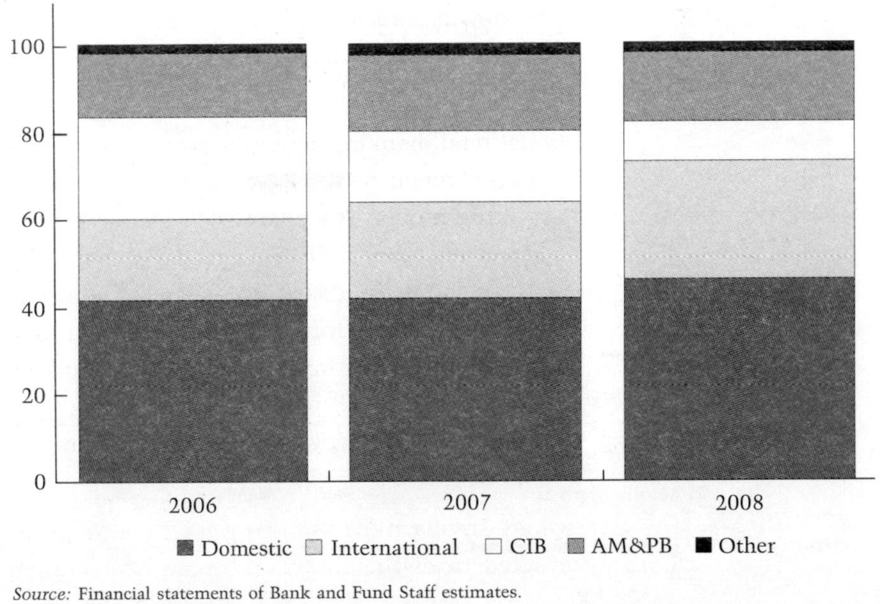

Source: Financial statements of Bank and Fund Staff estimates.

although to a lesser degree than for CIB activities. With the partly offsetting income from private banking, the contribution from combined asset management and private banking (AM & PB) fell back to its pre-crisis level.

French banks' exposure to foreign markets is not excessive and tilts towards mature markets. Foreign claims on an immediate borrower basis represented 34 per cent of bank assets and 128 per cent of GDP at the end of 2008 while foreign claims on an ultimate risk basis were slightly lower. The exposure in terms of the size of the national economy aligns with countries such as Austria, Germany, Sweden and the United Kingdom (UK) and lies between the very low level of the US and the very high level of Switzerland. Banks' exposure to mature market dominates, representing 86 per cent of total foreign claims. Exposure to the US, Italy, the UK and Germany accounts for more than half of the total exposure to mature markets. The mature market bias suggests that potential spillovers from these markets may have a material impact on French banks.

French banks' exposure to offshore financial centres and emerging markets is limited. Exposure to emerging markets on either an immediate borrower basis or an ultimate risk basis represented about four per cent of bank assets and 14 per cent of GDP at the end of 2008, only higher than the US and UK. Exposure to offshore financial centres is even smaller.

Figure 9.9

Foreign Exposure (% of GDP)

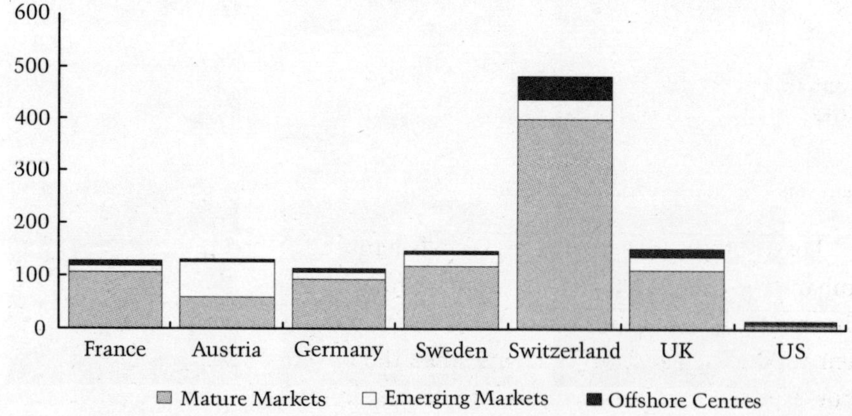

Source: BIS, IFS, WEO and Fund Staff estimates.

The exposure to emerging markets is geographically diversified. Exposure to Central and Eastern Europe (CEE) made up about 36 per cent of the total exposure to emerging markets, followed by Africa and the Middle East (28%) and Asia and the Pacific (24%) at the end of 2008. Among the exposure to CEE, exposure to the Czech Republic, Russia and Poland accounts for half of the total exposure. Among the three major French banks having exposure to CEE, only one bank has a sizeable exposure. Although pressure on French banks could be mounting with a worsening of the financial situation in the CEE region or emerging markets in general, the overall risks may be manageable.

Figure 9.10

Emerging Market Exposure

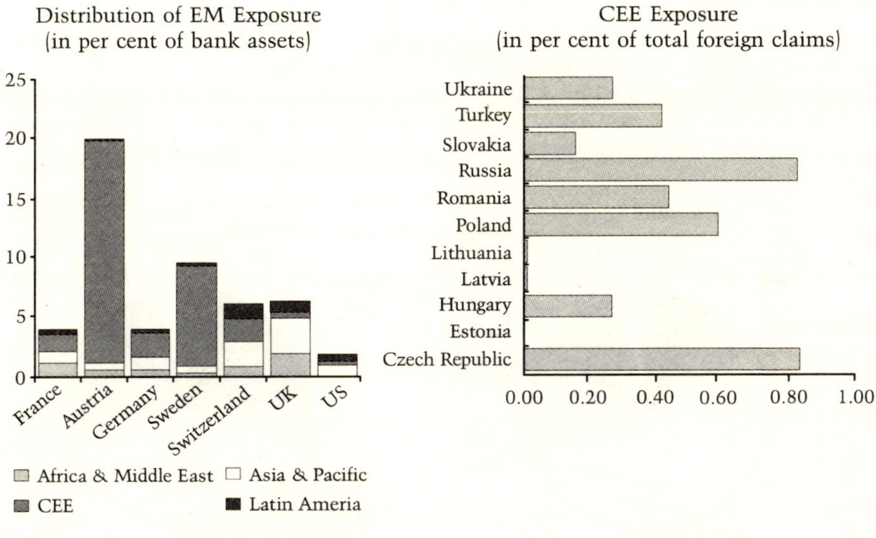

Source: BIS, IFS, WEO and Fund Staff estimates.

Losses and write-downs of French banks have been significant, but comparatively less than in the hardest-hit countries. French banks have written down a large proportion of assets relative to their initial value. Their total losses and write-downs since the onset of the crisis account for about 3 per cent of losses and write-downs around the globe, considerably less than those of banks in the US (55%), the UK (12%), Germany (9%) and Switzerland (7%) and also less than the share of French banks in the global

100 basis points recently. Throughout most of the crisis period, senior CDS spreads of French banks have been lower than those of peers, as measured by the iTraxx Euro Senior CDS index. In the case of junior CDS spreads of French banks, spreads have surged from less than 30 basis points before the crisis to more than 150 basis points recently. As in the case of senior CDS spreads, throughout most of the crisis period, junior CDS spreads of French banks have been lower than those of peers measured by the iTraxx Euro Junior CDS index. Moreover, the difference is more striking. For example, junior CDS spreads of French banks were 36 per cent below those of the iTraxx Euro Junior CDS index at the peak of the crisis in March 2009 and 24 per cent lower in June. Senior CDS spreads of French banks were 17 per cent and 8 per cent below those of the iTraxx Euro Senior CDS index in March and June 2009, respectively. The market perception of French banks as being less risky than their peers, even for the lower class of debt, may indicate that markets put a premium on national champions.

An Event Study of the French Banking Sector Support

Before the deepening of the crisis in September 2008, the French government focussed on increasing the efficiency and competitiveness of the financial sector domestically and advocated regulatory and supervisory reforms internationally. In particular to liberalise and reform the financial sector, the government rolled out a flurry of measures under the Paris-Place Financière initiative and the Loi de Modernisation de l'Économie (LME). In the aftermath of the trading fraud at Société Générale (SG), the government took actions to strengthen internal controls and operation risk management. During the 2008 French Presidency of the EU, it proposed 30 recommendations for Europe to combat the crisis.

The bankruptcy of Lehman Brothers intensified the crisis and fuelled the worst bout of financial contagion since WWII. Concerns about exposures to Lehman sparked massive turmoil in global financial markets with the freezing up of interbank, senior unsecured, covered bond and securitisation markets. The financial shock in the US reverberated internationally, fuelled the global 'flight-to-quality', and resulted in surging spreads, collapsing equity prices and spiking volatility.

The deepening of the crisis prompted large-scale sovereign interventions. Governments around the world took unprecedented support measures to recapitalise banks and unfreeze credit. Global government measures include recapitalisation, guarantees, deposit insurance, asset swaps, asset purchases, as well as direct lending and crisis liquidity facilities. Measures in some countries came with strings attached such as conditions on dividends, salary restrictions, lending rules, code of ethics and government appointed Board members.

As part of the global actions, the French government created two separate agencies to recapitalise banks and provide government guarantees for bank refinancing. Recapitalisation is handled by the Société de Prise de Participations de l'État (SPPE), a fully state-owned agency. Refinancing operations are undertaken by the Société de Financement de l'Économie Française (SFEF), owned jointly by the French state (34%) and seven leading French banks (66%).

SPPE has provided solvency support through the availability of Tier-I capital instruments. It earmarked €40 billion of funds. In addition to the injection to Dexia (a European banking group) along with other governments, €10.5 billion of the first tranche in the form of deeply subordinated debt securities were injected into six banks, boosting their Tier-I ratios by about 50 bps. SPPE also supported the merger between GCE and GBP with an additional €3 billion. The second tranche in the same amount to the same banks was announced, but has not been taken by all the banks yet.

There are several improvements of the new recapitalisation scheme over the original one. For example, banks are given the option of issuing preference shares. Preference shares are new core Tier-I instruments established by the French Law. They have the following characteristics: non-cumulative dividend, no voting rights, non-convertible, preferential but capped remuneration, limited dilution and loss-absorbing capacity. The new scheme also offers incentives for banks to buy back securities as the redemption amount would increase over time.

SFEF has provided liquidity support through the provision of government-guaranteed refinancing. It can raise market financing by issuing state-guaranteed bonds, the proceeds of which are then used to on-lend to banks in proportion to the market share of each bank in terms of customer loans and assets for a period of 1 to 5 years. SFEF can issue up to €265 billion of guaranteed term debt (maximum maturity five years), which enjoys 'AAA' rating as the French government. Debt must be issued before the end of 2009. Before the creation of the SFEF, the government also issued guarantees on Dexia's obligations (a maximum of €55 billion) along with the rescue package arranged for the bank with other governments.

SFEF has proved to be popular with investors as reflected in the very tight spreads of its bonds. Its issuance, second only to the US and about one-third denominated in US dollars, represents 20 per cent of the global issuance of government guaranteed bonds. Its ability to attract a wide range of investors from various market segments may result from its skillful set-up. By pooling liquidity, the agency has enhanced the visibility and reduced the liquidity premium of its bonds. In addition, by construction, investors are not exposed to bank risks. The guarantor, the French government, is perceived to be capable of standing behind its promises. With the recent market improvement, French banks have tapped markets by issuing bonds without government guarantees.

There have been several theoretical studies of best government support schemes, but very few empirical studies. The crisis provides good natural experiments of various government support schemes, but there seems to be only one empirical study by Veronesi and Zingles (2008) to examine the impact of the US plan. To bridge this gap in the literature, this paper uses a similar method to analyse the French plan. The event window is between October 10 and October 14 in 2008, one day before and after the announcement of the French schemes on October 13, which was also the day when the US government announced its revised Paulson plan and the UK government announced its own schemes.

The study aims to explore the impact of the French financial sector support plan by combining both balance sheet and market information. Specifically, it intends to: (i) gauge the market impact on debt using senior and subordinated CDS spreads and linking these to the maturity structure of the bank debt; (ii) gauge the market impact on equity using capital asset pricing model (CAPM); (iii) take into account other events happening at the same time by measuring the relative impact besides the gross impact and

(iv) reverse engineer the Black-Scholes-Merton model, as in Xiao (2008), to measure the proportion of equity injection transferred to debt holders.

Following Veronesi and Zingles (2008), the impact on debt is calculated as follows:

(i) The default probability from the CDS (RR is recovery rate) is backed out.

$$DP = \frac{CDS/10000}{1-RR}$$

(ii) The gross impact on debt is equal to the difference between the present value of debt before the plan and after the plan (rf is the risk-free rate, b and a indicate before and after, respectively).

$$\Delta PV = \sum_{t=0}^{T} \frac{(1-DP_b)t\frac{CDS_b}{10000}*D_t}{(1+rf)^t} - \sum_{t=0}^{T} \frac{(1-DP_a)t\frac{CDS_a}{10000}*D_t}{(1+rf)^t}$$

(iii) To control for other things happening at the same time, an adjusted impact is measured by subtracting debt changes in *Scor* Group, a re-insurance firm not receiving government money but experiencing narrowing spreads.

$$Adjusted\Delta PV = \Delta PV - PV_b \times \frac{\Delta PV^{SC}}{PV_b^{SC}}$$

The results show that the French support plan drove down banks' credit risk significantly. The debt value of banks appreciated across the board after the announcement of the plan, with the gross appreciation ranging from 21 per cent to 38 per cent. As expected, taking into account other events happening at the same time lowered the impact, but the positive effects of a value increase of at least 9 per cent were still pronounced. In addition, subordinated debt benefitted more than senior debt. On average, the value of the banks' subordinated debt went up by 35 per cent on gross terms and by 25 per cent on adjusted terms, while the value of the banks' senior debt went up by 26 per cent and 14 per cent, respectively.

Figure 9.13

Impact on Debt

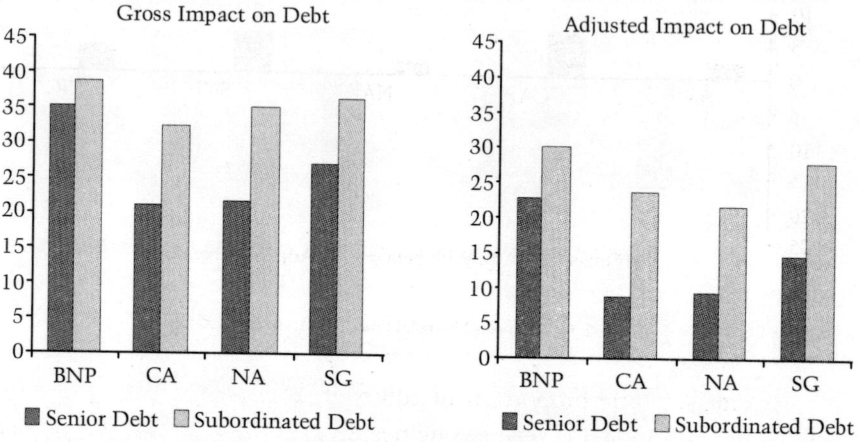

Source: Bloomberg, Datastream, Thomson Financial, and Fund staff estimates.

The impact on stock values is calculated as follows. The gross impact is measured by raw stock returns and the adjusted impact is measured by using abnormal returns from the CAPM. Beta is estimated from daily stock prices during the period 1/1/07-10/09/08. Both market benchmarks, CAC40 and SBF250, are used. Adjustments are done with beta equal to one and the estimated betas.

The results show that the plan had a mixed impact on equity. The gross impact was positive, with the equity value of the banks experiencing a modest increase of 2-7 per cent. However, the adjusted impact was negative across the board, regardless of the benchmarks and beta estimation methods used. The loss of the equity value of the banks ranged from one to 23 per cent. With the exception of one bank, the estimated betas produced larger equity value reduction than assuming betas equal to one. The different impact on debt and equity suggests the possibility of equity injections being transferred to debt, as analysed in Myers (1977).

Figure 9.14

Impact on Equity

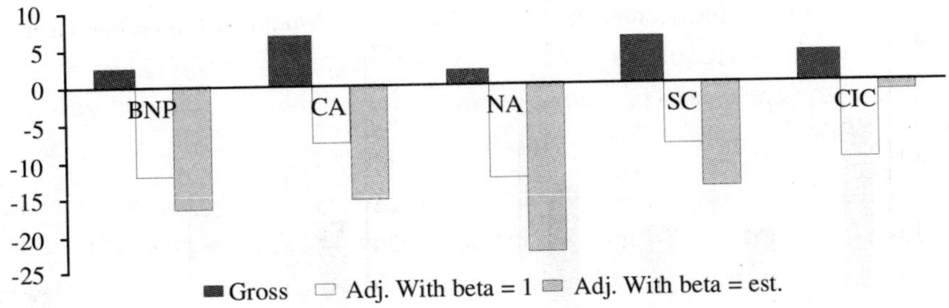

Source: Bloomberg, Datastream, Thomson Financial and Fund Staff estimates.

To measure the proportion of equity injections into debt, the Black-Scholes-Merton model is reverse engineered (See Xiao, 2008). In the Black-Scholes-Merton model, asset value follows a geometric Brownian motion:

$$dA/A=\mu_A dt+\sigma_A dw$$

Equity is a call option and debt is a put option on bank assets. Specifically,

$$E=\max(A-DB,0)=\int_{DB}^{\infty} e^{-rT} E(A-DB) f(A) dA$$

$$D=DB-\max(DB-A,0)=\int_{DB}^{\infty} e^{-rT} D(A-DB) f(A) dA$$

where

E is the market value of equity,

A is bank assets,

D is the market value of debt,

DB is the distress barrier,

μ_A is the expected rate of return of assets,

T is the time to maturity on debt in years,

σ_A is the standard deviation of assets,

dw is the Weiner process,

f(A) is the asset distribution function.

To obtain the share of equity injections into debt, the following procedure is followed: (i) calibrating the Black-Scholes-Merton model to market data of bank equity and volatility; (ii) backing out the implied value and volatility of bank assets; (iii) calculating *ex-ante* the market value of bank bonds and equities after the announcement of the plan and (iv) determining the share of equity injection into debt by the value difference between the pre- and post-plan market values relative to capital injections.

The results demonstrate that the share of transfer varies with the riskiness of banks. For the three largest French banks, the proportion of the transfer ranges from 13 to 56 per cent. Moreover, the transfer dovetails with the credit risk of banks measured by the average of the CDS spreads of the banks' senior and subordinated debt. The riskier the debt, the higher the share of capital injections into debt. It indicates that capital injections may benefit debt holders at the expense of shareholders, arguing for the necessity of injections by the government.

Figure 9.15

Share of Capital Injections Transferred into Debt

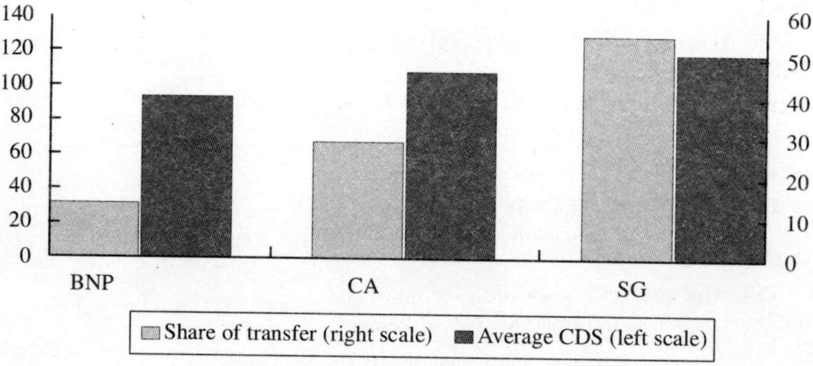

Sources: Bloomberg, Datastream, Thomson Financial and Fund Staff estimates.

Conclusions

French banks have demonstrated relative resilience to the global financial crisis so far. The crisis has put the banks to an unprecedented test and they are not immune to the severe fallout of the crisis. However, the banking model featuring diversification in business, funding and geography has helped to contain risk to a manageable level. In addition, benefitting from the comprehensive supervision, proactive regulation and timely information sharing among regulatory authorities, the banks enjoyed better initial conditions and have withstood the crisis thus far relatively well.

Government measures are necessary and beneficial, but challenges still lie ahead. Recapitalisation and refinancing measures have helped stabilise the system by reducing the risk and decreasing the financing cost considerably. Going forward, banks' earnings and profitability may continue to be under pressure with subdued CIB activities, potential losses and write-downs from risky assets, the still low interest margins, as well as the rising counterparty risk and the cost of risk. With the global crisis still unfolding and the international debate on capital adequacy still evolving, the impact of the banks' reduced comparative advantage in capital buffers remains to be seen. Rising to the challenge would call for continued vigilance and enhanced risk management.

References

BIS (2004). *BCBS Compendium of Documents-Volume II: Advanced Supervisory Methods*. Basel.

Black, Fischer and Myron S. Scholes (1973). "The Pricing of Options and Corporate Liabilities", *Journal of Political Economy* 81: 637–654.

Choulet, Céline (2009). "Banques Européennes: Les Plans de Soutien à l'épreuve de la Recession", *Conjoncture* 51. BNP Paribas.

Commission Bancaire (2009). *Rapport de la Commission bancaire pour l'année 2008*. Paris.

Direction des Journaux Officiels (2008). "de finances rectificative pour le financement de l'économie", *Journal Officiel de la République française*, Loi No. 2008-1061 du 16 Octobre 2008.

Federal Reserve (2009). *The Supervisory Capital Assessment Program: Design and Implementation*. Washington DC: Federal Reserve.

FSA (2009). *The Turner Review*. London: Financial Services Authority.

Gapen, Michael T., Dale F. Gray, Cheng Hoon Lim and Yingbin Xiao (2005). "The Contingent Claims Approach to Corporate Vulnerability Analysis: Estimating Default Risk and Economy-Wide Risk Transfer", in Michael Pomerleano & William Shaw (ed.), *Corporate Re-structuring: Lessons from Experience*. World Bank.

———. (2008). "Measuring and Analyzing Sovereign Risk with Contingent Claims", *IMF Staff Papers* 55: 109–148.

IMF (2009). *Global Financial Stability Report 04/09*. Washington DC: International Monetary Fund.

Lagarde, Christine (2008). *Le plan français pour assurer le financement de l'économie et restaurer la confiance*. Communiqué de presse du Conseil des Ministres, Paris.

Merton, Robert C. (1973). "Theory of Rational Option Pricing", *The Bell Journal of Economics and Management Science* 4: 141–83.

———. (1974). "On the Pricing of Corporate Debt: The Risk Structure of Interest Rates", *The Journal of Finance* 29: 449–70.

———. (1977). "An Analytic Derivation of the Cost of Loan Guarantees and Deposit Insurance: An Application of Modern Option Pricing Theory", *Journal of Banking & Finance* 1: 3-11.

Myers, S.C. (1977). "Determinants of Corporate Borrowing", *Journal of Financial Economics* 5: 147-75.

Noyer, Christian and Nouy Danièle (2009). *Audition devant la commission des finances du Sénat.* Paris: Comptes Rendus De La Commission Des Finances.

Ricol, René (2008). *Rapport sur la crise financière - Mission confiée par le Président de la République dans le contexte de la Présidence française de l'Union européenne 2008*. Paris.

Veronesi, Pietro and Luigi Zingles (2008). "Paulson's Gift" *(Mimeo)*. University of Chicago.

Xiao, Yingbin (2008). "Financing and Risks of French Firms", *IMF Selected Issues Paper* 08/74. Washington DC: International Monetary Fund.

10 The German Banking System and the Global Financial Crisis

Causes, Developments and Policy Responses

Hans-H. Bleuel

The German Banking Structure

The German financial system is based on banks. Accordingly, these financial intermediaries play an important role in channelising funds from lenders to borrowers. This is highlighted by the amount of bank assets, which were double the GDP figure in 2007 (IMF, 2008), a very high ratio in an international perspective. Beyond its economic importance, the German banking industry is characterised by the predominance of universal banks. These institutions engage in all fields of bank business activity. Universal banking in Germany is closely linked to the so called *Hausbank* approach. A *Hausbank* is the prime lender for companies, particularly small and medium-sized enterprises. Typically it has a long-term relationship with the corporations and offers a wide range of services (Benston, 1994: 121-31). Additionally, many commercial banks have traditionally been represented in the supervisory bodies of large corporations with a related corporate governance system that is based on insider control mechanisms. This so-called 'Deutschland AG' was characterised by equity holdings of manufacturing enterprises by the financial intermediaries. By the same token, banks and insurance companies were represented in the supervisory bodies of the enterprises. Following the trend of shareholder value management, these equity stakes have been reduced substantially in the last decade (Kellermann, 2005). So banks and insurance companies have concentrated on their core business. Accordingly, there are signs of convergence of the bank-based German financial system towards the market-based Anglo-American model. These revisions bring up questions in the scientific community as to whether the elements of the German financial system are still coherent (Krahnen and Schmidt, 2004).

The universal banks are classified into three groups that differ by legal form and ownership structure. These form the so-called 'three-pillar banking system', a term often used to describe the German banking industry as a whole. The structure of those three pillars plus the specialised bank sector is highlighted in Table 10.1.

Table 10.1

Structure of the German Banking Industry in 2008

	Number	*Assets (€ billion)*	*Average Assets/Bank (€ billion)*
First pillar: Commercial banks	272	25,30,694	9,304
Big banks	5	15,20,699	304,140
Regional or other commercial banks	164	8,09,667	4,937
Branches of foreign banks	103	2,00,328	1,945
Second pillar: Savings banks	448	26,82,317	5,987
Primary savings banks	438	16,19,614	3,698
Landesbanks	10	10,62,703	106,270
Third pillar: Cooperative banks	1,206	9,53,579	791
Primary cooperative institutions	1,204	2,90,725	241
Regional cooperative central banks	2	6,62,854	331,427
Specialised banks	62	19,26,638	31,075
Mortgage banks	20	8,26,572	41,329
Building and loan associations	25	1,88,984	7,559
Banks with special functions	17	9,11,082	53,593
Total	1,988	80,93,228	4,071

Source: Bundesbank (2008).

Commercial banks (*Kreditbanken*) are privately owned and have the principal intent to realise profits. Commercial banks only account for 14 per cent of the total number of banks, but own 31 per cent of the banking assets. These figures indicate that the best-known big German banks belong to this group. According to the statistical classification of the Bundesbank, five banks form this sub-group of big banks: the Deutsche Bank, the Dresdner Bank, the HypoVereinsbank, the Commerzbank and the Deutsche Postbank. These banks are active on a national and international level. The second sub-group of commercial banks comprises smaller institutions. Together with the branches of foreign banks as the third sub-group, they offer various bank services on a national or regional level. Their market share is however far below the figure of the five big German commercial banks.

The second pillar of the universal bank sector is the savings bank group consisting of the primary saving banks (*Sparkassen*) and their head institutions called *Landesbanken*. These intermediaries operate on a regional basis only and are owned by public law institutions such as cities, districts or federal states. Banks of this group have an autonomous legal status, yet their supervisory bodies (*Verwaltungsrat*) are manned with representatives of the respective public owner. According to the savings bank law, the institutions are obliged to serve the public interest of their region. This is to foster savings and economic development in a regional perspective. However, even if an explicit profit target is not the first priority of the savings banks, it has become the factual objective of banking operations.

Public guarantees that exist for the saving banks due to the public ownership have been discussed intensively. In fact, the public entities are liable without restriction in the event of a default. This guarantee has two facets. Firstly, there is a maintenance obligation (*Anstaltslast*) as a commitment to equip the institution under public law with the necessary means to fulfil its public mission. Secondly, a bailout obligation (*Gewährträgerhaftung*) exists. This is an unlimited responsibility of the public owner for the liabilities of its public law institutions. This bailout obligation is only relevant in case of a liquidation of a savings bank, as the maintenance obligation applies as a first line of defence in case of financial distress. As these two guarantees back the savings banks completely, a solvency risk is virtually non-existent with ensuing lower refinancing costs. This results in a clear distortion of competition. The European Commission assessed the guarantees as the equivalent of subsidies and initiated two agreements in 2001 and 2002 with Germany to abolish both *Anstaltslast* and *Gewährträgerhaftung* by 2005. However, liabilities incurred before July 2005 and maturing before 2016, in addition to all liabilities incurred before July 2001, will be grandfathered. Accordingly, the savings bank group is currently in a state of transformation to adapt to competitive conditions. Yet, the savings bank group is still immune to takeovers and thus protected from other forms of competitive pressure. Savings banks are not for sale. A takeover by a commercial bank would imply losing the aspect to serve the public interest as defined by saving banks laws. The regional principle also impedes competition between saving banks, as each institution is prohibited from operating outside its local area. So competition in rural areas is typically with cooperative banks and in municipal cities with commercial banks (Siebert, 2004: 12-15).

The primary saving banks only operate on a local level. They may typically not hold shares outside the savings bank group, trade money market, equity and foreign exchange instruments on their own account or take part in an underwriting consortium. These fields of business are covered by the Landesbanks that are mainly active on the regional level. Yet, following their investment banking activities these institutions have become increasingly involved in international business including some foreign subsidiaries. In addition to those commercial and investment banking activities the Landesbanks serve as a *Hausbank* to their federal states. As such they provide cash management services and grant loans, which are mainly refinanced by bonds. Further, they act as a central clearing institution for the interbank transfers of primary savings banks. Together the Landesbanks and primary saving banks offer a truly universal banking service. The Landesbanks are currently in a process of consolidation. The Landesbank of Rheinland-Pfalz merged with the Landesbank Baden-Würtemberg (LBBW). In 2008, the LBBW also took over the state bank of Saxony, the Sachsen LB.

The third pillar of the universal bank sector is the credit cooperatives sector (*Genossenschaftsbanken*). Credit cooperatives are typically owned by their clients and profits are distributed as dividends to the members owning the cooperative. The number of credit cooperative members is currently close to 16 million. Usually, a broad ownership is required by the statutes and shares cannot be sold. For raiders it is almost impossible to gain control over cooperative banks, as each member only has one vote irrespective of the value of his share. Thus, the cooperatives are not subject to the market of corporate control (Siebert, 2004: 17).

The cooperative sector shares many features of the savings banks group. Primary cooperative institutions operate according to the regional principle. As such, they mainly provide retail banking services to their customers. Since 1974, loans can also be granted to non-members. The role of the two central institutions of the credit cooperative group (DZ-Bank and WGZ-Bank) is comparable to the Landesbanks of the savings bank group. They provide cash management services, enable deposits and credits within the credit cooperative group and offer additional commercial and investment banking services (Hackethal, 2004: 83-5).

The institutions of the three pillars differ significantly regarding their business models. The commercial banks have a relatively high share of international financing, whereas the primary savings banks and co-operatives are financed domestically, mainly by deposits of the non-financial sector. Thus, the primary savings banks will not suffer significantly from the abolishment of state guarantees. This is quite different for the Landesbanks that source one-third of their financing from bonds. Interest rates for these bonds have been traditionally 25 to 40 basis points below market level, an advantage that will phase out (Brunner *et al.*, 2004: 24-5). Assets also mirror the differing business models of the universal banking group. Commercial banks as well as the head institutions of the savings banks show a high degree of internationalisation. The international links are particularly high for the big five commercial banks, with the Deutsche Bank being the only German bank in a top 20 ranking of the world's biggest banks by assets (Bankersalmanac, 2009). In contrast, granting loans to domestic individuals and companies is the major business of primary savings banks and cooperatives. The Landesbanks have the highest market share for credits to companies, followed by the big five commercial banks and the primary savings banks (Bofinger *et al.*, 2008a: 91).

the cause for low profitability. To sum up: in spite of the structural particularities of the German banking market which cushions some competitive mechanisms, there appears to be a sufficient degree of competition.

Table 10.2

Return on Equity of German Banks

	1994-1999 (%)	*2000-2006 (%)*
First pillar: Commercial banks		
Big banks	14.6	5.3
Regional and other commercial banks	12.6	7.2
Second pillar: Savings banks		
Primary saving banks	19.3	10.1
Landesbanks	9.8	4.3
Third pillar: Credit cooperatives		
Primary cooperative institutions	15.5	10.2
Regional cooperative central banks	14.9	5.0

Source: Bofinger *et al.* (2008a).

Causes of the Financial Crisis

Global financial markets have faced disruptions since the year 2007. As the financial turmoil had harsh consequences for Germany and its financial market policy, it makes sense to review the development of the crisis briefly. In current economic commentaries there is a surprising consensus about the major mechanisms that wreaked havoc on the global financial system.[1] Today, there is a clear agreement that a hype in the housing markets of the US was the root of the crisis. Originally, the boom of real estate markets was induced by the monetary policy of the Federal Reserve Bank resulting in low interest rates (Bofinger *et al.*, 2008b: 119-121). Thus, cheap money was available resulting in a high real estate demand. Accordingly, real estate prices rose constantly. This motivated high levels of borrowing, because individuals anticipated further price increases.

1. Unfortunately for the economic profession, this is a mere retrospective consensus.

This speculative occurrence was bolstered by financial intermediaries. Credit to house owners was granted generously. Fair value accounting of banks also anticipated increasing real estate prices—a procedure that justified elevated credit approvals. In consequence, typical credit checks or ceilings were undermined. As credit approval procedures lacked prudence, substantial high-risk lending in sub-prime segments was the result. Such procedures have been fostered by the new 'originate-to-distribute' business model. Whereas banks traditionally had loans on their balance sheets (originate-to-hold), the new approach was to sell the generated loans to outsiders transferring the risks simultaneously. This was enabled by means of structured finance or more precisely: the securitisation. Housing loans were polled in portfolios and sold as securities of several tranches on the financial market. In the bottom line, long-term loans have been refinanced with short-term securities.

In this way the famous asset backed securities (ABSs) of today emerged, with the assets behind being the claims for the blend of the original mortgages. With this business model, a formidable expansion of housing loans was possible (Blundell-Wignell *et al.,* 2008: 3-8). By selling the portfolios, the underlying loans were removed from the balance sheets of the originators. One implication was that the transfer of loans to third parties hampered the incentive for a cautious risk evaluation of borrowers. This furthered lending activity in sub-prime segments. As a second effect of securitisation, the equity requirements for granted loans, as defined in the Basel accords, were circumvented. Originating banks achieved the off-balance sheet situation even for unsold parts of the loan portfolios by transferring assets to the special purpose vehicles (SPVs). So, the available equity of banks was no limit for risky lending activities anymore resulting in a high leverage of financial intermediaries. Furthermore, low interest rates as a result of monetary policy induced high leverage ratios of banks (Wehinger, 2008: 2-6). These financial structures of banks increased return on equity and shareholder value in times of favourable business climate, yet to the burden of negative leverage effects in the case of an unfavourable business environment.

Selling the ABSs to other financial intermediaries was only possible due to the apparent low-risk characteristic profile of the structured products. Risk reduction was on the one hand accomplished through diversification of the portfolio and on the other hand through financial engineering. Here, the concept of tranching is of prime importance. A key goal of this process is to create assets with higher ratings than the average rating of the underlying assets. This is achieved by prioritisation of payments to so-called senior notes, followed by junior or mezzanine notes and finally the equity notes. Accordingly, losses of the portfolio are born by the different tranches in the opposite direction. The different tranches are the so-called collateralised debt obligations (CDOs), which cascade interest rates from senior to equity notes. The distilled senior tranches with excellent risk ratings accounted for up to 90 per cent of the portfolio with this figure illustrating the extent of apparent risk reduction. This judgement was delivered by credit rating agencies based on statistical methods such as the value-at-risk. The latter estimates a maximum loss of a portfolio at a given time horizon with a defined probability. To calculate this risk, historical data are used. Yet, the relevant sub-prime loan default data were only available over a short period, which moreover was a period without adverse effects. With the excellent risk ratings, the respective asset backed securities spread out in the financial systems, both domestically in the US and internationally. The misjudged risk evaluation once again resulted in the absence of a sound risk provision by equity of financial intermediaries.

Against the background of this inadequate risk management, the financial system bore an inherent instability at the onset of the crisis. With several subsequent increases of the federal funds rate, mortgage rates experienced a similar upwards trend. This caused a higher debt service for households. Loan defaults swelled correspondingly in 2007 and the housing bubble burst. Increasing default rates required a re-evaluation of the ABSs. The consequent write-offs caused losses of financial intermediaries, particularly in the US and Europe. In Germany, this first wave of the financial crisis affected especially the IKB Deutsche Industriebank AG and several Landesbanks such as the Sachsen LB. Due to the sharp decline of demand for ABSs the originators came under pressure. The revolving short-term refinancing was disturbed and credit lines at the originating banks were used to bridge the gap. Stressed liquidity of some financial intermediaries was the result.

As a reflection of a changed risk perception and because of doubts about the solvency of banks, interbank markets came under pressure. The trigger point for this second wave of the financial crisis was the collapse of the American investment bank Lehman Brothers in August 2008, when not only equity holders but for the first time also borrowers experienced losses in the course of the crisis. Damaged trust in interbank business disrupted money markets (Fender and Gyntelberg, 2008: 4-13). Interbank rates rose to levels well above the returns on bank assets. Chiefly banks with mismatching maturities of assets and liabilities such as the German Hypo Real Estate Group ran into liquidity problems. At the same time, doubts were raised about the soundness of other US assets of financial intermediaries, such as credit card debt, corporate loans and derivative products. The melange of these bad positions is often referred to as 'toxic assets'. In several steps, banks announced write-downs which amounted worldwide to a total of 518 € billion. by the end of the year 2008. The losses are concentrated in Europe and North America, as shown in Figure 10.1. Yet, it is certainly advisable to be extremely cautious with the interpretation of any data due to both the dynamics of the crisis and the piecemeal approach of banks to announce write-downs.

Figure 10.1

Bank Write-downs by Region (€ bn; 11/09)

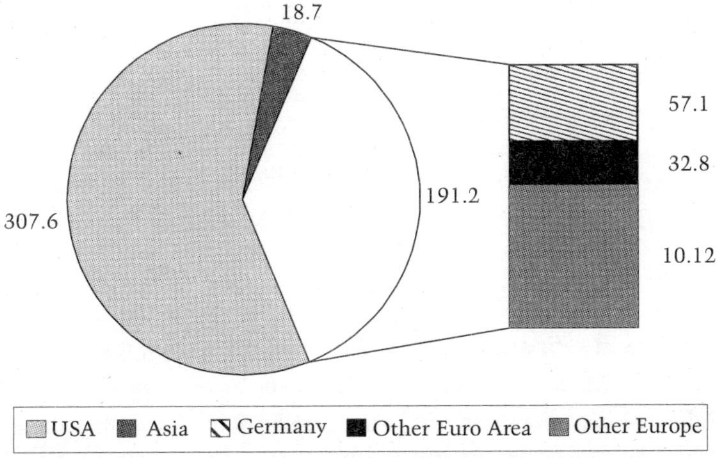

Note: US-$ values converted at 1.37 US$/€.
Source: ECB (2008b).

With the foregoing financial crisis, effects on the real economy ensued. As the write-downs reduced the equity of banks, the scope of lending has been reduced. This causes worse loan conditions for the private as well as the corporate sector and reduces aggregate demand. Investment activities of the corporate sector are further hampered by increasing interest rates, which result from the credit crunch in the interbank markets despite of expansionary monetary policy of central banks worldwide. Furthermore, the present situation in early 2009 is characterised by a loss in confidence of economic subjects resulting in a deep recession.

Effects on Germany and Policy Responses

As already shown, the financial crisis had substantial effects on Germany despite its distinct financial market setting. The situation in Germany rather resulted from international contagion than from domestic developments. Prices on real estate markets have been stable in Germany (Kholodilin *et al.*, 2008), so that there is no parallel to the origin of the crisis in the US. Additionally, financing in the housing sector is still conservative: mortgages are typically fixed rate annuity loans and have a typical credit ceiling of 60 per cent of the purchasing price. With this environment, the situation in Germany is less complex as opposed to other countries, which had a housing boom prior to the crisis. As the crisis was transmitted internationally to Germany, the fragmented banking structure of Germany had unexpected positive effects. A low concentration of the banking industry resulted at first in diversification effects of the banking industry as a whole. Large parts of the banking system such as the primary saving banks and the credit cooperatives remain unaffected by write-offs. Only international players such as the big private banks, the Landesbanks and some special banks were victims of the first wave of financial crisis.

First instances of major write-downs are linked to two banks. In August 2008, the Sachsen LB reported first losses owing to a subsidiary that was active in refinancing ABSs. After an emergency rescue package to ensure liquidity, the Sachsen LB was taken over by another Landesbank, the LBBW. Likewise the majoritarian private IKS Deutsche Industriebank AG ran into liquidity problems as it was unable to refinance its special purpose vehicles via short-term commercial papers. By an increase in capital stock, the KfW augmented its share from 40 to 91 per cent and sold its share to the financial investor Lone Star (Dallas-based private equity firm) a year later. In this early period, economic policy was based on a case by case approach aiming to prevent a breakdown of the affected banks.

Figure 10.2

Write-downs and Losses of German Banks (12/09)

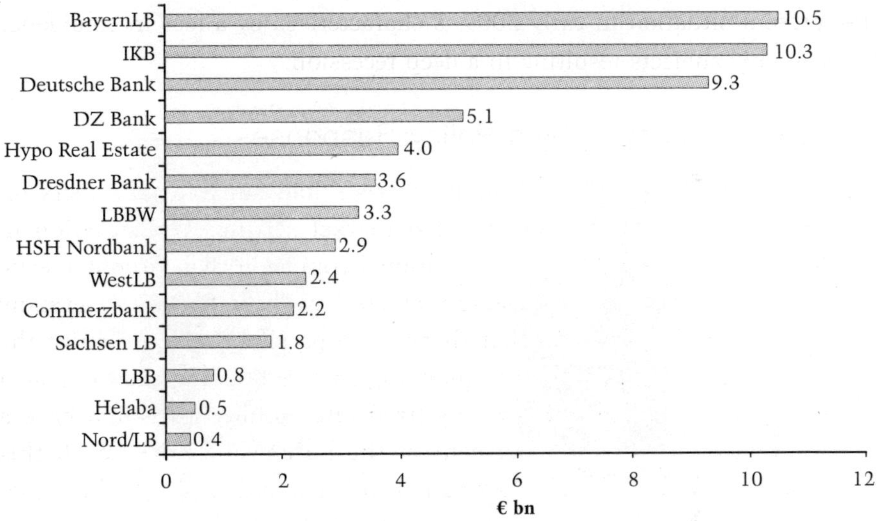

Source: Ramthun *et al.* (2009).

With the spreading crisis, other banks also experienced losses. As Figure 10.2 shows, the BayernLB was heading the list of write-downs by bank by the end of 2008. The figures presented are, however, prior to any news that may come out as soon as annual reports for 2008 are published. Given this preliminary basis, the realised write-downs of the savings banks group are disproportionate to their share of assets of the total banking industry. Corresponding data by pillar of the banking system are shown in Figure 10.3. Write-downs of the savings banks group only result from the Landesbanks with their international operations. This indicates that high risk taking and governance problems were present at least in some of the Landesbanks. The financial crisis fostered the reorganisation of the Landesbanks with the LBBW taking over two partner institutions. Similar discussions are currently taking place for another Landesbank, the WestLB of North Rhine-Westphalia. This bank has been subject to public discussion since 2003 due to its risky investment banking activities followed by losses in 2006 due to proprietary trading.

Figure 10.3

Distribution of Assets and Write-downs by Banking Group

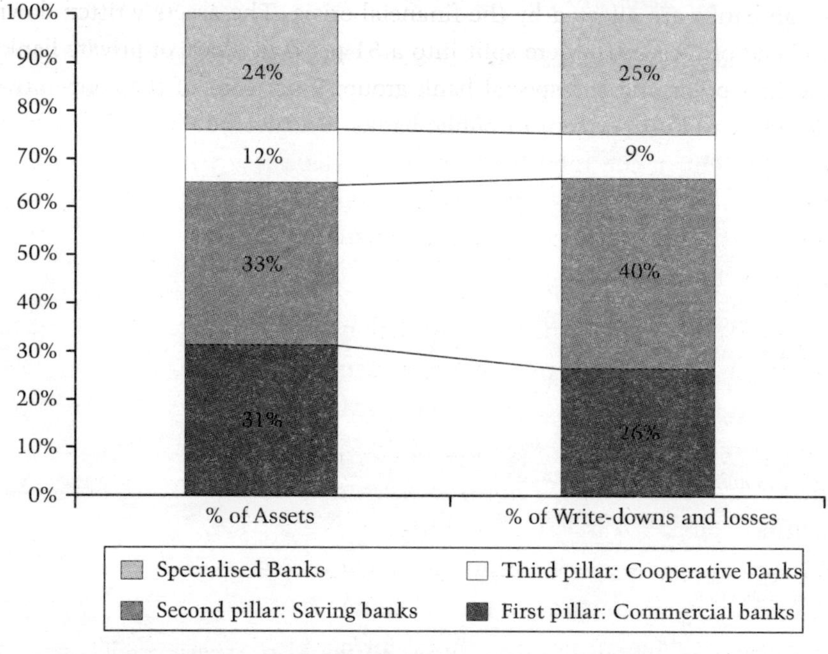

Source: Bundesbank (2008) and Ramthun (2009).

However, in the course of the year 2008, things began to move fast with subsequent announcements of banks' write-downs. The private banks did not make an exception to this process. Since autumn 2007, when first write-downs were revealed, quarterly results included ever mounting figures for losses following the subprime crisis spread to more and more types of assets. The Deutsche Bank experienced the highest losses of all commercial banks, which result from its size and internationalisation. The write-downs of Dresdner Bank and Commerzbank were substantially lower, also if compared to their lower assets. The private bank being most threatened by insolvency in 2008 is the Hypo Real Estate that belongs to the group of specialised banks. Apart from write-downs of € 4 billion, the bank ran into refinancing problems with its subsidiary Depfa, an intermediary active in government financing. At first the possible default of the Hypo Real Estate was politically handled as another special case. Guarantees of € 50 billion were granted in early October 2008. These events show that all types of German banks are affected by the financial crisis. The assets written down by the end of December were split into a 51 per cent share of private banks of the first pillar and the special bank group, 9 per cent of the cooperative bank group and 40 per cent of public banks. Because public banks account for 42 per cent of the total bank assets in Germany, present data do not support the opinion that excessive risk taking has been limited to the public sector. Governance problems existed apparently irrespective of ownership structures.

The repeated emergency support actions for banks and the mounting pressure on money markets gave rise to a more systematic framework for bank support, the Financial Market Stabilisation act (*Finanzmarktstabilisierungsgesetz* or in short : FMStG). Whereas the legislation in Germany normally is a semi-fluid process due to federal structures, the act was approved with astonishing speed on October 17, 2008, after a tight week of consultation. The main objective of the FMStG is to stabilise money markets and banks accordingly, the so-called *Rettungsschirm* (emergency parachute) for banks. With an overall volume of € 480 billion this rescue pack is of larger scale in the international perspective when compared to the realised write-downs and losses of the financial sector, as shown in Table 10.3. With € 400 billion, by far the larger part of the rescue pack is designated for guarantees of bonds and loans of banks. The remaining € 80 billion are for purposes of recapitalisation as well as purchases of non-performing assets (NPAs) for a term of three years.

Table 10.3

Comparative View of Financial Rescue Packages

	Capital Injection	*Asset Purchases/ Swaps*	*Guarantees/ Loans/ Credit Lines*	*Total*	*Bank Write-downs*	*Rescue Pack as % of Write-downs*
Germany	80	0	400	480	57	12
Other Euro Area	121	98	1,283	1,502	33	2
Other Europe	68	42	497	607	101	17
USA	683	1,318	1,559	3,560	308	9
Total	952	1,458	3,739	6,149	499	8

Note: The € 80 billion for both asset purchases and capital injection in Germany are assigned to capital injection for the sake of simplicity. US-$ values for write-downs converted at 1.37 US-$/€.

Source: ECB (2008).

The financial rescue fund (*Sonderfonds Finanzmarktstabilisierung* or SoFFin) is administrated by the Die Bundesanstalt für *Finanzmarktstabilisierungsanstalt* (FMSA), a public institution especially set up for this purpose. By February 2009, a total amount of € 117 billion of guarantees has been granted to banks. For an overview by bank refer to Figure 10.4. The Hypo Real Estate with its ongoing solvency problems accounts by far for the largest share. Rumours about a planned nationalisation of this bank do not cease. The option of asset purchases was not used; apparently due to the fixed term schedule which would necessitate to record contingent liabilities on banks' accounts and thus impede the disburdening balance-sheet effect. The first capital injection was made at the Commerzbank in order to stabilise its situation after taking over the Dresdner Bank from Allianz in January 2009. A 25 per cent share of the Commerzbank now belongs to the German state, representing a blocking minority for any decision subject to approval of the shareholders' meeting. A different kind of government support was taken up by the Deutsche Bank in the course of the Postbank takeover. Following a renegotiation of 22.9 per cent acquisition of the Postbank shares, the Deutsche Bank achieved payment via an exchange of stocks. Accordingly, the parent of Postbank, the Deutsche Post AG, still state-owned by 30 per cent, now owns up to 8 per cent of the largest German commercial bank, officially a short-lived construction. So there is indirect state support for the external growth of Deutsche Bank as well, whereas the bank is currently insisting on not resorting to the rescue pack of SoFFin.

Figure 10.4

SoFF in Disbursements (€ bn) as of February 2009

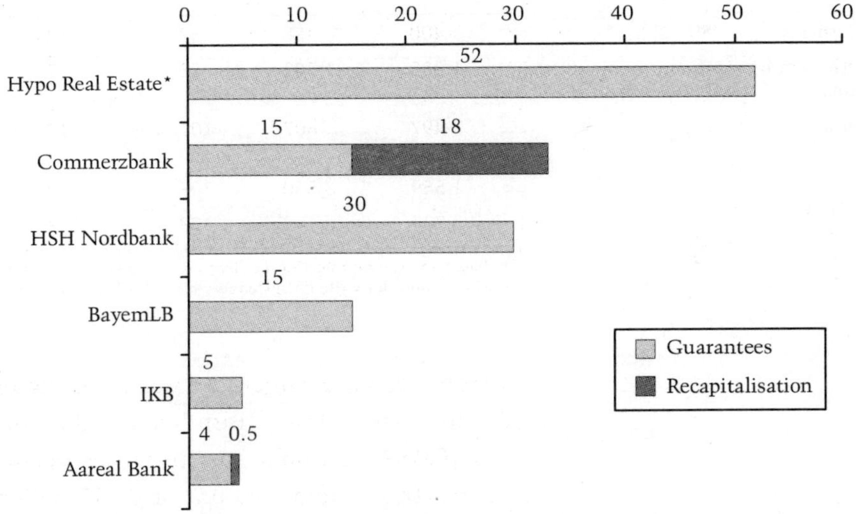

Note: * Figure for Hypo Real Estate excluding guarantees of 50 € bn granted in 10/08.
Source: Ramthun (2009) with update for Aareal Bank.

By mid of February 2009, there are applications pending for SoFFin support from the Landesbanks of Bavaria, Baden-Wurttemberg, North Rhine-Westphalia and Hamburg/Schleswig-Holstein. The Volkswagen Bank, a commercial bank subsidiary of the Volkswagen Group, also filed an application. In spite of these procedures, the interbank markets are not yet recovering. The reluctance of banks to engage in money market transactions with each other goes along with ever increasing estimates about the amount of toxic assets owned by German banks. The latest forecasts estimate a total of € 97 billion of bad assets which are still in the balance sheets of German banks. Further discussions on how to shore up financial markets are underway. A bad bank aimed at taking over NPAs was heavily discussed in January 2009, but finally rejected by political decision-makers (FAZ, 2009). With the deep recession clouding the business climate, even further political interferences into the capital markets appear most likely.

Aims of a Future Financial Market Policy

Deriving adequate future market policies requires a prior diagnosis of the recently misguided development of financial markets. The major symptom is a misallocation of financial resources, as revealed by the current wave of write-downs. To put it clearly: as the risk of failure is intrinsically tied to entrepreneurship, it is not the event of non-performing bank assets that is of relevance, but the extent of this occurrence. The latter signifies that financial intermediaries have failed to perform in their core competency, which normally is a superior evaluation of risks. The misevaluated risks have been produced in the financial market of the United States (US) with their exorbitant foreign debt (El-Shagi, 2008: 19). Deficient financial market regulation in the US and international regulatory arbitrage towards the US market has prepared the ground for the crisis (Winkler, 2008: 2-4). Here, the innovations of financial intermediaries turned out to be destructive for the market system instead of the productive effect entrepreneurship should have (Baumol, 1990: 893-921). Such misguided entrepreneurship of banks results from deficient incentive structures. The latter existed in spite of speed and scope of financial market reforms in the last decades. Thus, reforms lacked the right focus or direction in industrial countries. In the following Section it is argued that insufficient liability and transparency as well as undesirable concentration of financial intermediaries are the core challenges.

A deficient liability scheme for the bank management is the first core problem (Broll *et al.*, 2008: 1350-51). Lacking liability results in higher risk-taking, as gambling is a profitable individual strategy in case losses are bailed out by third parties. Yet, this practice does not comply with the social risk preference. Deficient liability can be detected in management remuneration that is sharing profits but no losses. Even in casc of bank management failures, there is hardly a sanction, but rather a 'golden handshake'. Corporate governance mechanisms are thus not working efficiently yet (Rehm, 2008: 307); this problem obviously exists both in market-based and bank-based financial systems. A more intense acceptance of risk by the top management itself is an aim of new corporate governance schemes. Another detriment to the principle of liability is a lack of sufficient bank equity to cover the taken risks. In general, high equity ratios will work as a buffer to adverse developments. Related to this, equity requirements of the Basel accord need to be adjusted, in order to increase banks' equity even in a boom. Currently, low default probabilities of bank assets in these periods result in low equity requirements. This is reversed in a recession, with the higher bank equity required resulting in lower bank lending and thus a procyclical effect (Bofinger *et al.*, 2008b: 170-1). Finally, unrealistic return on equity targets—as for example, the 25 per cent put forward by the Deutsche Bank until 2007—need to be revised. Achieving such profitability targets is possible in the long term only through competitive advantage for banks. Rather, high return on equity targets are often realised by high leverage; a risky and undesirable situation as the financial crisis showed (Hartmann-Wendels, 2008: 708).

An increase in transparency is a second reform target. Transparency enables the functioning of the price mechanism, which is in the bottom line processing information (Hayek, 1945: 519-30). Information can only be processed, if it is available to economic agents. Thus, transparency is a crucial factor. A multi-step securitisation process is evidently not enhancing transparency. As explained, banks are currently struggling with the appraisal of their assets. If even banks—the best informed economic agents in the financial markets—face these problems, products appear to be too complex. A certain standardisation might be of advantage (Wehinger, 2008: 29). Further, risk measures used by financial intermediaries are apparently deficient, as they did not incorporate the behavioural risks that are relevant to financial markets like herding effects (Broll *et al.*, 2008: 1350-1). Likewise, liquidity risks have been underestimated, as the re-financing problems of banks show. A proper functioning of rating agencies is also necessary for transparency, particularly for structured financial products. A part of the related problems are certainly associated to the methods and procedures used so far. A more fundamental reform is to unbundle consulting and rating activities because of the incorporated conflict of interests. Another issue is to tie the remuneration of rating agencies to the accuracy of their forecasts. By doing so, a short-termism of rating agencies can be prevented. This appears necessary, because the rational long-term target of a rating agency to build up reputation by adequate ratings has obviously become subordinate recently.

This brings us to the third reform challenge: reducing concentration. As a starting point one should keep in mind that financial markets will never be stable. They should even be the contrary: (financial) innovations always inherently have the risk of failure. This is an integrated part of the concept of a dynamic development in a competitive market process. Banks with non-viable concepts adapt or exit the market. If the latter raises a problem to the financial markets as a whole, banks become 'too-big-to-fail' (Brewer and Jagtiani, 2007). This is exactly the way the second wave of the global financial crisis arose. The collapse of Lehman Brothers aggravated the crisis strongly, because the bank was 'relevant to the system' (Bofinger *et al.*, 2008b: 122-3). If one single bank is relevant to the world financial markets, a lack of competition is evident. Here, a lower concentration would have resulted in diversification and stabilisation of the financial market. Unfortunately, corresponding views are currently not *en vogue*. Concentration in the banking industry is increasing in Europe and the US (Schildbach, 2008: 2), a coincidence with the regions most affected by the financial crisis. In Germany, the financial crisis spurs on the concentration process, as the mentioned mergers of private and public banks show. These procedures are already questionable from a corporate point of view, because most Landesbanks and all big commercial banks already have a considerable size. Empirical studies do not prove that additional largescale economies can be realised by further growth of these banks (Bos and Kolari, 2005). Additionally, gaining in size is apparently confused with socially desirable business models. Large banks already have substantial threats to the state (Funk, 2009: 76) and there is hardly any reason to worsen this situation even more. Especially in financial markets economies of size have the striking opportunity cost of banks' attempts to gamble for state intervention in case banks' business policies fail.

Apart from these principles for future financial market reforms, the current rescue efforts for banks require further attention. Despite the extent and the speed of state support, interbank markets are not functioning yet. This is illustrated by the differences of insured to uninsured money market rates as shown in Figure 10.5. Whereas the European rescue packages achieved bringing the rampant spread in the third quarter of 2007 down to a level in line with the figures of the period from mid-2007 to mid-2008, it is still far above the long-term average. This is not due to missing liquidity, as the deposit facilities at the central bank are increasing sharply. Yet, distrust is still present among banks hampering interbank lending. It is to be feared that banks as insiders to the market have the best forecasts on outstanding write-downs. So a substantial part of the necessary support for banks may be ahead.

Figure 10.5

Spread Euribor to Eurepo 3-month in Basis Points

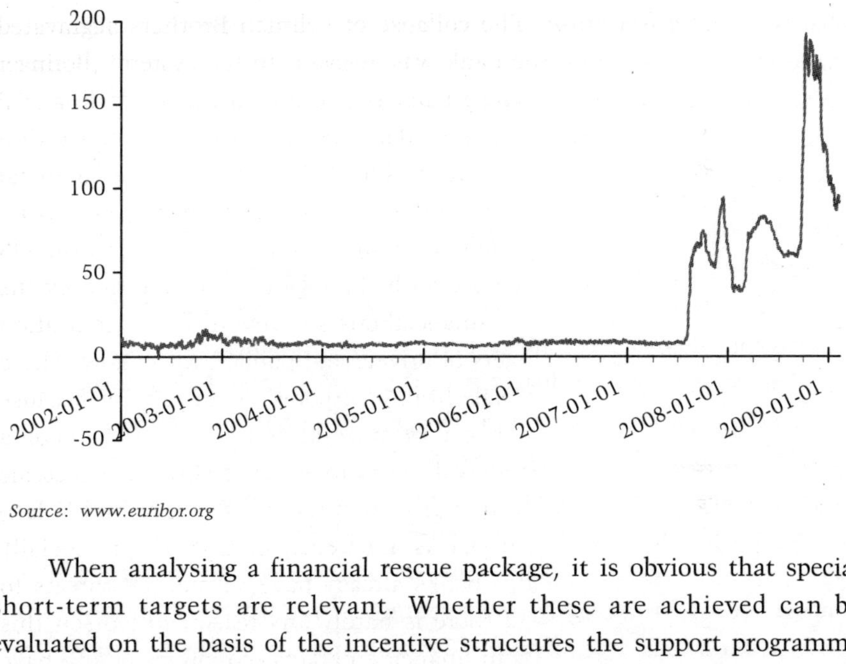

Source: *www.euribor.org*

When analysing a financial rescue package, it is obvious that special short-term targets are relevant. Whether these are achieved can be evaluated on the basis of the incentive structures the support programme sets. Fundamental considerations on the design of economic policy in the long run are secondary in this regard. Accordingly, transitional state guarantees for banks are justifiable, even if these represent soft budget constraints with adverse effects for managerial decisions like less diligence (Kornai, 1986: 3-30). However, to put it metaphorically: one does not rescue someone who is drowning by giving him swimming lessons! Nevertheless, it is advisable to find solutions that do not undermine long-term targets. In this context, one should also avoid any undesirable development that is hard to reverse. With these considerations in mind, some shortcomings of the Germany rescue scheme can be detected.

First, the rescue package does not tackle the lack in transparency sufficiently yet, as evidenced by the persistent interbank spread. There are two explanations for this occurrence: either banks face problems with NPAs to unforeseen extent or the degree of banks' financial soundness is simply not appraisable. To obtain information about the real situation as soon as possible would be highly useful for the public. One might hope that official financial statements for the year 2008 will clear conditions up. There is certainly also some additional insight in the course of requests to the SoFFin, also currently not published by this institution yet. Means are simple though. Just a special audit is missing that might be better based on the accounting principle of prudence. Such a specification valid for all banks is strikingly easy to define by the legislator.

Second, the German rescue package neglects challenges of concentration in the banking industry. Landesbanks are merging on a large scale and an acquisition within the big commercial banks was supported by injecting capital into the Commerzbank. This development impacts competition intensity, is hard to reverse and thus unfavourable in the long run. Competition is also distorted in the short term. This is illustrated by the case of Aareal Bank's request for approval of SoFFin support. The bank is financially healthy, but runs for SoFFin's shelter as did competitors in financial distress before. This decision aims at lowering the cost of capital. Consequently, the state becomes a surrogate for capital markets, not just in case of financial distress, but widely used. Evidently, the costs for SoFFin support are too low, a fancy way to paralyse the market mechanism. Here, the legal act suffers from a basic flaw, as it mentions 'fees in line with the market'. However, there currently is no market for such financial services and the defined yardstick misses accordingly. The resulting scope of discretion is apparently improperly used. Of course, increasing costs for capital supply and guarantees by the SoFFin should not be contradictory to the liquidity targets of banks. So it is certainly not sensible to augment annual fees and payments. An equity investment or even nationalisation, as discussed fiercely, is also not necessary. Adequate future profit sharing suffices.

Third, the principle of liability requires some attention, as it is important not to outrange the original concept of the rescue package. The original legal basis of the SoFFin is clear in this perspective. Bank guarantees, by far the largest part of the rescue package, were to expire by the end of 2012. The legal act also envisages an exit of the state in case of recapitalisations, yet without a timetable. This clearly has recourse to the re-establishment of the liability concept after a transitory period. To define a clear-cut end and limit of government support is of prime importance in order to avoid any adverse incentives to bank management that expected future bailouts will have. Not surprisingly, the debate on adjustments of the rescue package began right after release of the act. The government withstood calls for a 'bad bank', taking over NPAs from the banks at a large scale. Yet, the original act was supplemented in February, 2009 (by the FMStErgG or the Bank Nationalisation Act with a first draft released on February 18th). Guarantees now can have a prolonged life-span of five years, compared to the three years of the original act. Whether this adjustment is right or wrong can hardly be evaluated with the current lack of information on banks' real situations. However, the peril is that floodgates have been opened for ongoing political support and interference in the financial markets. This is also illustrated by the now new option to nationalise banks, currently limited until mid of 2009. It is not the neglect of property rights that is remarkable, because the option to nationalise is only feasible in case of a bankruptcy threat, but the increasing direct economic power of the state. Finally, nationalisation can be seen as an act to prevent acquisitions of banks in financial distress by foreigners, yet with alarming allusions to protectionism.

Conclusion

The German financial system underwent substantial change in the last decade. Many of its traditional characteristics like the close personal network between banks and non-financial corporations, the reliance on bank financing and the conservative accounting principles do not exist any more. The overall concept of these reforms was a more market-oriented approach. This unilateral adjustment assumed advantages of the Anglo-Saxon approach, based both on theoretical insight and empirical evidence, for example a higher productivity of the financial industry in the US and the UK. Yet, due to the current financial crisis, this model has lost quite a lot of its appeal. While the superiority of the market mechanism is beyond theoretical doubt, some empirical results of comparative financial market studies remain to be reassessed. In fact, the key issue is to identify the preconditions for a proper functioning of financial markets. According to the German *Ordnungstheorie* (Leipold, 1990), an adequate order or framework of the market mechanism has to be taken into account.

Thus, regulation of financial markets is a hot topic again. Rules need to be set that induce bank decisions that are based on long-term risk-return profiles of business activities. Regulation also needs to tackle the problems of systemic crisis and the related issue of banks that are too big to fail. However, regulation of financial markets is only viable in case of international harmonisation. Accordingly, an international rule system for financial markets is to be established (Siebert, 2008). This may result in true convergence, as the direction of adaption needs to turn, because some regulatory deficits in the US are at the bottom of the problems. One might argue that international policy coordination will be doomed due to national special interests. Those special interests are certainly a challenge, but the radical changes that are underway also draw a 'veil of ignorance' (Buchanan, 1986) over the special interests of lobbies. Hence, the current situation offers an extraordinary opportunity for international regulatory consent.

For the German financial markets there are challenges ahead. Despite the scope of recent reforms an end of the process is not in sight. Current turmoil will only end after necessary regulations have been incorporated. Of prime importance will be to reverse the direct state influence that the rescue package involves. Concentration constitutes a particular risk for a market-oriented approach towards the banking industry. Sheer size will not help make banks function again, no matter if the public or the private banking sector is concerned. More creative business models for future financial services should be the starting point.

References

Bankersalmanac (2009). "Top 50 Banks in the World". Available at *http: <http://www.bankersalmanac.com/addcon/infobank/wldrank.aspx>* (accessed 15 January, 2009).

Baumol, W.J. (1990). "Entrepreneurship: Productive, Unproductive and Destructive", *Journal of Political Economy* 72: 893-921.

Benston, G.J. (1994). "Universal Banking", *Journal of Economic Perspectives* 8: 121-43.

Blundell-Wignall, A., P. Atkinson and S. Lee (2008). "The Current financial Crisis: Causes and Policy Issues", *OECD Financial Market Trends* 95: 1-21.

Bofinger, P., W. Franz, B. Rürup, B. Weder di Mauro and W. Wiegard (2008a). "Das deutsche Finanzsystem", Effizienz steigern: Stabilität erhöhen. Expertise im Auftrag der Bundesregierung Online. Available at *http: <http://www.sachverstaendigenrat.org/>* (accessed 4 January, 2009).

Bofinger, P., W. Franz, B. Rürup, B. Weder di Mauro and W. Wiegard (2008b). "Die Finanzkrise meistern: Wachstumskräfte stärken", (Jahresgutachten 2008/09). Online. Available at *http: <http://www.sachverstaendigenrat.org/>* (accessed 4 January, 2009).

Bos, J.W. and J.W. Kolari (2005). "Large Bank Efficiency in Europe and the United States: Are there Economic Motivations for Geographic Expansion in Financial Services?", *Journal of Business* 78: 1555-92.

Brewer, E. and J. Jagtiani (2007). "How much would banks be willing to pay to become 'Too-Big-to-Fail' and to Capture other Benefits?", *Federal Reserve Bank of Kansas City Research Working Paper* No. 07.

Broll, U., V. Bieta and H. Milde (2008). "Die Ursachen der Finanzkrise", *WISU* 38: 1350-58.

Brunner, A., J. Decressin, D. Hardy and B. Kudela (2004). "Germany's Three Pillar Banking System: Cross-Country Perspectives in Europe", *IMF Occasional Paper* No. 233. Washington D.C.: IMF.

Buchanan, J.M. (1986). *Liberty, Market and the State: Political Economy in the 1980s*. New York: New York University Press.

Bundesbank (2008b). *Monatsbericht Dezember* 60(12). Frankfurt: Bundesbank.

El-Shagi, M. (2008). "Weltweite Ansteckung: Berechtigte Sorge oder grundlose Panik?", *Aus Politik und Zeitgeschichte* 7: 15-20.

European Central Bank, (2008). *Financial Stability Review* No. 2. Frankfurt: ECB.

Fender, I. and J. Gyntelberg (2008). "Global Financial Crisis Spurs Unprecedented Policy Actions", *BIS Quarterly Review* 4: 1-24.

Frankfurter Allgemeine Zeitung (2009) "Nationale Bad Bank praktisch vom Tisch" (30.01-2009). Available at *http: <http://www.faz.net/s/ Rub58241E4DF1B149538 ABC24D0E82A6266/Doc~EC5341A4143044C65AD3FAC9E6BA959B0~ATpl~E common~Scontent.html>* (accessed 12 February 2009)

Funk, L. (2009). "Grundpositionen zur Finanzmarktkrise", *WISU* 39: 74-76.

Hackethal, A. (2004). "German Banks and Banking Structure", in J. Krahnen and R.H. Schmidt (eds.), *The German Financial System*. New York Oxford: University Press. pp.71-105.

Hackethal, A., R.H. Schmidt and M. Tyrell (2006). "The Transformation of the German Financial System", *Revue d'Economie Politique* 117: 431-56.

Hartmann-Wendels, T. (2008). "Geringe Eigenkapitaldecke, Mangelhafte Transparenz und Fehlanreize", *Wirtschaftsdienst–Zeitschrift für Wirtschaftspolitik* 88: 707-11.

Hartmann-Wendels, T., A. Pfingsten and M. Weber (2007). "Bankbetriebswirtschaftslehre". Fourth ed. Heidelberg: Springer.

Hayek, F.A.V. (1945). "The Use of Knowledge in Society", *American Economic Review* 35: 519-30.

International Monetary Fund (2008). *Global Financial Stability Report* No. 2. Washington D.C.: IMF.

Kellermann, C. (2005). "Disentangling Deutschland AG", in S. Beck, F. Klobes and C. Scherrer (eds.), *Surviving Globalization? Perspectives for the German Economic Model.* Netherlands: Springer. pp.111-132.

Kholodilin, K.A., J-O. Menz and B. Siliverstovs (2008). "Immobilienkrise? Warum in Deutschland die Preise seit Jahrzehnten Stagnieren", *DIW Wochenbericht* 75: 214-20.

Kornai, J. (1986). "The Soft Budget Constraint", *Kyklos* 39: 3-30.

Krahnen, J.P. and R.H. Schmidt (2004). "Tacking Stock and looking Ahead: The German Financial System at the Crossroads?", in J.P. Krahnen and R.H. Schmidt (eds.) *The German Financial System*. New York: Oxford University Press. pp.485-515.

Leipold, H. (1990). "Neoliberal Ordnungstheorie and Constitutional Economics: A Comparison between Eucken and Buchanan", *Constitutional Political Economy* 1: 47-65.

Ramthun, C., A. Große Hallbuer and C. Welp (2009). "Die nächste Welle", *Witschaftswoche* 6: 20-8.

Rehm, H. (2008). "Das Deutsche Bankensystem: Befund, Probleme, Perspektiven (Teil II)", *Kredit und Kapital* 41: 305-31.

Schildbach, J. (2008). "U.S. and European Banks: Two Sides of the Same Story?", *American Institute for Contemporary German Studies Issue Brief* No. 28, Washington D.C.: AICGS.

Siebert, H. (2004). "Germany's Capital Market and Corporate Governance", *Kiel Working Paper* No. 1206.

———. (2008). "An International Rule System to avoid Financial Stability", *Kiel Working Paper* No. 1461.

Wehinger, G. (2008). "Lessons from the Financial Market Turmoil: Challenges Ahead for the Financial Industry and Policy Makers", *OECD Financial Market Trends* 95: 1-40.

Winkler, A. (2008). *Geld-oder Finanzsektorpolitik: wer trägt die Hauptschuld an der Finanzkrise?*. WISO direct–Friedrich-Ebert-Stiftung.

11 A Fiscal Stimulus to Address the Effects of the Global Financial Crisis on Sub-Saharan Africa

Ray Barrell, Dawn Holland and Dirk Willem te Velde*

Introduction

The global financial crisis (GFC) will have a major impact on developed and developing countries alike. The developed and richer developing countries have begun to address the consequences of the crisis and have announced various fiscal stimuli. The G-20 countries have announced fiscal stimuli worth around 1.5 per cent of gross domestic product (GDP) or some US$ 2 trillion, to cushion the consequences of the GFC. It will matter greatly for poor countries (non-G-20), such as African countries, whether part of such a stimulus is provided in poor countries, or whether the entire stimulus is kept in the G-20. This paper examines the effects of various fiscal stimuli on growth in the world, in developed and Sub-Saharan African (SSA) countries and uses a calibrated macroeconomic model of the world economy.

Several recent studies discuss a fiscal stimulus for the developing countries. The World Bank president, Robert Zoellick, has argued that 0.7 per cent of the developed country stimulus, worth around US$ 15 billion, should be used to finance a vulnerability fund for developing counties to spend on infrastructure, safety net and small and medium enterprise (SME)

* We are grateful for support and comments from One. We thank Miriam Lima for assistance and Simon Maxwell, Jeff Chelsky and Marijn Verhoeven for comments. The views expressed are those of the authors alone.

projects. The campaigning organisation suggests that 1 per cent or some US$ 20 billion should be provided to Africa. International Monetary Fund (IMF) (2009) provides current baseline projections for 2009 which suggest an aggregate additional financing need for LICs of about US$ 25 billion. However, much larger financing needs, up to US$ 140 billion, would result if various downside risks were to materialise. The World Bank (2009) suggests that developing countries face a financing gap of US$ 270-US$ 700 billion depending on the severity of the crisis and the strength and timing of the policy responses. Birdsall (2009) discusses the financial resources for a cash injection into the world economy and suggests that US$ 1 trillion could be resourced, though this is not based on needs. Te Velde (2009) uses the revisions in growth forecasts by the IMF (July 2008 to present) and suggests that the GFC has already led to an estimated output loss (assuming that the revisions can be attributed only to the crisis) of US$ 2.7 trillion in the world (around 5 per cent of world GDP), US$ 737 billion in developing countries and US$ 51 billion in SSA.

This paper examines the effects of providing an aid financed fiscal stimulus in SSA. Section II provides a brief review of the literature on aid, public expenditure and growth in Africa. Section III discusses the policy scenarios. Section IV explains the results of the model simulations. Section V provides the conclusions.

Aid, Public Expenditure and Growth in Sub-Saharan Africa

There is a large literature on aid, public expenditure and growth and poverty in SSA. This Section first describes the macroeconomic literature on fiscal expansion and growth in SSA and then reviews the different effects in different sectors such as investment in infrastructure, agriculture, energy efficiency and then conclusion.

Aid, Fiscal Expansion and Growth

The macroeconomic literature on aid, fiscal expansion and growth deals with two issues (apart from fungibility of aid concerns). The first is whether aid is actually absorbed and spent, and the second is how aid is spent: on non-tradeables or long-run productive capacity. Killick and Foster (2006) examine the effects of aid on growth. Recent aid surges improved GDP growth in four countries and good growth performance (*albeit* slightly slower) was maintained in Mozambique and Uganda. Slow growth in Ethiopia was due to drought. Inflation remained under control in three countries, and showed progress towards stabilisation in further three countries. Only Mozambique experiences some inflation potential. The aid surge was accompanied by higher investment in six countries and little change in Ghana, but (private investment) fell in Tanzania and Ethiopia. Increased aid responded to the ending of wars in Sierra Leone and Ethiopia, introduction of improved economic performance and policies in Mauritania and Tanzania and continued good performance in Uganda and Mozambique, while it fluctuated with variable economic policy performance in Ghana.

Different impacts and challenges for macroeconomic management depend on whether the aid is absorbed (increase in the current account deficit in the absence of aid) and/or spent (increase in fiscal deficit in the absence of aid). There is a fear that the absorption process may require an exchange rate rise, which may induce a 'Dutch disease' problem that exchange rate appreciations (due to inflationary pressures coming from the non-tradeable sector) will hamper the export sector. Spending can also have the same effect by raising the relative prices of non-tradeables (shifting production preferences for non-tradeables and affecting the prospects of positive long-term growth).

The authors survey an IMF study that identifies full absorption and spending as the best aid management option. When aid finances additional imports and the increase in domestic demand is, therefore, matched with increase in net imports, there is no change in the domestic supply-demand balance. But the authors add that such a scenario depends on different factors: quality of spending; elected channels for spending; initial state of the public finances; overall macroeconomic situation and expectations from sustainability of aid flow. There is no evidence of a 'Dutch disease' in most countries, but it is hypothesised that it may be due to the fact that exports in those countries are driven mostly by infrastructure and market structure determinants, rather than by prices.

Adam and Bevan (2006) provide model experiments to examine the magnitude and distributional consequences of the effect of aid and public expenditure. Can the medium period gains offset the 'Dutch disease' effect? Additional aid flows are used exclusively to finance an increase in public infrastructure. They find that when public infrastructure augments the productivity of private factors and when there is an initial scarcity of public infrastructure, there are potentially large medium-term welfare gains from aid-funded increases in public investment, despite the presence of short-run Dutch disease effects of aid. In the current context of the crisis, aid might well be spent on imports but not domestic consumption.

There is a large macroeconometric literature on the macro relationships amongst aid, growth and investment. Burnside and Dollar (2000) argue that aid has no identifiable additional effect on growth once other factors have been accounted for including economic policies. Aid raises growth only in countries with 'good' policies. Hansen and Tarp (2001) use different econometric specifications and find that aid is effective and that the results do not depend on policy. In a number of recent studies, Rajan and Subramanian (2005 and 2007) use longer time spans and show that the impact of aid on growth is less positive. Using a large panel of countries and instrumentation strategy to correct for the bias in conventional OLS estimation, Rajan and Subramanian (2007) do not find any positive relationship between aid and growth. After analysing 97 different empirical studies on the impact of aid on growth, Doucouliagos and Paldam (2007) conclude that the impact of aid on growth is not significant. A number of factors may explain the inconclusiveness of these research efforts. Bourguignon and Sundberg (2007) argue that these mixed results are not surprising given the heterogeneity of aid motives and the complex causality chain linking foreign aid to growth.

Importantly, there are a number of studies that disaggregate aid by type or category. McPherson and Rakovski (2001) use a multi-equation system and find that the impact of aid on GDP per capita growth is positive but indirect through investment. Also emphasising that aid affects growth through investment, Gomanee *et al.* (2002) find on the basis of 25 SSA countries over 1970-1997 that each one percentage point of the ratio of aid to gross national product (GNP) contributes one-third of one percentage point to growth. Clemens *et al.* (2004) split aid into different types and identify the type of aid that could plausibly stimulate growth in the short run. They include budget and balance of payments support, investments in infrastructure and aid for productive sectors. They find a large positive effect of this type of aid on short-term growth: a US$ 1 increase in aid raises the present value of output by US$ 8, although this effect is decreasing at the margin. By focussing the analysis on aid *via* investment (infrastructure, agriculture, energy efficiency), we can depart from the aid-growth conundrum by isolating the impacts of specific types of aid which have been found to be more effective. Cali and te Velde (2008) find positive and significant effects of various types of aid for trade on exports and the investment climate (e.g., the costs of exporting).

Two further considerations are worth mentioning before discussing rates of return for different types of investment. First, finding $50 billion of productive investment in SSA (particularly over a short time horizon) might be difficult. It is not always easy to get new projects off the ground. Having said this there is quite a demand for 'aid for trade' projects. Secondly, the developing countries may not possess the institutional capacity to significantly scale up public spending to implement a major fiscal stimulus. We recognise these issues and the analysis reported below must be viewed with these caveats in mind.

Infrastructure Spending and Growth

Much of the literature on the effects of infrastructure estimates rates of return using macroeconomic growth regressions. Estache (2006) suggests that economic returns on investment projects average 30-40 per cent for telecommunications, more than 40 per cent for electricity generation and more than 200 per cent for roads but when the outliers are excluded, the average is about 80 per cent for roads. Returns tend to be higher in low-income than in middle-income countries (see Canning and Bennathan, 2000; Briceño *et al.*, 2004). Table 11.1 provides the social rate of returns on World Bank projects in infrastructure and we take this to be around 20 per cent.

Table 11.1

Social Rates of Return on World Bank Projects: Unweighted Average (1960-2000)

Region	*Energy/Mining*	*Telecom & Information*	*Transport*	*Urban*	*Water & Sanitation*
Africa	14.1	20.6	25.5	21.3	7.5
East Asia	18.3	19.5	24.8	20.3	10.5
Eastern Europe	30.9	31.1	25.8	15.7	9.8
Latin America	12.8	16.6	22.4	19.2	11
Middle East	12.3	26.9	25.1	16.5	7.8
South Asia	23.2	22	24.1	14.9	9.8
Developing World	18.4	21.5	25.4	19.2	9.2

Source: Briceño *et al.* (2004).

World Bank (2006) suggests that financial rates of return for railway concessions have been low. For Cote d'Ivoire, the average annual return on equity is 9.2 per cent and for Cameroon it ranged from 14-22 per cent. Economic rates of return would be greater than financial rates of return as they should include cost savings for those using more expensive trucking, but on the other hand, investment by railway concessionaires is almost always based on loans with low interest rates from development finance institutions. Thus, it seems likely that the economic rate of return of properly costed private investment in railways is not very high. A low financial rate of return is also one of the reasons for the low level of private sector investment attracted to railways over the period 1990-2004.

The cross-country estimates by Esfahani and Ramirez (1999) suggest an elasticity of per capita output with respect to power generation capacity of 0.15. Deininger and Okidi (2004) examine growth and poverty reduction in Uganda during the 1990s. They also suggest that while improving access to basic education and health care is important, progress depends on complementary investments in electricity and other infrastructure.

The regression for Uganda results suggest that a doubling of electricity coverage (through a doubling in generating capacity) from 7 to 14 per cent would lead to an annual increase in incomes of 3.6 per cent. Such estimations suggest that the effects are not just one-off but also long-run.

Calderon and Serven (2008) provide new empirical estimates on the effects of infrastructure on growth in Africa using econometric regressions for a wider panel of 100 countries. They consider a scenario that raises the level of infrastructure development for each SSA country, so as to reduce by half its infrastructure gap relative to the average country in other regions in the relevant per capita income group. They estimate the costs of being between 7 and 15 per cent of GDP (reported in Figure 6 in their paper), suggesting 10 per cent of GDP as a rough average for SSA.

The estimate of the scenario (halving the gap) for the effect on real GDP per capita also varies, between 1.2 per cent and 2.3 per cent per annum and we suggest 1.5 per cent as a rough average for SSA. Costs of 10 per cent of Sub-Saharan GDP would be around US$ 80 billion. If around US$ 50 billion of infrastructure funds were added, this would be 63 per cent of the scenario implied by Calderon and Serven. Carrying this through, 63 per cent of a 1.5 per cent growth rate is around 0.9 per cent per annum permanent change in real per capita GDP. A US$ 20 billion would increase per capita growth by one-third of a per cent each year.

Investment in Agriculture

The World Bank's *World Development Report 2008* discusses the role of agriculture in development. It suggests that agricultural growth and poverty reduction depend critically on investments in rural infrastructure (irrigation, roads, transport, power and telecommunications), as well as on investments in markets, rural finance and research and extension. In SSA, returns on irrigation projects now often reach 15-20 per cent, as in the rest of the world. Evidence from rural China, India and Uganda shows that the highest returns in growth and poverty reduction come from investments in agricultural research, rural roads and education.

Current levels of agriculture investment in SSA are insufficient for sustained growth, New Partnership for Africa's Development (NEPAD) advocates a 10 per cent increase in agriculture spending in the national budget to try to reverse that. Much of the underinvestment in agriculture is driven by mis-investment practices (spending on private goods, such as inputs subsidies).

Subsidies for agriculture are often appropriated by the richest farmers; the quality (efficiency and equity) of the scarce resources spending is often more of a fundamental issue than the level of spending itself. Subsidies can be good complementary policies, as they can help overcome immediate constraints from market failures (as part of a broader strategy), offset costs of infrastructure and reduce risk. But most frequently subsidies have been used for different purposes, in detriment of high potential returns from investment in public goods (as fiscal resources are scarce). In Zambia, where 37 per cent of the agricultural budget is spent on fertiliser subsidies, only 15 per cent of the 2003/04 budget was spent on research, extension services and rural infrastructure investments that have shown high payoffs. In order to improve the spending efficiency and equity of public resources, political economy pressures on the budget allocation need to be addressed. Economic sectors/interest groups that gather higher proportions of national wealth often have the means to influence policies in their favour. A strategy to deal with this issue is to strengthen the voice of a wider group of stakeholders, particularly smallholders and provide gains of transparency and accountability.

Allston *et al.* (2000: Table 17) summarise 683 rate of return studies on agriculture research spending. They suggest that agricultural research and extension tend to generate the highest returns of any form of agricultural spending, suggesting that the returns to agricultural research average 50 per cent in Africa, 78 per cent in Asia and 53 per cent in Latin America although variability of outcomes is high especially in Africa.

Fan *et al.* (2004) provide information for returns of different spending categories on agriculture output by region in Uganda. They suggest that one shilling invested in feeder roads will result in agriculture output of 7.2 shillings for Uganda as a whole, less than agriculture research and development (R&D) (12.4 shillings) but much more than education (2.7

shillings) and health (0.9 shillings). For further details on output increases as a result of agriculture spending more see Table 11.2. Rates of return will depend on the efficiency of spending which depends on political drivers.

Table 11.2

Returns to Investment in Agricultural Public Goods

Spending Category	*China*	*India*	*Thailand*	*Uganda*	*Vietnam*
Research	9.6	13.5	12.6	12.4	12.2
Irrigation	1.9	1.4	0.7	0.4	-
Roads	2.1	5.3	0.9	-	3
Electricity	0.5	0.3	4.9	-	-
Education	3.7	1.4	2.1	2.7	2.1

Note: Returns = $ increase in agricultural output per $ of incremental spending.

Source: Fan *et al.* (2004).

Green Investment

Many researchers suggest that rules and institutions that promote investing in energy efficiency also help productivity enhancements vital to promote development and reduce poverty (see, for example, Porter and van der Linde, 1995). They argue that energy efficiency improvements provide a means to reduce costs without adversely affecting output or eroding a firm's competitive edge. In addition, energy efficiency is also considered to reduce the unpredictability of earnings associated with the current volatility of energy prices in the present day world economy.

Another hypothesis is that investing in technical change may automatically lead to greater energy efficiency if this incorporates the latest, more energy efficient techniques (Inhaber, 1997; Huber and Mills, 2005). This trend is referred to as the 'autonomous energy efficiency improvement technological change'. For example, Hogan and Jorgenson (1991) estimate that technological change alone caused a reduction in the US energy intensity by about 0.3 per cent per year, independent of changes in energy prices or standards. Koopmans and te Velde (2001) find that energy efficiency improved by 1.1 per cent a year in the Netherlands. There is, however, very limited evidence available for developing countries on the link between energy efficiency and technical change, although the issue is becoming increasingly important for them. te Velde (2008) suggests that productivity and energy inefficiency in China are negatively related, implying that greater productivity leads to higher energy efficiency. He also finds a positive but insignificant effect of physical capital intensity on energy efficiency.

Many stimulus programmes to combat the current global financial crisis have green elements. For example, 69 per cent of the US$ 38.1 billion stimulus in South Korea will go to green investments, 34 per cent of the US$ 581.2 billion in China but 0 per cent of the US$ 6.8 billion in India. In the United States (US), the green stimulus will create two million jobs by investing in four energy efficiency and renewable energy strategies:

- Retrofitting buildings to improve energy efficiency;
- Expanding mass transit and freight rail;
- Constructing a 'smart' electrical grid transmission system and
- Developing renewable energy, i.e., wind power, solar power, next-generation biofuels and other bio-based energy.

Only 2.3 per cent of the projects of the clean development mechanism (CDM) go to Africa. A UNEP report (a *Global Green New Deal*, from February 2009) suggests around one-third of the US$ 2.5 trillion worth of planned stimulus packages should be invested on 'greening' the world economy to assist in powering the global economy out of recession and onto a 'green' 21st century path. Stern (2009) suggests around 20 per cent of the stimulus should go to environment. There is no general study on the relationship between growth and energy efficiency in developing countries.

Conclusions for SSA and the Rest of the World

This brief literature survey suggests that investment infrastructure can increase growth in SSA and that aid can support this process through faster investment and especially aid for trade or increased budget support. Studies suggest that social rates of return are around 20 per cent for investment in infrastructure.

Further we should also emphasise that we live in an interdependent world and that growth in Africa is also good for others. The benefits of faster growth in Africa are non-economic (less conflict and more stability, fewer communicable diseases, etc.) but also economic. There is for instance a relationship between bilateral aid and bilateral exports, not because aid is tied but because aid can lead to additional growth and imports. Massa and te Velde (2008) estimate the effects of bilateral aid loans and aid grants on exports based on a sample panel of all Development Assistance Committee (DAC) providers of aid and all DAC developing country receives over the period 1980-2006, taking into accounts fixed country effects as well as other normal determinants of bilateral trade such as GDP, trade, distance and language ties (see the Appendix A-11.2 for regression results).

According to the estimation, a 100 per cent change in bilateral aid grants leads to a 1.7 per cent increase in bilateral exports from that country. In 2006 (according the Organisation for Economic Co-operation and Development (OECD) DAC and IMF DOTS database), UK bilateral aid was US$ 3.2 billion in 2006, and UK exports were US$ 27 billion in 2006. A 100 per cent change in aid (from US$ 3.2 to 6.4 billion) would lead to a US$ 475 million change in exports from the United Kingdom (UK) to the developing countries. Thus, for every US$ 6.7 a country provides in bilateral aid grants, it receives US$ 1 in bilateral export revenues. The rest of this paper describes how a fiscal stimulus in SSA financed by aid could help SSA and also the rest of the world.

Policy Scenarios

This paper suggests that 1 per cent of the G-20 fiscal stimulus can be directed towards SSA with the aim to offset the impact of the GFC in that region. This amounts to approximately $20 billion, or 2.2 per cent of SSA GDP in 2008.

A larger fiscal stimulus to SSA can be justified by the costs that the region has sustained as a result of the GFC. To estimate the impact of the financial crisis on SSA, we compare National Institute of Economic and Social Research (NIESR), UK, projections for real GDP in the region produced in January 2009 to a 'pre-crisis' scenario based on information available to August 2008 (Barrell and Holland, 2009). This suggests that the GFC has reduced growth prospects in SSA by 4-5 per cent per annum in 2009 and 2010 or roughly $40 billion per annum.

Both the short and long-term impacts of a fiscal stimulus to SSA will depend not just on the size of the stimulus itself, but on how the money is spent. There are essentially three different ways in which the fiscal stimulus can be enacted.

- The first scenario treats the funds as debt relief and reduces the stock of foreign debt. This has no immediate impact on domestic demand in the economy, but its effects on demand will built up as it will reduce the outflows from SSA to finance the stock of foreign debt.
- The second scenario is to use the funds to finance current consumption. For example, to shore up social protection schemes as economic conditions deteriorate. This has a noticeable direct impact on domestic demand and will support growth in the short term.
- The third scenario is to use the funds to finance productive investment, to raise the long-run productive capacity of the economy. This has a direct impact on domestic demand in the short term and also raises the level of potential output in the long run, so that we are not simply shifting output forward from subsequent years.
- As a final scenario, it may be possible to direct the investment expenditure in a way that speeds productivity growth and the process of convergence on a longer-term basis. Calderon and Serven (2008) suggest that investment in infrastructure can raise productivity growth for a sustained period in SSA, speeding the process of technology adoption from the advanced economies. If this can be done, World Bank studies suggest that there may be a social rate of return of 20 per cent on top of the capacity effects in the previous scenario.

Model Estimations

In order to assess the impact of the different approaches to fiscal expansion, we have run a series of model simulations, using NIESR's global econometric model, National Institute Global Econometric Model (NiGEM). Most of the OECD countries are modelled separately within NiGEM, as are China, Russia, Hong Kong, Taiwan, Brazil, Estonia, Latvia, Lithuania,

Slovenia, Romania, Bulgaria and South Africa. The rest of the world is modelled through regional blocks, and the results presented in this paper are based on the NiGEM regional block for Africa (see Appendix A-11.1 for details). All country and regional models in NiGEM contain the determinants of domestic demand, a supply side, export and import volumes, prices, current accounts and net assets. Economies are linked through the effects of trade and competitiveness and are fully simultaneous. There are also links between countries in their financial markets as the model describes the structure and composition of wealth, emphasising the role and origin of foreign assets and liabilities.

As discussed above, we estimate that the GFC has reduced the prospects for growth in SSA in 2009 and 2010 by about 4-5 percentage points per annum. This is before taking into account any of the fiscal stimulus packages that have recently been announced in the G-20 economies. However, the planned fiscal packages will have significant spillover effects on SSA and will partially offset the anticipated negative impact of the financial crisis on African exports.

We have incorporated the following fiscal packages from the G-20 economies into our model simulations, the bulk of which affect budgets in 2009 and 2010:

- A US fiscal expansion worth $797 billion, about 75 per cent of which will come through higher spending and 25 per cent of which will come through lower taxes;
- A fiscal expansion in Japan amounting to $110 billion, the bulk of which comes through higher consumption spending;
- Fiscal expansion in the Euro area worth $270 billion, with by far the biggest stimulus implemented in Germany;
- A fiscal package in Canada worth $33 billion;
- A UK fiscal expansion worth $22 billion and
- A fiscal expansion in China amounting to $586 billion.

Together, these fiscal packages are expected to raise growth in SSA by 1-1.5 per cent per annum in 2009-10, offsetting about 25 per cent of the impact of the financial crisis on the region. The level of GDP is just over 1 per cent higher in 2009 than without the fiscal stimulus and about 2.5 per cent higher in 2010. Exports from the region will be nearly 5 per cent higher than they would be in the absence of these fiscal packages. This gradually spills over into domestic demand, which is about 2 per cent higher in 2010 than it would have been in the absence of the fiscal packages.

Figure 11.1

Impact of Current G-20 Fiscal Packages on the Level of GDP in Sub-Saharan Africa

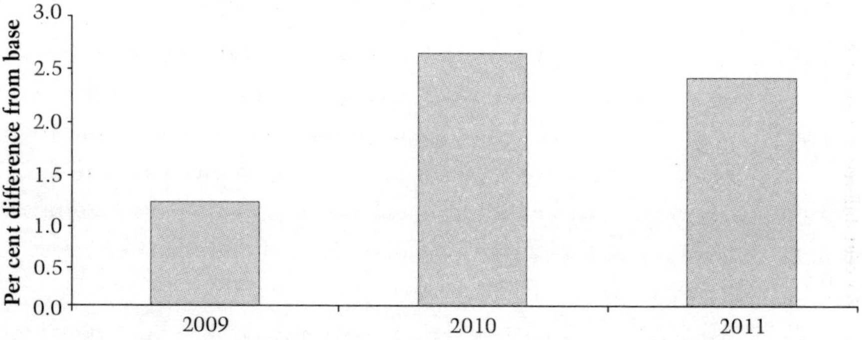

Source: Barrell and Holland (2009).

On top of the G-20 fiscal expansions illustrated in the figure above, we consider a direct fiscal expansion in Africa, financed through aid flows from the developed economies. We first consider a fiscal stimulus of $20 billion, in line with the current call for 1 per cent of global fiscal stimuli to be directed towards SSA. In this simulation we assume the stimulus is spent on current consumption, to support social safety net programmes. The package is financed by the G-7 economies, with costs distributed across countries according to the size of their domestic fiscal packages (57 per cent financed by the US, 12 per cent financed by Japan and Germany, respectively, 8 per cent financed by France, 6 per cent financed by Italy, 3 per cent financed by Canada and 2 per cent financed by the UK). Figures 11.2-11.7 illustrate the impact on the level of GDP in SSA on top of the spillover effects on growth of the agreed G-20 domestic fiscal expansions.

A $20 billion fiscal stimulus spent on consumption raises growth by 1.4 percentage points in 2009 and 0.5 percentage points in 2010, bringing the level of GDP about 2 per cent above base in 2010. The productive capacity of the economy is unchanged in this scenario, so in the long run the level of GDP is unchanged.[1] As a result, GDP growth will be somewhat lower in 2011-2013, as the level of GDP returns to its pre-stimulus (and pre-crisis) baseline.

Figure 11.2

Impact of $20 Billion Stimulus to Consumption on the Level of GDP in Sub-Saharan Africa

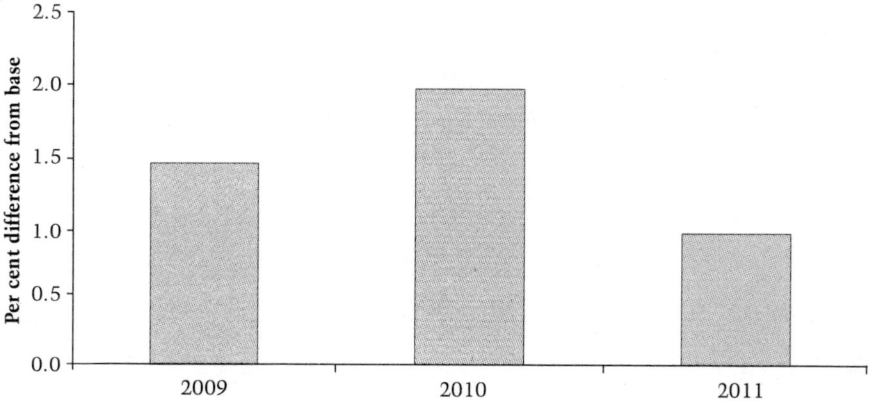

Source: Barrell and Holland (2009).

Taken together, the developed countries' domestic fiscal stimuli and a $20 billion SSA stimulus spent on current consumption offset about half of the impact of the global financial crisis on GDP growth in SSA in 2009 and 2010 (4-5 per cent per annum). This still leaves a significant gap in GDP, which could be filled by increasing the size of the stimulus package.

The following sets of simulations increase the size of the stimulus package to $50 billion. The financing of the package is distributed according to the same proportions above, with the bulk of spending coming in 2009. We consider each of the policy scenarios described in the previous Section.

1. While the level of GDP is unchanged in the long run, the level of GNP will remain somewhat elevated, as net interest payments abroad to finance external debt will be lower.

In the first scenario, the fiscal stimulus is treated purely as debt relief. This has a very modest positive impact on growth over the next few years, does little to offset the sharp slowdown attributable to the financial crisis, but the growth effects build up over time. Debt relief reduces outflows from SSA to finance debt payments, leaving income for spending on the domestic economy. The impact is small and builds up gradually over a few years, with the level of GDP expected to be about 0.8 per cent higher than it would have been in the absence of debt relief in 2011. This is not a useful channel for offsetting the short-term impact of the financial crisis on output.

Figure 11.3

Impact of $50 Billion Debt Relief on the Level of GDP in Sub-Saharan Africa

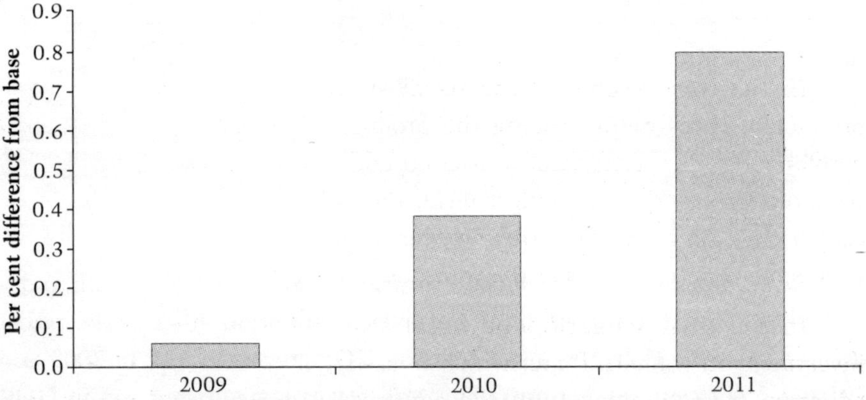

Source: Barrell and Holland (2009).

In the second scenario, the fiscal stimulus is affected through current consumption through social safety nets and the like. In this case, there is a strong impact on GDP growth in 2009, bringing the level of output back towards where it might have been in the absence of the financial crisis. As discussed above, the productive capacity of the economy is unchanged in this scenario, so in the long run, the level of GDP will return to its pre-stimulus base, implying lower growth for a few years.

Figure 11.4

Impact of $50 Billion Consumption Stimulus on the Level of GDP in Sub-Saharan Africa

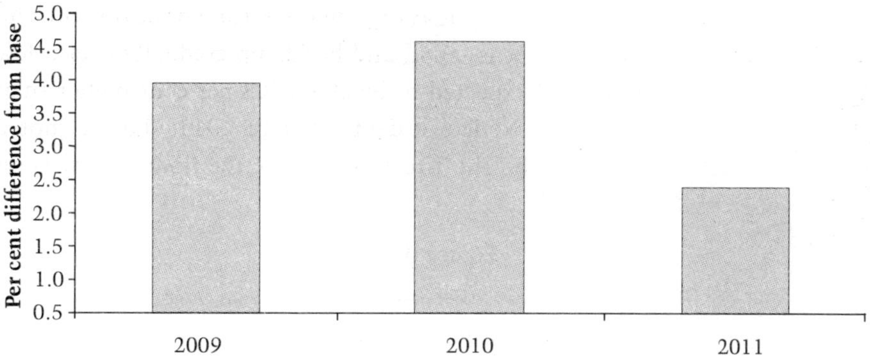

Source: Barrell and Holland (2009).

In the third scenario, the fiscal stimulus comes in the form of productive investment, raising the productive capacity of the economy permanently. The short-term impact on output is in line with the previous scenario. However, in the longer term, the level of output remains 1.5 per cent higher than it would otherwise have been. This allows positive long-term spillovers to the rest of the world as well.

In the final scenario, the fiscal stimulus comes in the form of investment in infrastructure, which is assumed to raise the speed of the adoption of technology from the advanced economies, allowing faster productivity growth for five years and assuming a 20 per cent social rate of return on investment in infrastructure. The impact on GDP growth in the first three years is very similar to that of the previous simulation. However, the long-run level of GDP is higher in this scenario, with a permanent increase in the level of output of 2.5 per cent.

Figure 11.5

Impact of $50 Billion Investment Stimulus on the Level of GDP in Sub-Saharan Africa

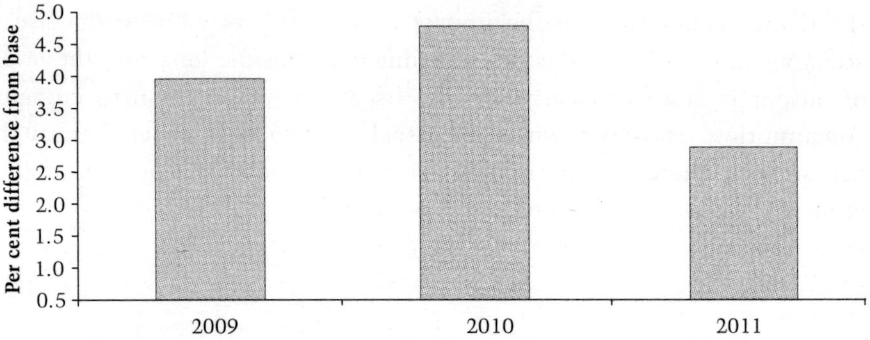

Source: Barrell and Holland (2009).

Figure 11.6

Impact of $50 Billion Infrastructure Investment Stimulus on the Level of GDP in Sub-Saharan Africa with Productivity Spillovers

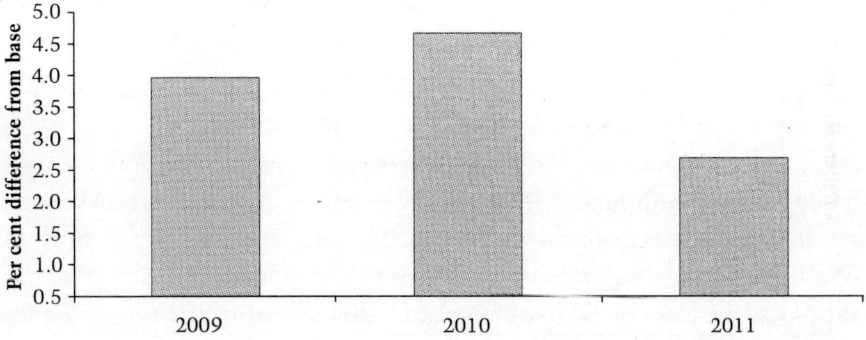

Source: Barrell and Holland (2009).

The impact of the three last scenarios on growth in the first three years is very similar, and in all cases is more or less is sufficient to offset the impact of global financial crisis on Sub-Saharan African output in 2009, offsetting more than 85 per cent of the impact of the crises. In fact, these simulations slightly overshoot the pre-crisis level of output in 2009, and some fine-tuning could shift some of this stimulus from 2009 into 2010 to smooth the outlook further.

The long-run impacts of the different fiscal scenarios do differ, and in the figures below we plot the impact on the level of GDP of the fiscal scenarios until 2021 to illustrate this difference. In the long run, the level of output is close to base when the fiscal expansion finances current consumption. However, when the fiscal expansion is enacted through investment, there is a permanent rise in the potential output in the economy. The level of output is 1.6 per cent higher in the long run than when the funds are spend on current consumption. If there are additional social spillovers associated with infrastructure investment, this may raise the long-run level of output by a further 1 per cent. Financing productive investment, and in particular productivity enhancing infrastructure investment, could help SSA move towards the United Nation's Millennium Development Goals (MDGs).

Figure 11.7

Impact on Sub-Saharan African GDP of $50 Billion Fiscal Expansion in Sub-Saharan Africa

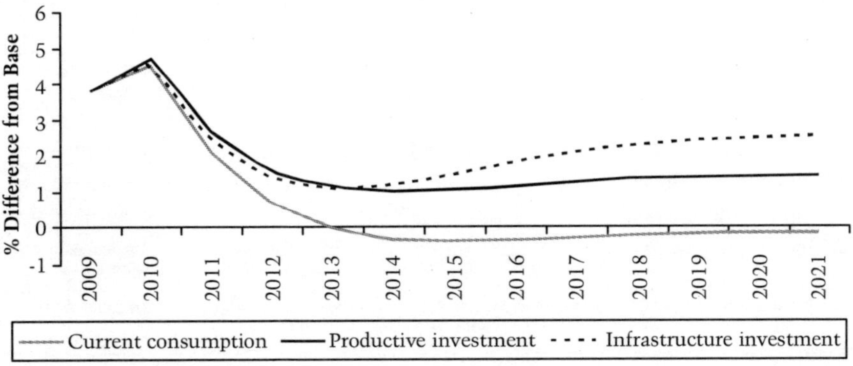

Source: Barrell and Holland (2009).

Table 11.3 summarises the findings discussed above, in terms of the growth rates of real GDP expected for SSA under the various scenarios. Under a pre-crisis scenario, real GDP in SSA could have been expected to rise by about 6.5 per cent per annum (2008-2010). The crisis has reduced prospects significantly, with growth expected to be just 1.75-2.25 per cent per annum (2009-10). Announced fiscal packages in the G-20 economies will offset some of this loss, raising the prospects for growth to about 3.25 per cent per annum in these years. On top of this, a fiscal stimulus of $20 billion raises growth to average 4.2 per cent in the two years, while a fiscal expansion of $50 billion raises growth to an average of 5.6 per cent in the two years, largely offsetting the impact of the financial crisis on SSA.

Table 11.3

Summary of Growth Projections for SSA[a]

	Real Growth (%)				
	2007 (Current Prices US$)	*2008*	*2009*	*2010*	*Long-Run Impact*
Pre-crisis	855.8	6.5	6.5	6.5	Base
Post-crisis		5.4	2.2	1.7	Returns to base
G-20 fiscal packages			3.3	3.2	Returns to base
$20 billion debt reduction			3.3	3.3	Returns to base
$20 billion consumption			4.7	3.7	Returns to base
$20 billion investment			4.8	3.8	Increased by 0.6 per cent
$20 billion infrastructure			4.7	3.8	Increased by 1 per cent
$50 billion debt reduction			3.4	3.5	Returns to base
$50 billion consumption			7.2	3.9	Returns to base
$50 billion investment			7.2	4.1	Increased by 1.4 per cent
$50 billion infrastructure			7.2	4.0	Increased by 2.5 per cent

Note: [a]: Growth rates for the $20 billion and $50 billion fiscal expansions in SSA also include the spillover impact of currently agreed fiscal programmes in the G-20 economies.

Source: ODI (2009).

A fiscal expansion in SSA financed by the developed economies does necessarily entail some costs to domestic demand in the financing countries. However, these costs are small relative to the size of the economies and the impact on GDP is at least partially offset by higher exports from the financing countries to SSA. The size of the offset will differ across countries, depending on the openness of the economies and the exposure of their export markets to SSA. In 2003, less than 1 per cent of US exports were directed towards SSA, while more than 4 per cent of Euro area exports were directed towards the region. Figure 11.8 illustrates the impact of a $50 billion fiscal expansion used to finance investment in infrastructure in SSA on export volumes emanating from the financing countries. Exports rise in all countries in the first two years, at least partly offsetting the costs to domestic demand.

Figure 11.8

Impact of SSA Fiscal Expansion Spent on Infrastructure on the Level of Export Volumes in Financing Countries[2]

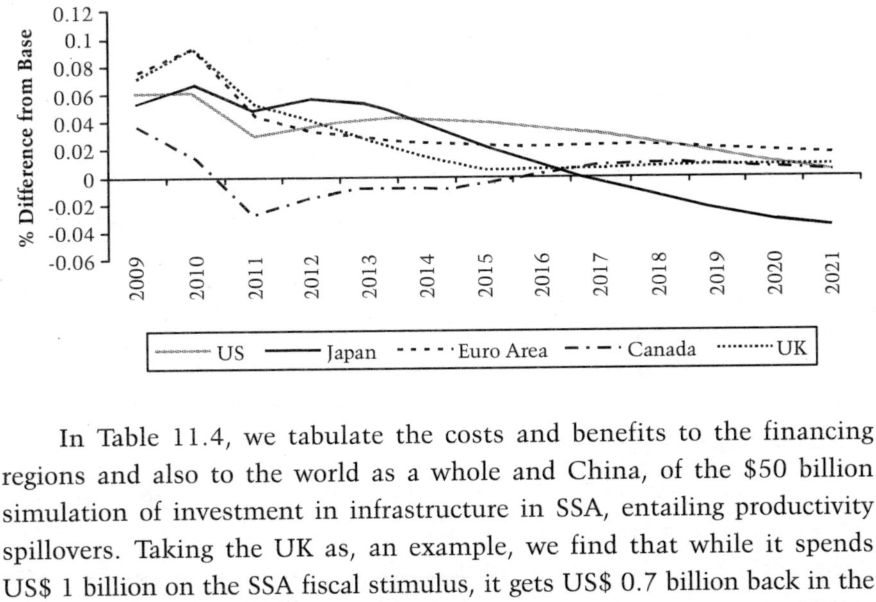

In Table 11.4, we tabulate the costs and benefits to the financing regions and also to the world as a whole and China, of the $50 billion simulation of investment in infrastructure in SSA, entailing productivity spillovers. Taking the UK as, an example, we find that while it spends US$ 1 billion on the SSA fiscal stimulus, it gets US$ 0.7 billion back in the form of exports in the first year. If the UK can persuade G-20 countries to contribute a fixed percentage to a stimulus in SSA, there will be a 20 per

2. The impact on Canada is small and even negative for a few years, reflecting both the low exposure of Canadian exporters to Africa and their high exposure to the US, which bears the highest share of the costs.

cent rate of return on its own investments (0.011 per cent net GDP impact compared to a 0.05 per cent of GDP investment) in 2009. The number has to be treated with caution because it depends on a particular allocation in contributions to the fiscal stimulus.

Table 11.4

Impact of SSA Fiscal Expansion on Financing Countries in 2009

	Direct Costs	*Additional Exports*	*Net Impact on Real GDP (%)*
US	$28.5 billion (0.20 per cent of GDP)	$1.4 billion	+0.003
Japan	$6 billion (0.11 per cent of GDP)	$0.6 billion	+0.005
Germany	$6 billion (0.18 per cent of GDP)	$1.8 billion	+0.007
France	$4 billion (0.15 per cent of GDP)	$1.6 billion	+0.025
Italy	$3 billion (0.14 per cent of GDP)	$0.7 billion	+0.007
Canada	$1.5 billion (0.12 per cent of GDP)	$0.3 billion	+0.006
UK	$1 billion (0.05 per cent of GDP)	$0.7 billion	+0.011
China		$1.4 billion	+0.016
World		$20.4 billion	+0.073

Source: Authors own calculations.

In 2009, the impact on output in all the financing countries is positive, but very small. The slight rise in exports is partly offset by lower domestic demand to finance the additional aid to SSA and this negative impact on domestic demand increases in 2010 and 2011. Nonetheless, the impact remains imperceptibly small, and would not materially affect the outlook for GDP growth in any of the financing economies. In the long run, the level of GDP is slightly above base in all countries, reflecting a permanent rise in global productive capacity.

The essentially negligible size of the impact on financing countries is an important finding, as the positive impact on the African economy is substantial, at little cost to the financing economies. If rising unemployment were to provoke social unrest, the negative impact on SSA of a recession may prove significantly higher than our economic model can capture, implying that the benefits of stabilising growth in the region may far outweigh the estimates presented here.

The figures reported in the Table 11.4 show that some countries benefit from a stronger Africa more than others, and it would be possible to design a financing package that entails a slightly more equitable impact across countries. For example, there is an argument for France and the UK and possibly even China, financing a slightly higher proportion of the package, as they reap the greatest benefits. However, it must be borne in mind that the impact of the aid package on the financing countries is so small, that the time and effort required to design a more equitable package may prove more costly than it is worth.

Another important factor to be borne in mind is that for the fiscal package to be fully effective, the funds must be spent in a productive manner that helps to maintain employment levels in the short term and also increases the productive capacity of SSA over the longer term. It can be difficult to design appropriate spending plans in a short period of time, as it takes time and research to determine how the funds can most usefully be spent.

Conclusions

The global financial crisis will have a major impact on development. We suggest that the output loss of the global financial crisis for SSA alone is around US$ 40-50 billion in 2008-09. Developed countries have announced fiscal packages worth close to US$ 2 trillion to address the effects of the global financial crisis—the effects of these packages help to smooth income losses in SSA in 2009-10, offsetting about a quarter of losses due to the financial crisis.

Developed countries can also support a fiscal stimulus in developing countries through increased aid. The literature suggests that productive investment in infrastructure increases growth in developing countries and specifically SSA, and the results in this paper confirm that further infrastructure spending raises growth for a sustained period.

We used a quarterly macroeconomic model (NIESR's NiGEM) to simulate a US$ 20 and a US$ 50 billion fiscal expansion in SSA. Both are illustrative and chosen because respectively $50 billon is approximately the output loss to SSA caused by the series of exogeneous shocks initiated by the GFC; and $20 billion is approximately 1 per cent of the $2 trillion sum of all national stimulus packages in developed and emerging economies. Taken together, the developed countries' domestic fiscal stimuli and a US$ 20 billion SSA stimulus spent on current consumption can offset about half the impact of the GFC on GDP growth in SSA in 2009 and 2010. In turn, increasing growth in SSA by some 2 per cent in 2009-10. This still leaves a significant gap in GDP, which could be filled by increasing the size of the stimulus package to around US$ 50 billion.

If US$ 50 billion goes as debt relief in SSA, the initial growth effects are small. If the stimulus is spent on consumption (income transfers, social safety nets etc.) it can smooth income losses and increase incomes by 4 per cent in 2009 and a further 1 per cent in 2010. If the stimulus goes to productive investment, there is a similar income smoothing effect over the short term. In addition there is a long-term positive impact on the level of output, which remains about 1.5 per cent higher, while other stimuli do not shift the long-run level of potential output.

A stimulus in SSA of US$ 50 billion has positive effects on global trade and world GDP would be 0.1 per cent higher in 2009-10 as a result (this is equivalent to US$ 44 billion worldwide and of this around 15 per cent or US$ 6 billion goes to the rest of the world outside SSA). US and Chinese exports would increase by about US$ 1.4 billion in 2009; German exports would increase by about US$ 1.9 billion and UK exports by US$ 0.7 billion. If the UK can persuade other G-20 countries to contribute a fixed percentage to a stimulus in SSA, there will be a 20 per cent rate of return on its own investments (0.011 per cent net GDP impact compared to a 0.05 per cent of GDP initial investment). The overall rate of return of the US$ 50 billion stimulus to the rest of the world is around 15 per cent.

Assuming that it is possible to find US$ 50 billion of productive investment in SSA infrastructure and based on the rates of return we have seen in the past for infrastructure projects and that funds are provided in the form of well-managed aid with capable local institutions implementing the investment, the simulations on the model suggest that world output would increase by US$ 250 billion, with much of it in SSA and around $20 billion in the rest of the world. The cumulative impact after 10 years of a fiscal stimulus in consumption is around US$ 60 billion in world GDP.

References

Adam, Christopher S. and David L. Bevan (2006). "Aid and the Supply Side: Public Investment, Export Performance and Dutch Disease in Low-Income Countries", *World Bank Economic Review* 20(2): 261-90. Oxford University Press.

Allston, J.M., C. Chan-Khan, M.C. Marra, P.G. Pardy and T.J. Wyatt (2000). "A Meta-Analysis of Rates of Return to Agricultural R&D", *IFPRI Research Report* No.113. Washington, DC: International.

Ayogu, M. (2007). "Infrastructure and Economic Development in Africa: A Review", *Journal of African Economies* 16 (Supplement 1): 75-126.

Barrell, Ray and Dawn Holland (2009). "A Fiscal Stimulus to Address the effects of the Global Financial Crisis on sub-Saharan Africa", *NIESR Discussion Paper* 331. UK: National Institute of Economic and Social Research.

Birdsall, N. (2009). "How to Unlock the $1 Trillion that Developing Countries Urgently Need to Cope with the Crisis", *http://www.cgdev.org/content/publications/detail/1421143/*

Bourguignon, F. and M. Sundberg (2007). "Aid Effectiveness–Opening the Black Box", *American Economic Review P&P* 97(2): 316-21.

Briceño-Garmendia, C., Estache Antonio and Nemat Shafik (2004). "Infrastructure Services in Developing Countries: Access, Quality, Costs and Policy Reform", *World Bank Policy Research Paper* No. 3468, December.

Burnside, C. and D. Dollar (2000). "Aid, Policies and Growth", *American Economic Review* 90 (4): 847-68.

Calderon, C. and L. Serven (2008). "Infrastructure and Economic Development in Sub-Saharan Africa", *Policy Research Working Paper Series* 4712.

Cali, M. and D.W. te Velde (2009). "Towards a Quantitative Assessment of Aid for Trade", *Commonwealth Economic Paper*. London: Commonwealth Secretariat.

Canning, David and Esra Bennathan (2000). "The Social Rate of Return on Infrastructure Investments", *Policy Research Working Paper Series* 2390. The World Bank.

Clemens, M., S. Radelet and R. Bhavnani (2004). "Counting Chickens when they Hatch: The Short-Term Effect of Aid on Growth", *CGD Working Paper* No. 44.

Deininger, K. and J. Okidi (2004). "Growth and Poverty Reduction in Uganda, 1999–2000. Panel Data Evidence", *Development Policy Review*: 481-509.

Doucouliagos, H. and M. Paldam (2007). "The Aid Effectiveness Literature. The Sad Result of 40 Years of Research", *University of Aarhus, Department of Economics Working Paper* 2007-2015.

Esfahani, Hadi Salehi and Maria Teresa Ramirez (2003). "Institutions, Infrastructure, and Economic Growth", *Journal of Development Economics* 70(2): 443-77.

Estache, Antonio (2006). "Infrastructure: A Survey of Recent and Upcoming Issues", *World Bank Draft*.

Fan, S. and C. Chan-Kang (2004). "Returns to Investment in Less-Favoured Areas in Developing Countries: A Synthesis of Evidence and Implications for Africa", *Food Policy* 29: 431–44.

Fan, Shenggen, Xiaobo Zhang and Neetha Rao (2004). "Public Expenditure, Growth and Poverty Reduction in Rural Uganda", *Development Strategy and Governance Division Discussion Paper* No.4. Washington, DC: International Food Policy Research Institute.

Foster, M. and T. Killick (2006). "What would Doubling Aid do for Macroeconomic Management in Africa?", *ODI Working* Paper 264, April.

Gomanee, K., S. Girma and O. Morrissey (2002). "Aid, Investment and Growth in Sub-Saharan Africa", Paper prepared for the 10th General Conference of EADI, Ljubljana in *Journal of International Development*.

Hansen, H. and F. Tarp (2001). "Aid and Growth Regressions", *Journal of Development Economics* 64: 547-70.

Hogan, W.W. and D.W. Jorgensen (1991). "Productivity Trends in the Cost of Reducing CO_2 Emissions", *The Energy Journal* 12(1): 67-85.

Huber, P.W. and M.P. Mills (2005). *The Bottomless Well: The Twilight of Fuel, The Virtue of Waste and Why we will Never Run Out of Energy*. New York: Basic Books.

IMF (2009). "The Global Financial Crisis and Low Income Countries", see *http://www.imf.org/external/pubs/ft/books/2009/globalfin/globalfin.pdf*

Inhaber, H. (1997). *Why Energy Conservation Fails*. Westport, CT: Quorum Books.

Killick, T. and M. Foster (2006). "What Would Doubling Aid Do for Macroeconomic Management in Africa?", A synthesis paper, *ODI Working Paper* 264. London: ODI.

Koopmans, C.C. and D.W. te Velde (2001). "Bridging the Energy Efficiency Gap: Using Bottom-up Information in a Top-down Energy Demand Model", *Energy Economics* 23: 57-75.

Massa, I. and D.W. te Velde (2008). "The Trade Distortion Implications of Loans and Grants", Draft Paper for KfW.

McPherson, M.F. and T. Rakovski (2001). "Understanding the Growth Process in sub-Saharan Africa : Some Empirical Estimates", *African Economic Policy Discussion Paper* No. 54, March.

ODI (2009). *A Development Charter for the G-20*. UK: Overseas Development Institute.

Porter, Michael E. and Claas van der Linde (1995). "Toward a New Conception of the Environment-Competitiveness Relationship", *The Journal of Economic Perspectives* 9(4): 97-118.

Rajan, R.G. and A. Subramanian (2007). "Aid and Growth: What Does the Cross-Country Evidence Really Show", *Review of Economics and Statistics* 90(4): 643-65. MIT Press.

———. (2005). "What Undermines Aid's Impact on Growth?", *NBER Working Paper* No. 11657.

Stern, Nicholas (2009). "Nicholas Stern's Reaction to Green Budget Measures", *The Guardian* (Environment Blog). April 22.

te Velde, D.W. (2009). "A Rainbow Stimulus", *ODI Opinion* 125. *http://www.odi.org.uk/resources/odi-publications/opinions/125-fiscal-stimulus-global-recession-downturn.pdf*

———. (2008). "Promoting Green Growth–Evidence from Firm Level Analysis in China", *Preliminary Note,* July.

World Bank (2009). "Swimming against the Tide: How Developing Countries are Coping with the Global Crisis", *Background Paper* for the G-20 Finance Ministers Meeting on March 13-14.

———. (2006). "Review of Selected Railway Concessions in Sub-Saharan Africa". *http://www4.worldbank.org/afr/ssatp/Resources/WorldBank-WorkingPapers/ESW-RailwayConcessions.pdf*

Acknowledgement: © National Institute of Economic and Social Research and Overseas Development Institute.

Appendix A-11.1

Details of Model for SSA in NiGEM

The model simulation results reported in this paper are based on the behaviour of NiGEM's regional model of Africa. There are a few technical factors to consider in the interpretation of the results.

Country Composition

NiGEM's model of Africa consists of the following countries:

Angola
Benin
Botswana
Burkina Faso
Burundi
Cameroon
Cape Verde
Central African Republic
Chad
Comoros
Congo, Dem. Rep. of
Congo, Rep. of
Côte d'Ivoire
Djibouti
Equatorial Guinea
Ethiopia
Gabon
Gambia, The
Ghana
Guinea
Guinea-Bissau
Kenya
Lesotho
Madagascar
Malawi
Mali
Mauritania
Mauritius
Morocco
Mozambique, Rep. of
Namibia
Niger
Rwanda
São Tomé and Príncipe
Senegal
Seychelles
Sierra Leone
Sudan
Swaziland
Tanzania
Togo
Tunisia
Uganda
Zambia

Nigeria is in OPEC and Morocco in Africa. In order to apply this model to illustrate a shock to Sub-Saharan Africa, we have to make the assumption that on an average the behaviour of included/excluded economies, in terms of price and demand elasticities and speed of response, is in line with that of the rest of the region. While this may prove a strong assumption, the level of GDP for NIESR's African region plus South Africa shows less than a 10 per cent deviation from the IMF's SSA definition historically.

PPPs *versus* Exchange Rates

For regional aggregations, the NiGEM model sums together real GDP data levels in terms of purchasing power parities, rather than current exchange rates. This corrects for price level differences across countries and more accurately captures the size of an economy relative to the rest of the world. However, this makes it less straightforward to apply an absolute transfer in US$ terms from one country to another. In order to account for this, we calculate the size of the shock (i.e., $50 billion) as a share of nominal domestic demand in current US$. We then raise domestic demand by an equivalent percentage, to capture the buying power of $50 billion in SSA. In percentage terms, the results are straightforward to interpret. However, some care must be taken when converting these impacts into level terms.

Key Model Relationships

Aid inflows into Africa enter the economy through balance of payment transfers. This is assumed to improve the current account balance and reduces the stock of net foreign debt. A decline in net foreign debt has a positive impact on domestic demand in Africa, which in turn raises African import demand and hence global exports to Africa.

If aid inflows are treated as debt relief, the shock simply entails a rise in balance of payment inflows to Africa, matched by a rise in outflows from the financing countries. If this is financed by government borrowing in the financing countries, the budget deficit widens by the same amount, and this will entail an offsetting rise in tax rates in the financing countries to maintain solvency. Meanwhile there is a small rise in domestic demand in Africa as the net stock of foreign debt declines, leading to a rise in global exports to Africa, which at least partly offsets the negative impact on domestic demand of financing costs.

If aid inflows are spent on either consumption or investment, this also involves a direct shock to domestic demand in Africa, and hence a more significant rise in African import demand and global exports.

If aid inflows are spent on investment, this raises the level of capacity output, entailing a direct shock to capacity output. This feeds into the rest of the economy through the price system, as prices adjust to equate actual output (demand) with potential output (supply).

If aid inflows are spent on infrastructure and this has productivity spillover effects, this entails an additional shock to the level of technical progress in Africa, speeding the approach to the technology frontier. This raises capacity output, and feeds into the rest of the economy through the price system as described above.

Some of the key equations on the model are described below:

AFCBV Current balance, US$ million

#i afcbv = afbpt + afxval – afmval + afipdc – afipdd

where afbpt is balance of payment transfers, afxval is African exports in US$, afmval is African imports in US$, afipdc is interest payments received by Africa and afipdd is interest payments paid by Africa.

AFPXCOM Price of commodity exports, US$, 2000 = 100

afpxcom = 0.04873* wdpmm + 0.251114* wdpanf +

0.042418* wdpfdv + 0.32965* wdpfld

+ 0.328086* wdpo

where wdpmm is the price of metals and minerals, wdpanf is the price of agricultural non-foods, wdpfdv is the price of food, wdpfld is the price of beverages and wdpo is the price of oil.

AFPXNCOM Price of non-commodity exports, US$, 2000=100

log(afpxncom)= log(afpxncom(-1)) + 0.136269

- 0.173991*(log(afpxncom(-1)) - 0.442582*log(afcpx(-1))

- (1.-0.442582)* log(afcedd(-1)))

+ 0.105890* log(afpxncom(-1)/afpxncom(-2))

+ (1.-0.105890)* log(afcpx(-1)/afcpx(-2))

where afcpx is competitor's export prices, afcedd is domestic prices in US$ terms.

AFPX Deflator, exports of goods and services, US$, 2000=100

#i afpx = 0.27694*afpxcom + (1.-0.27694)*afpxncom

AFDD Domestic demand, US$ billion, 2000 prices

log(afdd) = log(afdd(-1))

+ 0.451 - 0.132189*(log(afdd(-1))

- 0.60*log(afxvold(-1))

+ 0.0059783*afnar(-1))

+ 0.5*log(afpopt/afpopt(-1))

where afxvold is African export volumes in terms of domestic consumer prices, afnar is net foreign debt as a share of GDP and afpopt is total population.

AFMVOL Imports of goods and services, US$ billion, 2000 prices

log(afmvol) = log(afmvol(-1)) - 0.284631

- 0.092493* (log(afmvol(-1)) + 0.68077* log(afrpm(-1))

- 1.24* log(afdd (-1) + afxvol (-1)))

+ 1.1*log((afdd+afxvol)/(afdd(-1)+afxvol(-1)))

-0.06147*log(afrpm/afrpm(-1))

where afrpm is import prices relative to domestic prices.

AFXVOL Exports of goods and services, US$ billion, 2000 prices

log(afxvol) = log(afxvol(-1)) +0.11185

-0.172654*(log(afxvol(-1)) +1.350605*log(afrpx(-1))

-1.0*log(afs(-1)))

+1.08*log(afs/afs(-1)) -0.268*log((afrpx)/(afrpx(-1)))

where afrpx is African export prices relative to competitor's, afs is external demand.

AFY GDP, US$ billion, 2000 PPP

#i afy = afdd + afxvol - afmvol

AFCED Consumer expenditure deflator, 2000=100

log(afced)= log(afced(-1))+ 0.001774

-0.02545*(log(afced(-1))-log(afpmd(-1))-1.490*afog(-1))

+ 0.201981*log(afpmd/afpmd(-1))

+ 0.106133*log(afpmd(-1)/afpmd(-2))

+ (1.-0.201981-0.106133)*log(afinf)

+0.22897*(afog-afog(-1))

where afpmd is import prices in domestic currency, afog is the output gap (afy/afycap), afinf is inflation expectations.

AFYCAP Trend output for capacity utilisation

log(afycap) = log(afycap(-1)) - 1.566 - 0.2*(log(afycap(-1)) - aftechl

- log(afpopt(-1)))

where aftechl is the level of technical progress and afpopt is total population

Appendix A-11.2

Bilateral Aid and Trade Relationships

Bilateral aid leads to more exports without aid being tied. Massa and te Velde (2008) estimate:

$$In(Exp_{ijt}) = \alpha + \beta_1 \ln(Y_{it}) + \beta_2 \ln(Y_{jt}) + \beta_3 \ln(Ypc_{it}) + \beta_4 \ln(Ypc_{jt}) +$$
$$\beta_5 \ln(Dist_{ij}) + \beta_6 X_{ijt} + \delta_3 \ln(Grants_{ijt}) + \delta_4 \ln(Grants_{All-j,\ it}) + \varepsilon_{ijt}$$

where i stands for the exporting country (donor), j for the importing country (recipient) and t for the time span. The dependent variable Exp_{ij} represents the export flows from country i to country j. Among the explanatory variables, Y measures the gross domestic product of country i and j respectively, Ypc stands for the GDP per capita of each of the two countries, $Dist_{ij}$ is the distance between the exporting and importing country, and X_{ij} is a vector which usually includes dummies indicating whether the two countries share a common border, a common language or other. ε_{ij} is the error term, normally distributed, with mean 0 and variance σ_{ε}^{2}.

$Grants_{ij}$ and $Grants_{All-i,j}$ are respectively the grants country j receives from country i, and the grants country j receives from all the countries other than country i.

The vector X_{ij} in equation includes the following set of dummy variables commonly used in the international trade gravity model literature:

- Colony which is a binary variable taking value 1 if one country in the trade pair was colonised by the other, and 0 otherwise;
- Comlang which is a binary variable taking value 1 if the two countries have a common language, and 0 otherwise.

Table 1

Variable Description

Variables	*Number of Observations*	*Definition*	*Sources*
Exp_{ijt}	1688	Exports from country i to j in real terms in USD	IMF
Y_{it}	1688	GDP of country i in real terms in WDI	USD
Y_{jt}	1688	GDP of country j in real terms in USD	WDI
Ypc_{it}	1688	GDP per capita of country i in real terms in USD	WDI

contd...

...contd...

Variables	*Number of Observations*	*Definition*	*Sources*
Ypc_{jt}	1688	GDP per capita of country j in real terms in USD	WDI
$Grants_{ijt}$	1688	Grants disbursed in real terms in USD	OECD
^{Grants}All-i, jt	1688	Grants from all the countries other than country i in real terms inUSD	OECD
$Loans_{ijt}$	1688	Loans disbursed in real terms in USD	OECD
^{Loans}All-i, jt	1688	Loans from all the countries other than country i in real terms in USD	OECD
$Dist_{ij}$	1688	Distance between country i and j	CEPII
$Colony_{ijt}$	1688	Dummy for a previous colonial relationship	CEPII
$Comlang_{ijt}$	1688	Dummy for common language	CEPII

Note: The dataset covers the period 1980-2006.

Table 2

The Effects of Bilateral Aid (Disbursements) on Bilateral Trade, 1980-2006

Dependent Variable: Exp_{ijt}	*Fixed Effects*	*Random Effects*
	(6)	(7)
^{Y}it	-1.74	0.820***
^{Y}jt	2.267***	0.907***
Ypc_{it}	1.696	-0.450*
Ypc_{jt}	0.251	0.350***
$Grants_{ij,t}$	0.017*	0.020***
^{Grants}All-i,jt	-0.014	-0.021
$Dist_{ij}$		-1.007***
$Colony_{ijt}$		0.818***
$Comlang_{ijt}$		0.609***
Constant	127.142***	37.436***
N	1688	1688
N_g	319	319
R^2_within	0.280	0.248
R^2_overall	0.408	0.783
R^2_between	0.226	0.774

Note: All variables in natural logarithms. * significance at 10 per cent, **significance at 5 per cent, *** significance at 1 per cent. All regressions include a time trend not reported.

Source: Massa and te Velde (2008).

12 Reducing the Administrative Expenditures as Source for Increasing the Efficiency of Local Governance under Conditions of the Global Financial Crisis

Ani Matei and Lucica Matei

Introduction

The period we are going through in recent years is marked, economically speaking, by effects of financial crisis. These effects, felt in different proportions by each world state, overlapped other old economic processes that focus on bureaucracy high costs, costs that affect the economic efficiency both in the private sector and in the public sector. Evans and Rauch (1999) established the direct connection between the quality of bureaucracy and economic development.

The measurement instruments kept in mind the so called 'weberianness scale' (Evans and Rauch, 1999: 761-762) made after bureaucracy principles declared by Weber (1904-1911, 1968).

The evolutions specific to contemporary period lead to réglementations and obligations abundance that highly affect economic results, especially in the private sector. In this context, numerous states such as the United States of America (USA), the Netherlands, Germany, the United Kingdom (UK), Australia, Denmark, Sweden, Norway etc., and European and international organisations like European Union (EU), Organisation for Economic Co-operation and Development (OECD), World Bank etc., established methodological structures and activation system in order to reduce costs, especially for private firms, intended to cover some informational obligations imposed by national or transnational state legislation. Identified by the 'administrative burden' name, these costs were evaluated in the best projects aiming to reduce them. They are the object of some professional networks and their cover area is getting larger. We mention here SCM Network comprising over 24 states and organisations. Its main objective is the dissemination and development of cooperation itself regarding the administrative burdens reduction.

The strong connections between public and private sectors, currently sustained and developed by public economies and extended area of appliance of the new public management (NPM), determine the necessity of public sector preoccupation for administrative costs reduction, including administrative burden. This was imposed also by the financial crisis. Most of the world states' reality shows preoccupations in the two directions previously mentioned and the elaboration of new aggregated economic mechanisms capable to evaluate the efficiency and efficacy of administrative costs reduction structures. When local and Central governments aim to maintain a certain level of production, the economic mechanisms that may best sustain and describe the strategic objectives are those of production factors substitution. Economic analyses emerged from here may offer the necessary information to fulfil the objective of administrative costs reduction, referred to reduction levels, economic structure etc.

The proposed research objectives keep in mind to fundament new modalities to approach economic processes related to administrative costs reduction policies and strategies and to decrease the financial crisis effects. The main hypotheses refer to:

- extending administrative costs reduction topic in public sector;
- integrating the mechanisms of sustaining production factor and the model of production functions in the explanatory step that assures the economic support for politics and mentioned structures and
- evaluating local government efficiency in the actual conditions and applying some concrete measures to reduce the administrative costs.

The approached methodology comprises both descriptive and bibliographic administrative and economic analyses and certain statistic data analysis instruments.

Reducing the Administrative Costs: Programmes and Mechanisms

The General Conceptual Framework

For the public sector, the field literature reveals a certain specificity regarding the expenditures' efficiency. Thereby, Stiglitz (2000: 205) presents explanations of inefficiency in the public sector that refer to the organisational and individual differences, among which: the role of political concerns, absence of competition, absence of incentive pay, difficulty of firing etc., reduces incentives, as well as the pursuit of bureaucratic objectives—maximising the size of the organisation. Similar analyses can be found in Bailey (2002), Connolly and Munro (1999) or Matei (2003). With regard to the structure of the governmental expenditures, for the OECD countries, for example, this comprises: government consumption (20-25%), transfer payments (15-18%), subsidies (2-4%), interest paid (7-8%) and capital expenditure (2-4%). By analysing the weight of the public expenditures in the gross domestic product (GDP), Connolly and Munro (1999: 320-330) reconfirm their growth tendency in accordance with Wagner's Law, as well as in the theories regarding 'fiscal illusion' or Baumol Effect (Connolly and Munro, 1999: 14-15; Andrei *et al.*, 2009: 320-330). For Romania, Andrei *et al.* (2009) test the validity of Wagner's Law for the aggregated governmental expenditures, the average elasticity being non-linear and top-heavy.

Public expenditure represents 'the ensemble of annual expenditure with public nature of a country, financed on the basis of public budgetary resources' (Dobrotã *et al.*, 1999: 98). In fact, public expenditure reflects the political choices of the government, representing costs of the elements of economic policy aiming to deliver public goods. These costs relate to delivering goods through the budget of the public sector or represent expenditure in the private sector, induced by regulations and laws made by the public sector.

What we called in the introduction as the administrative burden of private companies can be framed in this second category of expenditure. The costs from the first category are in fact public expenditure as such, of which a part represents the costs of bureaucracy in any public administration. In an extended meaning for the administrative burden, the costs of bureaucracy are in this category for a public administration.

In the structure of the national or local budgets we find:

- Exhaustive public expenditure focussed on procurement of goods and services (for example: labour, consumables) and capital goods (for example: investments of the public sector in streets, schools, hospitals) and

  Transferable public expenditure, such as public expenditure for pensions, subsidies, interests, unemployment allowances.

In the general context of the public expenditures, a series of concepts are introduced and used, which are important for the analysis we are carrying out. Thus, in accordance with the International Standard Cost Model (ISCM) manual and the EU Standard Cost Model (EU SCM) methodology we will have (EU, 2006: 1):

- Administrative costs (AC) are defined by SCM as the costs of administrative activities that businesses are required to conduct in order to comply with the information obligations that are imposed through regulation (DTF, 2007: 4);
- Information is to be explained in a broad sense, i.e., including costs of labelling, reporting, monitoring and assessment needed to provide the information and registration and
- An important distinction must be made between information that would be collected by businesses even in the absence of the legislation and information that would not be collected without the legal provisions. The costs induced by the latter are called administrative burdens (AB). Some of the ABs are necessary if the underlying objectives of the legislation and prescribed level of protection defined in the treaties are to be met effectively; for instance, where information is needed to make market transparent. But there are also many cases where burdens can be streamlined and reduced without affecting the underlying objectives as such—the latter burdens are clearly unnecessary (DTF, 2007: 4). The ABs are that part of the administrative costs which are only incurred as a result of the regulations. Such costs are called incremental costs

because, in the absence of regulation, they would not be incurred. Conversely, the business as usual (BAU) costs are the costs of the activities which businesses would continue to carry out even if the regulatory requirements were removed.

Administrative cost	=	Business as usual costs	+	Administrative burden

Source: DTF (2007: 4).

or AC = BUC + AB

BAU costs are not considered in a baseline measurement because the reductions in regulatory requirements that are considered businesses' usual activities, will not result in actual reductions in business costs because businesses will continue to incur the costs to meet their own needs. Reducing the costs for business requires that the focus be on administrative burden. Third-party information obligation costs arise from regulation requiring business to provide information to third parties such as employees or consumers. The Netherlands and Denmark included third-party information obligation costs in their SCM baseline measurement. However, the UK SCM manual (BRE, 2005) states that third-party costs are excluded from the baseline.

DTF (2007: 5) describes a scheme intending to determine the share of different administrative costs categories in GDP.

SCM baseline mesurement	-	Business as usual costs (BAU)	-	3 rd party information obligation costs	=	Administrative burden as a % of GDP

Source: DTF (2007: 5).

Concrete estimations extracted from different strategic documents are illustrative also.

Table 12.1

Estimated Administrative Costs, Structure and Percentage of GDP

Country	*Measured Administrative Costs (%)*	*Estimated Administrative Burden (or Moving BAU)*	*Estimated Administrative Burden (Excl. 3rd Party Costs)*
United Kingdom	2.5	1.6	1.0
The Netherlands	3.6	2.3	1.4
Denmark	2.2	1.4	0.9
Czech Republic	3.0	1.9	1.1

Source: DTF (2007: 6).

For the mentioned states it can be observed that the estimated share of administrative burden is between 0.9 per cent to 1.04 per cent from GDP.

EU Policies and Programmes for Reducing the Administrative Costs

Better Regulation Programme

Regulation, a phenomenon happening at local, national or international level, is a mean to answer the challenges triggered by the free movement of goods, services, people and capital, serving several purposes: to protect health by ensuring food safety, to protect the environment by setting air and water quality standards, to set rules for companies competing in the marketplace to create a level playing field.

The European Commission (EC) launched a 'Better Regulation' programme in 2002, to simplify and generally improve the regulatory environment. It is designed to cut red tape, improve the quality of regulation and design better laws for consumers and businesses alike.

The Better Regulation programme included a mix of different actions:

- introducing a system for assessing the impact assessment and improving the design improvement of major Commission proposals;
- implementing a programme of simplification of existing legislation;

- testing Commission proposals still being looked at by the Council of Ministers and the European Parliament, to see whether they should be withdrawn;
- factoring consultation into all Commission initiatives and
- looking at alternatives to laws and regulations (such as self-regulation or coregulation by the legislator and interested parties).

The Commission's ongoing effort is to regulate better results in examining administrative costs in specific policy areas. The EC set out a method for measuring administrative costs (the EU's net administrative cost model), inspired by the best practice in the member states, such as the Netherlands and the UK.

The alternatives to regulation, which can be more cost-efficient and effective ways to address certain policy objectives than the classic legal tools, are:

- Coregulation: entrusting the achievement of the goals set out in law, for example to the social partners or to NGOs and
- Self-regulation: voluntary agreements between private bodies to deal with their own problems by taking mutual actions.

On 23 March 2005, the European Council requested 'the Commission and the Council to consider a common methodology for measuring administrative burdens with the aim of reaching an agreement by the end of 2005'.

On 16 March 2005, the Commission's communication on 'Better Regulation for Growth and Jobs in the EU' included, as a companion Staff Working Paper, a detailed outline of a possible 'EU Net Administrative Cost Model' (EC, 2005a) based on SCM.

The outline of an EU Net Administrative Cost Model was amended and refined through a pilot phase carried out from April to September 2005 that led the Commission to present a revised methodology, also called the 'EU SCM' (EC, 2005b). The Commission listed a number of possible improvements to the EU SCM, while making clear that such optimisation was no pre-condition for its application. An operational manual for applying the model was included on 15 March 2006, in the Impact Assessment (IA) guidelines and translated in all EU official languages to ease methodological convergence. The EU SCM has been applied in a number of published or upcoming IAs to ensure that any administrative burdens generated by new legislation are justified and minimised.[1]

Action Programme to Reduce the Administrative Burden

In November 2006, the Commission proposed launching an ambitious action programme to reduce the administrative burden of the existing regulation in the EU. As part of this, the Commission proposed that the 2007 Spring European Council fix a reduction target of 25 per cent, to be achieved jointly by the EU and member states by 2012. This underlines the Commission's commitment to better regulation as part of the 'growth and jobs' strategy.

The joint target to reduce administrative burdens by 25 per cent in 2012, covers Community legislation as well as national regulatory measures. Achieving this objective could lead to an increase in the level of EU GDP of approximately 1.4 per cent or € 150 billion in the medium term (Gelauff and Lejour, 2005).

The mentioned document also assesses the administrative costs of the EU member states that vary between 6.8 per cent in Greece, Hungary and RE (Baltic states, Malta and Cyprus) and 1.5 per cent (United Kingdom, Finland or Sweden), the EU average being of 3.5 per cent (the percentages refer to GDP)(EC, 2006). The prospects of reducing 25 per cent of the administrative costs will lead to a reduction of 1.3 per cent of their weight in GDP, on average for EU.

OECD: The Costs of Regulation—Financial and Administrative

Regulation has a number of consequences for businesses. Administrative costs are only one type of costs that regulation can entail.

1. Though they share a common methodology, the administrative burden (AB) reducing exercise is different from normal IA practice. This AB exercise aims to provide a comprehensive *ex-post* measurement of legislation in a policy area for all levels of legislation and then subsequent identification of reduction targets. IA, on the other hand, measures all the costs and benefits of available policy options, while the AB methodology is only a partial measurement tool which is to be applied proportionately and used only in assessing *ex-ante* impacts of proposed changes of legislation (marginal approach).

Figure 12.1 illustrates the different types of costs that regulation can impose on businesses.

Figure 12.1

Types of Costs Imposed by Regulation

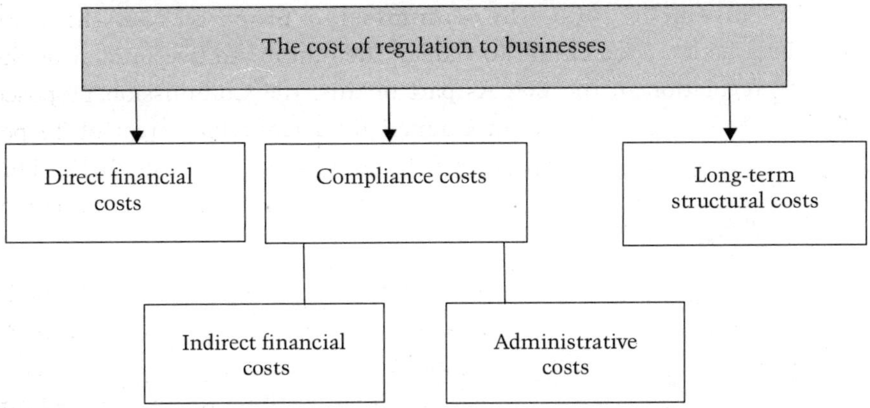

Source: OECD (2010: 10).

Direct financial costs are the result of a concrete and direct obligation to transfer a sum of money to the government or the competent authority. These costs are, therefore, not related to a need for information on the part of the government. Such costs include administrative charges, taxes, etc., For example, the fees for applying for a permit would be a financial cost of the regulation.

Compliance costs are all the costs of complying with regulation, with the exception of direct financial costs and long-term structural consequences. In the context of the SCM, these can be divided into 'substantive compliance costs' and 'administrative costs'. Examples of substantive compliance costs include:

1. Filters in accordance with environmental requirements and
2. Physical facilities in compliance with working conditions' regulations.

Examples of administrative costs include:

1. Documentation of the installation of a filter and
2. Annual report on working conditions.

ABs are the part of administrative costs that businesses sustain simply because of requirement. The ABs are thus a subset of the administrative costs in that the administrative costs also encompass the administrative activities that businesses will continue to conduct if the regulations were removed.

Standard Cost Model (SCM)

SCM network comprises for the time being over 24 states and organisations and recently also Romania. In fact, for Romania, the 'Strategy for Better Regulation at Central Government Level, 2008-2013' comprises, as priorities on medium-term, 'preliminary analysis of the issue of AB, development of a general methodology to assess the administrative costs and to elaborate a concrete action plan in order to implement the Standard Administrative Cost Model'.

There are measurement/estimating methodologies for quantifying the AB imposed by tax regulations:

Standard measurement methodology, such as what has become known as the SCM, which consists of four stages:

1) Information obligations (IOs) for each tax are specified. (IOs are the obligations arising from regulation to provide information and data to the public sector or third parties. An IO does not necessarily mean that information has to be transferred to the public authority or private persons, but may include a duty to have information available for inspection or supply on request. A regulation may contain many IOs);
2) The data requirements applicable to each information obligation are identified;
3) The administrative requirements are established; and
4) Cost parameters (i.e., price, time and quantity) for each administrative activity are collected:

- Price consists of a tariff, wage costs plus overhead for administrative activities done internally or hourly cost for external service providers;
- Time, the amount of time required to complete the administrative activity and
- Quantity comprises the size of the population of businesses affected and the frequency that the activity must be completed each year.

SCM Formula

Cost per administrative activity (or per data requirement) = price x time x quantity.

(population x frequency)

Tailor-made approach, such as those as employed by the New Zealand and Swedish revenue authorities when quantifying the AB of their respective VAT systems.

Taxes that contribute most to overall administrative burdens:

- Personal income;
- Social contributions—received largely from employers in the form of withholdings from employees' wages—is administered by separate social security agencies (in some countries, multiple agencies), while in other countries (e.g., Finland, Ireland, the Netherlands, Norway, Sweden and the UK) it has been integrated with the collection of personal income tax administered by the main revenue body;
- Corporate;
- Value added tax (VAT)—imposes the most significant level of burden (in absolute terms) of any tax in most countries and
- Excise.

Integrating the collection of social contributions and personal tax collections should trigger a reduction in the AB of businesses, 'placing responsibility for collection (of social contributions) with the tax administration can also significantly reduce compliance costs for employers, with less paperwork as a result of common forms and book-keeping systems and a common audit program covering income, VAT and payroll taxes, and social contributions based on income and payrolls. The increasing use of internet-based electronic filing and payment systems with the tax administration also lowers taxpayers' and contributors' compliance costs. This simplification can also improve the accuracy of calculations made by employers and therefore compliance levels' (IMF, 2004).

SCM Network disseminates and makes compatible the good practices from AB decreasing domain. Table 12.2 presents a synthesis of the main initiatives and proposals assumed by national governments.

Table 12.2

Synthesis of Initiatives and Proposals for Cost Reduction

Country	*Period/Term*	*Objective*	*Targetted Area*	*Comments*
Australia	2006-2012	25%	Businesses and not for profit	- Up to July 2011 was provided a 256 million $ decrease. -In September 2009, the target was revised to 500 million $ until July 2012 (including substantive compliance and delay costs).
Austria	2007-2012	25%	- Ministries -Austrian businesses	- Global evaluation – € 1 billion - Two phase reduction: 2010 for national induced burdens and 2012 for EU induced burdens.
Belgium	2007-2012	17-33%	Organisations from six governmental domains	- Global evaluation – € 61,120,467 - Reduction is made by projects implementation simplification.
Czech Republic	2005-2010	20%	Business organisations	In 2008, the government re-confirms the 2005 objective.
Denmark	2001-2012	25%	- Businesse organisations. - 15 invest with attribution in business réglementation	- The initial target of 15% was

contd...

...contd...

				recalculated in 2002 up to 25%. - E-government strategies keep in mind business but also public authorities reductions.
France	2006-2012	25%	Business organisations	3% of GDP (€ 60 billion).
Germany	2006-2012	25%	- Businesse organisations - Citizens - Public administration	- In 2009, the Federal government extended the topic. - Reducing administrative costs for public administration.
Italy	2008-2012	25%	Business organisations	The objectives were set up in accordance with Lisbon Strategy and European Target.
The Netherlands	2002-2007	25%	Business organisations	In 2007, the ABs for business were represented by € 9.3 billion, the equivalent of 1.7% of GDP and comes in equal parts, from national and European legislation.
Poland	2010	25%	Business and public organisations	Domains like environment, spatial planning, tourist services, labour law, business activity law, social security were targetted.
Spain	2008-2012	30%	- Business organisations - Citizens	- It will increase by 1.4 per cent of GDP. - 10 ministries are targetted.
The UK	2005-2015	25%	- Business organisations - Policy costs - The third sectors	- In the first phase, 2005-2010, the target was a redution evaluated to 3.3 billion £ - In 2009, the government established new objectives for 2010-2015.

Source: SCM Network. *http://www.administrative-burdens.com*

The synthesis proves the preoccupation of the majority of European states and also from other continents, in order to reduce the administrative costs. We refer to administrative costs because many states focus their governmental efforts towards them, overcoming the strict objective of administrative burden.

World Bank: Economic Benefits for Administrative Reform

The World Bank has developed a series of administrative reform projects that aimed at reducing the administrative and compliance costs (WB, 2007). These projects benefit society if they reduce administrative and compliance costs.

Macroeconomic Benefits

Trade liberalisation will implicate a loss in trade tax revenue that can be substituted with an increase in the domestic tax revenues.

Reduction in Administrative Costs of Collecting the Taxes

The modernisation of tax administration should lead to lower costs per amount of revenue raised as:

i. the tax administration is streamlined;
ii. tax officials are better trained;
iii. tax payers become more compliant as a result of enhanced tax payer education and the establishment of taxpayer support centres, process simplification and improved automation and
iv. a simpler tax policy results.

Reduction in Compliance Cost for the Taxpayer

These costs which tend to be higher than the cost of administering the tax itself, include the cost individuals and enterprises incur in preparing their tax declaration and dealing with tax audits (in-house costs, bribes) (Evans, 2003).

Support Trade Liberalisation

These benefits have been estimated for period 1997-2015 at $500 billion (1997 dollars), three quarters of which would result from the dismantling trade barriers in low and middle-income countries (World Bank, 2002).

Reduction in Distortions of the Present Tax Regime

Strengthening the capacity of the tax administration.

The Administrative Costs in the Public Sector

An Extension of the Conceptual Framework

The extension of this issue towards the public sector will lead to an extension of the content of the administrative burden to include 'compliance costs for enterprises, services and citizens, including administrative and bureaucratic (operational) costs as well as capital costs'.

Consequently, the administrative costs in the public sector comprise, mainly, the costs for purchasing goods and support services for bureaucracy, as well as payments of some charges etc. The model that will be presented follows the ideas from Matei (2008) and it was used for assessing the public sector performance (Matei, 2008: 69-73) or substantiating the marketing strategies under the reduction of the administrative costs (Matei *et al.*, 2009: 17-27).

The weight of the public expenditure is different and depends on the development level of the public or of the private sector. Reported to the latter, the administrative burden of the public sector has a non-linear evolution. From this perspective, it is worth mentioning that the models formulated by Musqrave (1974) and Rostow (1960), stating that in the earlier stages of growth and economic development, investments in the public sector are high, providing the core social infrastructure. The purpose of these investments is to help economy to reach higher development stages, where, although the state will continue with the investments, their role will be to complete the private investments. The conclusions of the two economists are relevant also for the evolution of the administrative costs, both in the public and private sector:

- While total investments increase as proportion from GDP growth, the relative share of the public sector decreases (Musqrave, 1974: 35);
- When economy reaches the maturity stage, the mix of public expenditure will be oriented from the expenditure for infrastructure to the expenditure for education, health and welfare services (Rostow, 1960: 9-10).

Therefore, if we take into calculation, the total administrative costs (AC_{tot}) obtained by summing up those from public and private sector:

$$AC_{tot} = AC_{public} + AC_{private} \quad (1)$$

it will have the following characteristics:

- AC_{tot} can be considered constant, for certain periods of economic development;
- AC_{public} and $AC_{private}$ vary in time and
- between AC_{public} and $AC_{private}$ there is bidirectional transfer due to effects of dislocation between public and private expenditure, specific for different periods of economic and social development.

The above assertions are based on Peacock-Wiseman analyses, stating that 'governments have the trend to spend more money and the citizens do not wish to pay many taxes. Consequently, the governments should take into consideration the wishes of their citizens' (Payne, Ewing and Mohammadi, 2006).

In this context, it occurs the so called effect of dislocation, namely the public expenditure dislocates the private expenditure in certain periods, such as crises periods.

By using (1.1) and (2.1), we obtain:

$$BUC_{public} + BUC_{private} = const.- (AB_{public} + AB_{private}) \quad (2)$$

Which lead us to the idea that, at least on a macroeconomic level, the customary costs of the public and private affairs depend directly on the administrative burden.

Evolution of Public Expenditures during Financial Crisis

OECD Analyses

In the last half century, specialised literature increased its concern towards public expenditure's evaluation, directly related to economical performance. Saunders (1985) analyses public expenditure's extent and its impact on GDP in OECD states. What characterises the period 1960-1981, was the existence of budget deficits on a large scale in the mid-1970s after a strong public expenses increase. Recently, Olugbenga (2009) explores the Wagnerian-Keynesian debate over the direction of the causal relationship between government expenditure and economic growth, not only in the developed countries but in the developing ones also. This exploration is made by examining the relations between dynamic properties of public expenditures and economic growth for 30 OECD countries during 1970-2005.

In fact, OECD preoccupation towards closely monitoring public expenses, towards the expenditures allocation mechanism and the way they contribute to attain a public policy goal are well known.

Some data are relevant for the financial crisis period. For Germany, the conclusion in OECD (2010a: Ch.3) is that public finances quickly decline. To be more concrete, it is thought that after a period in which general budget deficit was reduced to a level close to equilibrium (in 2007 and 2008), in 2009, it substantially increased. For 2010, it reaches over 5 per cent of GDP. Deficit reduction method should be reducing public expenditures through an ambitious programme. 'In reducing the expenses, improving the public administrative efficacy should have priority since this would allow expenses reduction without decreasing services' quality and availability'.

For Poland, OECD (2010b: Ch.1) presents another perspective: 'Poland registered in 2009 the best performance of GDP increase among the OECD countries'. Although the crisis effects were felt from the adaptation of European currency point of view, the public institutions empowerment remains an essential problem of this country.

For Norway, OECD (2010c: Ch.1) observes a strong resistance towards crisis effects. Nevertheless, after the crisis, it is necessarily a macro-production approach in order to coordinate with other European and international institutions. It is also mentioned (OECD, 2010c: Ch.21) 'the existence of an unexploited potential for providing efficient public services on lower prices, especially in municipal services, such as education, health and even fiscal expenditures'.

Bearing in mind the high recession level in Hungary, OECD (2010d: Ch.1) says that 'the crisis was a catalyst for applying decisive structural reforms'. The same source, in Chapter 3 talks about 'enhancing financial stability through better regulation'.

Obviously, OECD comprised 30 states' fundamental analysis of recent data concerning the financial crisis effects on public expenditures. These offer us the input for sustaining the main idea of this paper: the necessity for an integrated approach on policies and statistics for public administrative costs and expenditures reduction in times of financial crisis.

Public Budgets' Contraction

In order to continue the shortly presented analyses from OECD studies, we shall, consequently present some statistic data concerning the financial equilibriums at governmental level. The presented period, 1995-2011 highlights cyclical evolution. Moreover, after 2008 and 2009, a new cycle of budget deficit or surpluses measurement would occur and it would be characterised by an accentuated increase/decrease.

On account of OECD (2010e), Annexure A-12.1 presents, in per cents, the evolution of national budgets including a foresight for 2010 and 2011.

A more detailed analysis of national tendencies highlights a number of particularities. These resulted also from the calculation of Pearson correlation coefficient for thc analysed interval (Annexure A-12.2).

For most of the OECD states, the correlation's intensity is strong, generally overcoming the value of 0.6. The evolution under the correlation mean of most of the OECD states can be found in Czech Republic, Switzerland, Slovakia or Japan.

Negative correlations are being highlighted in the case of Hungary or Slovakia. It is also interesting that there is a correlation with the mean at OECD level or EURO zone. The proven overtime emergence of the economy in most of the OECD states is being underlined at high correlation level. Once more, Hungary and Slovakia are the exceptions since they have negative correlation both with OECD and also with Euro zone mean. Japan has positive correlation just under the mean of the other OECD states.

A general analysis of the mentioned states' budget evolution emphasises a pronounced contribution of national budget that is visible mainly starting with 2008 and even more in 2009.

Most states, both from OECD and also others, have public expenditure reduction strategies in a developing phase. Therefore, deficits are supposed to decrease and their economies to confirm, starting with 2011, positive evolutions. These strategies correlate with older administrative cost-reduction strategies. Hence, the extension of administrative cost-reduction subject towards public sector and integrated approach of private and public sector may lead to a more realistic image of economic efficiency maintenance and GDP-increased scenarios.

Administrative Expenditures' Reduction Impact on Local Government Efficiency

The financial crisis determined the overlapping of substitution effects of administrative expenditures' reduction with overcoming the financial crisis strategies that aim to decrease public expenditures.

In both the situations, the governmental objectives focussed on were those concerning the growth of economic efficiency. Or as in the case of crisis situation, to preserve these levels for a convenient period of time to cover the crisis.

A more profound economic analysis emphasise applicable economic mechanism that may explain and fundament the processes that characterise crisis times.

A New Explanatory Model of Production Factors Substitution during Financial Crisis

Specialised literature shows new approaches towards production factors substitution aiming to state economical models that describe, closer to reality, different economic processes specific to the present days.

In this context, Arow *et al.* (1961), Klump and Grandville (2000), Karagianis *et al.* (2004), Lovell (1973), Sato and Hoffman (1968), Zaman and Goschin (2007) focus especially on work and capital production factors, the actual absorptions incorporating technological progress evolutions that on the one hand determine 'the growth of factors consumption' and, on the other hand, caused 'the growth of complex highly qualified work' and 'the capital consumption at high technological level' (Zaman and Goschin, 2007: 3-4).

These tendencies generate significant changes in substitution elasticity of different production factors depending on the one hand, on the level of socioeconomical development and on the other, on the factors such as market globalisation, connectivity and interdependences growth in world economy as a result of information and communication technology extension, new managerial approaches and best practices generalisations and market competency growth etc.

Now-a-days (Zestos, 1996; Klump *et al.*, 2005; Karagianis *et al.*, 2004) the production factors substitution is analysed from its direct nature point of view—referring to one factor type replacement with another factors or its indirect one—several production factors replacement with other factors with different functions but complementary to productive processes.

Crisis periods emphasise the connection between substitution processes of productive factors and technological progress. The objectivity of such a connection is being currently offered by the restrictive characteristic of natural resources, by the necessity to fight pollution at local and global level and, in general, the 'global problems' effects on humankind. The financial crises add to these determinations other elements decreasing the financial resources.

The need for sustainability growth under economic, social and environmental aspects and in general, for the growth/conservation of production and consumption models, efficiency or eco-efficiency overlaps with objectives commonly reachable in most of the strategies for financial crisis effects reduction.

Nevertheless, indirect substitution that is specific for financial crisis times is equivalent with saving in order to maintain and/or to consolidate economic equilibriums. At the present time, the most important substitution between capital and work refers to information and communication technology (ICT). According to Zaman and Goschin (2007: 4-5), ICT becomes a real capital with modernisation significance, 're-structuring factors of a significant part of traditional work capital in all social compartments as a result of positive externalities created especially in costs reduction domain'. (Zaman and Goshim, 2007: 4-5)

The continuous growth of workforce qualification, the production 'dematerialisation' or the corporate management extension in public sector represent as many restructuring and sustaining factors as production factors substitutions.

Administrative costs or public expenditure reduction policies and strategies determine changes in the mechanisms of production factors substitution.

Arrow *et al.* (1961), Miller (2008), Sato (1967), Morishima (1967) and Matei (2008) show theoretical and methodological instruments for macroeconomic analysis of production factors substitution and Cobb-Douglas production factors with their variants constant elasticity of substitution (CES) and variable elasticity of substitution (VES).

As it is known, production functions are non-linear expression of production factors: capital and work to which it can be added or not technical progress. Production factors show production (output) maxim contribution that can be obtained starting from a series of production factors (input) and allow to define and to measure some economic effects related to factors' performance and to possible substitution between: scale elasticity, factors elasticity, substitution elasticity or, if the case, technology progress rate. We shall focus in our analysis on CES and Cobb-Douglas production factors without technical progress.

According to Andrei and Bourbonnais (2008: 180-184), non-linear model represented by CES is different based on:

$$Y_t = \gamma^{-\theta}[\delta k_t^{-\theta} + (1-\delta)L_t^{-\theta}]^{-\mu} e^{\Sigma t} \qquad (3)$$

where:

- Y_t – the variable that modifies the outputs from the system,
- k_t – fix capital, L_t – human capital,

- γ,δ,μ,θ – models' parameters and
- ε_t – residual variable with N repartition (0, σ_Σ^2)

CES model parameters significances are:

- $\gamma > 0$ – the parameter of production process efficiency,
- $\delta\varepsilon(0,1)$ is known as the parameter of production process distribution,
- $\mu > 0$ – scale parameter for the process and
- $\theta \geq -1$ – parameter for the two process factors substitution.

Two proprieties are relevant for the CES function:

- production factors substitution elasticity is determined by θ substitution parameter, the relation being:

$$e=\frac{1}{1+\theta} \tag{4}$$

Usually, the elasticity of a production factors substitution ratio greater than one means a greater probability of their optimal combination. On the contrary, a less than one ratio shows an inequality of efficient compensation variety of production factors, as a consequence of absorption delay or incapacity and investments in technological progress.

- scale performance is determined through μ parameter. The scale performance of production factors represents the sum of production factors' performance, each performance being equal to the ratio between factors' marginal productivity and mean productivity.

If μ ε (0,1) production function has a descending scale performance. If μ > 1 we have an ascending function of scale performance. For μ = 1, the scale performance is constant. Cobb-Douglas production function is a particular CES case. The expression of Cobb-Douglas function is:

$$Y_t = AK_t^a L_t^\beta e^{\Sigma t} \tag{5}$$

Y_t, k_t, γ_t have the significance mentioned earlier and A,α,β represent the real parameters in ε_t, the residual variable.

To be more precise, α will represent productivity partial elasticity related to fix capital e_K. And β – productivity of partial elasticity related to human capital e_L. Scale elasticity equals the sum of two partial elasticity cases.

$$e = e_k + e_L \quad (6)$$

If $e < 1$, the productive process increases the output in a lower proportion than the increase of production factors. If $e > 1$, the productive process generates a greater increase of output than in the case of production factors. In the case of competition markets, the elasticity is greater than one ratio.

Therefore, substitution or scale elasticity measures the percentage change in factors proportion due to change in the technical substitution marginal rate. Substitution elasticity shows the proportional variance of quantitative ratio of resulted factors from the proportional variation of marginal rate of technical substitution of one factor related to another. In other words, represents an ease measure of the variable factor to be substituted by another (Hicks, 1932: 117).

In the described context, the determination of CES or Cobb-Douglas production factors may offer information concerning the aggregation flexibility of the two important production factors, work and capital and the capacity to overtake and portray the inclusion level of technical progress as the main resource for efficiency and production conservation in crisis conditions.

An Empirical Analysis

Empirical research estimates, in Romania's case, the Cobb-Douglas production function model using as statistic data:

- GDP as a measure of output;
- Gross fixed capital formation (GFCF) as an expression of fix capital production factors and
- Employed population (EMPL) for human capital production factor.

The utilised statistic data are those in Annexure A-12.3. Making use of the mentioned data series for parameters estimation:

- Trans-log representation for CES function and

- Linearisation through logarithm function for Cobb-Douglas function.

Therefore, the result is:

$$GDP^{0.25} = (4.10^{-6})^{0.25}\left[1.305GFCF^{0.25} - 0.305EMPL^{0.25}\right]^{-2.014} \times e^{0.307}$$

$$R^{2-}0.961, F = 64.650 \quad (7)$$

$$GDP = 8.07(GFCF)^{0.775}.(EMPL)^{0.367}.e^{0.338} \quad (8)$$

$$R^2 = 0.957, F = 92.414$$

where substitution elasticity becomes:

- For CES, e=1.33; and
- For Cobb-Douglas model, e=1.142.

In both of the situations, the scale performance is ascending and the differences resulted from the relative number of utilised statistical data. After calculating CS and CA indicators, we can conclude that Cobb-Douglas model offers more likely results than CES model. Trying to make an evaluation according to the proposed model for the Romanian development regions, we find the following value for the elasticity of sustainability.

Table 12.3

The Elasticity of Production Factors Substitution according to Romanian Development Regions

No.	*Region*	*e*
1	North-West	-2.103
2	Centre	1.327
3	North-East	-0.125
4	South-East	-1.397
5	South-Muntenia	1.165
6	Bucharest-Ilfov	1.965
7	South-West Oltenia	-1.143
8	West	-0.587

Source: Authors own calculations.

The Romanian development regions analysis was made for the statistical data from 2003-2009. The situation shows strong imbalances, the scale performances being ascending in only three regions, the others having a decreasing aspect, with the special mention for North-West (-2.103), South-East (-1.397) and South-West Oltenia (-1.143).

Conclusions

Making use of fundamental economic analysis on production factors substitutions during financial crises, determined by strategic measures in order to reduce administrative costs and public expenditures offer relevant information concerning public policies formulation for national and local government in those mentioned periods.

Zaman and Goschin (2007: 10) highlight the conclusion according to which the mentioned analysis 'was an important instrument to fundament decision at micro and macroeconomic level when it comes to the policy of raising the efficiency and eco-efficiency, to income distribution and to assuring a framework for optimal combination of production factors in conditions of globalization and of an economy based on knowledge'.

Production factors elasticity is variable according to which time interval is being taken into consideration. On long-term, it has the tendency to stabilise at aggregate level.

Crises impose generally negative leaps, therefore, the stabile value of the strategies aiming to reduce crisis effects must actually watch for the comeback at the former stabilisation and to impose a new ascending trend.

Substitution of production factors due to public expenditures reduction is based on a mechanism that takes place in two stages.

First stage consists of human capital reduction which would lead, under the reallocation in production of resulted sums, to the growth of fixed productive human capital. In the second stage, the growth of fixed productive capital would determine the workforce growth in private sector, workforce with other qualifications and usually better qualified.

In this mechanism we can see two types of substitutions. On the one hand, the substitution of human capital/fixed capital and on the other, human capital/better qualified human capital. All these types of substitutions depend, as mentioned in the literature, on their elasticity level. Only in the condition of supra-unitary elasticity, the described substitutions is preferred. Administrative costs' reduction strategies overlapping with crisis effects become an important mechanism to preserve or to eventually increase the production efficiency during crisis times.

References

Andrei, T., A. Matei, I. Stancu and C. Andrei (2009). *Socioperformanþa reformei sistemului public de sãnãtate*. Bucharest, Romania: Economica Publishing House.

Andrei, T. and R. Bourbonnais (2008). *Econometrie, Editura Economicã*. Bucureºti, Romania.

Arow, K.J., H.B. Chenerz, B.S. Minhas and R.M. Solow (1961). "Capital-Labor Substitution and Economic Efficiency", *Review of Economics and Statistics* 43: 225-50.

Bailey, St. J. (2002). *Public Sector Economics, Theory, Policy and Practice*. Second edition. New York: Palgrave.

Better Regulation Executive, UK (2005). *Measuring Administrative Costs: UK Standard Cost Model Manual*. Version 1.01.

Connolly, S. and A. Munro (1999). *Economics of the Public Sector*. London, New York, Paris: Prentice Hall Europe.

Dobrotã, N. (coord.) (1999). *Dicþionar de economie*. Bucharest, Romania: Economica Publishing House.

DTF (2007). "Estimate of Victoria's Administrative Burden", *DTF Internal Working Paper*. Government of Australia.

European Commission (2005a). "Communication on Better Regulation for Growth and Jobs in the European Union, Minimizing Administrative Costs Imposed by Legislation", *Staff Working Paper* SEC(2005).175.

———. (2005b). "EU Common Methodology for Assessing Administrative Costs imposed by Legislation", COM(2005), 518.

———. (2006). "Measuring Administrative Costs and Reducing Administrative Burdens in the European Union", *Commission Working Document* COM(2006), 691.

Evans, C. (2003). "Studying the Studies: An Overview of Recent Research into Taxation Operating Cost", *Journal of Tax Research* 1(1): 64-92. Atax, University of New South Wales.

Evans, P. and J.E. Rauch (1999). "Bureaucracy and Growth: A Cross-National Analysis of the Effects of 'Webberian' State Structures on Economic Growth", *American Sociological Review* 64(5): 748-765. ABI/INFORM Global. October.

Gelauff, G.M. and A.M. Lejour (2005). "Five Lisbon Highlights: The Economic Impact of Reaching these Targets", *CPB Document* 104, The Hague, CPB.

Government of Romania (2008). *Strategy for Better Regulation at Central Government Level, 2008-2013. www.sgg.gov.ro*

Hicks, J. (1932). *The Theory of Wages*. 1963 edition. London: Macmillan.

IMF (2004). "Integrating Tax and Social Security Contributions Collection within a Unified Administration", *IMF Working Paper*, December.

Karagianis, G., T. Palivos and C. Papageorgiou (2004). *Variable Elasticity of Substitution and Economic Growth: Theory and Evidence*. Greece: Department of Economics, University of Macedonia.

Klump, R. and de la O. Grandville (2000). "Economic Growth and the Elasticity of Substitution: Two Thesaurus and Some Suggestions", *American Economic Review* 90: 282-91.

Klump, R., P. McAdam and A. Willman (2005). *The Long-term Success of the Neoclasical Growth Model.* ASSA/AEA Session, Boston, USA.

Lipsey, R.G. and K.A. Chrystal (1999). *Economie pozitivă,* Romanian translation. Bucharest, Romania: Economica Publishing House.

Lovell, C.A.K. (1973). "CES and VES Production Functions in a Cross-Section Context", *Journal of Political Economy* 81: 705-20.

Matei, A. (2003). *Economie publică. Analiza economică a deciziilor publice*. Bucharest, Romania: Economica Publishing House.

———. (2008). "Performance of the Public Expenditure Management at Local Level in Romania", *Transylvania Review of Administrative Sciences* 23E, Cluj–Napoca, Romania.

Matei, A., L. Matei and T. Dinu (2009). "Marketing of Local Public Services under the Reduction of Administrative Expenditures", *Theoretical and Applied Economics* 3: 532, March. Bucharest: Romania.

Matei, L. (2005). *Management Public*. Second Edition. Bucharest, Romania: Economica Publishing House.

Miller, E. (2008). *An Assessment of CES and Cobb-Douglas Production Function,* Congressional Budget Office (CBO), June.

Morishima, M. (1967). "A Few Suggestions on the Theory of Elasticity", *Keizai Hyoron (Economic Review)* 16: 149-50.

Mourre, G. (2008). *What Drives Income Differentials, Underutilisation of Labour and Economic Growth in Europe?* A Detailed GDP Accounting Exercise, Manuscript, Free University of Brussels, taken from COM (2008). 774 final.

Musqrave, R.A. (1974). *Expenditure Policy for Development.* USA: University of Florida Press.

OECD (2010a) *Economic Survey of Germany 2010*. OECD. *www.oecd.org/eco/surveys/germany*

———. (2010b). *Economic Survey of Poland 2010*. OECD. *www.oecd.org/eco/surveys/poland*

———. (2010c). *Economic Survey of Norway 2010*. OECD. *www.oecd.org/eco/surveys/norway*

———. (2010d). *Economic Survey of Hungary 2010*. OECD. *www.oecd.org/eco/surveys/hungary*

———. (2010e). *OECD Economic Outlook 86 Database*, Annex Table-27. General Government Financial Balances. *www.oecd.org/eco/statistics*

OECD-CTPA (2008). "Program to Reduce the Administrative Burden of Tax Regulation in Selected Countries", Forum on *Tax Administration: Taxpayer Services Sub-Group Information Note*.

Olugbenga, A.O. (2009). "Public Expenditure and Economic Growth: New Evidence from OECD Countries", *The 67th International Atlantic Economic Conference,* Rome, Italy.

Rostow, W.W. (1960). *The Stages of Economic Growth: A Non-Communist Manifesto. U.K.: Cambridge University Press.*

Sato, K. (1967). "A Two-Level Constant: Elasticity of Substitution Production Function", *The Review of Economic Studies* 34(1): 201-18.

Sato, R. and F. Hoffman (1968). "Production Functions with Variable Elasticity of Substitution: Some Analysis and Testing", *Review of Economics and Statistics* 50: 453-60.

Saunders, P. (1985). "Public Expenditure and Economic Performance in OECD Countries", *Journal of Public Policy* 5(1): 1-21.

SCM Network (2005). *International Standard Cost Model Manual: Measuring and Reducing Administrative Burdens for Business.*

Stiglitz, J.E. (2000). *Economics of the Public Sector,* Third edition. New York/London: W.W. Norton & Company.

Tuan, Minh Le, Duc Minh Pham and Luc De Wulf (2007). "Estimating Economic Benefits for Revenue Administration Reform Projects", *World Bank PREM Note,* Public Sector Governance, March, No. 112.

Weber, M. [1904-1911] (1968). *Economy and Society,* edited by Guenther Roth & Claus Wittich, New York, Bedminster.

WIFO-CEPS (2006). *Pilot Project on Administrative Burden,* October.

World Bank (2002). *Global Economic Prospects and the Developing Countries*. Washington, DC: World Bank.

Zaman, Gh. and Z. Goschin (2007). "Elasticity of Substitution for Production Functions in Romania and other Countries", *Theoretical and Applied Economics* 2 (507): 3-12.

Zestos, G. (1996). "The Elasticity of Substitution as a Proxy Measure of Economic Integration", *Atlantic Economic Journal* 24(1): 43-51.

Annexure A-12.1

	Australia	*Austria*	*Belgium*	*Canada*	*Czech Republic*	*Denmark*	*Finland*	*France*	*Germany*	*Greece*	*Hungary*	*Iceland*	*Ireland*	*Italy*	*Japan*	*Korea*
Australia	1,000	0,768**	0,893**	0,923**	0,510*	0,835**	0,848**	0,819**	0,612**	0,835**	-0,326	0,615**	0,725**	0,784**	0,121	0,466
Austria	0,768**	1,000	0,804**	0,802**	0,457	0,767**	0,878**	0,775**	0,689**	0,716**	-0,109	0,365	0,516*	0,740**	0,318	0,513*
Belgium	0,893**	0,804**	1,000	0,895**	0,369	0,754**	0,894**	0,885**	0,574*	0,844**	-0,246	0,579*	0,766**	0,791**	0,215	0,597*
Canada	0,923**	0,802**	0,895**	1,000	0,585*	0,876**	0,902**	0,906**	0,734**	0,862**	-0,143	0,670**	0,785**	0,848**	0,229	0,598*
Czech Republic	0,510*	0,457	0,369	0,585*	1,000	0,577*	0,521*	0,351	0,834**	0,362	0,349	0,247	0,171	0,571*	0,293	0,150
Denmark	0,835**	0,767**	0,754**	0,876**	0,577*	1,000	0,841**	0,785**	0,644**	0,686**	-0,242	0,597*	0,615**	0,645**	0,496*	0,569*
Finland	0,848**	0,878**	0,894**	0,902**	0,521*	0,841**	1,000	0,797**	0,766**	0,721**	-0,041	0,425	0,568*	0,840**	0,202	0,539*
France	0,819**	0,775**	0,885**	0,906**	0,351	0,785**	0,797**	1,000	0,562*	0,917**	-0,247	0,700**	0,898**	0,677**	0,273	0,747*
Germany	0,612**	0,689**	0,574*	0,734**	0,834**	0,644**	0,766**	0,562*	1,000	0,535*	0,374	0,218	0,290	0,814**	0,193	0,304
Greece	0,835**	0,716**	0,844**	0,862**	0,362	0,686**	0,721**	0,917**	0,535*	1,000	-0,312	0,810**	0,899**	0,687**	0,143	0,679*
Hungary	-0,326	-0,109	-0,246	-0,143	0,349	-0,242	-0,041	-0,247	0,374	-0,312	1,000	-0,446	-0,422	0,123	-0,092	-0,177
Iceland	0,615**	0,365	0,579*	0,670**	0,247	0,597*	0,425	0,700**	0,218	0,810**	-0,446	1,000	0,860**	0,379	0,228	0,637*
Ireland	0,725**	0,516*	0,766**	0,785**	0,171	0,615**	0,568*	0,898**	0,290	0,899**	-0,422	0,860**	1,000	0,484*	0,185	0,727*
Italy	0,784**	0,740**	0,791**	0,848**	0,571*	0,645**	0,840**	0,677**	0,814**	0,687**	0,123	0,379	0,484*	1,000	0,077	0,410
Japan	0,121	0,318	0,215	0,229	0,293	0,496*	0,202	0,273	0,193	0,143	-0,092	0,228	0,185	0,077	1,000	0,445
Korea	0,466	0,513*	0,597*	0,598*	0,150	0,569*	0,539*	0,747**	0,304	0,679**	-0,177	0,637**	0,727**	0,410	0,445	1,000
Luxembourg	0,494*	0,680**	0,694**	0,656**	0,085	0,515*	0,622**	0,853**	0,458	0,731**	-0,044	0,471	0,714**	0,578*	0,258	0,716*

contd...

...contd...

	Australia	Austria	Belgium	Canada	Czech Republic	Denmark	Finland	France	Germany	Greece	Hungary	Iceland	Ireland	Italy	Japan	Korea
The Netherlands	0,782**	0,794**	0,742**	0,904**	0,788**	0,804**	0,851**	0,800**	0,914**	0,745**	0,132	0,461	0,573*	0,804**	0,240	0,488*
New Zealand	0,628**	0,586*	0,640**	0,620**	0,197	0,783**	0,596*	0,669**	0,215	0,548*	-0,547*	0,584*	0,659**	0,249	0,596*	0,600*
Norway	0,368	0,509*	0,347	0,461	0,626**	0,667**	0,604*	0,245	0,608**	0,188	0,242	0,144	0,022	0,451	0,539*	0,351
Poland	0,605*	0,572*	0,580*	0,695**	0,361	0,742**	0,584*	0,773**	0,571*	0,706**	-0,123	0,585*	0,636**	0,582*	0,462	0,678*
Portugal	0,744**	0,685**	0,855**	0,749**	0,274	0,610**	0,707**	0,829**	0,515*	0,722**	-0,226	0,417	0,722**	0,672**	0,311	0,571*
Slovak Republic	0,196	0,043	0,050	-0,012	0,033	0,288	-0,003	-0,120	-0,218	-0,155	-0,355	0,018	-0,116	-0,080	0,338	-0,201
Spain	0,899**	0,743**	0,880**	0,897**	0,420	0,862**	0,814**	0,845**	0,475	0,858**	-0,403	0,810**	0,822**	0,648**	0,327	0,645*
Sweden	0,777**	0,732**	0,705**	0,848**	0,779**	0,821**	0,875**	0,648**	0,889**	0,630**	0,177	0,408	0,409	0,838*	0,172	0,361
Switzerland	0,378	0,549*	0,382	0,410	0,515*	0,632**	0,611**	0,303	0,642**	0,260	0,268	0,059	-0,005	0,480	0,490*	0,319
The United Kingdom	0,735**	0,670**	0,834**	0,847**	0,211	0,643**	0,726**	0,966**	0,494*	0,896**	-0,216	0,684**	0,915**	0,655**	0,115	0,716*
The United States	0,594*	0,506*	0,684**	0,724**	0,139	0,523*	0,518*	0,901**	0,368	0,869**	-0,245	0,750**	0,922**	0,506*	0,129	0,699*
Euro Area	0,879**	0,738**	0,792**	0,922**	0,683**	0,819**	0,834**	0,799**	0,840**	0,798**	-0,093	0,567*	0,669**	0,850**	0,253	0,524*
OECD	0,753**	0,705**	0,823**	0,885**	0,376	0,744**	0,730**	0,976**	0,584*	0,921**	-0,187	0,755**	0,910**	0,680**	0,313	0,761

contd...

...contd...

	Luxem-bourg	*Nether-lands*	*New Zealand*	*Norway*	*Poland*	*Portugal*	*Slovak Republic*	*Spain*	*Sweden*	*Switzer-land*	*United Kingdom*	*United States*	*Euro Area*	*OECD*
Australia	0,494*	0,782**	0,628**	0,368	0,605*	0,744**	0,196	0,899**	0,777**	0,378	0,735**	0,594*	0,879**	0,753**
Austria	0,680**	0,794**	0,586*	0,509*	0,572*	0,685**	0,043	0,743**	0,732**	0,549*	0,670**	0,506*	0,738**	0,705**
Belgium	0,694**	0,742**	0,640**	0,347	0,580*	0,855**	0,050	0,880**	0,705**	0,382	0,834**	0,684**	0,792**	0,823**
Canada	0,656**	0,904**	0,620**	0,461	0,695**	0,749**	-0,012	0,897**	0,848**	0,410	0,847**	0,724**	0,922**	0,885**
Czech Republic	0,085	0,788**	0,197	0,626**	0,361	0,274	0,033	0,420	0,779**	0,515*	0,211	0,139	0,683**	0,376
Denmark	0,515*	0,804**	0,783**	0,667**	0,742**	0,610**	0,288	0,862**	0,821**	0,632**	0,643**	0,523*	0,819**	0,744**
Finland	0,622**	0,851**	0,596*	0,604*	0,584*	0,707**	-0,003	0,814**	0,875**	0,611**	0,726**	0,518*	0,834**	0,730**
France	0,853**	0,800**	0,669**	0,245	0,773**	0,829**	-0,120	0,845**	0,648**	0,303	0,966**	0,901**	0,799**	0,976**
Germany	0,458	0,914**	0,215	0,608**	0,571*	0,515*	-0,218	0,475	0,889**	0,642**	0,494*	0,368	0,840**	0,584*
Greece	0,731**	0,745**	0,548*	0,188	0,706**	0,722**	-0,155	0,858**	0,630**	0,260	0,896**	0,869**	0,798**	0,921**
Hungary	-0,044	0,132	-0,547*	0,242	-0,123	-0,226	-0,355	-0,403	0,177	0,268	-0,216	-0,245	-0,093	-0,187
Iceland	0,471	0,461	0,584*	0,144	0,585*	0,417	0,018	0,810**	0,408	0,059	0,684**	0,750**	0,567**	0,755**
Ireland	0,714**	0,573*	0,659**	0,022	0,636**	0,722**	-0,116	0,822**	0,409	-0,005	0,915**	0,922**	0,669**	0,910**
Italy	0,578*	0,804**	0,249	0,451	0,582*	0,672**	-0,080	0,648**	0,838**	0,480	0,655**	0,506*	0,850**	0,680**
Japan	0,258	0,240	0,596*	0,539*	0,462	0,311	0,338	0,327	0,172	0,490*	0,115	0,129	0,253	0,313
Korea	0,716**	0,488*	0,600*	0,351	0,678**	0,571*	-0,201	0,645**	0,361	0,319	0,716**	0,699**	0,524*	0,761**
Luxem-bourg	1,000	0,589*	0,437	0,095	0,747**	0,755**	-0,279	0,542*	0,435	0,265	0,888**	0,866**	0,567*	0,872**
Nether-land	0,589*	1,000	0,437	0,557*	0,655**	0,627**	-0,173	0,702**	0,907**	0,538*	0,714**	0,600*	0,900**	0,791**
New Zealand	0,437	0,437	1,000	0,376	0,538*	0,631**	0,329	0,802**	0,360	0,304	0,557*	0,464	0,555*	0,609**

contd...

...contd...

	Luxembourg	*Netherlands*	*New Zealand*	*Norway*	*Poland*	*Portugal*	*Slovak Republic*	*Spain*	*Sweden*	*Switzerland*	*United Kingdom*	*United States*	*Euro Area*	*OECD*
Norway	0,095	0,557*	0,376	1,000	0,312	0,097	0,235	0,433	0,712**	0,839**	0,076	-0,067	0,457	0,230
Poland	0,747**	0,655**	0,538*	0,312	1,000	0,680**	-0,022	0,614**	0,579*	0,534*	0,726**	0,733**	0,747**	0,822**
Portugal	0,755**	0,627**	0,631**	0,097	0,680**	1,000	-0,023	0,684**	0,472	0,244	0,813**	0,704**	0,767**	0,798**
Slovak Republic	-0,279	-0,173	0,329	0,235	-0,022	-0,023	1,000	0,181	0,061	0,193	-0,276	-0,306	-0,066	-0,186
Spain	0,542*	0,702**	0,802**	0,433	0,614**	0,684**	0,181	1,000	0,682**	0,366	0,758**	0,651**	0,785**	0,803**
Sweden	0,435	0,907**	0,360	0,712**	0,579*	0,472	0,061	0,682**	1,000	0,697**	0,548*	0,404	0,830**	0,632**
Switzerland	0,265	0,538*	0,304	0,839**	0,534*	0,244	0,193	0,366	0,697**	1,000	0,152	0,023	0,470	0,283
United Kingdom	0,888**	0,714**	0,557*	0,076	0,726**	0,813**	-0,276	0,758**	0,548*	0,152	1,000	0,953**	0,740**	0,963**
United States	0,866**	0,600*	0,464	-0,067	0,733**	0,704**	-0,306	0,651**	0,404	0,023	0,953**	1,000	0,628**	0,943**
Euro Area	0,567*	0,900**	0,555*	0,457	0,747**	0,767**	-0,066	0,785**	0,830**	0,470	0,740**	0,628**	1,000	0,808**
OECD	0,872**	0,791**	0,609**	0,230	0,822**	0,798**	-0,186	0,803**	0,632**	0,283	0,963**	0,943**	0,808**	1,000

Note: ** Correlation is significant at the 0.01 level (2-tailed).

* Correlation is significant at the 0.05 level (2-tailed).

Source: Authors own calculations.

Annexure A-12.2

Australia	*Austria*	*Belgium*	*Canada*	*Czech Republic*	*Denmark*	*Finland*	*France*	*Germany*	*Greece*	*Hungary*	*Iceland*	*Ireland*	*Italy*	*Japan*
-3.7	-5.9	-4.5	-5.3	-13.4	-2.9	-6.2	-5.5	-9.7	-9.1	-8.7	-3	-2	-7.4	-4.7
-2.4	-4.1	-4	-2.8	-3.3	-1.9	-3.5	-4	-3.3	-6.6	-4.6	-1.6	-0.1	-7	-5.1
-0.7	-2	-2.3	0.2	-3.8	-0.5	-1.3	-3.3	-2.6	-5.9	-6.1	0	1.4	-2.7	-4
1.6	-2.5	-1	0.1	-5	0	1.6	-2.6	-2.2	-3.8	-7.9	-0.4	2.3	-3.1	-11.2
2	-2.4	-0.7	1.6	-3.7	1.4	1.6	-1.8	-1.5	-3.1	-5.4	1.1	2.6	-1.8	-7.4
0.9	-1.9	-0.1	2.9	-3.7	2.3	6.9	-1.5	1.3	-3.7	-3	1.4	4.8	-0.9	-7.6
-0.1	-0.2	0.4	0.7	-5.6	1.2	5	-1.6	-2.8	-4.4	-4.1	-0.7	0.9	-3.1	-6.3
1.3	-0.9	-0.2	-0.1	-6.8	0.2	4.1	-3	-3.5	-4.8	-8.9	-2.6	-0.3	-3	-8
1.8	-1.6	-0.2	-0.1	-6.6	-0.1	2.4	-4.1	-4	-5.7	-7.2	-2.8	0.4	-3.5	-7.9
1.2	-4.5	-0.4	0.9	-2.9	1.9	2.2	-3.6	-3.8	-7.4	-6.4	0	1.4	-3.6	-6.2
1.7	-1.7	-2.8	1.5	-3.6	5	2.6	-3	-3.3	-5.3	-7.9	4.9	1.7	-4.4	-6.7
1.9	-1.4	0.2	1.6	-2.6	5	3.9	-2.3	-1.6	-3.2	-9.4	6.3	3	-3.3	-1.6
1.8	-0.7	-0.2	1.6	-0.7	4.5	5.2	-2.7	0.2	-4	-5	5.4	0.2	-1.5	-2.5
1	-0.5	-1.2	0.1	-2	3.4	4.4	-3.4	0	-7.8	-3.7	-13.6	-7.2	-2.7	-2.9
-4	-4.3	-5.7	-4.8	-5.7	-2.5	-2.3	-8.2	-3.2	-12.7	-4.3	-15.7	-18.2	-5.5	-7.4
-3.5	-5.5	-5.6	-5.2	-5.6	-5.4	-4.8	-8.6	-5.2	-9.8	-4.1	-10.1	-12.2	-5.4	-8.2
-2.6	-5.8	-5.2	-4.5	-5	-4	-5.2	-8	-4.6	-10	-3.6	-5.8	-11.6	-5.1	-9.4

contd...

...contd...

Korea	*Luxem-bourg*	*Nether-lands*	*New Zealand*	*Norway*	*Poland*	*Portugal*	*Slovak Republic*	*Spain*	*Sweden*	*Switzer-land*	*UK*	*US*	*Euro Area*	*OECD*
3.8	2.4	-9.2	2.8	3.2	-4.4	-5	-3.4	-6.5	-7.3	-2	-5.8	-3.3	-7.6	-4.8
3.4	1.2	-1.9	2.8	6.3	-4.9	-4.5	-9.9	-4.9	-3.3	-1.8	-4.2	-2.3	-4.3	-3.1
3.3	3.7	-1.2	1.4	7.6	-4.6	-3.5	-6.3	-3.4	-1.6	-2.8	-2.2	-0.9	-2.7	-1.7
1.6	3.4	-0.9	0.4	3.3	-4.3	-3.4	-5.3	-3.2	1.2	-1.9	-0.1	0.3	-2.3	-1.9
2.7	3.4	0.4	0	6	-2.3	-2.8	-7.4	-1.4	1.2	-0.5	0.9	0.7	-1.4	-0.8
5.4	6	2	1.9	15.4	-3	-3	-12.3	-1	3.7	0.1	3.7	1.5	-0.1	0.2
4.3	6.1	-0.3	1.8	13.3	-5.1	-4.3	-6.5	-0.7	1.7	-0.1	0.6	-0.6	-4.9	-1.3
5.1	2.1	-2.1	3.8	9.2	-5	-2.9	-8.2	-0.5	-1.4	-1.2	-2	-4	-2.6	-3.3
0.5	0.5	-3.2	4	7.3	-6.3	-3	-2.8	-0.2	-1.2	-1.7	-3.7	-5	-3.1	-4.1
2.7	-1.1	-1.8	4.1	11.1	-5.7	-3.4	-2.4	-0.4	0.6	-1.8	-3.6	-4.4	-3	-3.4
3.4	0	-0.3	5.2	15.1	-4.1	-6.1	-2.8	1	2	-0.7	-3.3	-3.3	-2.6	-2.7
3.9	1.3	0.5	5.9	18.5	-3.6	-3.9	-3.5	2	2.4	0.8	-2.7	-2.2	-1.3	-1.3
4.7	3.7	0.2	5	17.7	-1.9	-2.7	-1.9	1.9	3.8	1.6	-2.7	-2.8	-0.6	-1.3
3.3	2.5	0.7	3.1	18.8	-3.7	-2.8	-2.3	-4.1	2.5	1.6	-5.3	-6.5	-2	-3.5
-1.8	-2.3	-4.5	-1.2	9.6	-6.4	-6.7	-5.9	-9.6	-2	-0.7	-12.6	-11.2	-6.1	-8.2
0.4	-4.3	-5.9	-3.3	9.9	-7.8	-7.6	-6.3	-8.5	-3	-1.3	-13.3	-10.7	-6.7	-8.2
1.1	-3.6	-5.3	-3.9	10.8	-6.8	-7.8	-5	-7.7	-2	-1.3	-12.5	-9.4	-6.2	-7.6

Source: Authors own calculations.

Annexure A-12.3

Production Factors and GDP Evolution during 1990-2009

Year	*GDP (100 Million Euro)*	*EMPL (Population Outputs) (Thousand Persons)*	*GFCF (Gross Capital Formation) (1,000 Million Euro)*
1990	44.5	12025	1,557
1991	39	11965	1,065
1992	35	11604	1,182
1993	36	11159	1,280
1994	37	11099	1,544
1995	40	10522	1,652
1996	41	10402	1,745
1997	39	10005	1,775
1998	37	9776	1,674
1999	33	9343	1,593
2000	40	9572	1,680
2001	45	9500	1,851
2002	48	9235	2,004
2003	53	9223	2,174
2004	61	9158	2,413
2005	80	9147	2,720
2006	98	9313	4,606
2007	121	9353	9,438
2008	130	9369	6,370
2009	121	9115	5,850

Source: Authors own work.

13 Local Employment Policies in the Context of the Economic Crisis

Influences of the European Community Structural Instruments

Lucica Matei and Ani Matei

The New Context of the Employment Policies in Europe

Europe is facing an economic and financial crisis that affects the citizens and the European economic activity. The crisis effects are registered on the level of population and labour market, local economies, quality of life, local governance and economic and social increasing disparities. In general, the crisis generates a decrease of the economic activities and an unemployment increase (Table 13.1).

The end of year 2008 is marked by the reduction of the main socio-economic indicators (the gross domestic product (GDP) growth rate, the employment growth rate, the investment flows growth rate), by significant transformations of the labour market with regard to the decrease of active population and employment, creation of new jobs etc. This crisis affects the 'real economy' of jobs.

In the middle of the 90s, problems have been identified in the European labour market, like the one presently occurring due to the economic and financial crisis, namely unemployment, a problem that has been approached in the European Employment Strategy (EES) initiated through the 'Luxembourg Process' (1997)—a meeting exclusively dedicated to employment. During that same period, namely the second half of the 90s, the Treaty of Amsterdam (1997) introduced provisions referring to the employment policy and social protection and the assemblies on the

Table 13.1

The Evolution of the Unemployment Rate in Certain States
(Percentage of Labour Force)

	2007	2008	2009
The European Union	7.1	7.0	8.9
Australia	4.4	4.2	5.6
Austria	4.4	3.8	4.8
Belgium	7.5	7.0	7.9
Canada	6.0	6.1	8.3
Czech Republic	5.3	4.4	6.7
Denmark	3.8	3.3	6.0
Finland	6.9	6.4	8.2
France	8.4	7.8	9.5
Germany	8.4	7.3	7.5
Greece	8.3	7.7	9.5
Hungary	7.4	7.8	10.0
Iceland	2.3	3.0	7.2
Ireland	4.6	6.4	11.9
Italy	6.2	6.8	7.7
Japan	3.9	4.0	5.1
Korea	3.2	3.2	3.6
Luxembourg	4.2	4.9	5.4
Mexico	3.7	4.0	5.5
Netherlands	3.2	2.8	3.4
New Zealand	3.7	4.2	6.1
Norway	2.5	2.5	3.1
Poland	9.6	7.2	8.2
Portugal	8.1	7.8	9.6
Slovak Republic	11.2	9.5	12.0
Spain	8.3	11.4	18.0
Sweden	6.1	6.2	8.3
Switzerland	3.6	3.5	4.4
Turkey	8.8	9.7	12.6
United Kingdom	5.3	5.6	7.6
United States	4.6	5.8	9.3

Source: OECD (2010). *Harmonised Unemployment Rates.* News Release, February.

employment policies topic from Cardiff (1998—the Cardiff Process—the economic and internal market reform), Köln (or Cologne) (1999), Lisbon and Stockholm (2000 and 2005), Barcelona (2002), consecrate the principle of collaboration between the European Union (EU) member states in the field of employment policy and its accordance with the economic policies, thus creating a direct link between employment and economy.

In December 2008, the European Council approved the 'European Plan to Re-launch the Economy', aiming at supporting the actions that can combat the crisis in the EU states. The cohesion policy's instruments of EU—European Regional Development Fund (ERDF), European Social Fund (ESF), Cohesion Fund (CF), represent one-third of the total EU budget and are the biggest source of investment in the EU real economy.

The issue of employment approached on a regional level confers realistic arguments in developing the strategies by taking into account the local features.

The ESF is the main financial instrument for structural actions, financing member states' actions comprised in the National Action Plans for Employment that aim at preventing and combating unemployment, human resource development and labour market integration, equality of chances between men and women, sustainable development and economic and social cohesion.

The employment policies of the EU member states must facilitate the participation to employment of all persons able to work, being related to other economic policies, of regional development, covering the EES objectives:

a) Full employment;
b) Improving quality and labour productivity and
c) Consolidating social and territorial cohesion.

The EU member states, in the framework of the National Reform Programmes (NRP), design the employment policies in accordance with the 'Integrated Guidelines for Growth and Jobs' (COM (2009) 34).

The community (EU) dimension of the employment policies, education and training must be used in a creative manner by the member states for developing the strategies of acquiring new competences, improving the jobs' quality and providing support to those who lost their jobs.

The European Structural Instruments

EU acts through these financial instruments in order to eliminate the economic and social disparities between regions, aiming at reaching an economic and social cohesion, economic growth, competitiveness and employment.

Table 13.2

Planned Cohesion Policy Interventions (2007–2013) by Member States in Million Euro 2004 Prices

Country	*2007*	*2008*	*2009*	*2010*	*2011*	*2012*	*2013*	*Total*
Poland	7,680.0	8,024.9	8,365.9	8,405.0	8,747.9	9,073.7	9,401.1	59,698.6
Czech Rep.	3,136.0	3,222.9	3,305.9	3,391.2	3,472.0	3,547.7	3,621.6	23,697.2
Cyprus	158.2	128.9	99.7	70.4	41.2	41.2	41.2	580.8
Estonia	355.7	379.7	405.4	432.8	462.6	494.4	527.5	3,058.1
Greece	2,914.8	2,803.8	2,692.9	2,582.0	2,471.2	2,407.9	2,344.6	1,8217.2
Spain	5,947.0	5,329.7	4,712.8	4,196.2	3,879.6	3,783.5	3,687.4	31,536.3
Ireland	199.9	167.4	134.9	102.4	69.9	70.0	70.1	814.5
Italy	2,774.0	2,869.0	2,753.0	2,744.0	2,690.0	2,724.0	2,714.0	19,268.0
Latvia	480.0	513.0	549.0	584.0	619.0	655.0	691.0	4,091.0
Lithuania	725.3	771.5	819.6	867.8	918.3	971.5	1,023.0	6,097.0
Hungary	2,868.0	2,990.9	3,121.4	3,227.4	3,302.7	3,414.4	3,526.6	22,451.5
Malta	108.1	108.5	108.8	109.1	109.2	108.8	108.3	760.8
Portugal	2,807.2	2,783.1	2,759.2	2,735.3	2,711.4	2,687.4	2,663.4	19,146.9
Slovenia	523.9	527.3	530.7	534.1	537.5	540.9	544.3	3,738.7
Slovakia	1,227.9	1,303.3	1,385.7	1,479.7	1,558.0	1,631.5	1,678.2	10,264.3
East Germany	2,310.0	2,264.0	2,234.0	2,196.0	2,157.0	2,118.0	2,079.0	15,358.0
Bulgaria	486.0	682.9	900.6	929.4	974.0	1,016.9	1,057.5	6,047.3
Romania	1,261.2	1,774.2	2,339.3	2,752.5	2,906.6	3,063.4	3,219.4	17,316.6
Total	35,963.2	36,645.1	37,218.5	37,339.5	37,628.1	38,350.3	38,998.2	2,62,142.9

Source: DG Regional Policy 2007 in Bradley *et al.* (2007: 12), Table 2.2.

The ESF, the main instrument of EU for investments in the human resources, is one of the structural funds that aim at reaching the strategic objectives of the EU employment policy. During 2007-2013, ESF will invest almost 76 billions of Euros in the member states (Table 13.2) for projects on employment support and increasing the level of education and competences.

ESF encourages change and adaptation to change and support Europe's economic recovery.

The ERDF is one of the structural funds. Its main objective is promoting the economic and social cohesion inside EU through reducing the imbalances between regions or social groups. The CF is a structural instrument that helps the EU member states to reduce the economic and social discrepancies and to reach a stability of their economies as far back as 1994.

The main objective of the EU's cohesion policies is promoting the economic growth and job creation in accordance with the Lisbon Strategy (the percentage increase to 70%).

The key feature of the cohesion policy is that it is based on an efficient programming system, which establishes the way the funds shall be spent on a seven years period. On a national level, that of the EU member states, the use of the cohesion policy's funds influences the national or regional development paths. The programming process thus becoming an important mechanism for planning the development in 2007-2013 period.

The ERDF, the ESF and the CF contribute to reaching three objectives (Table 13.3):

1. 'Convergence' supports the economic growth and employment in 84 regions from 17 states of the EU-27, with 154 million inhabitants, where the value of the gross domestic product (GDP) per capita is under 75 per cent of the community average. This objective can be found in all the three European funds, having different values of financial contribution. Through 'phasing out', another 16 regions with a population of 16.4 million inhabitants and with a GDP per

Table 13.3

Objectives and Priorities of Community Structural Instruments

Convergence	*Regional Competitiveness and Employment*	*European Territorial Co-operation*	*Objective* / *Instrument*	*Priorities*											
				Lisbon Strategy	*Infrastructure*	*Investments*	*R&D*	*Small and Medium Enterprises*	*Training*	*Employment*	*Institutional Capacity and Administrative Efficiency*	*Environment and Transport Infrastructure*	*Abroad Transport*	*Urban Transport*	*Energy*
√	√	√	ERDF	√	√	√	√	√							
√	√		ESF	√					√	√	√				
√			CF 85%									√	√	√	√
75-85 %	50-85 %	75-85 %	Financing coefficient												

capita slightly above the 75 per cent limit. CF applies for the 15 member states.

2. 'Regional competitiveness and employment' consolidates the regions' competitiveness and attractiveness, the employment capacity, through a dual approach that assumes, on the one hand, development programmes for supporting the regions in anticipating and being favourable to economic changes by stimulating innovation, knowledge society, entrepreneurship and environmental protection, and, on the other hand, the increase in the number and quality of jobs by adapting the labour force and making investments in human resources. This objective is found in 138 regions from EU-27, with 314 million inhabitants (states which are not eligible for Objective-1). This objective is financed by ERDF and ESF.
3. 'European territorial cooperation' is designed on three axes: cross-frontier cooperation, transnational and interregional.

The European structural funds have an impact upon the development of the infrastructure, human resource or directly for economic actions, depending on the absorption capacity.

The programming of the structural and cohesion funds on a national level (Romania) is done through the National Strategic Reference Framework (NSRF) 2007-2013 and the operational programmes (OPs).

The convergence objective is accomplished in Romania through seven OPs applicable to the eight Romanian development regions, established by the Law No. 315/2004 on regional development, abiding the EC Regulation No. 1059/2003 referring to establishing a common system for statistical classification of the territorial units (Matei, 2004).

The distribution of funds in development regions in Romania was differentiated in terms of their degree of development, using a 'development index', which reflects the economic and social disparities of the region, and using the GDP per capita, adjusted by a population density coefficient (Table 13.4).

Table 13.4

Feature Dimensions of the Development Regions in Romania

Regions	*Area(km²)*	*GDP*		*Population*		
		Millions lei Current Prices 2007	*Per Inhabitant*	*Inhabitants July 1, 2008*	*Urban (Per cent)*	*Rural (Per cent)*
Macroregion 1	68.259	1,00,140.8	19,090	52,45,573	56.3	43.7
North-West Region	34.159	50,724.1	18,610.5	27,22,063	53.3	46.7
Centre Region	34.100	49,416.7	19,579.5	25,23,510	59.4	40.6
Macroregion 2	72.612	90,263.1	13,804	65,38,667	48.3	51.7
North-East Region	36. 850	45,990.1	12,340.9	37,19,102	43.2	56.8
North-East	35.762	44,273.0	15,641.8	28,19,565	55.1	44.9
Macroregion 3	36.274	1,47,811.7	26,717	55,32,551	62.0	38.0
Bucharest–Ilfov Region	18.21	95,798.2	43,037.3	22,48,026	92.2	7.8
South–Muntenia Region	34.453	52,013.5	15,757.8	3284525	41.4	58.6
Macroregion 4	61.246	77,415.6	18,486	41,87,651	54.7	45.3
South–West Oltenia	29.212	34,419.6	15,097.3	22,62,274	47.5	52.5
West region	32.034	42,995.7	22,341.9	19,25,377	63.1	36.9
Romania	238.391	4,16,006.8	19,315.4	2,15,04,442	55.0	44.0

Source: Romanian Statistical Yearbook 2009, p.86.

The Cumulative Multiplier of Employment

The labour market plays a very important part in transmitting the policies' mechanisms. Recognised as the ensemble of the governmental measures of intervention on the labour market, aiming at creating new jobs, improving the human resource adaptation to the economic needs and ensuring the fluidity and flexibility of the labour force in order to reduce the imbalances and malfunctions, the employment policy became the topic of many scenarios, of modelling. These take into consideration the wage policies, regulations on the labour market, indicators like employment, labour participation rate and constraints on the labour market.

The local employment policy goes through changes determined by the effects of the economic and financial crisis upon the national and local economies, upon the governmental allowances at the local level for supporting the economic and social development, upon the investments, the change of the production conditions, etc., the labour force migrates from the less developed regions towards those under a sustainable development and jobs' creation, inside the same region from one community to another, from one country to another, from the urban environment towards the rural one, or the other way around, from one economic sector to another. There is registered unemployment increase (Table 13.5), professions lost for certain categories of population with high qualifications (determined by the lack of jobs or disappearance of some economic activities represented at local, county or regional level). At the same time, we are witnessing an increase of the local authorities' responsibilities, of the social and economic actors with regard to the development of the local community, from the point of view of accessing the development and cohesion structural funds, the European funds for economic growth, infrastructural development, environmental protection, professional conversion, human resource investment growth, new jobs' creation, etc.

Our theoretical argument begins from the premises of the general equilibrium theory, where we identify the following local features: the demand 'D' and supply 'Y' and the relation (1):

$$Y = D \qquad (1)$$

The demand D is represented by the demand for goods and services on a local level C and by the demand for investment goods ë.

The supply Y is intended for the consumption of goods and services C and the savings E.

$$D = C + \lambda \qquad (2)$$

$$Y = C + E \qquad (3)$$

By applying the general equilibrium theory and replacing relation (1), D and Y with relations (2) and (3), we obtain:

$$C + E = C + \lambda \qquad (4)$$

$$E = \lambda \qquad (5)$$

Table 13.5

The Evolution of the Indicators on the Labour Market in the Development Regions from Romania during 2007-08

Macroregion Development Region	*Economically Active Population (Thousand Persons)*		*Employment (Thousand Persons)*		*ILO Umemployed (Thousand Persons)*		*Activity Rate (Per cent)*		*Employment Rate (Per cent)*		*ILO Unemployment Rate (Per cent)*	
	2007	*2008*	*2007*	*2008*	*2007*	*2008*	*2007*	*2008*	*2007*	*2008*	*2007*	*2008*
Macro-region	2298	2295	2153	2155	145	140	60	60.3	56.1	56.5	6.3	6.1
NW1	1198	1172	1147	1128	51	44	59.6	58.7	57.0	56.4	4.3	3.8
Centre	1100	1123	1006	1027	94	96	60.4	61.9	55.1	56.6	8.5	8.5
Macro-region	3047	2999	2851	2830	196	169	62.7	61.9	58.4	58.2	6.5	5.6
NE	1785	1753	1696	1674	89	79	64.8	63.6	61.3	60.5	5.0	4.5
SE	1262	1246	1155	1156	107	90	60.1	59.8	54.7	55.3	8.5	7.2
Macro-region	2661	2661	2486	2517	175	144	65.8	65.7	61.3	62.0	6.6	5.4
S-Muntenia	1600	1593	1468	1485	132	108	66.3	65.9	60.5	61.1	8.2	6.8
B-If	1061	1068	1018	1032	43	36	65.1	65.5	62.4	63.3	4.1	3.4
Macro-region	1988	1989	1863	1867	125	122	63.7	63.8	59.5	59.7	6.3	6.1
S-W Oltenia	1103	1112	1028	1040	75	72	64.1	64.6	59.3	60.0	6.8	6.5
W	885	877	835	827	50	50	63.2	62.9	59.6	59.3	5.6	5.7
Romania	9994	9944	9353	9369	641	575	63.0	62.9	58.8	59.0	6.4	5.8

Source: *Romanian Statistical Yearbook 2009.*

We point out that relation (5) is valid only in an optimum situation, where the demand for goods and services is equal to the supply.

The local supply (Y) also includes the imports of goods and services (C′), and the demand (D) includes the exports of goods and services (C″). The equilibrium conditions become:

$$Y + C' = D + C'' \tag{6}$$

$$C + E + C' = C + \lambda + C'' \tag{7}$$

$$E + C' = \lambda + C'' \tag{8}$$

$$E - \lambda = C'' = C' \tag{9}$$

Relation (9) represents the condition of local economic equilibrium, where we locate the role of the community structural instruments with regards to the degree of employment and local income.

During 2007-2013, Romania benefits from non-reimbursable financial assistance from EU through the following structural instruments: ESF, ERDF and CF.

The differentiated repartition of the funds on the development regions of Romania (Table 13.6) aimed at supporting the Regional Operational Programme (ROP) with regard to assisting a well-balanced development of all Romanian regions, ensuring that all the areas have a minimum level of business, social and human resource infrastructure, which allows the economic growth, by using the gross domestic product (GDP) per capita economic indicator in order to measure the development degree of the regions (Table 13.4). The regions with a low level of GDP per capita will benefit of a greater share of the total funds of the ROP programme (for example, the Eastern region with a 16.32 per cent allocation), while the share of the financial allocation will be smaller for the regions with a higher GDP per capita (for example, Bucharest-Ilfov Region with an allocation of 8.86 per cent—Table 13.6).

At regional level, the sectoral operational programmes (SOPs) are also developed, the National Programme for Rural Development (NPRD), complementary to the priority axes of ROP. The development of a regional employment multiplier based on the impact of ROP and SOP starts from the development capacity of jobs in the economic sectors: manufacturing industry (T), agriculture (A), market services (N), governmental services (G), using the total working labour equation on a regional level:

$$L_R = L_i + \sum_{j=1}^{4} L_j + L_k + L_z \tag{10}$$

L_R = employment in the region,

L_i = employment in the activities developed through the ROP project,

Table 13.6

Financial Allocation to Development Regions and Priority Axes ROP (2007–2013)

Priority Axes ROP	*Funds Allocated on Axes (ERDF and Co-financing 2007-2013)*		*Regions*							
			NE	*SE*	*S*	*SV*	*V*	*NV*	*C*	*B-I*
			(Per cent in the Total Funds Allocated)							
	Million Euro	*Per cent*	*16.32*	*13.25*	*14.23*	*14.01*	*10.34*	*12.09*	*10.90*	*8.86*
			Allocated Funds (ERDF and Co-financing): Million Euro							
1. Supporting the sustainable development of cities	1391.17	31.73	227.04	184.33	197.96	194.90	143.85	168.19	151.64	123.26
Potential growth poles, ERDF	1117.81		182.43	148.11	159.07	156.60	115.58	135.14	121.84	99.04
2. Improving the regional and local transport infrastructure	876.71	20.00	143.08	116.16	124.76	122.83	90.65	105.99	95.56	77.68
of which: ERDF	758.36		123.76	100.48	107.92	106.25	78.41	91.69	82.66	67.19
3. Improving the social infrastructure	657.53	15.00	107.31	87.12	93.56	92.12	67.99	79.50	71.67	58.26
of which: ERDF	558.90		91.21	74.06	79.52	78.30	57.80	67.58	60.92	49.51
4. Supporting the development of the local and regional business environment	709.89	16.19	115.86	94.06	101.02	99.45	73.40	85.83	77.38	68.89
of which: ERDF	633.42		103.39	83.92	90.13	88.74	65.50	76.58	69.04	56.12

contd...

...contd...

Priority Axes ROP	*Funds Allocated on Axes (ERDF and Co-financing 2007-2013)*		*Regions*							
			NE	*SE*	*S*	*SV*	*V*	*NV*	*C*	*B-I*
			(Per cent in the Total Funds Allocated)							
	Million Euro	*Per cent*	*16.32*	*13.25*	*14.23*	*14.01*	*10.34*	*12.09*	*10.90*	*8.86*
			Allocated Funds (ERDF and Co-financing): Million Euro							
5. Sustainable development and tourism's promotion	616.77	14.07	100.65	81.72	87.77	86.41	63.78	74.57	67.23	54.64
of which: ERDF	558.90		91.22	74.05	79.53	78.30	57.79	67.57	60.92	49.52
Total Axes 1-5	4252.07	-	693.94	563.39	605.07	595.71	439.67	514.08	463.48	376.73
of which: ERDF	3627.39		592.01	480.62	516.17	508.19	375.08	438.56	395.38	321.38
6. Technical assistance	131.51	3.00	The funds of the technical assistance priority axis are not regionally allocated							
of which: ERDF	98.63									
Total ROP (Axes 1-6)	4383.58	100.00								
of which ERDF	3726.02									

Source: Annual Implementation Report 2008, ROP 2007–2013. Romanian Government, MDRL, June 2009, p.14.

$\sum_{j=1}^{4} L_j$ = employment in the activities (jobs created) through the SOP projects (four projects: transport, environment, human resource development and competitiveness),

L_k = employment in the activities (jobs created) through the NPRD project (one project for rural development),

L_z = employment in the region's economy.

We assume that the activities and the infrastructure of the region's economy serve all the economic interventions of the ROP, SOP and NPRD programmes, and this relation can be expressed as follows:

$$L_z = \alpha(L_i + \sum_{j=1}^{4} L_j + L_k) \qquad (11)$$

Where α is a positive constant specific to each programme that signifies the cumulative effects of all the programmes upon the level of employment.

A global analysis at Romania's level shows us that in the context in which until 2020 it is foreseen that there will be 550,000 jobs created, as an effect of the macroeconomic impact of the 'Community Support Framework 2007-2013' for the year 2009, α coefficient will have the value $\alpha_{2009} = 6.19 \times 10^{-3}$.

By substituting (11) into (10), we obtain:

$$L_R = (L_i + \sum_{j=1}^{4} L_j + L_k) + \alpha(L_i + \sum_{j=1}^{4} L_j + L_k) \qquad (12)$$

$$L_R = (1+\alpha)(L_i + \sum_{j=1}^{4} L_j + L_k)$$

By considering the time variation of labour, we obtain:

$$\Delta L_R = (1+\alpha)\Delta(L_i + \sum_{j=1}^{4} L_j + L_k) \qquad (13)$$

$$\frac{\Delta L_R}{\Delta(L_i + \sum_{j=1}^{4} L_j + L_k)} = (1+\alpha)$$, or, at limit

$$\frac{dL_R}{d(L_i + \sum_{j=1}^{4} L_j + L_k)} = (1+\alpha)$$

$(1+\alpha)$ is the cumulative multiplier of employment, which shows that one supplementary job created due to the activities developed through the ROP, POS and PNDR programmes will lead to an increase with $(1+\alpha)$ of the total employment in the region.

The HERMIN Model

The HERMIN model is designed for environments under structural change (Barry *et al.*, 2000) and used for estimating the impact of structural and cohesion funds upon the national economies of the EU member states (Table 13.2), presenting various aspects of these with regards to the absorption and distribution, difference in terms of destination (the infrastructure development, human capital development or directly for economic actions). The HERMIN modelling framework needed to be based on a fairly simple theoretical framework that permitted inter-county and inter-region comparisons.

The HERMIN model (Bradley *et al.*, 1995) used in the EU states for estimating the impact of structural and cohesion funds is characterised by the following features:

(1) It is a macroeconomic model with an annual time horizon and multisectoral coverage area that includes the following sectors: T sector—manufacturing industry, N sector—market services, A sector—agriculture and G sector—governmental services (Kejak and Vavra, 1998; Barry *et al.*, 2003);

(2) It can describe the functioning and flexibility of labour force in relation to the potential influences of the labour migration to inter-regional;

(3) It is a medium-scale model, empirical, entirely written in structural form, based on the conventional Keynesian mechanisms describing the functioning of the demand-product equilibrium for all the sectors;

(4) It ensures the assessment of the economic policies' impact upon the individual sectors, emphasising the sectoral changes and

(5) It is a structural model, based on microeconomic fundaments: the supply includes the main mechanisms incorporations through which the structural and cohesion funds influence the productive potential, the direct externalities (upon the output) and indirect (upon the production factors—capital and labour) (Bradley and Morgenroth, 2004). The model functions as an integrated system of equations with interrelations between all the sub-components.

The HERMIN model structure (Box 13.1), where many branches and economic operators can be found, emphasises the variations of the capital accumulation, of the technological progress, the relations between the stocks and flows and the retrospective expectations, is built on three blocks: a supply block, an absorption block and an income distribution block (Bradley *et al.*, 2007; Bradley *et al.*, 2004).

Box 13.1

The HERMIN Model Schema

Supply Aspects

Manufacturing sector (mainly tradable goods)

Output = f_1(world demand, domestic demand, competitiveness, t)
Employment = f_2(output, relative factor price ratio, t)
Investment = f_3(output, relative factor price ratio, t)
Capital stock = investment+(1-δ)capital stock_{t-1}
Output price = f_4(world price*exchange rate, unit labour costs)
Wage rate = f_5(output price, tax wedge, unemployment, productivity)
Competitiveness = national/world output prices

Building and construction sector (mainly non-tradable)

Output = f_6(total investment in construction)
Employment = f_7(output, relative factor price ratio, t)
Investment = f_8(output, relative factor price ratio, t)
Capital stock = investment + (1-δ)capital stock_{t-1}

contd...

...contd...

Output price = mark-up on unit labour costs)
Wage inflation = manufacturing sector wage inflation

Market service sector (mainly non-tradable)

Output = f_6(domestic demand, world demand)
Employment = f_7(output, relative factor price ratio, t)
Investment = f_8(output, relative factor price ratio, t)
Capital stock = investment+(1-δ) capital $stock_{t-1}$
Output price = mark-up on unit labour costs)
Wage inflation = manufacturing sector wage inflation

Agriculture and non-market services: mainly exogeneous and/or instrumental

Demographics and labour supply

Population growth = f_9(natural growth, migration)
Labour force = f_{10}(population, labour force participation rate)
Unemployment = labour force – total employment
Migration = f_{11}(relative expected wage)

Demand (absorption) aspect

Consumption = f_{12}(personal disposable income)
Domestic demand = private and public consumption + investment + stock changes
Net trade surplus = total output – domestic demand

Income distribution aspects

Expenditure prices = f_{13}(output prices, import prices, indirect tax rates)
Income = total output
Personal disposable income = income + transfers – direct taxes
Current account = net trade surplus + net factor income from abroad
Public sector borrowing = public expenditure – tax rate * tax base
Public sector debt = (1 + interest rate) $debt_{t-1}$ + public sector borrowing

Key exogeneous variables

External: world output and prices; exchange rates; interest rates.
Domestic: public expenditure; tax rates.

Source: Bradley *et al.*, 2007: 50, Figure 1.1.

In order to be able to estimate the effect of the structural instruments, which include a complex system of measures, their aggregation must take place in categories with economic significance represented by three types of expenditures regarding:

1) Physical infrastructure – PI;
2) Human resource – HR;
3) Direct aid to the productive sector (market services and agriculture)—APS, and the possible co-financing sources together with the national one must also be distinguished.

By applying the HERMIN model to the European states with regard to measuring the impact of the cohesion policy, Bradley *et al.* (2007) classifies the countries into three groups, based on the size of the cumulative multipliers:

1) High cumulative multipliers: Ireland (4.82); Romania (4.60); Czech Republic (4.38);
2) Medium cumulative multipliers: Estonia (3.65); Lithuania (3.36); Latvia (2.78); Slovakia (2.62); Greece (2.47); Poland (2.39); Hungary (2.37); Spain (2.40); Cyprus (2.21);
3) Low cumulative multipliers: Bulgaria (1.87); Slovenia (1.86); Portugal (1.84).

In Romania, the HERMIN model was implemented for the first time during 1997-1999 (Ciupagea, 2000), and a second version of the HEROM model is currently in use (Ţurlea, 2006), which is based on the specification of the standard HERMIN model (Bradley *et al.*, 1995). The model advances more than 240 equations formed by identities or pre-established functional relations between economic variables, being adapted to the specificities of the Romanian economy and answering the needs of the *ex-ante* studies of the impact of structural funds developed by the European Commission.

The simulation is done for two scenarios that are based on the standard HERMIN model for the 2007-2020 period, with the following hypotheses:

Hypothesis 1 (H1)—the structural funds are present with the material contributions which exists in the National Development Plan (NDP).

Hypothesis 2 (H2)—the contributions for the structural funds are not present in the NDP after, thus maintaining the ceiling to the level of the pre-adherence funds corresponding to 2006, considering an absorption rate of 100 per cent.

The results of the simulations on the indicators regarding the labour market (Table 13.7) emphasises differences between the two scenarios.

The modelling of labour market was accomplished through the analysis of the wage policies and regulations on the labour market (taxation), of the two indicators—employment rate and labour participation rate. The mechanism establishing the wages on the labour market take into account the labour cost and world prices (Charemza and Turlea, 1998).

The total employment in the four economic sectors T, N, A, G is equivalent to the labour demand used for estimating unemployment.

The total employment in the four sectors of the economy on the country level is equivalent to the labour force demand, as it is also of reference for estimating unemployment. The labour market will be significantly influenced by funds so that in the 14 years of the prognosis period, over 550,000 jobs will be created in H1. The annual growth rates in H2 are -0.25 per cent, while in H1 they have positive values of 0.42 per cent annually. These lead to a net difference of employment (L) in 2020 to almost 10 per cent against H2. The unemployment rate (UR) in 2020 will be in H1 almost half of its level corresponding to H2. The increase of the labour demand in H1 will be larger in the tradable goods sector, where in 2013 the number of jobs will go up by 23 per cent while in agriculture a fall will be registered, according to the two scenarios.

The Input-Output Model on Labour Market at Development Regions' Level

Another method used for studying the impact is the input-output model designed for local development (Matei, 2007; Matei *et al.*, 2009; McNicoll and Baird, 1980), for interregional economic development (Cardenoso and Oosterhaven, 2010) or for the effects of the European funds in Romania's regions (Bonfiglio, 2005).

Table 13.7

The Macroeconomic Impact of Structural Funds

(Per cent)

Year / Indicator	2007	2008	2009	2010	2011	2012	2013	2014	2015	2016	2017	2018	2019	2020
Employment (L)	1.93	1.75	2.57	3.39	4.01	4.60	7.46	7.04	6.98	7.38	7.61	7.68	8.40	9.74
Employment in N sector	0.66	1.31	1.94	2.54	3.12	3.66	4.57	4.50	4.45	4.40	4.40	4.34	4.28	4.21
Employment in T sector	7.70	5.82	8.54	11.23	13.09	14.29	25.87	23.96	23.75	26.20	27.33	26.73	30.09	36.27
Unemployment rate (UR)	-23.42	-27.87	-42.59	-46.43	-47.48	-50.27	-59.08	-47.59	-45.68	-43.90	-42.24	-44.78	-47.27	-3.95

Note: The percentage difference between the values obtained in H1 and H2.

Source: The National Development Plan 2007-2013, p.371.

The analyses determine the effects of the appearance or expansion of some activities in the economic process specific to local development, more precisely establishing the impact of a new activity upon the economic and social local development.

In theory, the input-output model (I-O) is designed with a simple, functional structure of the economy, incorporating the links between the flows of intermediary goods, the fact that the 'inputs are themselves current outputs for the other processes of the system' (Lancaster, 1973) being of essence. The I–O multiregional model (described by Bonfiglio, 2005) for the eight development regions (with a NUTS development level, Table 13.4) of Romania can be described as a model of interactions and transactions between the economic sectors and between regions, as follows:

$$\begin{vmatrix} x^1 \\ x^2 \\ x^3 \\ x^4 \\ x^5 \\ x^6 \\ x^7 \\ x^8 \end{vmatrix} = \begin{vmatrix} \underline{A^{11}} & A^{12} & A^{13} & A^{14} & A^{15} & A^{16} & A^{17} & A^{18} \\ A^{21} & \underline{A^{22}} & A^{23} & A^{24} & A^{25} & A^{26} & A^{27} & A^{28} \\ A^{31} & A^{32} & \underline{A^{33}} & A^{34} & A^{35} & A^{36} & A^{37} & A^{38} \\ A^{41} & A^{42} & A^{43} & \underline{A^{44}} & A^{45} & A^{46} & A^{47} & A^{48} \\ A^{51} & A^{52} & A^{53} & A^{54} & \underline{A^{55}} & A^{56} & A^{57} & A^{58} \\ A^{61} & A^{62} & A^{63} & A^{64} & A^{65} & \underline{A^{66}} & A^{67} & A^{68} \\ A^{71} & A^{72} & A^{73} & A^{74} & A^{75} & A^{76} & \underline{A^{77}} & A^{78} \\ A^{81} & A^{82} & A^{83} & A^{84} & A^{85} & A^{86} & A^{87} & \underline{A^{88}} \end{vmatrix} \times \begin{vmatrix} x^1 \\ x^2 \\ x^3 \\ x^4 \\ x^5 \\ x^6 \\ x^7 \\ x^8 \end{vmatrix} + \begin{vmatrix} fd^1 \\ fd^2 \\ fd^3 \\ fd^4 \\ fd^4 \\ fd^5 \\ fd^6 \\ fd^7 \\ fd^8 \end{vmatrix} \qquad (14)$$

Where,

X is the output column vector,

A is the coefficient's matrix,

F_d is the vector of the final demand,

A^{12}, A^{21}, ... refer to the flows between sectors and regions and

A^{11}, A^{22} ... A^{88} refer to the flows of goods and services on unit of output, and to the trade inside the region.

The multiregional model of I–O can be written in the form of the equation:

$$X = AX + f_d \qquad (15)$$

$$X = (1 - A)^{-1} \cdot f_d$$

The relation for determining the impact (Matei *et al.*, 2009) is

$$\Delta x = \left[1 - \overline{A}\right]^{-1} \Delta F, \qquad (16)$$

Where,

Δx is the modification in the local outputs derived from the operations specific to the new local activities. Δx will be a column vector with n+1 elements.

$\overline{A}$ is the extended I–O matrix of the intermediary flows' coefficients, which includes a line and a column correspondent to the local activities.

ΔF represents the changes in the final demand determined by the creation of a new local activity.

In terms of determining, from equation (16) of the outputs correspondent to the n+1 local activities, as well as to knowing the coefficients of the employees' need, for each output unity e_i, i=1, n+1, the impact of the new local activity upon the labour force need can be determined.

$$\Delta E_i = e_i \Delta x_i, i = \overline{1, n-1} \qquad (17)$$

Where ΔE_i measures the changes in employment from the *i* activity and is the ith element of the column vector *x*.

In the I–O model, replacing the flows of goods and services with those of labour and income has been the fundament of developing a study by Bonfiglio (2005), regarding the effects of using the European funds for the regional development in Romania. The author has developed an I–O multiregional model for Romania, assessing the effects upon the labour market and income as a result of the development policies promoted under the European funds for the 2007-2009 period, analysing the interrelations from and between (the economic branches) the development regions. The author's conclusions state the fact that the structural funds in general have a positive effect upon the degree of development and reducing the economic disparities, taking into consideration the economic sectors (agriculture, industry, services) and social sectors (labour market and income) between regions (Table 13.8).

Table 13.8

The Impact of Structural Funds upon Employment during 2007-2009 in Romania

	NE	*SE*	*S*	*SW*	*W*	*NW*	*C*	*B If*	*RO*
Agriculture	55.7	46.5	63.8	52.1	38.6	48.6	36.4	7.5	49.6
Industry	24.2	27.3	22.8	28.5	35.0	29.6	41.9	45.4	29.1
Services	20.1	26.2	13.4	19.4	26.4	21.8	21.7	47.0	21.3
Total	100.0	100.0	100.0	100.0	100.0	100.0	100.0	100.0	100.0

Source: Bonfiglio (2005: 26, Table 10).

Referring to the creation of new jobs, the distribution of half of the jobs is assigned between industry 29 per cent and services 21 per cent, the other half being in the agriculture and the income are at a level of 5.3 per cent in agriculture, 44.7 per cent in industry and 50 per cent in services. In terms of effectiveness, policy generates an increase in income by 32 per cent of public expenditure and in employment by 183 labour units for each one million Euro. At a sectoral level, policy demonstrates to be more effective in services, as for income and in agriculture, as for employment.

Conclusions

The assessment of the possible effects that the community structural instruments of EU can produce at the economic level in the development regions of Romania can be accomplished through the use of certain economical-mathematical modelling designed for simulating the national macroeconomic system in the multisectoral and multi-institutional variants.

Characterised by the sets' triplet (inputs I, system's status S and outputs O), the regional model is a multitude of parts interacting with one another, described as follows:

Where,

T – is the time for ordering events (as the system has a continuous time);

I – inputs' set;

F – the set of the segment input system;

E – outputs' set;

S – the set of the system's states (that we declare it to be the modelling concept of the internal structure of the system, which contains its 'history' and which affects its present and future and together with the inputs' form determine in an unique manner the system's outputs);

φ – is the function of response of the system,

$\varphi = I * S \rightarrow O$

That we use in our case, of the community structural instruments in the region, in the sense that: at a certain input I and a certain status of the system S can reach a certain response O.

γ - is the function of the states' transition.

The rule of the system's equilibrium, the behavioural equations and the macroeconomic identities have used annual data bases, appealing to Keynesian mechanism for describing the way of functioning of the demand-supply equilibrium for all the economic sectors.

The presented HERMIN model, the HEROM model, the cumulative multiplier of employment based on the community structural instruments and the multiregional I–O model are testing different scenarios for European financial instruments' allocation in a national economic structure, financial source, distributed at the level of the development regions on a 2007–2020 prognosis time horizon (2007-2013: European financing and 2014-2020: the post-transfer period), a period when employment changes will take place.

The experimented models (HERMIN, HERMON, I-O) or the cumulative regional employment multiplier justify the economic and social policy decision and allow the effects' quantification (credible) if we compare with what has been registered for the 2007-08 period, a period that for Romania represents the first, respectively the second year when the country's statute is that of EU member, with rights to access the structural and cohesion funds.

The I–O links at a regional level generate feedback effects, both direct (the increase in the number of jobs and of the employees' income as a result of the insertion of the structural instruments) and indirect (the increase of demand in the sectors supporting the new activities developed as a result of the European financial instruments, thus increasing the output, employment and income in these sectors) and induced (the employees from the new activities created through the European financial intervention spend a part of their income for buying goods and services on a local level, thus increasing the demand in that sector).

References

Allais, M. (1994). *Traité d'économie Pure* (Ed.). Paris: Clément Juglar.

Annual Implementation Report 2008. (2009). *www.inforegio.ro.*

Barry, Frank, John Bradley, Michal Kejak and David Vavra (2000). "The Czech Economic Transition: Exploring Options using a Macrosectoral Model", *Centre for Economic Research Working Paper* 00/03. University College Dublin.

Bonfiglio, A. (2005). *Analysing EU Accession Effects in Romania by a Multiregional I–O Model*. Universita Politecnica Delle Marche. February.

Boomsma, P. and J. Oosterhaven (1992). "A Double-Entry Method for the Construction of Bi-Regional Input-Output Tables", *Journal of Regional Science* 32(3): 269-84.

Bradley, J. (2006). "Evaluating the Impact of the European Union Cohesion Policy in Less-Developed Countries and Regions", *Regional Studies, Taylor and Francis Journals* 40(2): 189-200, April.

Bradley, J. and E. Morgenroth (2004). *A Study of the Macro-economic Impact of the Reform of EU Cohesion Policy*. ESRI, Dublin, Ireland.

Bradley, J., G. Untiedt and T. Mitze (2007). *Analysis of the Impact of Cohesion Policy. A note explaining the HERMIN–based Simulations*. Münster, Germany, Dublin, Ireland.

Bradley, J., L. Modesto and S. Sosvilla–Rivero (1995). "HERMIN. A Macro Econometric Modelling Framework for the EU Periphery", *Economic Modelling* 12.

Bradley, J., T. Mitze, E. Morgenroth and G. Untiedt (2005). "An Integrated Micro-Macro (IMM) Approach to the Evaluation of Large-Scale Public Investment Programmers: The Case of EU Structural Funds", *Papers* WP167. ESRI, Dublin, Ireland.

Cardenoso, F.E. and J. Oosterhaven (2010). *Hybrid Interregional Input-Output Construction Methods. Phase One: Estimation of RPCs*. April.

Charemza W. and G. Turlea (1998). *Internal Foreign Exchange Markets during Transition: An Empirical Analysis.* Research Memorandum Univ. Leicester.

Ciupagea, C. (2000). *Economic and Econometric Models for Romania* (Ed.). Bucharest: IEM.

Ciupagea, C., I. Ghizdeanu, V. Tudorescu and R. Voinescu (2007). *Macro-economic Models used in assessing the Effects of Structural Reforms in Romania*. IWE, Romanian Academy, Bucharest.

Cohesion policy of the European Union (2007). *Structural Instruments: Development Opportunities for Romania. www.fonduri-ue.ro.*

European Commission (2009). Recommendation of the Council on updating in 2009. The general orientations of the economic policies of the Member States and Community on the Employment Policies of the Member States, COM (2009). 34 final, Volume 1, Brussels, 28.1.2009.

Government of Romania (2007). *Regional Operational Program 2007-2013*. June. *www.gov.ro.*

———. (2005). *National Development Plan 2007-2013*, December. *www.gov.ro.*

Isard, W. *et al.* (1960). *Methods of Region al Analysis: An Introduction to Regional Science*. MIT Press.

Keynes, J. Maynard (2007). *The General Theory of Employment, Interest and Money*. The Royal Economic Society.

Lahr, M.L. and E. Dietzenbacher (eds.) (2001). *Input-Output Analysis: Frontiers and Extensions*. Palgrave.

Lancaster, K. (1973). *Analiza economicã matematicã*, Editura Stiintificã, Bucuresti, p.103.

Matei, A. (2007). "Empirical Approaches about the Input-Output Model for the Local Economic Development", *International Journal of Public Administration in Central and Eastern Europe* 1 (39–49), Budapest.

Matei, A., S. Anghelescu and C. Sãvulescu (2009). *Modele teoretice si empirice ale dezvoltãrii* locale, Editura Economicã, Bucuresti, pp.169-222.

Matei, L. (2004). "Strategii de dezvoltare economicã localã. Abordare managerialã", Editura Politeia-SNSPA, Bucuresti, pp.77-104.

Matei, L. and S. Anghelescu (2009). *Dezvoltarea localã. Concepte si mecanisme*, Editura Economicã, Bucuresti, pp.23-44.

McNicoll, I.H. and R.G. Baird (1980). "Empirical Application of Regional Input-Output Analysis: A Case Study of Shetland", *The Journal of the Operational Research Society* 31(11).

Monthly statistical bulletin, (2010). INSE, Bucharest.

Study of Interim Evaluation of the Regional Operational Programme for 01.01.07-30.06.09. (2009). *www.inforegio.ro.*

Turlea, G. (2006). "Modelul HEROM—Menþinerea în funcþionare si recalibrarea ecuaþiilor", *Studiu CEROPE*, Bucuresti.

United Cities and Local Governments (2009). *The Impact of the Global Crisis on Local Governments. www.cities-localgovernments.org.*

van Run, Pieter (2007). "Evaluare ex-ante România", *EUROPEAID/121373/DISV/RO*, Program operaþional de dezvoltare regionalã, Ministry of Finance, Bucuresti.

http://www.evalsed.info

http://www.insse.ro

http://www.mfinanþe.ro/fonduriUE

14 Micro, Small and Medium-Sized Enterprises and the Global Economic Crisis

Impacts and Policy Responses

Paul Vandenberg

Introduction

While losses and layoffs at large firms are making headlines, many micro, small & medium enterprises (MSMEs) are also severely affected by the global economic slump of 2008-09. Weak demand and tight credit are the chief pressures faced by these enterprises. Demand stimulus measures will assist all enterprises, whereas access to finance needs more specific targetting for small firms. Cooperatives (i.e., cooperative enterprises) appear to be the least affected by the crisis.

The employment pillar of the Decent Work Agenda (ILO), which promotes the creation and maintenance of productive employment opportunities, is certainly under threat during the current downturn. One or more of the other three pillars (rights at work, social protection and social dialogue) may also be affected, although in less obvious ways.

Many stimulus packages include specific measures for small and medium-sized enterprises. These measures include assistance with taxation, trade, credit and procurement. In addition, measures that apply to firms of all sizes support smaller enterprises operating in the formal sector. It is important that business owners are aware of these programmes and can access them easily and without undue bureaucratic delays or paperwork.

There is limited direct help for informal and microenterprises, which dominate the enterprise landscape in most developing countries. Microbusiness startups are likely to increase as laid-off workers and returning migrant workers seek to make a living. Success for these new businesses and indeed many existing ones will be difficult to achieve, given weak demand and limited credit access. Entrepreneurs will need to be entrepreneurial in seeking out and exploiting new business opportunities.

While government interest rates have fallen, credit is scarce because banks are risk averse and have difficulty screening even good clients in a downturn. Governments are attempting to reduce the shortfall by expanding loan programmes. Many governments have created or are expanding loan guarantee programmes for the MSME sector. These include developed countries such as the UK and the developing ones such as India.

Where possible, permanent layoffs are being averted through various measures including work-time reductions, temporary shutdowns, training schemes and employee retention subsidies. Unemployment insurance, where it exists, is being extended and used to fund training in some cases.

Employers' organisations and trade unions have added their voices to the debate about appropriate crisis management measures. Some countries have reached tripartite agreements to promote economic activity and reduce social tensions during the crisis.

The ILO's Five Point Crisis Response for MSMEs offers support to policymakers and enterprises through: (i) rapid assessments to pinpoint the constraints felt by MSMEs; (ii) advice through examples on managing credit; (iii) advice to policymakers on public procurement; (iv) advice and training on business development services, notably entrepreneurship and enterprise management training and, (v) advice and training on supporting small business associations to take an active advocacy and support role during the crisis.

The Evolving Crisis

The global economy is experiencing its greatest slowdown since the Second World War. Due to the increased integration of goods, services and financial markets, the crisis has spread from housing and credit sectors in the US to other markets and countries around the world. There are a few, if any, economies that have been left untouched by the crisis. The collapse of Wall Street investment banks and American mortgage lenders has had serious knock-on effects for commercial banks and non-financial companies around the world.

Credit everywhere is tight as lenders seek to shore up their financial positions and increase their precautionary reserves. Borrowers have become suspect as creditworthiness is difficult to assess. Businesses in the real economy have found it hard to survive, resulting in increased layoffs and closures. Retrenchment translates directly into a decline in the opportunities for women and men to engage in decent work. Thus, the credit crisis has developed, via weak demand, into a full-blown economic crisis. Many developed countries slipped into recession in the last quarter of 2008 and many developing countries have seen their growth rates plummet.

The crisis is affecting firms of all sizes. While large firms grab headlines when disclosing layoffs and dramatic declines in sales and earnings, many MSMEs are also trying to cope with weak demand, tight credit and reduced orders from larger companies. Small businesses across a range of sectors and organisational types have been affected, although preliminary evidence suggests that the cooperative form of enterprise is managing particularly well and many are adding new members.[1]

MSMEs, which account for over 90 per cent of enterprises in all countries, are an important source of output and employment.

They employ 33 per cent of the formal sector workers in low-income countries and 62 per cent of such workers in high-income countries (ILO, 2004). Because poor countries have large informal economies dominated by micro-businesses, the MSME portion of total employment is much higher. In India, for example, 86 per cent of the labour force is employed in the informal sector, including farming. The crisis has not only hit Wall Street and Main Street, but it has affected the side streets, the dirt streets and the markets where many small retailers and producers thrive.

This paper analyses the constraints faced by MSMEs during the current crisis and reviews the actions taken by policymakers. Section II focusses on the various aspects of finance, while Section III is dedicated to demand and employment and includes issues such as public procurement, changes in taxation policies and self-employment. Country examples are used frequently so that this paper can act as a means of sharing experiences and providing ideas to countries that have, as yet, focussed only limited attention on the needs of small businesses. Section IV outlines the ILO's Five Point Crisis Response for MSMEs so as to provide constituents with ideas of how they can best collaborate with the ILO in this area. Section V addresses more specifically the actions that the social partners can take to ensure that there is a shared approach to managing through the crisis, notably as it pertains to maintaining decent work. Section VI concludes. Cooperatives (i.e., cooperative enterprises) are not included in the analysis both because they appear to be weathering the current crisis better than other small businesses and because they are the subject of a companion ILO publication.

Many, if not most, of the stimulus packages announced by governments in late 2008 and early 2009 include measures for the MSME sector. This is true of both developed and developing countries. For example, an announcement by the Indian Prime Minister Manmohan Singh on the country's first stimulus package, stressed that 'The government attaches the highest priority to supporting the MSMEs sector which is critical for employment generation'.[2] Similarly, Peter Mandelson, the UK's business secretary, when outlining measures to increase credit to SMEs, stated that 'UK companies are the lifeblood of the economy and it is crucial that Government acts now to provide real help to support them through the downturn'.

The MSME sector is highly varied, both within a country and between richer and poorer countries. Formal sector firms, working within the framework of formal credit institutions, tax regulations and social security programmes can benefit from changes to the policy environment that are designed to assist enterprises during the downturn.[3]

Jobs Cuts at Small Industrial Firms in Pune, India

The Indian economy lost half a million jobs in the last quarter of 2008, according to a conservative estimate. Many of the affected firms are small ones which have grown up over the last decade as large Indian firms have taken eagerly to outsourcing as a competitive strategy.

'In Pune, in central India, small industrial firms have cut jobs as work from their buyers has fallen. As of now, over 40,000 workers have lost their jobs and we fear that number may increase', says Nitin Bankar, President of the local Small Scale Industries Association.

One of the companies that may be shutting down currently supplies Tata Motors, the home-grown car and bus manufacturer. Prakash Dhawale, who worked at the company until recently, is concerned that he will not be re-employed. 'Our children are studying, our daughters are yet to marry', he says. 'We are thrown out on the streets like this. The government must help'.

Workers have come to Pune from the small villages and towns in the rural areas over the years. They are finding it hard to survive and many are moving back. 'We used to have a lot of work here earlier', says Gagan, a carpenter. 'But now there is no work, so we are returning'. ('Big trouble for small industries in Pune' *www.ndtv.com*, 04.02.09)

Microenterprises, notably those operating in the informal sector, constitute the vast majority of businesses in the most developing countries. They include what are often called own-account workers, the self-employed and small family operations. They are unlikely to benefit directly from changes to the formal policy environment and from the efforts to expand credit through banks and other formal lenders. They will only benefit from procurement and infrastructure programmes if they are consciously included. In addition, small and medium firms engaged in export-related industries, producing either final products or components in a value chain, are being affected as recession hits importing countries.

Governments in many countries have responded with a range of policies, often combined together in fiscal stimulus packages. These policies are designed to stabilise the financial sector but also support companies and workers in the real economy. Many enterprise-related policies provide assistance to companies of all sizes, while others specifically target the MSME sector. Policy support is also designed for specific (notably exporting) sectors where smaller firms are known to be a significant part of the enterprise landscape.

Box 14.1

Voices of Shopkeepers in Delhi

It has been slow for the last several weeks, since Christmas', says the young man taking orders for freshly dressed chickens at INA Market. In upscale Khan Market, one grocer has seen a dramatic decline. 'We are about 25 per cent down', he says. The decline has been evident for the past six months. People are buying necessities (fruits and vegetables) but cutting backed on the higher-priced packaged goods.

'We are about 10 to 15 per cent down', says the owner of a durable goods supplier in Khannna Market. 'The Sunday afternoon crowd is down', he says. Large flat screen TVs are not selling well with the public or business clients. He supplied a building with 10 flat screens last year. The same client completed a similar building this year but wanted only one screen.

'Business is good', says the man handling the cash register at the popular Evergreen Sweets in Green Park. His 12-person sales crew is working at a brisk pace. Asked if the shop is affected by the economic slowdown, he replies, 'Yes, we are down a little, but not much.

Source: Interviews, 02.09, P. Vandenberg.

Finance

Access to finance and low demand are the chief factors affecting small businesses in the current downturn. Governments have responded by loosening monetary policy, strengthening banks, encouraging lending and providing demand stimulus through fiscal policies. It is too early to tell which policies will be effective in supporting recovery. This section sets out the various financial constraints faced by small businesses and the measures being taken by policymakers. Examples are provided from both the developed and the developing countries.

Credit has tightened in most countries and not only where banks held mortgage-backed securities (MBS) and collateralised debt obligations (CDO) linked to the US housing market. Most governments have cut interest rates, lowered reserve ratios and urged lenders to pass on lower rates to their customers. As few countries set the rates that are charged by commercial banks, lower rates in the interbank markets are not automatically passed on to commercial customers. In addition and in most cases more importantly—lenders are offering fewer loans.

Credit has tightened for small enterprises in many countries although the actual impact is not well-known. A survey of banking executives in 19

Latin American and Caribbean countries in late 2008 found that 58 per cent expected that less credit would be available to SMEs during the coming year. Just under half of the executives thought that the interest rates on loans to the sector would increase.[4] Many governments have anticipated this slowdown in lending and have sought to pre-empt it through measures in their stimulus packages.

Banks and non-bank financial institutions are consolidating their own financial positions by ensuring adequate reserves as a precaution against delinquency and default. These prudential measures have reduced the flow of new lending and the extension of existing lines of credit in many countries. Lenders are finding it difficult to assess creditworthiness in the downturn. A stable company last year may be risky this year, notably if demand has slumped for its products or services. Even enterprises with a good credit history are finding it difficult to obtain loans.

In the UK, where the number of small business closures rose dramatically to 85 per day in early 2009, the Federation of Small Businesses (FSB) summarised the problems succinctly: 'Costs are up, orders are down and banks are not being helpful'.[5] Smaller enterprises that can access credit in good times now face difficulties. Microenterprises and some small business which are unable to access credit under normal conditions will continue to be shut out during the crisis.

Box 14.2

Lobster Fisherman Needs Working Capital

Many small firms are in need of working capital during the downturn. Even though they may have a good credit repayment history, their bank may be short of funds to lend. This is the case of a Canadian lobster fisherman.

The fisherman from Prince Edward Island, on the east coast, supplies high-end restaurants in the region. With the downturn, many of his regular customers were becoming delinquent in their payments. The fisherman asked his bank to increase his working capital line of credit. Despite a good credit history and being current in his payments, the bank denied the increase, citing pressure on its own funds.

The fisherman was able to secure extra financing from a public sector financial institution that has received funds through the federal government's new Business Credit Availability Programme. The programme is providing C$5 billion for onlending to businesses during the global slump.

Source: *Canada's Economic Action Plan, Budget 2009*, 27.01.09 (p.82).

The following sub-sections discuss specific types of finance and the measures being taken by governments.

Investment Lending

Few small businesses are initiating new investment projects in sectors and countries where demand is weak. Existing projects, notably those that are more than three quarters finished, are likely to be completed because of the sunk costs and thus the need to begin generating a return.[6] In countries and sectors that are less affected by the crisis, the desire for investment loans will be stronger. Banks are scrutinising investment proposals more closely.

Many countries are ensuring that specialised lenders have sufficient resources to extend loans to small borrowers. For example, the central bank has provided $1.45 billion to the Small Industries Development Bank of India (SIDBI) to deal with the downturn. The Chinese government has eliminated credit ceilings imposed on commercial banks to channel more loans to various areas including small enterprises and to encourage investment in technical innovation. The European Investment Bank (EIB), which regularly provides about €5 billion annually to banks for onlending to SMEs, has increased the amount to €7.5 annually for 2008-2011. The increased allocation is designed partly to support SME sector during the global downturn and partly has a long-term effort to increase support to these enterprises.[7]

Credit Policy Options

- Continue with loose monetary policy to encourage low-interest rates;
- Ensure adequate MSME lending through state-owned development and commercial banks;
- Ensure adequate credit for working capital requirements;
- Increase lending through enterprise support programmes;
- Expand microcredit to microbusinesses, including those newly created by laid-off workers;
- Improve access to finance for exporters;

- Encourage prompt payment and enforce rules on late payment in the private sector;
- Ensure local, provincial and federal governments pay promptly their bills to MSMEs;
- Expand the coverage and decrease the enterprise cost of credit/loan guarantee schemes;
- Ensure access to equity finance and
- Assist enterprises in preparing high quality loan proposals.

Working Capital

A chief concern of enterprises is to ensure sufficient working capital, especially when payments for goods sold or services provided are delayed. This involves, in part, astute cash flow management, tight tracking of accounts receivable, maximising the use of supplier credit and managing overdraft facilities. Several countries have instituted programmes to support working capital, notably through loan guarantee schemes.

Credit Guarantees

Banks may have the funds but are restricting lending to enterprises due to the negative economic environment. As a result, governments have created or expanded guarantee schemes or reduced the costs paid by borrowers. For example, the size of loans covered under the Credit Guarantee Scheme in India has doubled to approximately $200,000. The guarantee covers half of the loan amount, but 85 per cent for microloans up to $10,000.

In the UK, two major programmes have been launched for small and medium firms.[8] The Working Capital Scheme provides a government guarantee for 50 per cent of the value of short-term loans provided by commercial banks. Total lending of £20 billion will be guaranteed and the scheme applies to firms with turnover of under £500 million. The Enterprise Finance Scheme is for smaller firms, with turnover up to £25 million and will provide guarantees for a total of £1.3 billion in bank lending for working capital or for investment loans of up to £1 million. It can also be used to covert existing overdrafts into loans to free up the overdraft.

Equity

Finance provided by venture capital funds and business angels has declined in several countries, although good data is generally not available (OECD, 2009). In most developing countries, this type of finance is not well-developed, especially for small firms. Governments have, however, taken equity positions in struggling banks and, in a few cases, in non-financial enterprises. These latter schemes allow a business to convert debt into equity to improve its financial position. In Mauritius, for example, the government is offering to take an equity stake in manufacturing firms, notably small and medium textiles firms, which need to restructure due to weak international demand (GoM, 2008). In the UK, the Capital for Enterprise Fund will finance the conversion of business debt into equity. The government will provide £75 million and the main commercial banks an additional £25 million. The scheme is open to large and small companies.[9]

Credit Support: Country Examples

- Mauritius: MUR 100 million directly to SMEs that need assistance with liquidity or to restructure.
- India: US$ 1.4 billion to the SIDBI for direct or indirect onlending to MSMEs.
- China: Government financial support and insurance to small textile and garment firms, hit by the sharp decline in export demand.
- UK: Loan guarantees for £20 billion in working capital to enterprises with turnover of over less than £500 million and guarantees for £1.3 billion of other bank lending to enterprises with turnover of less than £25 million.[10]
- Canada: Raised the maximum loan amount to C$ 350,000 and to C$ 500,000 for real property under the existing Canada Small Business Financing Programme, which should increase lending by C$ 300 million; the loans are guaranteed up to 85 per cent.

Facilitating Loan Applications in Singapore

The Financial Facilitator Programme was established in Singapore to provide free advice to small enterprises on finance and loans during the slump. Assistance will be given to: diagnose the health of the enterprise; understand financing options and, put together a high-quality loan application.

Png Cheong Boon, chief executive of SPRING, the government's business support agency, says, 'One common feedback from the banks is that many SMEs are unable to present their case to the banks'. The new service will be provided at the island's six business membership organisations, including the Association of SMEs.

SPRING also lowered rates on loan programmes for small enterprises. Interest rates were cut by 1.25 per cent, with the rate for loans of four years or less falling to 5 per cent. The changes will affect 13,540 existing loans and new ones. The government's portion of loan insurance is being raised from 50 per cent to 90 per cent. Thus, an enterprise will pay only 0.15 per cent of the loan amount for the insurance, which, in total, costs 1.5 per cent of the loan amount (SPRING website).

Export Finance

Recession in developed economies has reduced global trade and cut exports from developing countries. Exporters have sought relief in the form of reduced export financing costs. Labour-intensive goods from the developing countries have been particularly affected by the slump, notably in sectors with a heavy small enterprise presence. The textile sector has been particularly affected in India, China and other countries. To provide general relief to exporters, the government in India is providing an interest rate subsidy of two per cent on pre- and post-shipment export credit for labour-intensive exports and those produced by SMEs.

Receivables and Supplier Credit

The credit squeeze may be affecting interfirm finances, although it is hard to know the full extent of this problem. Small enterprises generally have difficulty receiving timely payment from larger firms, given the power imbalance. During a credit squeeze, accounts receivable may mount and reduce further the funds available for working capital. (As part of its crisis response, the Indian government has instructed all public sector departments and companies to ensure prompt payment to MSMEs). In addition, small firms rely regularly on credit from suppliers to meet working capital needs for inputs and sales inventories. In a crisis, such credit may be more difficult to secure or the terms may be more demanding. Small firms may need to try to compensate in other ways, either through the use of their overdraft (if they have such access), by securing new government lending or by better management of finance in other areas.

Microfinance

Household-based microbusinesses and some small businesses rely on microcredit for working capital and for needed investments in tools and machinery. The crisis is putting pressure on these lending operations but much depends on the nature of the microfinance institution (MFI) and its clientele. Deposit-based institutions are weathering the crisis better than non-deposit institutions, which instead rely for funds on outside sources including government development banks and foreign capital sources, including donors.

Financing has become scarcer and more expensive during the crisis and foreign finance is prone to the added risks of exchange rate movements. One Indian MFI reported that the cost of borrowing (for onlending to its clients) had recently risen by 2-3 per cent, while another institution noted that 'banks are taking more time to lend to MFIs'.

Some experts in the microfinance industry feel that the crisis may encourage a focus on sound microbanking practices and an increased emphasis on local funds generation through deposit-taking. The risk is that governments may meddle needlessly. Claudio Gonzalez-Vega, an expert at Ohio State University, sees the following risks: 'interest rate ceilings, mass loan forgiveness, the encouragement of delinquent borrower associations [and] the development of credit programmes in government agencies that lack financial experience.' Some of these practices are already in evidence.[11]

Demand and Employment

The financial crisis has evolved rapidly into a crisis of demand and employment. Reduced access to credit for businesses, home-owners and consumers, along with uncertainty, has stalled demand in the US and increasingly in other parts of the world. The American economy is set to shrink by 2.8 per cent and the Euro zone by 4.2 per cent in 2009. Together, these two markets account for more than a third of global demand. Overall, the world economy is likely to see output fall by 1.3 per cent.[12] The slump is having a profound affect on trade for both developed and developing countries. Trade flows grew by only 2 per cent in 2008 and are expected to fall by 9 per cent in 2009. Early in the crisis many commentators suggested that the developing world has become increasingly 'decoupled' from developed economies and would not be vulnerable. As the World Trade Organization (WTO) has noted recently, however, this 'has not turned out to be the case'.[13]

Export-oriented sectors felt the impact early, along with construction. The impact has been uneven, however. For example, manufacturing exports from China's coastal areas are down considerably but low-end ready-made garments from Bangladesh which supply to discount retailers such as Wal-Mart appear to be doing reasonably well.[14] Footwear and handicrafts exports have seen a decline. The commodities picture is more complex because prices for many goods, notably food, petroleum and steel, rose dramatically in the first half of 2008 before falling significantly as a result of the crisis.[15] Higher food prices tend to be good for rural producers but impact negatively on consumers—be they rural or urban.

The decrease in demand has put serious pressure on enterprises of all sizes to reduce staff. Indeed, the ILO estimates that global unemployment increased by 11 million people in 2008 and may increase by an additional 40 million in 2009.[16] In China, the steep decline in exports has resulted in the layoff of 20 million workers. The US economy lost 4.4 million jobs since the crisis there began in late 2007[17] and the Indian economy lost half a million jobs in the last three months of 2008 (Ministry of Labour and Employment, 2009). Unemployment rates are rising to levels not experienced for decades. The jobless rate in Spain reached 14.9 per cent in January 2009, for example. Layoffs in developing countries are pushing large numbers into poverty. As Michelle Bachelet, President of Chile said recently about the crisis, 'We need to focus on what is necessary and today, that is to guarantee employment'.[18]

The crisis is also impacting on the demand for migrant workers and reducing the remittances they send back home. It is currently unclear whether, globally, the net flow of migrants is positive or negative,[19] but certain countries, including Nepal and Bangladesh, do expect a large re-flow of migrants.[20] The pull factors that entice people to seek work abroad (vacancies, better pay) have certainly weakened. At the same time, however, the push factors have strengthened (few opportunities, low remuneration at home). Even where workers decide to remain in a foreign country, they face increasing difficulty in finding decent paying jobs and thus maintaining the flow of money home. In 2009, global remittances are expected to fall by 5-8 per cent, the first annual decrease in almost 25 years.[21] While some existing migrants are returning home after losing their jobs, others are shifting to different sectors. In the US for example, there has been a move from manufacturing and construction work into hotels and restaurants and wholesale and retail trade.[22]

Governments have responded to the slump with fiscal stimulus packages to boost demand and support employment. Such measures have taken the form of infrastructure and procurement measures, employment programmes and changes to tax policies. These programmes provided opportunities for MSMEs as well as large enterprises.

Infrastructure and Procurement

Many of the fiscal stimulus packages now being implemented include infrastructure development, such as the building of roads, ports, houses and schools. In some cases, they are designed to engage in needed development (rural infrastructure), the dredging of rivers (Korea) or the creation of green jobs. Such stimuli are designed to create employment either directly on the projects or indirectly through machinery and inputs that companies will supply to those projects. The speed at which governments can implement those projects will determine how quickly they can contribute to reversing the downturn.

For many of the larger projects, governments may seek to engage large firms, although high capital intensity will limit the employment creating benefits of such stimulus measures. Governments that use labour-intensive practices will see a greater employment impact. This approach may include the contracting of work to MSMEs.

Governments can also support procurement in other ways. For example, the Mexican stimulus package requires that at least 20 per cent of government purchases be made from small and medium companies.[23] Small tenders and the decentralisation of procurement decisions can also increase opportunities for small firms.

In the UK, the government launched a campaign in the midst of the crisis urging small businesses to register with its online procurement portal. In February 2009, there were over 100,000 supply opportunities, with many of the contracts valued at less than £100,000. About 3,000 new contracts are advertised every month and 123,000 firms are registered on the portal. According to Ian Austin, a Regional Minister, 'Every year the government spends billions of pounds with SMEs on public sector contracts. Many of them are lower-value contracts that until this website was created were difficult to find out about'.[24]

Infrastructure and Procurement Options

- Ensure there is no enterprise size minimum for bidding on projects, where feasible;
- Source MSMEs for small projects and components of large projects;
- Reserve a specific percentage of government contracts for MSMEs and
- Favour bids with high employment intensity.

Taxation

A reduction in tax can ease working capital constraints for businesses and stimulate demand among consumers. As taxes are levied at several levels—income, production, value added, sales and imports—there is considerable room for governments to make cuts. Many of these measures are applicable to enterprises of all sizes but governments are aware that in many cases they will benefit MSMEs.[25]

Anggito Abimanyu, Chief of Policy Affairs, Ministry of Finance in Indonesia, explained his country's approach to tax changes during the slowdown: '[Businesses] can save costs from not paying their taxes which will increase their profits'.[26]

Such cuts result in the loss of public revenues but a number of governments around the world are not particularly concerned about the size of deficits at the present conjunction. The benefits of keeping business operating and workers employed currently outweigh concerns about the effects of future public debt servicing. Egyptian Trade Minister Rachid Mohamed Rachid was echoing a common sentiment when he said, 'Everyone is willing to sacrifice an increase in the budget deficit to stimulate growth'.[27]

Tax cuts today will require additional taxation in the future, which, however, will be resisted by taxpayers and businesses. Policymakers need to decide judiciously how much cutting is feasible and to what extent debt accumulation will inhibit future growth prospects and future social spending.

Changes in taxation will affect formal sector businesses but are likely to have only limited direct effects on the fortunes of informal enterprises. The latter tend to fall outside of the tax net and their owners' income may also not be taxed. Informal operators may benefit indirectly, however, if purchasing supplies from formal firms which normally do pay tax.

In late 2008 and early 2009, governments in many countries cut taxes in a variety of ways. Some countries chose to cut corporate income tax that affected all sizes of incorporated firms. For example, Singapore cut the corporate tax rate by one per cent for all firms. Korea went much further, cutting the rate for small firms by three per cent over two years and by five per cent for larger firms over the same period in 2009 and 2010.

Value-added taxes are an important target of cuts. In India, the central value-added tax was reduced a full 4 per cent on all products, except for oil. Similarly in China, the value-added tax for small businesses was cut to a uniform 3 per cent from the existing 4-6 per cent. The government there is speeding up the process of moving away from the use of excise taxes (on production) to value-added taxes. Recent changes are estimated to reduce total taxes paid by companies by US$ 17.6 billion annually.

Many countries have found ways to promote exports by cutting the tax related to export production or by rebating duties on imports used in exports (duty drawbacks). Specific sectors that have been hit hard by the crisis, such as textiles and garments, have received specific attention from governments. For example, China increased the tax rebate for textile and garment exporters four times between August 2008 and February 2009. The most recent increase, of one per cent, raised the rebate to 15 per cent.

Taxation Policy Options

- Reduce the corporate tax rate;
- Reduce the tax rate for sole proprietorships and partnerships;
- Link tax rate reduction to employee retention;
- Reduce excise tax;
- Reduce value-added taxes;
- Allow multi-year income/loss smoothing;
- Increase duty drawback rates (rebate on duty for imports used in exports) and
- Bring forward property assessments (newer assessments will be lower thus lowering property tax payable).

Some countries have tax schemes that allow profit and loss to be smoothed over several years and are extending such provisions to reduce tax payments in 2009. Singapore has a unique scheme in which it is moving forward on property assessments because with lower property prices, assessments will be lower and will result in a lower tax burden on households and businesses.

Countries which recently made tax cuts (i.e., before the crisis) have found it difficult to do so again due to its impact on revenues. South Africa made changes in 2008 such that in early 2009, the government resisted calls for further cuts. Indonesia moved from progressive taxes to a flatter regime in 2008. While the changes decrease revenues, the government resisted calls to halt the cuts in 2009. It sees the cuts as part of its stimulus efforts.

Micro and small businesses that do pay taxes need to be aware of the changes and may need assistance to understand how they apply. In this regard, business associations, including sectoral ones, can play a role in explaining tax changes to their members. Enterprise promotion agencies may provide similar assistance. Business associations have also a critical role to play in advising governments on the hardships of their members and on where tax cuts can be most effective in stimulating output, exports and employment.

Tax Relief during the Crisis: Examples

- Korea: Tax rate for smaller businesses reduced by 2 per cent to 11 per cent in 2009 and a further 1 per cent the following year; the rate for larger businesses reduced by 3 per cent to 22 per cent and then further to 20 per cent.
- Egypt: As part of its stimulus package, government proposed tax rebates for loss-making small businesses.
- Indonesia: Due to the crisis, government resists calls that it may not proceed with historical corporate tax cuts programme (to a flat 28 per cent) for 2009 that were announced a year earlier.
- China: The value-added tax for small businesses and the self-employed reduced to a universal 3 per cent from either 4 per cent for commercial enterprises or 6 per cent for industrial ones.
- Mauritius: To protect domestic business, the government froze for two years its plan to lower import duties.
- India: Central government value-added tax was reduced by 4 per cent on all goods except oil or where the tax is already below 4 per cent; the cut affects enterprises of all sizes.
- Singapore: Corporate tax rate reduced by one per cent to 17 per cent; this measure, combined with existing Partial Tax Exemption Scheme in which a company pays no tax on 75 per cent of its first S$ 10,000 and no tax on 50 per cent of its next S$ 290,000, provides a low tax regime for MSMEs.
- Brazil: To boost demand, taxes on cars, personal income and industrial earnings lowered; cars with an engine size of less than one litre now have no tax.
- France: Complete corporate tax exemption on investments made between now and early 2010.
- Canada: The amount of small business income eligible for the lower 11 per cent tax rate has been increased to C$ 500,000 from C$ 400,000. It is expected to reduce the total tax bill for small business by C$ 45 million.

Employment

While layoffs reduce business costs, they put further downward pressure on consumption, thereby prolonging the downturn. Thus, efforts to maintain employment are of benefit both to the welfare of workers and to the prospects for economic recovery. Worker retention may also aid businesses if it allows them to avoid losing valuable human capital, although businesses are unlikely to retrench their best workers.

Firms are taking their measures to reduce labour costs. Many are implementing wage freezes or low wage rises. In the UK, for example, a quarter of wage settlements in January 2009 resulted in a year-long wage freeze and more than half had lower settlement (often lower rises) compared with a year earlier.[28] These measures also tend to dampen demand but if instituted in lieu of layoffs, they may provide a more acceptable alternative. This is especially true in countries where unemployment insurance and related welfare measures are weak or non-existent.

Employment Options

Business Strategies

- Shift workers to required training;
- Move workers to units, plants or offices where demand is stronger;
- Negotiate a reduction in length of the work week (to avoid layoffs);
- Temporary work stoppage and
- Negotiate wage freeze or low wage rise.

Government Support

- Use unemployment insurance benefits to cover work-time reductions;
- Subsidise new hiring or retention;
- Extend unemployment insurance benefits period;
- Subsidise training and
- Subsidise non-wage labour costs (payroll deductions).

To avoid permanent retrenchment, many firms have instituted work-time reductions, either in the form of a shorter work week or a temporary plant shutdown. Such measures ease pressure on the payroll while still allowing workers to bring home a pay cheque. Temporary shutdowns have been common in the past at North American automobile companies and other manufacturers when inventories build up. Bipartite and tripartite dialogue can play an important role in shaping socially acceptable employment solutions during the downturn.

Workers affected by time reductions or temporary layoffs can often avail of unemployment insurance in countries where such schemes exist. Governments have been innovative in adapting their schemes. In Canada, for example, an employee whose work-week has been cut to four days can receive unemployment insurance benefits for the fifth day.

In other countries, unemployment insurance funds are not only being used to provide passive assistance. In China, for example, funds are being used to train unemployed and migrant workers. As explained by Mr Zheng, Vice-Minister of Human Resources and Social Security, 'The unemployment insurance fund has topped 100 billion yuan ($14.5 billion), and it's high time it is used'.[29]

Subsidies to retain workers or hire new ones are provided in some countries including Singapore, Japan and the UK (see 'Employment schemes'). The Singaporean government is providing a cash grant equal to 12 per cent of the first S$ 2,500 in wages for each regular worker retained during the slowdown.

Employment Schemes

- Slovakia: Subsidies for new jobs and reduction of employment taxes for employers that might otherwise retrench workers.
- Brazil: Duration of unemployment insurance benefits has been extended by two months.
- China: Vocational training programme for the unemployed and migrant workers funded from unemployment insurance and related funds.
- Japan: $16 billion package to expand training for the unemployed; provide benefits to laid-off workers not covered by unemployment insurance; subsidise companies to retain workers and expand job creation schemes.[30]

- Singapore: Under a new Jobs Credit scheme, employers of all sizes receive a cash grant for each regular employee.
- Korea: $3.5 billion to create half a million temporary jobs, expand training schemes and fund unemployment insurance.
- UK: Companies will receive £ 2,500 for hiring workers who have been unemployed for more than six months.

Self-Employment

Some countries have realised the important role that business start-ups can play in easing the impact of the slowdown. New businesses can be started by locally retrenched workers, by migrants moving from urban to rural areas and by migrants returning from abroad. New businesses have a high potential to fail, however, and therefore, require planning and supportive measures to increase their chances of success. Ideas for new businesses should be grounded in the realities of market demands that either exist or can be developed in the rural or urban environments where they are established. Local Economic Development (LED) approaches, in which local communities come together to assess and determine local market potential, can be facilitative in this regard. Pinpointing the market potential can then be supplemented with training on how to start and manage a business, with skills training and with access to credit. The ILO has a number of programmes on LED, skills training (CBT-TREE) (Abella and Ducanes, 2009) and enterprise management (Start and Improve Your Business) that can be helpful in this area.

In the Philippines, the government has established 'help desks' in provinces to guide the returning migrants to new jobs and also advise them on self-employment. A total of 250 million pesos from the Overseas Workers' Welfare Fund has been allocated for livelihood support for returning migrants (Ibid). In China, governments are supporting the return of retrenched workers from cities and industrial zones to rural areas and helping them to start businesses with credit and other supports. In Canada, the government's stimulus package provides C$ 10 million to the Canadian Youth Business Foundation (CYBF) which mentors new entrepreneurs.

ILO's Five Point Crisis Response for MSMEs

The ILO has developed a Five Point Crisis Response to help existing MSMEs weather the crisis and to support unemployed workers, including migrants, in creating self-employment. The five points, detailed below, focus on assessing environments and on providing advice, examples and training to policymakers, businesses and business associations. The ILO stands ready to offer this assistance through its network of enterprise specialists at ILO offices around the world and through the network it has developed of SME experts who deliver its well-known package of enterprise training, the Start and Improve Your Business (SIYB) suite of programmes.

Rapid Assessments of the Enterprise Environment

The impact and severity of the crisis have caught employers, workers and policymakers by surprise. As such, a rapid assessment of the impacts and how they are making enterprises vulnerable is an important first step in designing appropriate responses. The crisis has had a general impact on all economies around the world, but there are sectoral and geographical (region, country, within-country) differences. The crisis has also hit economies and enterprises at different times and some will exit from the crisis more rapidly and in better condition than others. A rapid assessment will pinpoint problem areas.

Advice through Examples for Policymakers on Access to Finance

Access to finance is a key constraint for MSMEs during the crisis. The ILO has produced this guide, which in Section II focusses considerable attention on the credit issue and provides a range of examples drawn from countries in various parts of the world. These examples offer ideas for policymakers and social partners in other countries on how to take a proactive approach to unblocking the financing constraint. Each country will need to work out its own approach based on its own set of banking institutions (including development banks and small enterprise banks) and credit programmes and on its resources, expertise and regulatory environment.

Box 14.3

ILO's Five-Point Crisis Response for MSMEs

1. Rapid assessment of factors that make enterprises vulnerable.
2. Advice through examples for policymakers on enterprise financing strategies.
3. Advice on public procurement programmes.
4. Advice and training on business development services.
5. Advice and training on strengthening small business associations.

Advice to Policymakers on Public Procurement

The ILO promotes an approach to public procurement that seeks to both remove the constraints faced by MSMEs in gaining access to government contracts and by actively promoting these enterprises because of their high labour intensity. Many governments have responded to the crisis with demand stimulus measures that involve spending on public works. With adequate access, MSMEs in relevant sectors, notably road and building construction, can compensate for the decline in demand from private clients with increased servicing of public sector customers. Other micro or small businesses, which are not or have not been able to secure public contracts, may benefit by supplying or sub-contracting with other enterprises that have. The ILO has a training programme on public procurement by MSMEs that can be used to provide advice and ideas to policymakers.

Advice and Training on Business Development Services

Small enterprises need to cope with reduced demand in their traditional markets and develop products and services for new markets and new opportunities arising during the crisis. For this they need help to 'think outside of the box' and take initiatives to ensure that instead of being 'entrepreneurs in crisis', they are 'entrepreneurial in the midst of the crisis'. Entrepreneurship is a complex issue involving personal attributes, a supporting culture and an enabling policy environment. It can be assisted through training on how to start and manage a business. For many years the ILO has promoted entrepreneurs through its SIYB suite of course, which also includes 'Generate Your Business Idea and Expand Your

Business'. These programmes have been used for emergency situations, notably in Indonesia and Sri Lanka for tsunami survivors and in China, where the Emergency-SIYB programme was successful in assisting those whose lives were disrupted by the Sichuan earthquake of 2008.

The ILO has developed a network of 7,000 trainers and 277 licenced master trainers for the SIYB suite in over 500 partner organisations worldwide. Through 10 sub-regional workshops, the ILO is mobilising and reinvigorating this network for ready deployment during the crisis. It can provide training for entrepreneurs and would-be entrepreneurs on coping with reduced demand and seizing new opportunities.[31]

Advice and Training to Strengthen Enterprise Associations

Enterprise associations can be a valuable support mechanism for businesses during the downturn. They allow members to share ideas and knowledge, provide information on new policies and programmes and advocate on behalf of their members *vis-à-vis* governments. The effectiveness of such organisations varies considerably, depending on the ability to attract members, the level of funding and the leadership and management. The Federation of Small Businesses (FSB) in the UK and the Canadian Federation of Independent Business (CFIB) are two of the many effective organisations around the world. Unfortunately, there are also many small business associations which are less effective and thus the voice of small entrepreneurs is often inaudible. The ILO is ready to strengthen these associations through its training programme for small business associations so that these associations can play a more active role during the downturn.

Role of the Social Partners

The economic crisis has prompted the ILO's social partners to put forward suggestions on how their country can manage the crisis. In many cases, this involves advice to governments. There is some consensus on a need to moderate wage demands and to find ways to retain workers and to support those who are retrenched.

In a number of countries, the crisis has created social tensions that have boiled over into street protests. The government in Iceland resigned in

January 2009 after months of protests, while in Ireland, over 100,000 people protested the imposition of a pension levy on public sector workers during the recession. Protests have also occurred in France, Greece, Bulgaria, Lithuania, Latvia and elsewhere.

The tripartite parties have come together in several countries to seek agreement on how to manage through the crisis. For example, in Slovakia, the government and the umbrella trade union, along with employers, agreed to limit salary increases to productivity increases.[32] In Mexico, employers' and workers' organisations have publicly supported the country's stimulus package. In addition, the Confederación de Trabajadores de México, which represents workers, has pledged not to engage in strikes or protests related to the current economic crisis.[33]

Employers' organisations in many countries have added their voices to the debate about appropriate economic policies to help businesses weather the downturn. Small business associations and small business cells within larger organisations have an important role to play in keeping the concerns of MSMEs at the forefront of policymaking during the crisis.

Social Dialogue Initiatives

By Employers' Organisations

- Engage in high-level dialogue with workers' organisations;
- Suggest crisis management strategies that are in tune with the interests of workers and
- Set long-term goals that extend beyond the short-term stresses of the current crisis.

By Workers' Organisations

- Understand how the crisis is affecting business owners and managers;
- Defend decent work and
- Work with management to find ways to increase productivity in the current crisis.

Advocating for Indian Garment Exporters

Indian garment exports for 2008-09 are expected to be 9 per cent lower than a year earlier. India is the world's fifth largest exporter of readymade garments. The sector comprises small and large producers and provides employment to 33 million workers directly and 55 million indirectly. The industry estimates that 700,000 workers lost their jobs within five months in late 2008.

The Apparel Export Promotion Council (AEPC) has asked for an increase in the duty drawback, which was lowered in September to between 8.8 per cent and 10.5 per cent. AEPC has asked for it to be raised to 14.65 per cent.

AEPC also asked for a five-year income tax holiday, interest-free loans on machinery investments, zero duty on machine imports and a lower fringe benefit tax. In its stimulus package of late 2008, the government provided a 2 per cent interest subsidy on loans for exporters and a US$ 290 million allocation to the sector's technology upgrading fund (Press release, AEPC, 07.12.08).

Conclusion

Securing Recovery and Beyond

Many analysts expect the first signs of economic recovery to appear in 2009 with a more robust upturn in the following year. Certain countries and sectors may recover more quickly than others. In the interim, many jobs and enterprises will be at risk. As the examples in this paper have shown, governments have demonstrated a commitment to supporting small enterprises and the employment they provide.

We should not, however, view the current situation as merely a crisis to be survived. It also presents opportunities on three fronts. One, the recent efforts to support MSMEs may provide an opportunity for policy experiments. Reduced regulation for startups, better access to finance and improved methods for monitoring and sustaining decent work can be developed during the crisis and continued when growth revives. We may recall that important aspects of Western social security systems were initiated during the last great crisis: the depression of the 1930s.

Two, even in a downturn, true entrepreneurs will arise, finding profitable opportunities to fulfill consumer wants either by innovating new products and services or by devising ways to produce existing products or deliver existing services more cheaply. And three, demand stimulus packages present important opportunities for small businesses to build infrastructure and supply goods and services to governments.

Carpe diem: seize the day, even when it's gloomy!

Notes

1. According to the International Co-operative Alliance and the ILO's Co-operatives programme.
2. "Government announces measures for stimulating the economy", Press release, Prime Minister's Office, India, 7.12.08.
3. "Real help for business", Press release, UK. Department for Business, Enterprises and Regulatory Reform, 14.01.09.
4. IDB, IIC, Felaban pool shows continued SME credit interest despite crisis, *Business News Americas*, 13.02.09.
5. "Small business closures hit 280 a week", *The Guardian* (UK), 23.10.08 and "Banks have run out of excuses as government announces £1 billion fund for small business", press release, Federation of Small Businesses, 14.01.09. The number of UK closures rose from 280 per week in October 2008 to 85 per day in early January, according to FSB.
6. The idea that projects three-fourth completed would continue was provided by an industry expert in India. The figure is a rough estimate and relates to all sizes of business.
7. EIB rolls out SME funding scheme, *www.euractiv.com* 13.02.09.
8. See Note 3.
9. Ibid.
10. Ibid.
11. The Section is derived from a written summary of CGAP Virtual Conference, *Micro-Finance and the Financial Crisis*, 18-20.11.08.
12. See IMF (2009). For share of global expenditure, see World Bank (2007) for figures of 2009 PPP.
13. "WTO sees 9 per cent global trade decline in 2009 as recession strikes", WTO press release, 24.04.09.
14. This is according to experts that the author met in Dhaka in May 2009.
15. For example, the world export price of rice rose by May 2008 to over 130 per cent of the previous.
16. "The financial and economic crisis: A decent work response", ILO Governing Body, ESP Committee, 04.09.

17. "When jobs disappear", *The Economist*, 14.03.09.
18. "Chile's Bachelet sets date to combat unemployment", *La Nación* (Santiago), 4.03.09.
19. According to the World Bank, *World Development Indicators 2007*.
20. Opinions of researchers in Kathmandu and Dhaka as told to the author in May 2009.
21. Revised "Outlook for Remittance Flows 2009-2011", by D. Ratha and S. Mohapatra, *Migration and Development Brief* 9, World Bank, 23.03.09. Global remittances doubled over a five-year period beginning in 2003, reaching $305 billion in 2008, or 1.9 per cent of those countries' GDP.
22. Ibid.
23. "Stimulus plan to curb impact of crisis", *IPS News Agency*, 18.03.09.
24. "West Midlands SMEs urged to sign up for Government contracts", Press release, UK. Department for Business, Enterprises and Regulatory Reform (West Midlands), 04.02.09.
25. Many countries already provide lower tax rates for small businesses or for those with a low level of profit.
26. "Government to maintain income tax cuts as economic stimulus", *Antara News Agency*, 7.02.09, Embassy of Indonesia, Oslo.
27. Rachid details trade ministry's stimulus package, *Daily News Egypt*, 11.12.08.
28. More firms freeze annual pay rises, Virgin Media, website, 20.02.09. The article is based on figures of the Industrial Relations Services.
29. "Economic crisis and policy responses in China", ILO-Beijing, undated.
30. Japan and S. Korea seek to ease jobs pain, *FT.com*, 19.03.09. The package was being proposed at the time of writing.
31. Few governments have included business development services in their stimulus packages. There are exceptions, however. In Mauritius, the government will help SMEs develop plans to qualify for financing. It is also accelerating the implementation of its Manufacturing Adjustment and SME Development Fund (MUR 500 million) which supports standards upgrading, productivity improvement, marketing, export promotion and other aspects to expand markets. In Canada, the government's stimulus package provides C$ 30 million to the Canada Business Network which provides a single window for accessing information and tools for business, mostly smaller ones.
32. "Slovak government, unions agree to cap wage hike demands", Reuters 06.02.09.
33. "Stimulus plan to curb impact of crisis", IPS News Agency, 18.03.09.

References

Abella, M. and G. Ducanes (2009). "The Effect of the Global Economic Crisis on Asian Migrant Workers and Governments' Responses", *Technial* Note. Manila: ILO, February.

Government of Mauritius (2008). *Additional Stimulus Package: Shoring up Economic Performance.* Government of Mauritius, December.

ILO (2004). *World Employment Report 2004-05*. Geneva: ILO. p.228.

IMF (2009). *World Economic Outlook,* April. Washington.

Ministry of Labour and Employment (2009). *Report on Effect of Economic Slowdown on Employment in India*. Ministry of Labour and Employment, 01.09.

OECD (2009). "Turin Roundtable on the Impact of the Global Crisis on SME and Entrepreneurship Financing and Policy Responses", *Issues Paper.* Turin (Italy): OECD. 26.03.09. p.16.

World Bank (2007). *World Development Indicators*. World Bank.

Acknowledgement: Reproduced with permission from International Labour Organisation.

15 Stages of the Ongoing Global Financial Crisis

Is there a Wandering Asset Bubble

Lucjan T. Orlowski*

Introduction

The global financial crisis (GFC) of 2007 and 2008 is a complex and multifaceted process. Its underlying causes shall be attributed to the prevalent excess liquidity or, using the terms used by the Federal Reserve Chairman Ben Bernanke, the 'savings glut' in global financial markets, as well as to the unorderly proliferation of sub-prime mortgages in the United States (US), coupled with inadequate asset/liability and risk management practices of financial institutions. Its systemic complexity and far-reaching spillover effects into a wide-range of credit areas, global financial markets, real economy and commodity markets make this crisis seemingly more different and more multifarious than the financial crisis episodes of recent years.

Proliferation of this crisis can be explained in terms of changeable allocations of the global savings that have become increasingly illiquid.[1] As these allocations move across various types assets, they have produced varying asset bubbles. We call this process a 'wandering asset bubble'. Accordingly, this crisis has four distinctive stages. First, it has led to the housing bubble in the US that was increasingly inflated by indiscriminate mortgage loans to sub-prime and near prime (so called Alt-A) mortgage

* The author wishes to thank Halle Institute for Economic Research for sponsoring this study. He has benefitted from the feedback and discussions with participants of a special seminar on global financial instability on August 13, 2008, in particular from comments by Hubert Gabrisch and Axel Lindner. He remains solely responsible for all possible errors and omissions.

borrowers.[2] Second, it has spread into other types of assets and affected not only mortgage companies and specialised investment banks, but also universal banks. Third, it induced the global liquidity crisis accompanied by a massive pullout of liabilities from the most severely affected banks, i.e., Northern Rock and Bear Stearns and triggered anxiety about possible contagion effects on the global scale. Fourth, the collapse of structured investment products derived from the affected assets, mainly collateralised debt obligations (CDOs), shifted the global liquidity into commodity futures causing some bubble effects in this area as well.

The key factors contributing to the decline of the housing market and the sub-prime mortgages in the US are examined in Section II. The four distinctive stages of the crisis are identified in Section III. Possible theoretical explanations of the current crisis are discussed in Section IV. Interactions between different financial risk categories during the course of the crisis are analysed in Section V. Policy recommendations at the micro-level, i.e., for financial institutions are presented in Section VI. They are followed by recommendations at the macro level, i.e., for regulatory agencies and monetary authorities presented in Section VII, which also evaluates critically the actual actions of central banks aimed at containing the crisis and mitigating the resulting risks to global financial stability. Section VIII synthesises the main findings and arguments of the paper and provides suggestions for further research.

Origins of the Current Financial Crisis

The deep roots of the current crisis can be traced way back into the capital outflows from many emerging markets in the aftermath of the 1997/98 Asian and Russian financial crises and the corresponding liquidity buildup in the countries with growing current account surpluses. Although such a farsighted analysis would be reasonable, the aim of this study is to emphasise the more direct contributing factors and triggers of the current crisis.

This crisis has stemmed from an idiosyncratic combination of macroeconomic processes and micro-level institutional factors, all prevalent before the crisis outbreak in 2007. The macroeconomic contributors to the crisis include: monetary expansion in the US, large capital inflows to US securities (mainly government bonds) from high-savings countries, the US housing boom and mounting indebtedness of US households. The institutional characteristics encompass: developments of new structured finance products, emergence of hedge funds as well as other conduits and financial vehicles, and flawed credit risk assessment and asset valuation models.

The monetary expansion in the US was based on the supposition that the unprecedented productivity growth in the late 1990s and early 2000s (induced by the technological progress) was not matched by wage and costs adjustments. It was, therefore, non-inflationary. The monetary expansion contributed to high profits, is net interest margins for banks. As shown in Figure 15.1, the cost of funding for banks based on the federal funds rate was considerably below the 30-year mortgage rate at that time. With the US Federal Reserve (Fed) returning to a tighter policy stance in mid-2004, the profit margins of banks were subsequently reduced. In order to sustain long-term lending activity in the presence of the booming housing market, banks were more prone to resort to securitisation of increasingly risky mortgages.

Prior to 2006, the housing market in the US enjoyed a long period of steady expansion, which has been largely secured by new, structured financial products. Several characteristics of the US housing market boom can be highlighted. Among them is the strong increase in new privately-owned housing starts from the monthly level of 798,000 units in the beginning of 1991 to the peak of 2,273,000 in January 2006 (Figure 15.1). Concurrently, the number of new one-family houses sold rose from 401,000 in January 1991 to 1,389,000 in May 2005. Thus evidently, construction of new homes continued to grow during the May 2005-January 2006 period, but the actual purchases of new homes declined. Since their respective peak levels until June 2008, both the housing starts and the sales of new homes have dwindled to approximately by half (Figure 15.1). Similarly, the existing home sales have also declined from their monthly-average close to 7.1 million units in 2005 to 4.8 million in June 2008 (based on the National Association of Realtors data).

Further insights are derived from the analysis of the actual ratio of new housing starts to new houses sold, along with its Hodrick-Prescott trend and the cyclical component shown in Figure 15.2. The declining pattern of this ratio between 1990 and 2005 indicates a faster growth of

Figure 15.1

Total New Privately-owned, Housing Starts and New One-Family Houses Sold in the US (in '000), January 1990-June 2008 Series

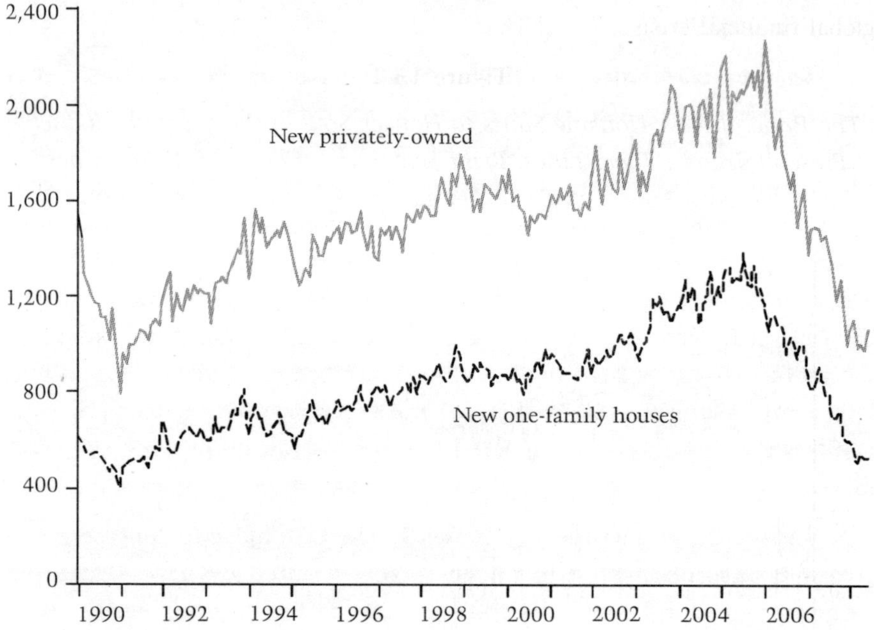

Source: Federal Reserve Bank of St.Louis–FRED.

demand for new homes relative to their supply, which contributed to the rising prices of new constructions. But the trend has been markedly reversed since 2005, implying a downward pressure on prices. The cyclical component shows increasing tendency in 2005, which stems from rising interest rates, including residential mortgage rates.

Evidently, the housing boom coincided with expansionary monetary policy of the Federal Reserve. The policymakers kept the benchmark federal funds rate at 1.0 per cent from July 2003 until July 2004, as shown in Figure 15.3. Then under the new leadership of Ben Bernanke, the Fed began a tightening cycle increasing the fed funds rate steadily to 5.25 per cent in January 2007. The benchmark rate was maintained at that level until July 2007, on the eve of the outbreak of the sub-prime mortgage crisis. Since then, the rate has been reduced to the current level of 2.0 per cent in several steps. It has become evident that the Fed created excessive liquidity during the 2001-2005 periods, which in turn became a strong contributing factor to lax lending practices of banks and the subsequent global financial crisis.

Figure 15.2

The Ratio of New Housing Starts to Houses Sold in the US with Hodrick-Prescott Trend (Upper Lines, Right Scale) and the Cyclical Component (Lower Line, Left Scale), January 1990-June 2008 Series

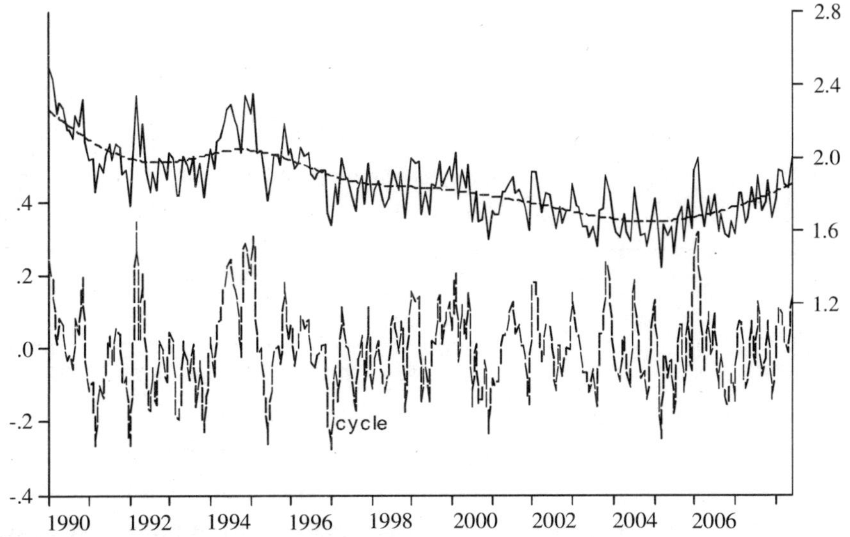

Source: Federal Reserve Bank of St.Louis–FRED.

Experiencing a very low cost of funding during the bountiful liquidity period, the financial institutions enjoyed high profit margins by generating mortgage loans, since the mortgage rates were considerably higher than the Fed funds rate, as shown in Figure 15.3. The tighter policy stance of the Fed in the following period reduced bank profits on traditional prime mortgages, i.e., those granted to borrowers with good credit, guaranteed repayments and fully-documented income. Under this scenario, the banks and mortgage brokers found very strong incentives to sustain their lending activities by reaching out to more risky borrowers with large mortgages at

Figure 15.3

The 30-Year Conventional Mortgage Rate and the Effective Federal Rate, January 1990-June 2008 Series

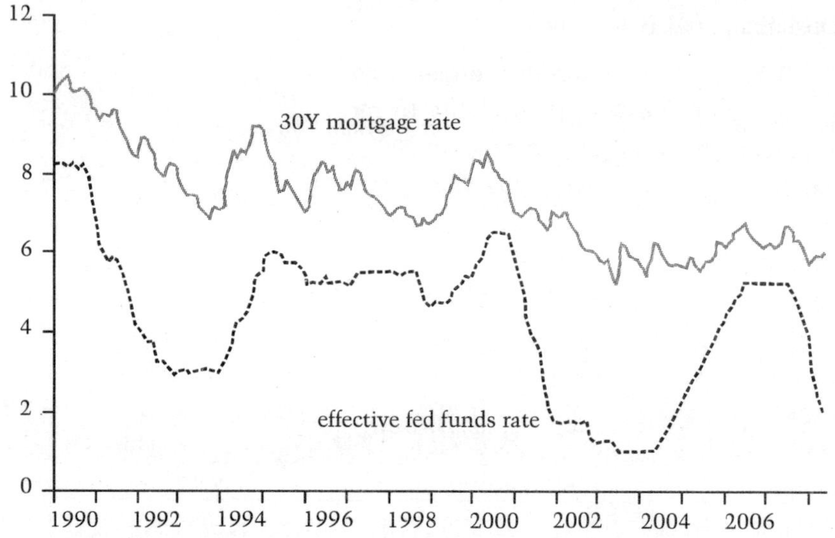

Source: Federal Reserve Bank of St. Louis–FRED.

adjustable interest rates. Mortgage brokers in a somewhat unethical manner reached out to low-income, higher-risk borrowers by offering them initially low (so called 'teaser') rates, knowing that the borrowers could no longer afford to repay their mortgages after increases in interest rates in the subsequent periods. On a widespread scale, the standard credit criteria based on maximum levels of total debt service (TDS) ratios for mortgage borrowers were extensively violated. Hence, the unprecedented expansion of high-risk non-traditional mortgage loans took place. More mortgages were extended to the least creditworthy applicants with low credit scores and uncertain income prospects, i.e., to sub-prime borrowers; as well as to the applicants who qualified for credit but were not able to document their incomes fully or to provide traditional down payments, i.e., to near-prime or, the so-called Alt-A borrowers. The share of sub-prime and Alt-A in total newly-originated securitised mortgages reached 40 per cent in 2006 while it was merely 9 per cent in 2001 (Tilton, 2007). This rush to high risk mortgage loans has been unprecedented, considering the fact that sub-prime loans constitute merely 14 per cent of total outstanding US mortgages, while the traditional prime loans prevail with 80 per cent share in total mortgages, with 6 per cent falling into the near-prime category (DiMartino and Duca, 2007).

The surge in non-prime mortgage loans was spurred by the confidence of originating banks in their ability to measure default risk accurately by employing standard quantitative models. The risk associated with these underlying securities was subsequently transferred to market investors in the form of residential mortgage-backed securities (RMBS) and their common derivatives such as CDOs.[3] These complex financial instruments have been differentiated by their riskiness and sold to market investors. They have allowed investors to choose assets with a precise risk profile. Through their applications, banks have managed to make liquid and marketable some of the underlying risky, illiquid and non-marketable assets. Their proliferation has been significant over the past several years, as shown in Figure 15.4. Quarterly issuance of global CDOs reached a peak of $186.5 billion in the first quarter of 2007. Since then, it has nearly collapsed, scoring merely $11.7 billion in the first quarter of 2008. Their total annual issuance was the highest in 2006 reaching $551.7 billion and it declined to $502.3 billion in 2007. As we have learned from the troubled banks, their risk management departments viewed CDOs as credit-risk and not market-risk instruments. Therefore, they customarily, yet incorrectly assumed that in case of market vicissitudes, CDO positions could be easily adjusted or liquidated, especially due to the fact that many of these risky derivatives were over-rated at AAA or AA levels by the rating agencies. Figure 15.4 shows also denomination of CDOs in US dollars and in euros. It is worth noting that their issuance in euros began declining already in the second quarter of 2007, that is, before the outbreak of the sub-prime mortgage crisis, while at the same time, their dollar issuance was still on the rise. At that time, the ECB demonstrated stronger commitment to containing inflation expectations that the Fed did. These different policies led to the euro appreciation against the dollar that reduced effective yield margins on euro-denominated CDOs.

Figure 15.4

Global CDO Market Issuance, Quarterly Series (2005QI-2008QI)

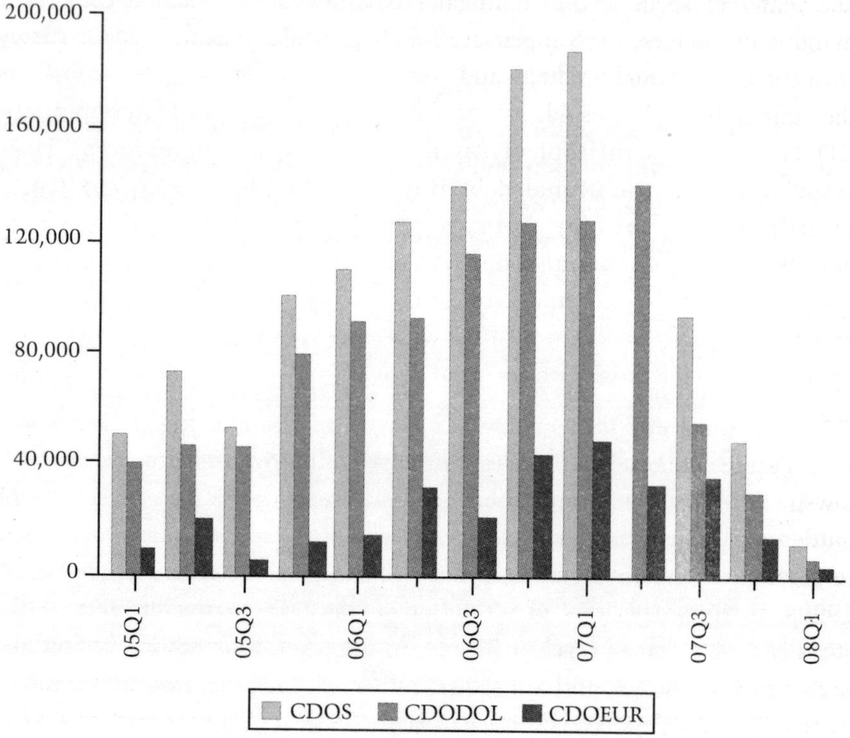

Notes: CDOS-total issuance in USD million, CDODOL-USD issues, CDOEUR- EUR issues.
Source: Securities Industry and Financial Market Association (SIFMA).

The short-lived success of CDOs was made possible due to the creation of the persistent global savings glut. International investors were eager to purchase these high-yielding structured products since yields on lower risk fixed income sureties, such as US Treasury bonds, were considerably lower. In fact, these yields were depressed by the heavy demand for the US long-term bonds in the first half of the present decade, which contributed to the inverted US Treasury yield curve. Consequently, the plentiful global liquidity in the hands of managed investment funds was reallocated into high-yielding CDOs, which initially offered savvy investors attractive returns. However, these structured products entailed significant asymmetric information. For investors, the information asymmetry was in the form of the adverse selection problem, i.e., before their purchase, investors believed in a relatively low risk embedded in their yield margins above risk-free securities, such as government bonds. In a one-year retrospect of the financial crisis, one may conclude that these margins did not nearly compensate for the *de facto* default risk associated with these structured products and stemming from the non-performance of the underlying assets, such as the sub-prime mortgages. In recent years, CDOs were a useful tool of financial innovation for reducing risks associated with traditional debt funding. They have been applied to securitisation of not only mortgages, but other debt instruments. They have been also an important source of funding for leveraged corporate buy-outs. Yet, CDOs have been oversold to market investors as indicated above, and the *de facto* risks associated with these complex derivatives with option-like characteristics have been grossly underestimated by the rating agencies.

The rising home prices along with the surge of mortgages originated to low-income borrowers and their securitisation have imposed a serious burden on US households. As shown in Figure 15.5, the share of mortgage re-payments in total household debt service was very high in the early 1990s, reaching the level of 90 per cent in 1992. Since then, it declined steadily to the lowest level of 72 per cent in 2002, but driven initially by high property values and subsequently by higher mortgage rates, it has increased to the recent levels exceeding 80 per cent. Larger and increasingly expensive mortgages are a serious contributing factor to a sharp increase in the ratio of household debt to disposable income that exceeded unity in 2001; but after the period of steady climbing, the US household debt now exceeds disposable income by one-third. These conditions have ultimately led to deterioration of household wealth. In addition, increasing interest rates in 2006 and 2007 increased failures of repayments of mortgages, thus also undermined the collateral base of CDOs. In consequence, a further growth of mortgages, property values, bank profit margins from mortgage loans and CDOs could not be rationally assumed already in 2006.

In sum, the sub-prime mortgage crisis has been an unavoidable result of a specific plot of macroeconomic conditions and microeconomic systemic failures. The macroeconomic triggers of the crisis include the global liquidity glut, the excessive liquidity created by the Fed and some other central banks and low yields on risk-free government bonds inducing

Figure 15.5

Total Outstanding Debt as a Share of Disposable Income and the Share of Mortgage Debt Service Payment in Total Debt Payment for US Households, Quartely Series (1990Q1-2008Q1)

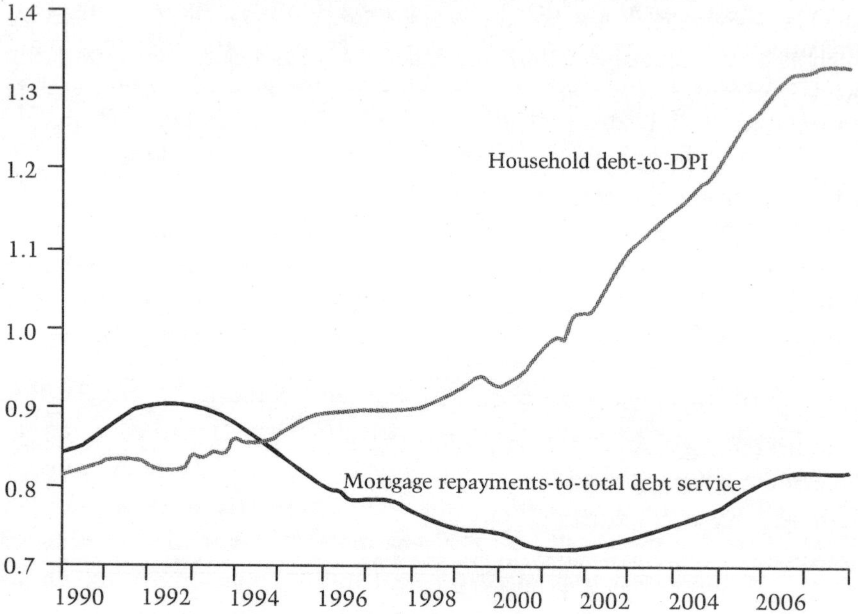

Source: Own compilation based on the Federal Reserve Board data.

attractiveness of higher yielding CDOs. The microeconomic flaws include unrecognised information asymmetry for investors in CDOs and other asset-backed securities (ABS), mistakes of the rating agencies in the assessment of risk associated with these securities, proliferation of sub-prime mortgage loans accompanied by ubiquitous violations of standard TDS safety benchmarks and, what will be discussed below, excessive leverage of banks.

Distinctive Stages of the Crisis

The macro and microeconomic triggers of the sub-prime mortgage crisis along with the systemic flaws in credit rating and risk management had to be recognised at some point. With the return of the Fed to the policy tightening cycle (see Figure 15.3), interest margins between CDOs and government securities narrowed, gradually eroding attractiveness of these derivative securities to global investors. At the same time, adjustable rate mortgages (ARM) interest rates reset higher, leading to a dramatic increase in defaults and foreclosure activity. Foreclosures on housing properties in the US rose by nearly 1.3 million in 2007, up by 79 per cent from 2006. As high as 43 per cent of the 2007 foreclosures were associated with sub-prime ARMs.

As a result, lending activity in the mortgage market fell sharply. The troubles in the housing market rippled into the wholesale markets in which banks raise short-term finance. In response, banks hoarded cash and withdrew credit from others, which elevated LIBOR rates. In essence, this was a sign of a widespread erosion of trust. Correspondingly, more expensive funds in capital markets and in some cases downgrades of financial institutions by risk rating agencies restricted the ability of conduits and structured investment vehicles (SIVs) to issue asset-backed commercial paper at short maturities.[4] These conduits and SIVs have been sponsored by investment banks. In sum, the outbreak of the sub-prime mortgage crisis lifted the LIBOR rates well-above risk-free interest rates (Figure 15.6) making some of the SIVs (for instance Cheyne or Victoria Finance) insolvent. As a result, the banks found it increasingly difficult to transfer some of their risky mortgages and mortgage-backed securities to SIVs.

In essence, tensions on the interbank lending market, thus also the intensity of the financial crisis can be best captured by the time series distribution of the spread between LIBOR and risk-free corresponding maturity government securities yields. Figure 15.6 shows a one-year series of the Treasury over Eurodollars (TED) spread captured by the difference between of three-month LIBOR over three-month US Treasury bill yields. Increasing spreads denote elevated counterparty risk or reluctance of banks to lend funds to each other. Over the one-year period displayed on the graph, the TED spread shows at least three major jumps.

The first one coincides with the outbreak of the sub-prime mortgage crisis on August 17, 2007, in response to the collapse of two hedge funds owned by Bear Stearns, which both had vast exposure to mortgage-backed securities. At the same time, three European investment funds were unable to price assets linked to sub-prime mortgages due to sudden illiquidity in these markets (DiMartino *et al.*, 2007). The funds in question froze redemptions, which induced panicky reactions in the broader markets. On August 20, 2007 the TED jumped to 240 basis points (bps)—the level that was previously experienced only during the 1987 market crash. The subsequent liquidity injection by the Fed helped reduce the TED spread to around 100 bps in October 2007. In addition, the spread was brought down by the initial write-offs by banks of losses, but on sub-prime loans only.

Figure 15.6

TED Spread (3M LIBOR minus 3M T-bill Rate), Daily Data for One-Year Period Ending August 4, 2008

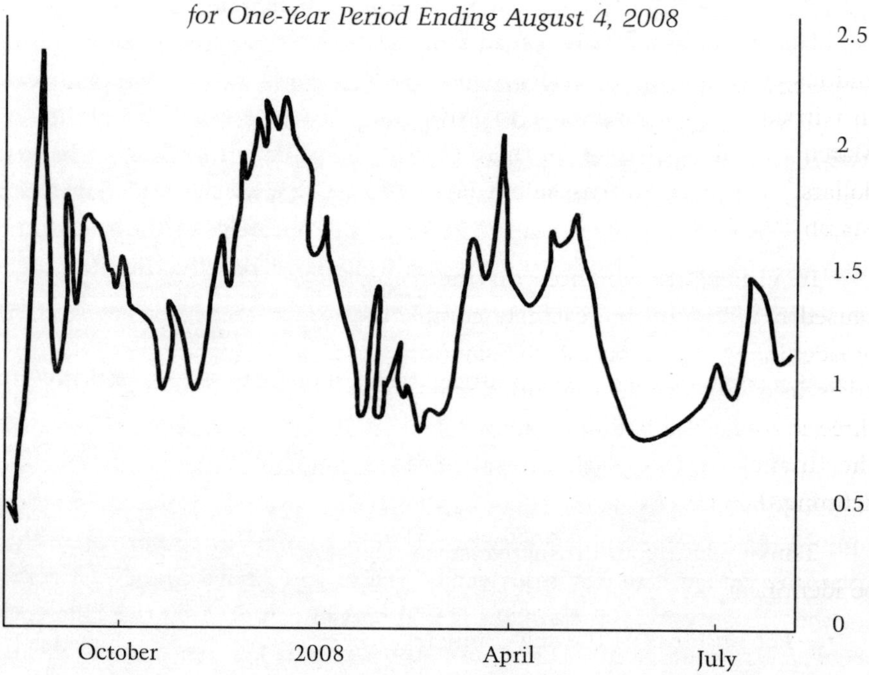

Source: Bloomberg.

The second outbreak took place in December 2007, when it became apparent that the financial crisis was spreading into other credit areas and a wide range of financial institutions. On December 11, 2007 the TED spread hit 221 bps. The steep lowering of the federal funds rate by the Fed (see Figure 15.3) during the December 2007 and February 2008 period did not halt the spreading of the crisis. It became apparent that the elevated market and credit risks were spreading over liquidity risk and the effects of this transmission were most severe at the most vulnerable institutions with vast exposure to CDOs, particularly those that failed to raise capital and reduce excessive leverage to reduce potential bank run threats. The proliferation of credit risk entailed expansion of credit default swaps (CDS) as credit risk hedging unfunded derivatives, while the funded derivates such as CDOs were declining.[5] The sharp increase in counterparty risk resulted in extensive losses of large dealers of derivatives, most notably, of Bear Stearns.

Hence, the third TED spread took off. The elevated counterparty risk and losses of derivative dealers induced severe liquidity problems at banks. In particular, they triggered a massive run on Bear Stearns' liabilities on March 13 and 14 of 2008. In these two days, its liabilities fell by 17 billion dollars.[6] The Bear Stearns fallout elevated the TED spread to 204 bps on March 19, 2008.

In hindsight, the three distinctive leaps in the TED spread were caused by different, increasingly complex factors. Their intricacy reflects broadening of the scope and the spillover effects of the sub-prime mortgage crisis into other credit categories and global financial institutions. These three idiosyncratic outbursts allow for identification of the initial stages of the financial crisis, with capital reallocation into commodity futures defining the latest stage.

Thus in sum, four distinctive stages of the ongoing financial crisis can be identified:

- The outbreak of the sub-prime mortgage crisis,
- The proliferation of credit risk, along with the broadening of losses of financial institutions,
- The eruption of liquidity risk highlighted by the run on Bear Stearns, with the spread of contagion effects on other investment banks with similar portfolio characteristics (most notably, on Lehman Brothers) and
- The commodity price bubble.

The heterogeneous roots and the complex sequence of the current crisis make it challenging to synthesise its underlying causes and global repercussions. It is, however, crucial to assume that the global savings glut persists, but allocations of global managed assets are changing in response to market signals and the dynamics of systemic risk. The overextended debt of US households (Figure 15.5) has engendered a gradual decline in real consumer spending, thus also a slowdown of the US economy and the correction of the housing market (Figures 15.1 and 15.2). At the same time, the monetary policy expansion at the late stage of Alan Greenspan era reduced the cost of funding for banks to near or even below zero in real terms. These conditions invoked indisciplined lending practices, additionally spurred by the rise in credit derivatives. Moreover, the credit derivatives were widely believed to be liquid and non-risky. Their optimistic outlook stemmed from their upbeat assessment in the IMF Global Financial Stability Reports (subsequently from 2004 until April 2007), as well as in the reports of various credit rating and supervisory agencies. In the aftermath of the outbreak of the crisis, the implicit low risk and safety of global financial markets, instruments and institutions proved to be illusive.

In such a fragile environment, assessing systemic risk and credit quality across many loan classes is fraught with difficulty for banks, credit rating agencies and investors. The asymmetric information and systemic risks associated with various asset-backed securities have proven to be more significant than previously assumed. In response, the international investors and managed-asset companies have been transferring their vast capital across various asset classes. Before 2007, residential property, mortgage-backed securities and CDOs were popular investment venues. Following the collapse of sub-prime mortgages, alternative market or 'plain-vanilla' securities were preferred. But proliferation of market risk and credit risk switched the investors' preferences into commodity futures.

These observations lead us to the argument of persistency of the 'wandering asset bubble' defined as a bubble or overvaluation of various asset classes attributable to the continuous reallocation of international liquidity. We, therefore, argue that the current credit crisis was originated by the emergence of this liquidity and its somewhat disorderly allocations across various unregulated markets and structured financial products. Until 2007, global financial markets enjoyed a subdued risk environment with falling credit spreads, low interest rates, low market volatility and the absence of defaults in credit instruments. Both the high-savings economies and the Fed contributed to the extraordinary creation of investment capital in recent years, which in turn fed the bubble wandering between credit, housing, derivatives and, more recently, commodity futures markets. In this environment, default risk has been migrating from sub-prime mortgages to credit cards, consumer loans, student loans and leveraged loans issued by private equity firms. Unfortunately, the recent liquidity injections by the Fed and other central banks aimed at rescuing, recapitalising troubled banks are likely to exacerbate the bubble problem.

The fourth stage of the crisis, i.e. the commodity futures bubble began to emerge at the beginning of 2008. After the global investors incurred huge losses on CDOs and other derivates, as well as on stocks of financial institutions, they switched some of their funds into commodity futures recognising that many of the futures markets were in a normal backwardation position.[7] This was in fact the case of a number of commodity futures markets, most notably, of the crude oil futures market. It seems that investors and speculators found strong incentives to purchase futures contracts, and their actions drove up futures prices to a high expected spot price. As a result, NYMEX oil futures prices nearly doubled from 75 dollars per barrel in the beginning of October 2007 to their peak of 147 on July 11, 2008 (Figure 15.7).[8] Since then, the oil futures markets have been in a contango situation, providing disincentives to invest in commodity futures thus contributing to declining tendency of futures prices.

Although a large portion of the commodity futures bubble seems to have been unloaded by the end of August 2008, the problem of the wandering bubble still persists as other assets might become temporarily overpriced due to a heavy investment. At this juncture, it is hard to predict which assets will be attractive for profitable investments. Regained price stability coupled with improvements in bank liquidity and credit market conditions in the US may bring some of the global financial capital back to US securities.

Figure 15.7

Light Crude Oil Futures Prices (NYMEX), One-Year Series Ending August 5, 2008

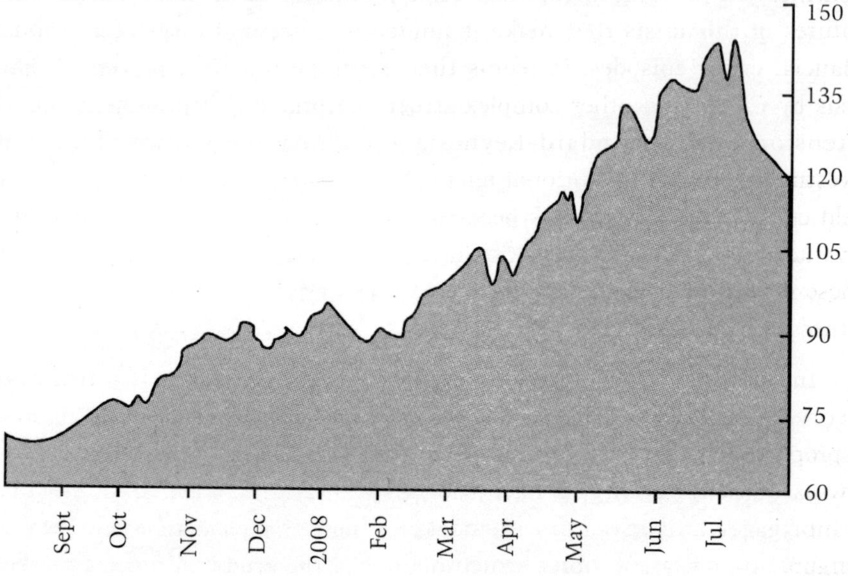

Source: Wall Street Journal Data Center.

Regardless of its actual placement among various asset classes or securities, an asset bubble always engenders excessive volatility of their prices. It can be therefore also argued that the episodes of surging capital investments lead to increasing leptokurtosis of the time series distribution of prices of the underlying securities. Therefore, under normal market conditions, volatility of prices of these securities is likely to be well-contained, but under turbulent markets such volatility will be exacerbated. If risk analysts apply assessment methods that are based on a normal instead of a leptokurtic data distribution of security prices, they are likely to seriously underestimate risk of investing in volatile securities, particularly at turbulent market times. In hindsight, the wandering bubble and the overvaluation of various types of securities have made the risk assessment methods that assume a normal data distribution highly inaccurate.

Plausible Theoretical Foundations

The analysis of the factors contributing to the current crisis allows for identification of some theoretical underpinnings that explain the special features of this crisis that make it unique in comparison to the previous financial crises episodes. It seems that the important role played in this crisis by CDOs and other complex structured financial vehicles engenders extension of the standard Keynesian liquidity preference theory of investments from its traditional reference to the term structure of the bond yield curve and the trade-offs between bonds and stocks into the liquidity advantage of these new securities in relation to 'plain-vanilla' securities.[9] These new complex securities have emerged on the scale that has not been witnessed before.

In addition to the extended application of the liquidity preference theory into new securities, a distinctive feature of this crisis is the disproportionate asymmetric information facing investors' decisions. The new asset-backed securities have widened the distance between borrowers of mortgages and investors in mortgage-backed securities. Also, yield margins on CDOs and other structured investment products over risk-free securities did not compensate for the *de facto* default risk of these esoteric securities. This has entailed a serious adverse selection problem for investors.

Moreover, investment in these new securities was accompanied by the herding behaviour of investors, whose theoretical foundations are prescribed by Scharfstein and Stein (1992). Considering the magnitude of the CDOs bubble, the scale of herding has been unprecedented. Based on scattered information from financial analysts, speculation and herding have been manifested mainly by unregulated managed funds. Their actions have escaped regulatory restrictions and statutory disclosure rules brought forth by the Sarbanes-Oxley Act of 2002.

Theoretical explanations at the early stages of the crisis focussed mainly on the timely debated about superior features of universal *versus* specialised or regional banking. As the crisis initially affected investment banks as originators of mortgage-backed securities, the universal banking model was considered to be more resilient. Among others, Buiter (2007) concludes that universal banks have a wider variety of assets than investment banks, which allows them to spread credit risk across a broader range of asset categories. More recently, however, large universal banks such as Societe Generale, UBS, ING-Barings, Wachovia, Credit Suisse and others also have shown large losses stemming from their vast exposure to risky mortgages and derivative securities. Therefore, the initially claimed merits of universal banking superiority seem rather unwarranted.

Adding to the debate generalising the roots and outcomes of this crisis, we attempt to explain it in terms of the 'wandering asset bubble'. It is, however, debatable whether the bubble is more persistent being occasionally subdued by central bank interventions in the form of liquidity injections or bailouts of financial institutions or it is more unbalanced due to disproportionate, herding behaviour of investors.

Transmission of Risks and Repercussions of the Credit Squeeze

The wandering asset bubble has generated serious distortions or dislocations in interest rates or effective yields among various money and capital market instruments. Prior to the outbreak of the crisis in August 2007, the Fed funds rate and other short-term rates were rising in relation to long-term rates (Figure 15.3), leading also to flattening of the US Treasury yield curve. At the same time, effective yields on CDOs were still outperforming US Government bond yields. With the progression of the crisis, the term spread on US treasuries has widened again and interest positive margins on CDOs have been wiped out. These changeable movements have contributed to misalignments in pricing of various types of mortgage loans. Since variable mortgage rates normally follow LIBOR or other short-to-medium bond rates, while fixed mortgage rates are priced on the basis on long-term bond yields, the linkages in pricing of different types of mortgages have been somewhat broken. This situation has exacerbated the overall credit risk since risk margins on all securities have generally risen due to their unstable and unpredictable path.

The crisis has also raised volatility of equities, thus contributed to propagation of market risk. This can be illustrated by a strong increase in market volatility VIX index.[10] Its average daily score from the beginning of

January 2007 to the end of July 2007 was 13.25, but it increased to 23.25 during the August 2007-March 2008 period. The elevated market risk has resulted in a slowdown in capital inflows to equity markets, at least in the US.

An important factor in the proliferation and transmission of risk was the securitisation of sub-prime mortgages. The new practice of assessing and securitising risk of such borrowers emerged in the first half of the current decade. The new method relied on a two-step process: assessment and pricing of credit risk and securitisation of default risk of sub-prime and Alt-A borrowers (DiMartino *et al.*, 2007). Accordingly, lenders first sorted out mortgage applicants by their creditworthiness by applying credit-scoring models (initially adopted from the auto loan market). They subsequently charged borrowers with appropriate risk-based interest. But the problem of default risk remained unresolved. At that juncture, financial innovation came to the rescue; loan repayments were divided into different risk classes, then consolidated in appropriate classes or tranches into CDOs. In hindsight, CDOs were originally devised as an effective and prudent vehicle of securitising default risk. They would probably maintain their soundness if not the overblown appetite of global investment funds for these new structured products, stemming from their attractive yield margins over US and other sovereign bonds. A rhetorical question can be asked whether their original intent unscathed by speculative investments would be preserved if the US monetary policy were tighter prior to 2005. In quintessence, CDOs were originally devised as effective default risk-mitigating vehicles.

There has been also a severe liquidity crisis sparked by the US housing market slump. The formerly-sound but now increasingly-fragile financial institutions have been hurt by a larger number and variety of underperforming assets thus by the elevated credit risk. These institutions have become vulnerable to a net drain (net cash outflow) or to a potential run on their liabilities, which are symptoms of a higher liquidity risk. They were trying to avert it by selling off some of their risky assets (to SIVs among others), by borrowing assets from other financial institutions or by raising more capital in the second half of 2007. Those with a vast exposure to CDOs found it increasingly difficult to employ these techniques. The liquidity indexes of the majority of banks were reduced by decreasing values of CDOs and the banks with the largest exposure to mortgage-backed securities were hurt the most. The explicit manifestations of the escalating liquidity risk were runs, i.e., massive liability withdrawals, on Northern Rock in the UK (Mizen, 2008) and on Bear Stearns in the US.

The impact of the ongoing crisis on the exchange rate risk is somewhat ambiguous. There is mixed evidence in support of the claim the crisis has exacerbated exchange rate risk. For instance, the average daily standard deviation of the euro in US dollar terms was 0.076 in the January 1, 2003-August 16, 2007 period. Since the outbreak of the crisis on August 17, 200, until August 6, 2008, the standard deviation actually declined to 0.069. The coefficient of variation for the same periods also fell from 0.061 to 0.046. However, the linear trend depreciation of the dollar against the euro got considerably stronger, the daily trend coefficient increased from 0.012 to 0.062 US cents per euro.[11] Thus in sum, the crisis has incited dollar depreciation, but not volatility.

On the basis of the above analysis, the earlier-identified stages of the crisis can be reconciled with the prevalent intensity of respective risks. It appears that the first stage (the outbreak of the sub-prime mortgage crisis) was accompanied by the surge in default risk. The second stage (spillovers into other credit areas) affected mainly the credit risk. The dominant risk factor during the third stage was the liquidity risk (the deepening liquidity crisis). The latest stage of the 'great escape' of capital into commodity futures might have exacerbated the exchange rate risk. In all, this crisis induced by heterogeneous factors seems to reverberate across various risk categories, which makes it particularly difficult to identify and to mitigate. However, this reasoning might be oversimplified and it needs to be tested thoroughly once complete information and data are available.

The broadening progression and the unbalanced intensity of the ongoing crisis have played a role in causal directions and the strength of interactions between various types of risks. The initial fallout of sub-prime mortgages and the downfall of CDOs denoted a surge in default risk. Spillover effects of the crisis into other asset categories exacerbated the credit risk. At the same time, widespread concerns about credit and sustainability of economic growth elevated market risk, which in turn deteriorated credit risk further. At the late stage, intensified investments in commodity futures have been accompanied by more pronounced depreciation of the US dollar and by elevated exchange rate risk. In all, the scope of proliferation of various types of risk, as well as their causal interactions have been almost impossible to ascertain and even more so to predict. Under such a mayhem, effective management of financial risk has been seriously impaired. This has posed a challenge for banks to rework their risk assessment models and management practices.

Challenges for Banks

The difficulties of banks to manage various classes of risk during the ongoing financial crisis have renewed debates over a most resilient model of banking. It seems that a universal banking model is emerging as a winner. Universal banks are those offering a wide range of commercial and investment lending activities; their balance sheets encompass diverse earnings streams and they raise funds in both wholesale and retail markets. The crisis has proven a necessity for banks to diversify sources of earnings so that losses in one area can be offset with gains in other functional areas. More specifically, the crisis has hit mainly the broker-dealer investment banks as they have operated with highly concentrated, over-leveraged balance sheets and have relied only on wholesale markets for funding. Prior to the crisis, they enjoyed extraordinary gains from asset securitisation and their own hedge fund activities, but the crisis made these areas most vulnerable. Furthermore, many investment banks moved to asset securitisation and hedge fund operation activities trying to mimic Goldman Sachs as the strongest and the most innovative of them.[12] The drive to follow the investment banking leader included Merrill Lynch—a traditional retail broker, as well as Lehman Brothers and Bear Stearns—known experts in fixed income securities. Their switch toward complex asset-backed securities has proven to be strategically unsound.

The evolution of credit derivatives and structured finance, particularly the securitisation of mortgages by Fannie Mae and Freddie Mac, have also broken the traditional 'originate and hold' model of banking (Buiter, 2007). Within the traditional scheme of operations, banks engaged in lending long and keeping their debt on their books, thus refraining from its securitisation. This new banking genre is commonly prescribed as an 'originate and distribute' scheme based on the practice of banks lending long, but instead of keeping their debt on their books, the banks structure it into new securities, thus instantaneously transfer the debt to market investors. The new model has a range of complex characteristics, some of which having a destabilising impact on financial markets and institutions (Mizen, 2008). Among them is the gap between the high risk of credit borrowers, in particular sub-prime mortgage borrowers and the perceived low risk of CDOs. Another feature is the remote distance between mortgage borrowers, dealers, banks and investors, which distorts information about the *de facto* risk of underlying assets (mortgages).

Another unanticipated result of the current crisis is the painful impact of various types of credit risk amplifiers, i.e., factors that contribute to larger *de facto* risk of certain asset categories as well as magnified losses during the periods of financial distress. These amplifiers include:

- Inability to rely on marked-to-market valuation in the presence of elevated market risk;
- Flawed algorithms for marked-to-model valuation due to increasing instability of model parameters;
- Excessive leverage and
- Unexpected increases in counterparty risk, as reflected by jumps in LIBOR rates that have an incapacitating impact on interbank credit market.

The amplifiers of gains of losses from assets pose a serious challenge for financial institutions in light of the ongoing crisis. The first of them, i.e., unreliability of marked-to-market valuation stems from a number of factors. Chief among them is non-marketability of an increasing number of assets. Progression of the financial crisis has made uncovered, or unmarketable a very large number of mortgages (not only sub-prime or Alt-A, but also prime) and mortgage-backed securities. Declining housing prices have contributed to higher debt-to-equity ratios. When this ratio exceeds unity, the mortgage borrowers face a negative equity situation, i.e., the nominal value of their mortgage being higher than the property value. When this happens, the mortgages become uncovered and the related securities are no longer marketable. They can be no longer marked-to-market, thus can be valued only on the marked-to-model basis. This process has been spread wider than previously anticipated. Increasing number of mortgage-backed securities have become unmarketable and have fallen effectively to the Level 3 asset category.

Classification of assets into three levels based on their valuation method was introduced by FAS 157 in November 2007.[13] The new standards require US banks to report assets falling into each category from the beginning of 2008. However, anticipating the new accounting rules, the major US banks began classifying and reporting their assets in this way already in 2007. The dangerous propagation of Level 3 assets is shown in Table 15.1. Based on Bloomberg estimation, the total value of Level 3 assets among US banks reached 500 billion dollars at the end of the first quarter of 2008. Such exorbitant holdings of risky, in part toxic assets cannot be easily erased, either through write-downs or especially through the Fed bailout. The Fed does not have sufficient funds available for their purchase and, candidly speaking, should not hastily and indiscriminately engage in their cleanup. To put it simply, the bankers mishaps should not be a subject to a social bailout.

Table 15.1

Ratio of Level 3 Assets to Equity

	2007 3rd Quarter	*2008 1st Quarter*
Morgan Stanley	2.51	2.35
Goldman Sachs	1.85	1.92
Lehman Brothers	1.59	1.71
Bear Stearns	1.54	3.13
Citigroup	1.05	1.17
Merrill Lynch	0.38	1.30
JP Morgan/Chase	0.30	0.58

Source: Own compilation based on Bloomberg data and bank earnings reports.

The data in Table 15.1 show that holdings of Level 3 assets are greater among the Big five investment banks than at JP Morgan/Chase--a universal bank. Their growth between third quarter of 2007 and first quarter of 2008 was the most pronounced at banks that were either unable (Bear Stearns) or unwilling (Merrill Lynch) to raise capital. As indicated above, their proliferation arises mainly from declining home values and uncovered position of mortgage-backed securities. However, according to some unofficial reports, reclassification of assets into Level 3 might have been also deliberate in order to inflate the need for potential bailouts. Bank executives might have also additional incentives to build up these assets because their return into market trading at some point in the future followed by reclassification into the Level 1 category is likely to result in special bonuses for them. Moreover, reclassification of some of the most 'toxic' assets into the Level 3 category allows hiding them, which certainly decreases banks' transparency.

In addition to non-marketability of assets, the difficulties of marked-to market valuation stem from the elevated volatility of asset prices in response to the higher market risk. Under such conditions, losses from riskier assets are amplified or augmented, which triggers a perpetual, self-reinforcing spiral of unwinding investments and a further downfall of asset prices.

If assets fall into the Level 3 category and markets are continuously volatile, management assumptions and algorithms for their valuation are imperiled. The widely used method of value-at-risk (VaR) does not really take into consideration leptokurtosis or prevalence of long-tailed distribution of risk at turbulent times. Hence the amplifying effect of VaR as periods of high volatility lift up VaR, thus send a signal to sell, which in turn exacerbates volatility further.

Perhaps the most serious amplifier of gains and losses is the excessive leverage. In general terms, a sharp decline in asset values cuts deep into equity and entails margin calls from lenders. This reaction prevails regardless of the source of high leverage, i.e., excessive liquidity, high debt, or elevated exposure to CDOs—all of which posing serious problems during the current financial crisis Excessive liquidity arises when banks rely too much on wholesale markets to borrow short-term (mainly from SIVs) and to invest in higher-yield long-term assets. Creation of debt took place prior to the outbreak of the crisis when asset prices were rising and the banks borrowed funds to take advantage of their upward trend. The vast exposure to CDOs is also a serious amplifier of losses, since it takes only a small decline in their value to escalate losses on underlying assets (Craig, 2007).

The current crisis has been in fact accompanied by a swelling leverage, as shown in Table 15.2. The asset-to-equity ratios for all Big five Wall Street investment banks increased sharply between during the 2005-2007 period. The (now-gone) Bear Stearns as well as Morgan Stanley have reached the highest ratios, while Goldman Sachs has scored its lowest, most comfortable level.[14] In all, such high leverage functions as a dangerous amplifier of losses during the period of declining asset prices and higher market risk, which makes deleveraging an urgent task for the bankers at the present time.

Table 15.2

Expanding Leverage: Asset-to-Equity Ratios

	2005	*2007*
Bear Stearns	26	33
Morgan Stanley	31	33
Lehman Brothers	25	31
Merrill Lynch	18	28
Goldman Sachs	25	27

Source: Own compilation from banks' earnings reports.

The last amplifier, i.e., unpredictable jumps in LIBOR that obfuscate counterparty risk may result in a standstill of freeze of interbank credit. This was in fact the result of the three surges in LIBOR and TED spread shown in Figure 15.6, which had an incapacitating impact on the interbank credit market and generated bank losses.

Recognising the dangers of amplified losses at the time of financial distress, the leading investment banks are now facing mounting tasks to revise their asset and liability as well as risk management strategies and tactics. Some valuable conclusions from the ongoing discussions in the international banking community on this broad topic area have been recently articulated in the July 2008 Report of the Institute of International Finance (IIF, 2008). The Report emphasises improvements in risk management as a highest priority for banks. It recommends assessing the bank's risk profile in relation to risks that are prevalent across all business activities. Other valuable suggestions for banks include not relying on a single risk methodology but using all available methods for this purpose and assigning ultimate responsibility for risk assessment with senior management. The IIF Report also emphasises the need to monitor sensitivity of providers of market liquidity to asset quality and credibility of ratings for structured vehicles—the sensitivity that has been grossly underestimated by banks during this financial crisis. The global financial Market Monitoring Group (MMG) is established by the IIF for this purpose. Ultimately, these efforts should lead to global standardisation and harmonisation of market definitions and structures. Among other valuable suggestions, the Report calls for due diligence process to ensure integrity of all stages in the originate-to-distribute banking.

A number of other micro-level institutional improvements in bank management can be derived from the current crisis. Chief among them is a more holistic approach to risk management emphasising overall balance of risks, not just the credit risk associated with individual assets. Risk management shall be viewed as a team effort thus portfolio managers shall be compensated for company-level balance of risks. Stress testing methods, i.e., an analysis of 'go-wrong' scenarios and their possible outcomes shall be employed with caution, as the crisis has proven that too many of these scenarios may be implausible under turbulent market conditions. It seems also that most of the banks will stick to 'plain-vanilla' debt securities, at least until more compelling methods of risk assessment for complex structured products are developed.

The above discussion of selected, presumably most crucial dilemmas of banks in response to the current financial crisis will likely result in major adjustment in the banking sector. Specifically, since the universal banking model has proven to be more resilient, one may expect a new wave of mergers or acquisitions of commercial banks by better-capitalised investment banks once their write-downs are completed and some of their Level 3 assets become marketable again. Moreover, the collapse of CDOs and some of the more esoteric derivatives seems to be permanent as investors have probably learned their lessons about asymmetric information and *de facto* risks embedded in these complex securities. One may also expect a better transparency of balance sheets of banks as their practice of risk transferring to SIVs will fall under the scrutiny of regulators.

Regulatory and Monetary Policy Responses: A Critical Evaluation

Valuable suggestions have emerged from the current financial crisis for regulators and monetary policymakers. It seems that the regulatory focus should be on restraining SIVs. They are in essence off balance sheet vehicles created by many major investment banks to facilitate securitisation of risky assets. SIVs are nothing more than balance sheet gimmicks that allow banks to shave off risky assets from their balance sheets, thus also to meet the regulatory minimum limits on their capital. As Buiter (2007) correctly points out, SIVs have little or no capital, no transparency and opaque governance. Without doubt, they should be a subject of a more rigorous regulatory scrutiny in terms of their minimum capital holdings and transparency (Schiller, 2008).

Even more important lessons for the regulators is the recognition of close linkages and inseparability between different types of risk. Credit, default, interest rate, liquidity, and exchange rate-risk are all integrated. Again, a more comprehensive, holistic institutional approach to risk should be promoted by regulators and required from supervised financial institutions. The crisis has shown that the models of dissecting of risk into various tranches were easier to devise in theory than to implement in practice, as they have not always adequately captured all *de facto* risks embedded in the underlying assets. A further, more integrated approach to modeling risk is crucial for advancing financial research.

The crisis seems to also underpin the importance of further elaboration and specification of capital adequacy standards. In terms of Basel II guidelines, it seems important to stick to the discipline of Pillar 1 (minimum capital requirements), while at the same time to expand the scope of both Pillar 2 (the supervisory review process) Pillar 3 (enhanced disclosure). Within Pillar 2, it seems imperative to require banks to improve internal procedures for assessing the institutional risk profile and to set up more elaborate guidelines for liquidity risk. The enhanced disclosure practices within Pillar 3 will likely require financial institutions to publish special reports on their financial stability. More work needs to be done also in the areas of developing standardised risk-assessment scorecards for individual credits, particularly mortgages, as well as standardised central clearing contracts on CDS. Along these efforts, it is imperative not to squander CDS as they are crucial for mitigating default risk.

Valuable lessons from this crisis should be drawn by monetary policy-makers. At the present time the Fed and some other central banks seem rather desperate to bail out the investment banks that have been hit hard by the crisis. However, as argued above, credit risk at specialised banks tends to follow a leptokurtic, long-tailed time distribution. Hence, investment banks that are over-leveraged and rely heavily on wholesale funding are experiencing amplified losses. Yet, their gains will be probably magnified at better market periods as well. If these banks are bailed out at hard times, does it also mean that their profits should be taxed more at good times? Both of these extreme solutions are unwarranted. In principle, there might be some legitimacy for a government to preserve one of the largest institutions in the country's banking system, since the collapse of one may drag down others as well. It is because large partner banks are entangled through various interest rate swap contracts. However, such bailouts shall be exercise with caution and implemented preferably through a fiscal stimulus, not through cash injections from a central bank. Vast liquidity injections are likely to hamper price stability thus subsequently hurt central bank's credibility. They also provide implicit guarantees for high-risk operations of banks in the future.

Instead of rectifying strategic mistakes of investment banks through liquidity infusions, the Fed and other central banks will be well-advised to direct their tactical efforts toward managing the 'wandering bubble' i.e., the liquidity glut, so that capital inflows to specific securities will not endanger price stability and will not hinder economic growth.

One shall assume that the bubble is here to stay, it cannot be bursted with taxes or other restrictions on capital inflows—it is simply too large. A prudent mix of regulations and monetary policy strategies can channel this capital into productive investments without inflationary consequences and harmful effects on real economy.[15]

Once the bank recapitalisation is over, it seems prudent to reinforce commitment of the Fed and other central banks to flexible, forward-looking inflation targetting. Flexible, in the sense of avoiding a radical, exclusive commitment to hitting the inflation target only, without consideration of alternative goals, such as growth in real national income and employment or exchange rate stability. The forward-looking or forecast-based approach to inflation targetting allows for smoothing nominal indexation (Svensson, 1999; Woodford, 2007). It is, therefore, likely to reduce volatility or risks associated with key policy variables, such as exchange rates, interest rates or inflation forecasts. Emerging market economies or in particular, the recently admitted EU members undergoing convergence to the euro, cannot target domestic inflation forecasts only. They will be well-advised to target differentials between domestic and the key underlying currency area, i.e., the Euro zone, inflation forecasts. Such policy framework for the euro-candidates is proposed by Orlowski (2008b) and prescribed as 'relative inflation-forecast targetting'. Incorporating the stable currency area's inflation forecast variable in the converging economy's central bank target or reaction function will likely result in absorption of lower market risk and inflation risk environment in these open, intrinsically volatile economies.

A crucial for a successful implementation of inflation targetting is the appropriate choice of the inflation target. It seems prudent for all central banks to specify the target in terms of headline, rather than core inflation. The late stage of the current crisis, i.e., capital inflows to commodity futures, has led to the wider gap between headline and core inflation (Orlowski, 2008a). The wider gap for the US is shown in Figure 15.8. Headline inflation seems to be a bigger problem at the present time and it is likely to pass-through onto other measures of inflation in the near future. However, the Fed tried to enact an implicit target for core inflation based on personal consumption expenditures (PCE). Chairman Bernanke in his February 17, 2007, Congressional Testimony disclosed the core PCE inflation target for the end of June 2008 in the range of 1.75-2.00 per cent. But large liquidity injections in response to the current financial crisis have curtailed the Fed plans for embracing inflation targetting. However, if such policy plans are restored in the future, headline rather than core inflation should be a basis for specification of inflation targets. After all, nominal indexation of wages, prices and interest rates is routinely adjusted to headline rather than core inflation.

Notes

1. The size of global savings is best captured by the total value of international managed assets companies (pension funds, mutual funds, insurance funds, official reserves, sovereign wealth funds, hedge funds and private equity) estimated by the International Monetary Fund (IMF) to have reached $76 trillion at the end of 2007. Total liquidity attributable to unregulated, more risk-prone sovereign wealth funds, hedge funds and private equity reached $9 trillion, the allocations of which are most prone to go with the flow.
2. Sub-prime mortgage borrowers are the least creditworthy applicants with low credit scores and uncertain income prospects, near-prime are those who qualify for credit but are unable to document their income fully or to provide traditional down payments.
3. In their abbreviated definition, CDOs are structured credit products backed by pools of other assets, with cash flows assigned to varying credit risk tranches: senior AAA-rated, mezzanine AA to BB-rated, and equity (unrated) tranche. Cash flows are going first to the lowest risk tranche. In exchange for purchasing CDOs, third-party investors receive a claim on the mortgage asset and related cash flows, which becomes collateral in the case of default. Forms of CDOs include: a cashflow CDO where underlying credit risks are bonds or loans held by the issuer, a synthetic CDO with the exposure to risk insured by the credit default swap (CDS), and CDOs-squared where each underlying risk is itself a CDO tranche.
4. SIVs are funds that borrow money typically by issuing commercial paper at rates close to LIBOR and lend this money to banks by buying bonds at higher interest rates. The bonds purchased by SIVs include securities backed by mortgage, credit cards and other credit instruments. If values of long-term securities bought by SIVs fall below the values of short-term securities sold by them, their solvency is at risk.
5. The total notional value of CDS increased from 10 trillion dollars in June 2005 to 62 trillion at the end of 2007.
6. The key contributors to the run on Bear Stearns included: renaissance technologies corp.—a hedge fund that withdrew 5 billion dollars of cash, Rabobank and ING—each of them pulled out 500 million of loan commitments.
7. 'Normal backwardation' in futures markets takes place when the expected spot price is above the futures price. Recognising that the futures price must converge to the expected spot price, speculators take 'net long' positions anticipating the futures price to increase. The adverse situation are 'contango' markets, where the expected spot price is below the futures price. In this case, speculators find incentives to sell futures, thus bringing their prices down to the expected spot price.
8. Valuable insights on the current escalation in expected spot prices of crude oil are provided by Brown *et al.* (2008). They attribute this increase to escalating demand expectations and to the US dollar depreciation. In addition, Stevans and Sessions (2008) show empirically that the real price of oil today is strongly determined by long-term futures contracts that are inherently speculative
9. 'Plain-vanilla' securities are those based on guaranteed reimbursement of the principal with the return not linked to derivatives.
10. VIX–Chicago Board Options Exchange volatility index is an implied 30-day forward volatility of S&P 500 index options. In general terms, it measures market expectations of volatility for the next one-month period.

11. Own calculations based on Bundesbank data.

12. It is not surprising that Goldman Sachs has weathered the current crisis more effectively than its competitors. It has a better liquidity and debt-maturity position than the others. At the end of the second quarter of 2008, it held 90 billion dollars of cash and liquid assets and its debt had an average maturity of eight years.

13. According to FAS 157, assets in Level 1 are those that have observable market prices, thus can be marked-to-market. Level 2 are assets that are not marketable and are marked-to-model with observable inputs (for instance, interest rate swaps which components are linked to observable yields on Treasuries). Level 3 are non-marketable assets that are marked-to-model with unobservable inputs. Their valuation is based on arbitrary management assumptions. Not only mortgage-related assets, but also other complex derivatives, credit card receivables, loans linked to leverage buyouts and asset-backed commercial paper fall into the Level 3 category.

14. The highly leveraged balance sheet was the key factor contributing to the loss of investors' confidence and to the run on Bear Stearns in March 2008. At the end of November 2007, the company had 28 billion dollars of Level 3 assets in comparison to its 12 billion equity. Both the large exposure to CDOs and the failure to raise capital since the collapse of two of its hedge funds in August 2007 contributed to Bear's excessive leverage.

15. Tong and Wei (2008) show empirically the scope and the transmission of harmful spillover effects of the current crisis into the real economy. These negative effects are transmitted through two channels: the declining real consumer demand and, more importantly, the liquidity constraint on non financial firms.

References

Brown, S.P.A., R. Virmani and R. Alm (2008). "Crude Awakening: Behind the Surge in Oil Prices", *Federal Reserve Bank of Dallas–Economic Letter* 3(5), May.

Buiter, W.H. (2007). "Lessons from the 2007 Financial Crisis", *CEPR Discussion Paper* No. DP6596, December.

Craig, J. (2007). *Financial Market Instability: A Many Sided Story*. Brisbane, Australia: Center for Policy and Development Systems, September.

DiMartino, D. and J.V. Duca (2007). "The Rise and Fall of Sub-prime Mortgages", *Federal Reserve Bank of Dallas–Economic Letter* 2(11), November.

DiMartino, D., J.V. Duca and H. Rosenblum (2007). "From Complacency to Crisis: Financial Risk-taking in the early 21st Century", *Federal Reserve Bank of Dallas–Economic Letter* 2(12), December.

Institute of International Finance (IIF) (2008). *Final Report of the IIF Committee on Market Best Practices: Principles of Conduct and Best Practice Recommendations*. IIF, July.

Mizen, P. (2008). "The Recent Credit Crunch", Paper to the 25th Symposium on *Money, Banking and Finance*. Luxembourg, University of Luxembourg. June 18-20.

Orlowski, L.T. (2008a). "Recent Turmoil in Financial Markets: Sources and Systemic Remedies", *E-brief* No. 4. Warsaw. Center for Economic and Social Research CASE.

———. (2008b). "Relative Inflation-Forecast as Monetary Policy Target for Convergence to the Euro", *Journal of Policy Modeling* (forthcoming).

Scharfstein, D.S. and J.C. Stein (1992). "Herd on the Street: Informational Inefficiencies in a Market with Short-term Speculation", *Journal of Finance* 47(4): 1461-84.

Schiller, R.J. (2008). *The Sub-prime Solution: How Today's Global Financial Crisis happened and what to do about it*. Princeton University Press. September.

Stevans, L. and D. Sessions (2008). "Speculation, Futures Prices and the US Real Price of Crude Oil", *Munich Personal RePEc Archive Paper* No. 9456.

Svensson, L.E.O. (1999). "Inflation Targeting as a Monetary Policy Rule", *Journal of Monetary Economics* 43(3): 607-654.

Tilton, A. (2007). "The Sub-prime Slump and the Housing Market", Goldman Sachs, February 23, pp. 4-6.

Tong, H. and S.J. Wei (2008). "Real Effects of the Sub-prime Mortgage Crisis: Is it a Demand or a Finance Shock?", *International Monetary Fund–Working Paper* No. WP/08/186.

Woodford, M. (2007). "The Case for Forecast Targeting as a Monetary Policy Strategy", *Journal of Economic Perspectives* 21(4): 3-24.

16 The Potential Impact of the Global Financial Crisis on World Trade

Warwick J. McKibbin and
Andrew Stoeckel

What this Study is About?

The September 2008 collapse of Lehman Brothers, a mid-size 'Wall Street' investment bank, sent a wave of fear around world financial markets. Banks virtually stopped lending to each other. The risk premium on interbank borrowing shot up to 5 per cent, whereas typically it was close to zero. Although authorities scrambled to inject liquidity into financial markets, the damage was done. The risk premium on corporate bonds shot up even more to over 6 per cent. Large capital expenditure (CAPEX) projects were shelved, the corporate sector virtually stopped borrowing, trade credit was hard to get and, with falling demand, particularly for investment goods and manufacturing durables like cars, trade volumes collapsed.

The result is that the global financial crisis (GFC) has seen the largest and the sharpest drop in global economic activity of the modern era. In 2009, most major developed economies found themselves in a deep recession. The fallout for global trade, both for volumes and the pattern of trade has been dramatic. The Organisation for Economic Co-operation and Development (OECD) predicts that world trade volumes could shrink by 13 per cent in 2009 from 2008 levels.[1]

The contraction in trade has several interrelated causes comprising both price and income effects as global financial flows readjust, real exchange rates realign, terms of trade change and domestic savings rise with a concomitant drop in domestic demand. That is, financial problems have had devastating real effects. Each of these effects reverberates around the world, some compounding and some offsetting each other.

Governments have responded with an easing of monetary and fiscal policy that in turn have their own effects on activity and financial and trade flows. The downturn in activity is causing unemployment to rise sharply and, with it, a political response to protect domestic industries through various combinations of domestic subsidies and border protection. There is potential for protectionism to rise further.

Both the causes of the crisis and the policy responses are reshaping the level and pattern of world trade. The objective of this study is to disentangle the various direct and indirect effects of the crisis on international trade and how events might unravel. To do this, a dynamic, intertemporal general equilibrium model that fully integrates the financial and real sectors of the economy is used to unravel and understand the mechanisms at work. The model incorporates wealth effects, expectations and financial markets for bonds, equities and foreign exchange as well as trade and financial flows. It is a suitable tool to analyse the impact of the crisis and policy responses on global trade and financial flows.

The paper is organised as follows. In Section II, the main linkages and mechanisms by which the financial crisis affects trade is given. This is necessary on two counts: it sets up the modelling approach and it also serves as a basis for developing the shocks to be imposed on the model that represent the financial crisis. The main features of the G-Cubed model that is used in this analysis are described briefly as the model is documented in full elsewhere.

In Section III, the simulations to represent the financial crisis are described and the justification for the size of the shocks chosen. It turns out six shocks which are needed: three for the crisis itself and three for the subsequent policy responses which cover monetary and fiscal stimulus as well as the trade protectionism that has emerged.

Results are then discussed in two separate parts to disentangle the various macroeconomic influences on world economies including trade. In Section IV, the effects of the crisis on world economies without the fiscal policy responses, that is the first three simulations, are described. Then in

Section V, the results from the three policy responses are described on their own to gauge their relative impacts. Finally, in Section VI, some of the main insights are highlighted and discussed.

How the Financial Crisis has Affected Trade Outcomes

The Mechanisms at Work

The financial crisis has affected trade outcomes through several channels, some obvious, some less so. One obvious one is the slowdown in demand both by business and households. As households spend less, imports will fall and hence someone else's exports will fall. But other effects are more complicated as set out in Figure 16.1.

A financial crisis causes a sharp reappraisal of risk by households and business. With any loss of confidence, banks are no longer happy to lend at the same rates as before, if they lend at all. Trade credit under these circumstances is harder to come by. Such upward reappraisals of risk cause the cost of capital to rise and, with widespread uncertainty, countries become reluctant to lend to other countries. Therefore, capital flows shrink and this means current account deficits and surpluses will contract. Such changes in current account balances affect trade balances and hence exports and imports. Facilitating all these adjustments will be changes in real exchange rates that affects the relative price of tradeables and non-tradeables and hence the supply and demand of exports and imports.

Falling output, trade and employment leads to unpleasant social consequences and so causes policymakers to counteract the effects and stimulate the economy. There are three ways in which policymakers look after their constituents. One is to ease monetary policy. Another is to stimulate domestic demand through expansionary fiscal policy. This can occur through handouts to households via tax breaks or direct payments, by extra government spending, often on infrastructure, or subsidies to producers, such as car makers. Extra spending by governments means extra borrowing in the first instance and this affects capital flows and trade once again. The third way is where governments sometimes choose to 'look after their own' by protection: either by overt border measures such as tariff increases or more subtle ones such as 'buy local' programmes. Financial protection, for example where banks or firms are directed to lend at home, can also occur. Financial protection will affect relative rates of return and hence capital flows and trade.

All of the above mechanisms affect trade. Some will compound each other, others will be offsetting. The only way to understand some of the key drivers is by the use of a model as set out below:

Figure 16.1

The Main Mechanisms Affecting Trade Outcomes

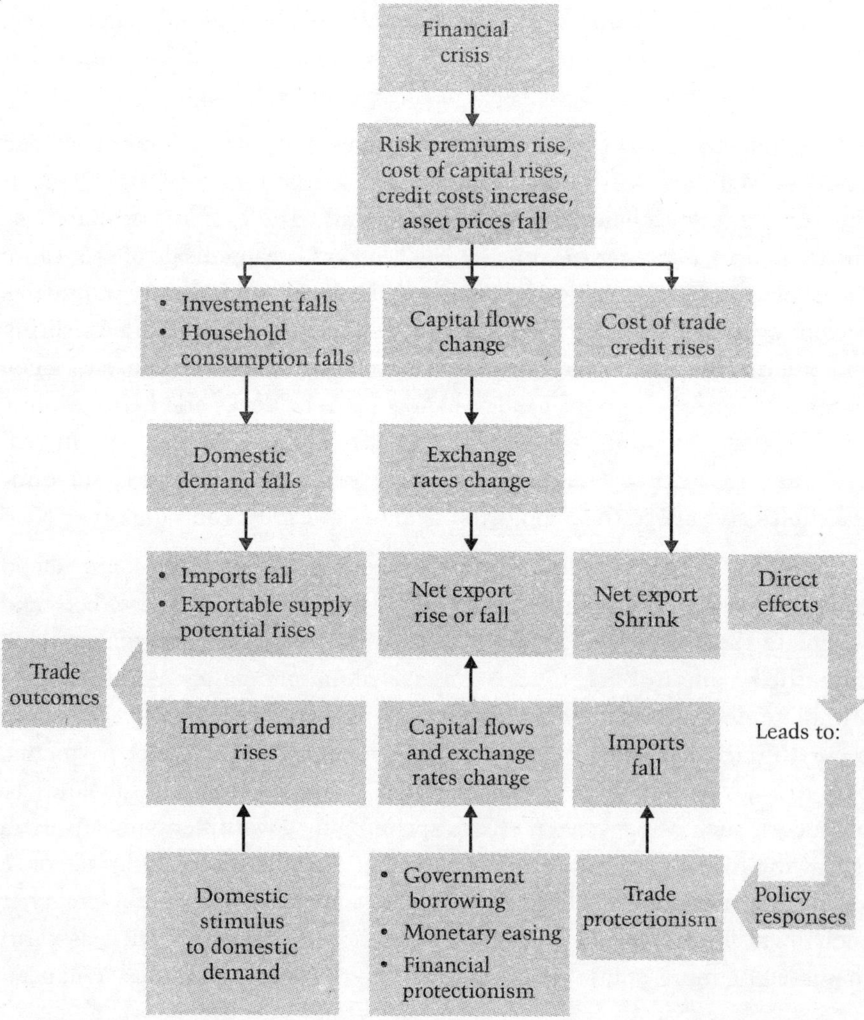

The Model

The G-Cubed model is an intertemporal general equilibrium model of the world economy. The theoretical structure is outlined in McKibbin and Wilcoxen (1998).[2] A number of studies—summarised in McKibbin and Vines (2000)—show that the G-Cubed modelling approach has been useful in assessing a range of issues across a number of countries since the mid-1980s.[3] Some of the principal features of the model are as follows:

- The model is based on explicit intertemporal optimisation by the agents (consumers and firms) in each economy (Blanchard and Fischer, 1989; Obstfeld and Rogoff, 1996). In contrast to static CGE models, time and dynamics are of fundamental importance in the G-Cubed model. The MSG-Cubed model is known as a dynamic stochastic general equilibrium (DSGE) model in the macroeconomics literature and a dynamic intertemporal general equilibrium (DIGE) model in the computable general equilibrium literature.
- In order to track the macro time series, the behaviour of agents is modified to allow for short-run deviations from optimal behaviour either due to myopia or to restrictions on the ability of households and firms to borrow at the risk-free bond rate on government debt. For both households and firms, deviations from inter-temporal optimising behaviour take the form of rules-of-thumb, which are consistent with an optimising agent that does not update predictions based on new information about future events. These rules-of-thumb are chosen to generate the same steady state behaviour as optimising agents so that in the long run there is only a single intertemporal optimising equilibrium of the model. In the short run, actual behaviour is assumed to be a weighted average of the optimising and the rule-of-thumb assumptions. Thus, aggregate consumption is a weighted average of consumption-based on wealth (current asset valuation and expected future after tax labour income) and consumption based on current disposable income. Similarly, aggregate investment is a weighted average of investment based on Tobin's q (a market valuation of the expected future change in the marginal product of capital relative to the cost) and investment based on a backward looking version of Q.

- There is an explicit treatment of the holding of financial assets, including money. Money is introduced into the model through a restriction that households require money to purchase goods.
- The model also allows for short-run nominal wage rigidity (by different degrees in different countries) and, therefore, allows for significant periods of unemployment depending on the labour market institutions in each country. This assumption, when taken together with the explicit role for money, is what gives the model its 'macroeconomic' characteristics. (Here again the model's assumptions differ from the standard market clearing assumption in most CGE models.)
- The model distinguishes between the stickiness of physical capital within sectors and within countries and the flexibility of financial capital, which immediately flows to where expected returns are highest. This important distinction leads to a critical difference between the quantity of physical capital that is available at any time to produce goods and services, and the valuation of that capital as a result of decisions about the allocation of financial capital.

As a result of this structure, the G-Cubed model contains rich dynamic behaviour, driven on the one hand by asset accumulation and, on the other, by wage adjustment to a neoclassical steady state. It embodies a wide range of assumptions about individual behaviour and empirical regularities in a general equilibrium framework. The interdependencies are solved out using a computer algorithm that solves for the rational expectations equilibrium of the global economy. It is important to stress that the term 'general equilibrium' is used to signify that as many interactions as possible are captured, not that all economies are in a full market clearing equilibrium at each point in time. Although it is assumed that market forces eventually drive the world economy to neoclassical steady state growth equilibrium, unemployment does emerge for long periods due to wage stickiness, to an extent that differs between countries due to differences in labour market institutions.

In the version of the model used here there are 6 sectors (energy, mining, agriculture, manufacturing durables, manufacturing non-durables and services) and 15 countries/regions as set out in Table 16.1.

Table 16.1

Countries/Regions

The US	China
Japan	India
The United Kingdom	Other Asia
Germany	Latin America
The Euro Area	Other LDC
Canada	East Europe & Former Soviet Union
Australia	OPEC
Rest of OECD	

Simulating the Effects of the Crisis

Events Leading up to the Crisis in 2008: The Baseline

The focus of this study is on disentangling the many influences of the financial crisis on trade outcomes. The 'crisis' is defined here as the bursting of the housing market bubble in late 2007, the ensuing collapse in the sub-prime mortgage market and related financial markets and the subsequent collapse of Lehman Brothers in 2008 which resulted in a sharp increase in risk premia around the world. The effect of the financial crisis on global trade is, therefore, the difference between a world where there was no crisis and one where there is. That is, to assess the effects of the crisis on trade, a baseline, or 'business as usual', view of a world without a crisis has to be produced.

There are two aspects to this baseline. One, is the exogeneous productivity and population trends going forward and the other is the underlying imbalances brewing in the world economy prior to the financial crisis itself. We assume that tax rates and the shares of government spending devoted to each commodity remain unchanged. In the G-Cubed model, projections are usually made based on a range of input assumptions. There are two key inputs into the growth rate of each sector in the model. The first is the economy-wide population projection which differs by country according to the UN mid-projection. The second is the sectoral productivity growth rates. How the sectoral productivity growth rates are calculated is detailed in Appendix A-16.1. In the long run, we take the underlying long-run rate of world population growth plus productivity growth to be 1.8 per cent per annum, and take the long-run real interest rate to be 4 per cent.

The second aspect of a baseline is some of the prior events to the crisis. The problem is that some of the seeds of the financial crisis were sown in the decade before the crisis. A series of large global events, such as the bursting of the dotcom bubble in 2001 and the rapid growth of China, were already reshaping the pattern and level of world trade before the 2007-2008 financial crisis hit. Some of these events, like the large disparities between savings and investment in China (a surplus) and in the US (a deficit) led to large differences between exports and imports for each nation so that large current account surpluses were accumulating in China and large deficits in America. Some people (Corden, 2009; Wolf, 2008) attribute these growing global imbalances as contributing causes of the crisis and there is some truth in that. But the focus of this study is on the impact of the crisis itself on world trade and not on trying to disentangle the various contributing factors to the crisis, as important as that issue is.

Therefore, besides population and productivity trends shaping the baseline for the world, some of the key events over the last decade influencing the baseline would be:

- First, there was the Asian financial crisis of 1997-98, which saw Asian economies generate large current account surpluses that had to be invested offshore to keep their nominal exchange rates low. Capital flowed out of Asia into the US dotcom stocks driving up equity prices.
- Next was the bursting of the dotcom bubble, which saw the booming NASDAQ over 1998–2000 burst in 2001.
- Fearing a downturn and possible deflation, the US Federal Reserve eased monetary policy in 2001 in a series of steps to 2004. Some argue that they eased too much for too long (See Taylor, 2008).
- But, with easy credit and a rising housing market, a boom in house prices followed and a period of high growth in credit and leveraged loans. Risk premia hit low levels and leveraged deals became common as investors chased yields in an environment of lax regulatory oversight.

- Rising demands from China (and, to some extent, India), plus a booming world economy saw commodity prices rise across oil, minerals and food from late 2004 to late 2007. The shock to the global economy from this commodity price boom was as big as the first oil shock in the 1970s.
- Rising prices and inflation caused monetary authorities to tighten policy from mid-2004 to June 2006.

Each of these major events set up their own dynamics for the course of the world economy and helped shape the underlying baseline. Some of these events such as the easing and tightening of monetary policy are endogeneous to the model and already incorporated in the baseline. It is important to appreciate that the results reported here are deviations from baseline from the financial crisis, as defined here. What is important is the relative contribution of different effects and to disentangle the impacts of the financial crisis on trade outcomes.

The Six Shocks to Represent the Crisis and the Policy Responses

The above events have led to the now well-known global downturn. All official forecasting agencies, such as the International Monetary Fund (IMF) and the Organisation for Economic Co-operation and Development (OECD), have described this downturn and so will not be expanded here. As the IMF (2009) notes 'Global Gross Domestic Product (GDP) is estimated to have fallen by an unprecedented 5 per cent in the fourth quarter (annualized), led by advanced economies, which contracted by around 7 per cent'. Japan has been particularly hard hit with a fourth quarter GDP (2008) plummeting by 13 per cent. Demand for durable goods has been particularly hard hit. With the downturn there has been a sharp upturn in savings by households (and commensurate reduction in consumption), driven by a reappraisal of risk by households and a loss of net worth with falling house prices and equity prices. So shocks need to be devised to account for three things:

- The bursting of the housing bubble and loss in asset prices and household wealth with consumers cutting back on spending and lifting savings.

- A sharp reappraisal of risk with a spike in bond spreads on corporate loans and interbank lending rates with the cost of credit, including trade credit, rising with a commensurate collapse of stock markets around the world.
- A massive policy response including a monetary policy easing, bailouts of financial institutions and fiscal stimulus. Also, signs of emerging trade and financial protectionism appear.

These three outcomes can be represented by six shocks—three for the crisis itself and three for the policy response.

Three main shocks capture the onset of the global financial crisis:

1. The bursting of the housing bubble causing a reallocation of capital and a loss of household wealth and drop in consumption.
2. A sharp rise in the equity risk premium (the risk premium of equities over bonds) causing the cost of capital to rise, private investment to fall and demand for durable goods to collapse.
3. A reappraisal of risk by households causing them to discount their future labour income and increase savings and decrease consumption.

Shock 1: The Bursting of the Housing Bubble

Falling house prices had a major effect on household wealth, spending and defaults on loans held by financial institutions. Events in the US typify a global phenomenon. From 2000 to 2006, house prices in some areas doubled to subsequently collapse (Figure 16.2). These changes in some areas have generated dramatic news headlines but, overall the US index of house prices has fallen by 6.2 per cent in real terms from the first quarter 2008 to the same quarter in 2009.[4]

While house prices were rising so strongly, credit was supplied liberally to meet the demand as perceptions of risk fell. The rising wealth boosted confidence and spending. The housing bubble was a global phenomenon centred mainly in the Anglo-Saxon world.

The housing bubble was the result of a long period of low interest rates by the US Federal Reserve. The Federal Reserve cut interest rates by a total of 550 basis points in a series of steps between 2001 and 2004. The

Figure 16.2

US House Prices Relative to Per Capita Household Income

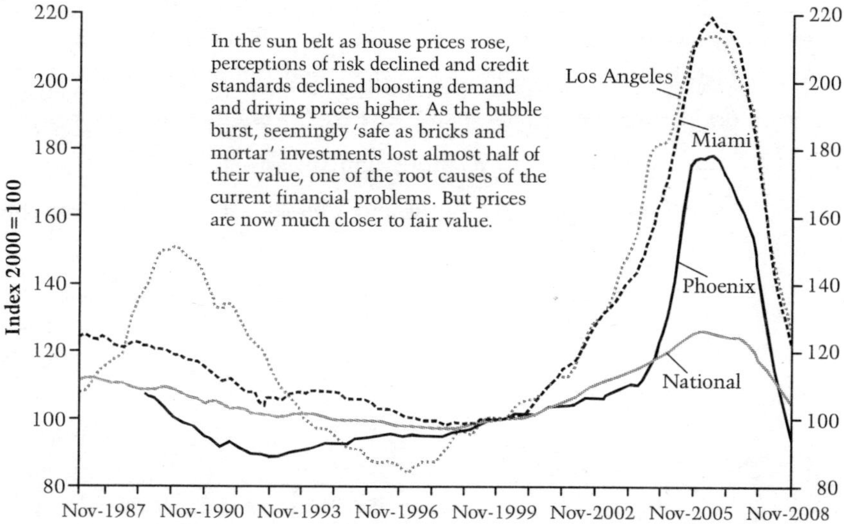

Notes: Series shown are house prices over per capita household income. For comparison series are indexed to a common base 2000=100. Individual cities are from the S&P Case Schiller index. National prices are from the OFHEO. OFHEO data has a complete coverage of the US while the Case Schiller index only covers the largest 20 cities. OFHEO and Case Schiller data for individual cities indicate similar movements – i.e. differences in the series largely reflect the coverage differences. (The widely reported Case Schiller index shows much larger falls than the OFHEO index.)

Source: Standard and Poors, Office of Housing Enterprise Oversight, *OECD Economic Outlook Database*.

easing, subsequent tightening and current easing are shown in Figure 16.2. Some believe (for example the 'Austrian school' and Taylor, 2008: 2), that monetary policy was too loose for too long and this is what gave rise to the asset price bubble and commodity price spike. Taylor argues that had the Federal Reserve followed the Taylor rule (actually the Henderson-McKibbin-Taylor rule), interest rates would have risen much sooner and the bubbles would not have appeared to the same extent (Figure 16.2).

The low interest rates were due to fears of deflation (Greenspan, 2007) and led to a boom in US housing, low interest rates were not just the result of the Fed's actions. US bond yields were also low because of low world rates (with Japanese bond yields at a little over 1 per cent and short-term interest rates at zero). There was also an international aspect to low US interest rates with Japan and Europe only recovering very slowly from the 2000-01 downturn and in turn placing pressure on the US to keep interest rates low. In Japan there were fears of re-emergent deflation. That is the principal reason why interest rates were kept low in the US for an unusually long term—until mid-2004 when the Fed began a very sharp tightening cycle.[5] The low interest rates through 2003-04—besides fuelling a boom in bank lending, rising asset prices and rising demand in China and other developing countries—also fuelled a commodity price boom.

Figure 16.3

Federal Funds Rate Actual and Counterfactual

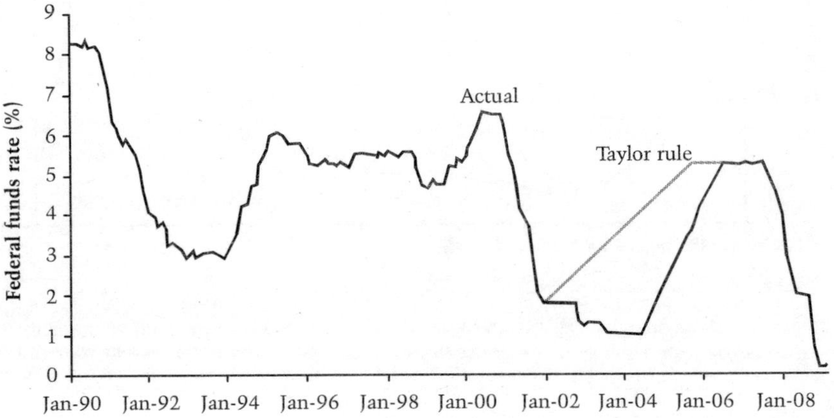

Note: The daily effective federal funds rate is a weighted average of rates on brokered trades. Weekly figures are averages of 7 calendar days ending on Wednesday of the current week; monthly figures include each calendar day in the month. Annualised using a 360-day year or bank interest.

Source: US Federal Reserve Statistical Release, *http://www.federalreserve.gov/releases/h15/data/Monthly/H15_FF_O.txt*, Accessed 5 March 2009.

However, only a part of the dwelling boom and the commodity boom can be attributed to the actions of the Fed. The up-trend in US house prices was evident as early as 2000. As small investors abandoned the stock market in 2001, they dived into the housing market, driving up and sustaining the price rises. Similarly, the surge in commodity prices through 2005 to 2008, which took most analysts by surprise, had as much to do with developments in China, and the lagged response of supply, as they did with an increase in demand in North America. Where the real problem lay was in the combination of the two.

The bursting of the housing bubble is modelled as a surprise fall in the expected flow of services from housing investment—larger in the US, the

UK and Europe but still significant throughout the world. In the model, the household in each economy is modelled as solving an intertemporal consumption problem subject to an intertemporal budget constraint. The result is a time profile for the consumer in each country of consumption of goods from all countries based on expected future income and expected relative goods prices. The household also chooses investment in a capital good. The household capital stock combines housing and other durable goods. For simplicity of exposition we will refer to this capital good as 'housing' from here on.

The investment decision by households is modelled analogously to how we model the investment decisions of firms within an intertemporal framework subject to adjustment costs for capital accumulation. The household invests in housing to maximise consumption from the stream of future service flows that housing provides. This stream of services is analogous to a production function based on inputs of capital and a productivity term. We model the housing part of the crisis as a fall in the productivity of the service flow from the housing stock. This fall in expected future productivity of housing means that the Tobin's q for housing drops when the shock occurs. The drop in housing productivity in the US is assumed to be 10 per cent lower in 2009 and is calibrated to give, along with the other shocks, a drop in house prices in the US of the order of 6 per cent, roughly what has been observed for the last year.[6] A plausible scenario is where productivity returns to 'normal' by 2013.

Shock 2: Rising Equity Risk Premia

The surprise upswing in commodity prices from 2003 but most noticeable during 2006 and 2007 led to concerns about inflation leading to the sharp reversal in monetary policy in the US. This tightening in the US policy also implied a tightening of monetary policy in economies that pegged to the US dollar. It was the sharpness of this reversal as much as the fall in the US house prices and the failures of financial regulation (for example, the mortgage underwriters Fannie Mae and Freddie Mac) that led to the financial problems for 2008-09.[7] Lehman Brothers' failure was primarily due to the large losses they sustained in the US sub-prime mortgage market. Lehman held large positions in the sub-prime and other lower-rated mortgage markets. But mortgage delinquencies rose after the

US housing price bubble burst in 2006-07. In the second fiscal quarter 2008, Lehman reported losses of $2.8 billion. It was forced to sell off $6 billion in assets.[8] The failure of Lehman Brothers in September 2008 and effect on risk premiums across markets can be seen clearly in Figure 16.4.

Figure 16.4

The Lehman Brothers' Bankruptcy and Risk Premia

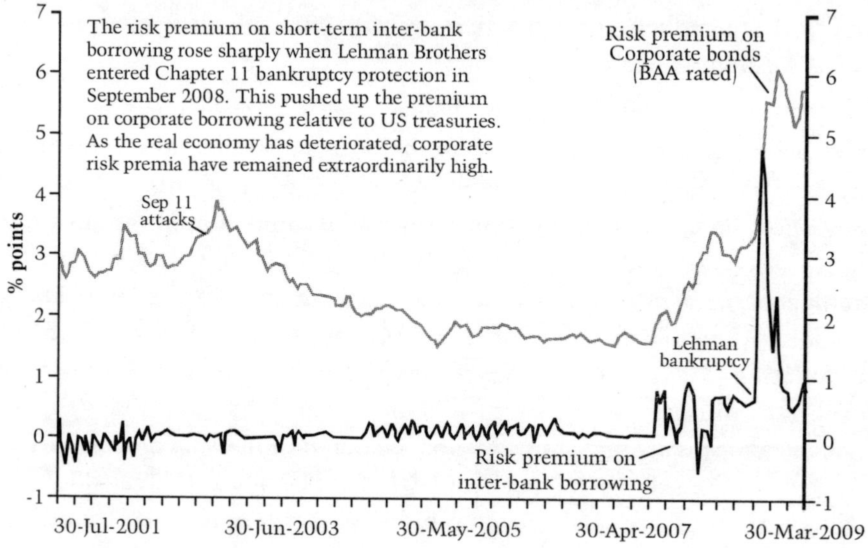

Notes: Weekly data. Risk premium on inter-bank borrowing approximated by the rate on one month Euro-dollar deposits less the Federal funds rate. Risk premium on corporate bonds measured as the yield on BAA rated corporate bonds less the 10 year Treasury bond yield.

Source: Federal Reserve Board.

The rise in the equity risk premium since the collapse of Lehman Brothers has been of the order of eight percentage points. A plausible scenario where confidence is gradually restored so things are back to 'normal' by 2013 is, therefore, assumed.

- Under this scenario, balance sheets of financial institutions are gradually restored through existing and new programmes to address distressed assets. Combined with new capital raising, confidence and lending returns. Also, investors learn to live with the 'new world' and economic recovery encourages new investment and a virtuous circle of further improvements in confidence.

– This scenario is plausible in the opinion of the authors. The world will recover but the size and speed of the drop in economic activity has been a salutary lesson for investors who are not likely to forget that quickly. So, to capture the collapse of commodity prices and the financial sector, an initial rise in the equity risk premium of eight percentage points for the US is taken for the six sectors in the model: the energy, mining, agriculture, durable and non-durable manufacturing and services sectors in 2009 and then dissipates in equal steps over the next four years but staying permanently higher by two per cent from 2012. The permanent rise in the risk premium reflects the baseline risk premium which is assumed to be close to zero in the projection based on the experience from 2003. Thus, there is an overshoot in the return to 'normal'.

Shock 3: A Rise in Household Risk

The reappraisal of risk by firms as a result of the crisis also applies to households. As households view the future as being more risky, so they discount their future earnings and that affects their savings and spending decisions. The increase in household risk in the US is assumed to be three percentage points in the 'plausible' scenario in 2009, half that in 2010 and back to 'normal' in 2011 and thereafter. The three shocks by sector in the US are shown in Table 16.2.

Table 16.2

Equity Risk Premium, Household Risk and Housing Productivity for the US under the Plausible Scenario

Plausible Scenario	*2009*	*2010*	*2011*	*2012*	*2013*	*...beyond 2014*
Equity risk premium by sector:						
– Energy	8	6	4	2	2	2
– Mining	8	6	4	2	2	2
– Agriculture	8	6	4	2	2	2
– Durable manufacturing	8	6	4	2	2	2
– Non-durable manufacturing	8	6	4	2	2	2
– Services	8	6	4	2	2	2
Household risk	3	1.5	0	0	0	0
Housing productivity	-10	-8	-6	-4	-4	-4

Source: Authors' calculations.

The shocks in Table 16.2 are for the US—the 'epicentre' of the crisis. But not all countries have been equally affected by the crisis. For example, durable manufacturing in Japan would be hit harder by the risk reappraisal given the collapse of their durable exports (dominated by cars) as a result of the combination of the global downturn and the appreciation of the Yen that resulted from the collapse in commodity prices and improvement in their terms of trade.

Also, Japan had their housing bubble a decade earlier than did the US, so over the last few years they never experienced a property bubble as in America. So, the shock to their economy from the bursting of the housing bubble would be less than for the US. Therefore, the shocks for equity risk, the housing bubble bursting and household risk are scaled off the US. Taking the US as 1, a series of weights for other sectors and economies appears in Table 16.3.

Table 16.3

Weight for Country and Sector Shocks

	USA	*JPN*	*GBR*	*DEU*	*EUR*	*CAN*	*AUS*	*OEC*	*CHI*	*IND*	*OAS*	*LAM*	*LDC*	*EEB*	*OPC*
Equity risk by sector															
– Energy	1	1	1	1	1	1	1	1	0.8	0.8	0.8	0.8	0.8	0.8	0.8
– Mining	1	1	1	1	1	1.2	1.2	1	0.8	0.8	0.8	0.8	0.8	0.8	0.8
– Agriculture	1	1	1	1	1	1	1	1	0.8	0.8	0.8	0.8	0.8	0.8	0.8
– Durable manufacturing	1	1.2	1	1.2	1	1	1	1	0.8	0.8	0.8	0.8	0.8	0.8	0.8
– Non-durable manufacturing	1	1	1	1	1	1	1	1	0.8	0.8	0.8	0.8	0.8	0.8	0.8
– Services	1	1	1.2	1	1	1	1	1	0.8	0.8	0.8	0.8	0.8	0.8	0.8
Household risk	1	0.3	1	0.5	1	0.5	0.5	0.5	0.5	0.5	0.5	0.5	0.5	0.5	0.5
Household productivity	1	0.1	1	0.5	1	0.5	0.5	0.5	0.5	0.5	0.5	0.5	0.5	0.5	0.5

Note: Three main shocks capture the policy responses.

On top of the above three financial crisis shocks, there has been an unprecedented policy response comprising three more elements:

1. An easing of monetary policy to near zero official rates of interest in major developed economies.
2. An easing of fiscal policy across countries and large run-up in government deficits.
3. A rise in trade and financial protectionism.

Shock 4: Monetary Easing

There is an endogeneous monetary response in the model for each economy where each economy follows a Henderson-McKibbin-Taylor rule as shown in equation (1) with different weights on inflation (π) relative to target, output growth (y) relative to potential and the change in the exchange rate (e) relative to target.

$$i_t = i_{t-1} + \beta_1(\pi_t - \pi_t^T) + \beta_2(\Delta y_t - \Delta y_t^T) + \beta_3(\Delta e_t - \Delta e_t^T) \quad (1)$$

Table 16.4

Coefficients in Henderson-McKibbin-Taylor Rule in Each Country

	Inflation (β1)	*Output Growth (β2)*	*$US Exchange Rate (β3)*
USA	0.5	0.5	0
JPN	0.5	0.5	0
GBR	0.5	0.5	0
DEU (*)	0.5	0.5	0
EUR (*)	0.5	0.5	0
CAN	0.5	0.5	0
AUS	0.5	0.5	0
OEC	0.5	0.5	0
CHI	0.5	0.5	-1
IND	0.5	0.5	0
OAS	0.5	0.5	-1
LAM	0.5	0.5	-1
LDC	0.5	0.5	-1
EEB	0.5	0.5	-1
OPC	0.5	0.5	-10

Note: (*) that Germany (DEU) and the rest of the Euro Zone (EUR) have a common interest rate with a weight on European-wide inflation and output gap.

The assumed parameter values are set out in Table 16.4. Note that China and most developing economies have a non-zero weight on the change in the $US exchange rate. The monetary easing that has occurred is close to the endogeneous monetary policy response already built into the model so any extra monetary stimulus is not required. Of course it is possible that authorities, being fearful of raising interest rates too early and pricking the nascent recovery, could end up easing too much for too long and would be an interesting simulation, especially if different countries chose different amounts of 'over-easing' which would set up capital flow changes and hence trade flow changes.

Shock 5: Fiscal Easing

There is an endogeneous fiscal policy response in the model but the rule is targetting of fiscal deficits as a per cent of GDP. The easing of fiscal policy announced by most economies has been an extra unprecedented stimulus in the modern era and expansion of fiscal deficits, has to be simulated.

Table 16.5

The Assumed Fiscal Policy Response (Per cent of GDP)

Country/Region	*2009*	*2010*	*2012*	*2013*	*Cumulative*
US	2.07	1.55	1.04	0.52	5.18
Japan	1.46	1.10	0.73	0.37	3.65
The United Kingdom	1.32	0.99	0.66	0.33	3.29
Germany	1.38	1.04	0.69	0.35	3.45
Euro area	1.30	0.98	0.65	0.33	3.25
Canada	1.68	1.26	0.84	0.42	4.20
Australia	2.48	1.86	1.24	0.62	6.21
Rest of OECD	1.00	0.75	0.50	0.25	2.50
China	4.80	3.60	2.40	1.20	12.00
India	0.50	0.38	0.25	0.13	1.25
Other Asia	2.00	1.50	1.00	0.50	5.00
Latin America	0.50	0.38	0.25	0.13	1.25
Other LDC	0.50	0.38	0.25	0.13	1.25
EEFSU	1.70	1.28	0.85	0.43	4.25
OPEC	3.00	2.25	1.50	0.75	7.50

Source: OECD (2009) and authors' calculations.

The discretionary stimulus packages announced by each country has mainly occurred over 2009 and 2010 and is usefully summarised by the OECD (2009). For the US, the cumulative stimulus is nearly 5 per cent of GDP and for China it is over 11 per cent of GDP. It is unlikely that such a stimulus will suddenly end in 2010 for two reasons: it is hard to crank up government spending on things like infrastructure quickly and governments usually find it hard to reign in spending quickly once programmes are announced. Therefore, whilst assuming the same cumulative fiscal response as outlined by the OECD and other studies, the fiscal response has been assumed to taper off quickly after 2010 but finishing in 2012. The assumed fiscal response is outlined in Table 16.5.

Shock 6: Rise in Trade and Financial Protectionism

Rising trade protectionism is a real threat. It occurred during the Great Depression and is attributed with making matters far worse. The main driver for this protectionism was to protect jobs. The Smoot-Hawley (1930) legislation in the US at the time of the Great Depression saw tariffs increase and help trigger the beggar-thy-neighbour round of tariff increases by other countries. Could it happen again?

The answer is that it has already started, *albeit* on a small scale so far. At the G-20 meeting in November last year, leaders affirmed their commitment to open trade and declared they would not put up more barriers. Yet within 36 hours, India and Russia, two attendees at the summit had put up some trade barriers.[9] Just about every major and minor car producer for that matter, has given its domestic industry various concoctions of subsidies, grants and soft loans. President Obama was implored to weed out the 'buy American' provisions in his fiscal stimulus package. Although 'softened', it got through.

It is worth remembering that at the time of the introduction of the Smoot-Hawley tariff during the Great Depression, over 1,000 economists petitioned about the harm the legislation would cause. Smoot-Hawley was nevertheless signed into law. Such is the power of politics! Actually, there are two political problems. One is the obvious loss of jobs and ability of narrow vested interest groups to look after themselves in times of crisis at the expense of the common good.

The other political problem is the free rider one. It goes as follows. When all countries are affected by the downturn, monetary policy is far less effective because all countries cannot devalue against each other. And with the drastic loss of confidence, business is reluctant to borrow and invest irrespective of the level of interest rates. Hence, countries have to rely on fiscal stimulus to encourage a recovery. But it is tempting for countries to free ride on others like the US, who need to implement big fiscal stimulus packages, part of which will spill over to imports. Taxpayers, bearing the future burden of the fiscal stimulus, naturally want to get the 'biggest bang for their buck' but wrongly think that is achieved by keeping the spending at home. Hence, the 'buy American' provisions in their stimulus bill. Other countries, most recently China, have followed suit.[10] But if there is global coordination of proportionally similar stimulus packages, most of the leakage washes out as gains elsewhere. Some of the protectionist sentiment is a result of a lack of global coordination of policy.

WTO members are only legally required to not increase tariffs above their 'bound' rates. However, there can be special exemptions invoked and there are ways to impose protection that raise effective rather than observed tariff rates.

Rising financial protectionism is a real threat as well and has already been observed. For example, some countries, faced with undercapitalised banks unwilling to lend on the same basis as before the crisis and with taxpayers shoring up bank reserves, have directed their banks to lend locally. Other restrictions on foreign bank operations are bound to emerge in the regulatory aftermath that is now bound to emerge in the regulatory aftermath that is now following the crisis. All of these actions have the effect of widening disparities between rates of return and therefore affect global capital flows and, in turn, trade. But modelling this effect requires estimates of how big this effect might be and, as none are readily available, the effect of financial protectionism has not been included in this analysis. The result is: trade impacts from the crisis are likely to be understated.

Two Potential Effects not Specifically Covered by the Six Shocks

There are two other potential effects on trade not specifically covered by the simulations. First is that the model is an annual one and while it allows for stock-adjustment dynamics across years, there can be important within-year effects, particularly on trade. The second is the effect of rising interest rates on trade credit. Again while the data in the model has embedded in it the cost of credit on all transactions, trade credit might involve relatively higher costs and has a depressing effect on international trade.

Inventory Cycle and Trade

Over the last 20 years, the globalisation of manufacturing production chains and the large increase in global trade has meant that a much greater proportion of inventories in any individual country are imported. Hence, a sharp down shift in the inventory cycle from the month of December 2008 onwards has probably been a significant factor behind the sharp downturn in world trade over the first quarter of 2009. It also appears to be a significant factor behind the downward revision of the OECD's forecasts for the global economy since November.

Figure 16.5

Japanese Manufacturing Stocks to Sales Ratio

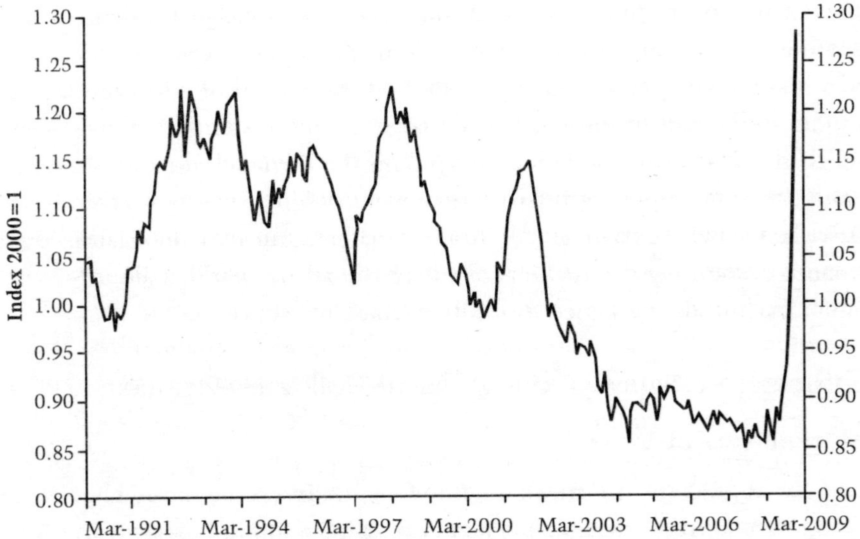

Source: OECD Main Economic Indicators and CIE calculation.

The sharp drop in global sales in December 2008 led to a sharp increase in the stock-to-sales ratio, particularly for OECD economies. Typical of the pattern in the stock-to-sales ratio is highlighted by Japan (Figure 16.5). This pattern was repeated internationally with particularly large increases in most major OECD economies. In the Euro area and Japan, in the December 2008 quarter, retailers and manufacturers built up stocks, as the drop in sales caught them by surprise. The opposite was true in countries like the UK, Korea and Australia where inventories were run down relatively quickly.

The large increases in stock-to-sales ratios in Japan, the Euro area and the rest of the world, will mean that there were significant rundowns in stocks in the first half of 2009. These added to the impact of the falls in sales on production.

The key feature about the inventory cycle for this study is that it will account for some of the large monthly drops in trade volumes that have generated headline grabbing attention. Year-on-year effects, the focus of this model, are likely to be much less.

Trade Credit

At the time of the onset of the financial crisis in September 2008, there was much publicity given to the shortage of credit as banks stopped lending. For example, Auboin (2009) from the WTO Secretariat described a $25 billion shortfall in trade credit in November 2008. A shortage of trade credit would impact on world trade on the supply side but it also seems much of the contraction was a collapse on the demand side as orders were cancelled once business realised they were holding excess inventories as described above. A study by the World Bank estimates the shortfall in trade finance accounting for 10-15 per cent of the fall in world trade.[11] Being of small magnitude, this effect is omitted from this study.

Effects of Crisis without a Fiscal Policy Response

Mechanisms at Work

To appreciate the mechanisms at work from the three shocks, an illustrative scenario where shocks affect the US alone is shown in Figure 16.6. The bursting of the housing bubble has the biggest negative impact on real consumption, which being roughly 70 per cent of the domestic economy, has the biggest negative impact on real GDP. The permanent loss in wealth causes consumption to fall sharply and because the housing shock is assumed to be permanent, consumption is permanently lower in all periods as shown on Figure 16.6.

Figure 16.6

Impact of a US only Financial Crisis on the United States

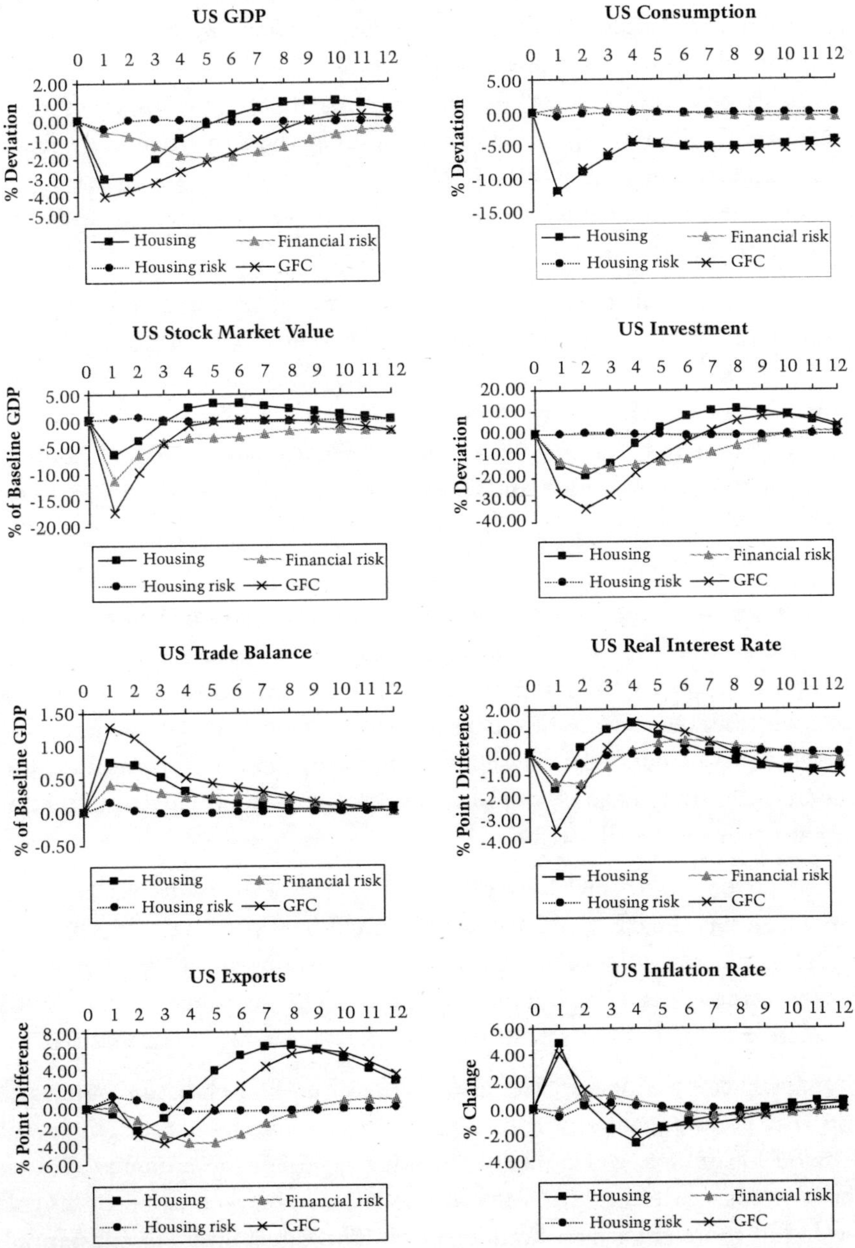

Source: G-Cubed model simulations.

The financial shock has the largest negative impact on stock market values from baseline in 2009 and an equally large impact as the bursting of the housing bubble on investment. The equity risk shock causes a shift out of equities into other domestic assets, such as housing and government bonds as well as to asset purchases overseas. The shift into government bonds drives up their prices and pushes down real interest rates substantially. This surprisingly raises human wealth because expected future after tax income is discounted at a much lower real interest rate. Thus in the US, the equity shock alone is positive rather than negative for consumption in the short run.

Investment on the other hand falls sharply. The equity shock reduces US investment by about 15 per cent below baseline. The rise in equity risk implies a sharp sell-off of shares due to a large rise in the required rate of return to capital. The higher equity risk premium implies that the existing capital stock is too high to generate the marginal product required from the financial arbitrage condition and investment falls and, over time, due to the existence of adjustment costs, the capital stock falls and potential output is permanently reduced.

Under this simulation where the US alone is assumed to be affected by the crisis, there is little impact on US exports (bottom left hand panel of Figure 16.6) because there is little net impact on the rest of the world. The negative trade effects are offset by positive effects from US capital going elsewhere as elaborated below. But as the drop in US consumption hits imports, the trade balance improves over baseline especially in 2009 and remains that way until 2013.

Each of the three shocks has a negative effect on the US and, combined, has the effect of lowering real GDP by 4 per cent below baseline in 2009 and real GDP does not return to baseline until 2017, nearly a decade later. That is sufficient to put the US into recession in 2009 (baseline growth is 3.4 per cent) but will allow positive growth in 2010.[12]

A key compositional effect also occurs when household discount rates and risk premia generally rise. The effect is a much sharper fall in the demand for durable goods relative to other goods in the economy. This is shown clearly in Figure 16.7. Imports and domestic production of durable goods fall more than non-durable goods. The differences are substantial.

The high risk adjusted cost leads to a reduction in the flow of services from durables and, therefore, the demand for these goods drops sharply. This compositional effect is critical for the trade outcomes. Countries that export durable goods are particularly affected by a crisis of the type modelled.

The recession in the US has two main effects on the world economy. One is the negative knock-on effect from the loss in activity with those economies most dependent on the US market most affected. The second effect runs counter to the first. As prospects dim in the US, so the returns on investment look better elsewhere. Money flows out of the US (or strictly in the case of the US, less inflow than otherwise) and into other economies where it stimulates investment and economic activity. This is illustrated by the effect on China (see Figure 16.7). The US is a large importer from China. As US imports fall, China's exports fall (see bottom left hand panel of Figure 16.8), with a combined effect from the three shocks of a drop in exports of 5 per cent below baseline in 2009. China's trade balance worsens, but note how small the effect is: barely 1 per cent below baseline (as a per cent of GDP).

Figure 16.7

Impact of a US only Financial Crisis on Durable versus Non-Durable Goods in the United States

Production and Imports of Durables and Non-Durables

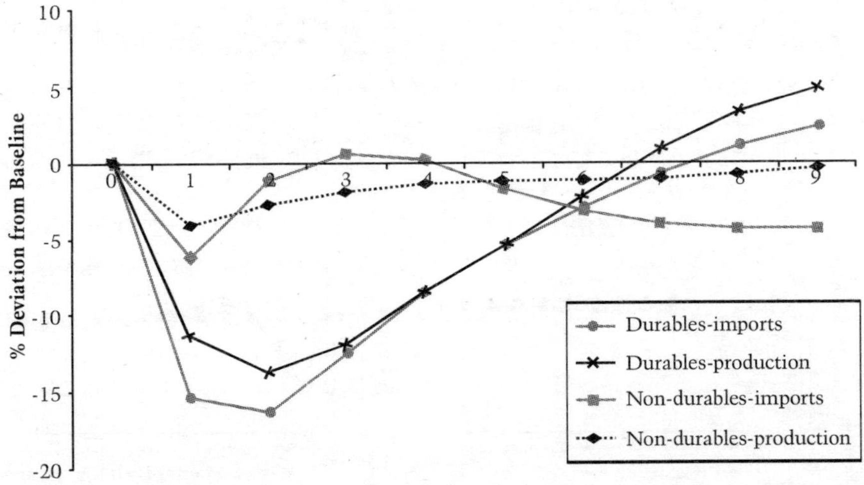

Source: G-Cubed model simulations.

Figure 16.8

Impact of a US only Financial Crisis on China

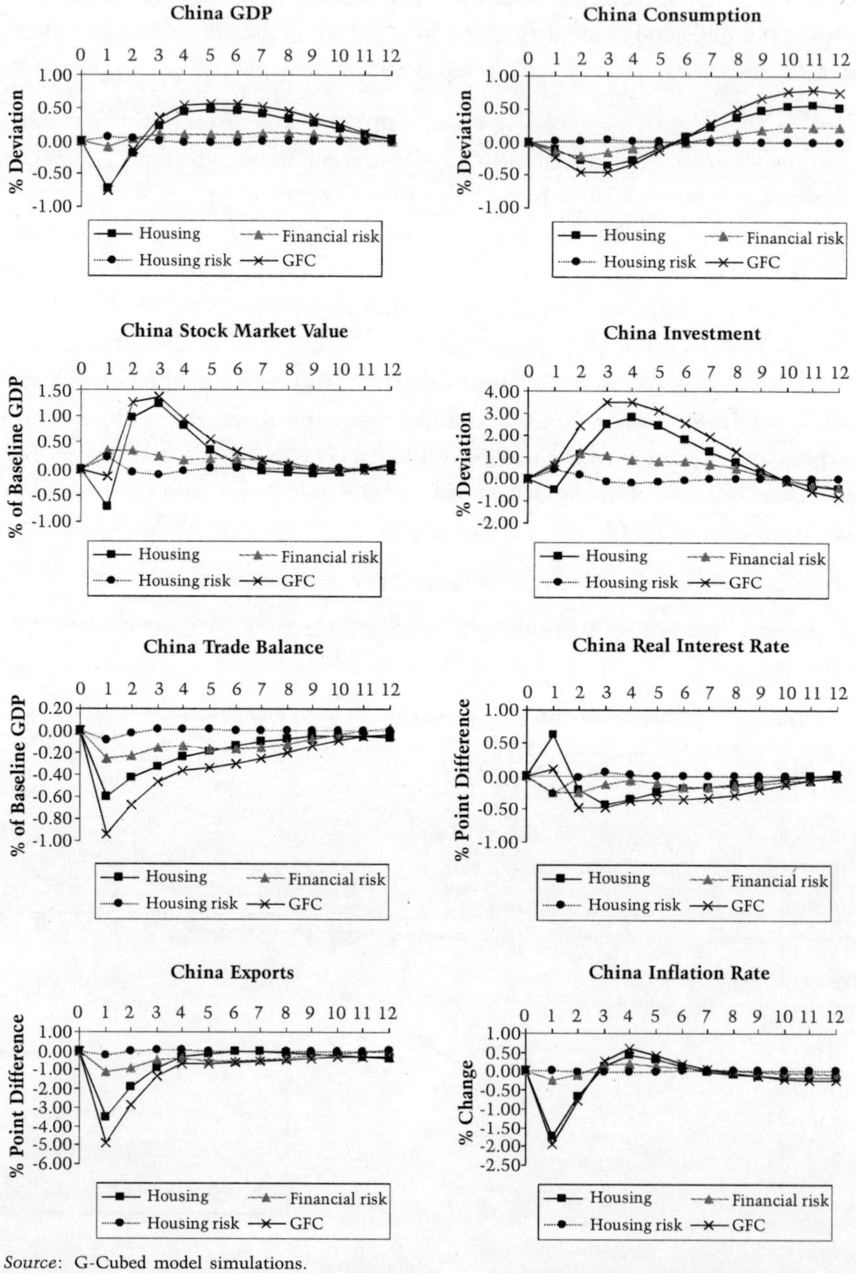

Source: G-Cubed model simulations.

Note also the net small effect on China's real GDP even though China's exports are a large proportion of their GDP. When the US alone is affected by the crisis, there is a small combined effect on China of a reduction in real GDP of 0.75 per cent below the baseline in 2009 and a positive effect from 2011 onwards. Looking at China's real investment provides the answer. Because investment prospects in the US are now dire under the combined scenario, money flows elsewhere, one recipient of which is China. China's real investment could be 3.5 per cent above baseline in 2011 and 2012, in response to the relatively better investment prospects. China gains at the US' expense. The favourable stimulus from extra investment largely offsets and eventually outweighs the negative effects from the loss of exports to the US.

The conclusion is that the financial crisis which started in the US, had it been confined to the US alone, would not have had dire consequences for the world economy. Of course the real story is different. Contagion and rising risk premiums everywhere have caused a different scenario. When everyone is affected, the consequences for the US also depends on who and how other countries are affected.

Projected Outlook from the Global Financial Crisis without Fiscal Stimulus

When all the economies are affected by the GFC through global changes in risk premia and loss of consumer confidence, other countries like China are adversely affected. When other economies are also adversely affected by the reappraisal of risk, the cost of capital for them also rises and, in effect, causes the existing capital stock to be too large. Investment plummets, but not everywhere because it is relative effects that matter. The impact on investment is shown in Figure 16.9. Whereas Chinese investment rose when just the US was assumed to be affected by the crisis, now Chinese investment falls to a low of over 8 per cent below baseline in 2010. Real interest rates fall everywhere by over 400 basis points both reflecting a long-run decline in marginal product of capital but also reflecting a response of monetary authorities in lowering nominal interest rates.

Under the assumptions of the smaller rise in risk premia across Latin America and less developed countries (LDCs), these regions gain relatively

Figure 16.9

Investment Effects of GFC

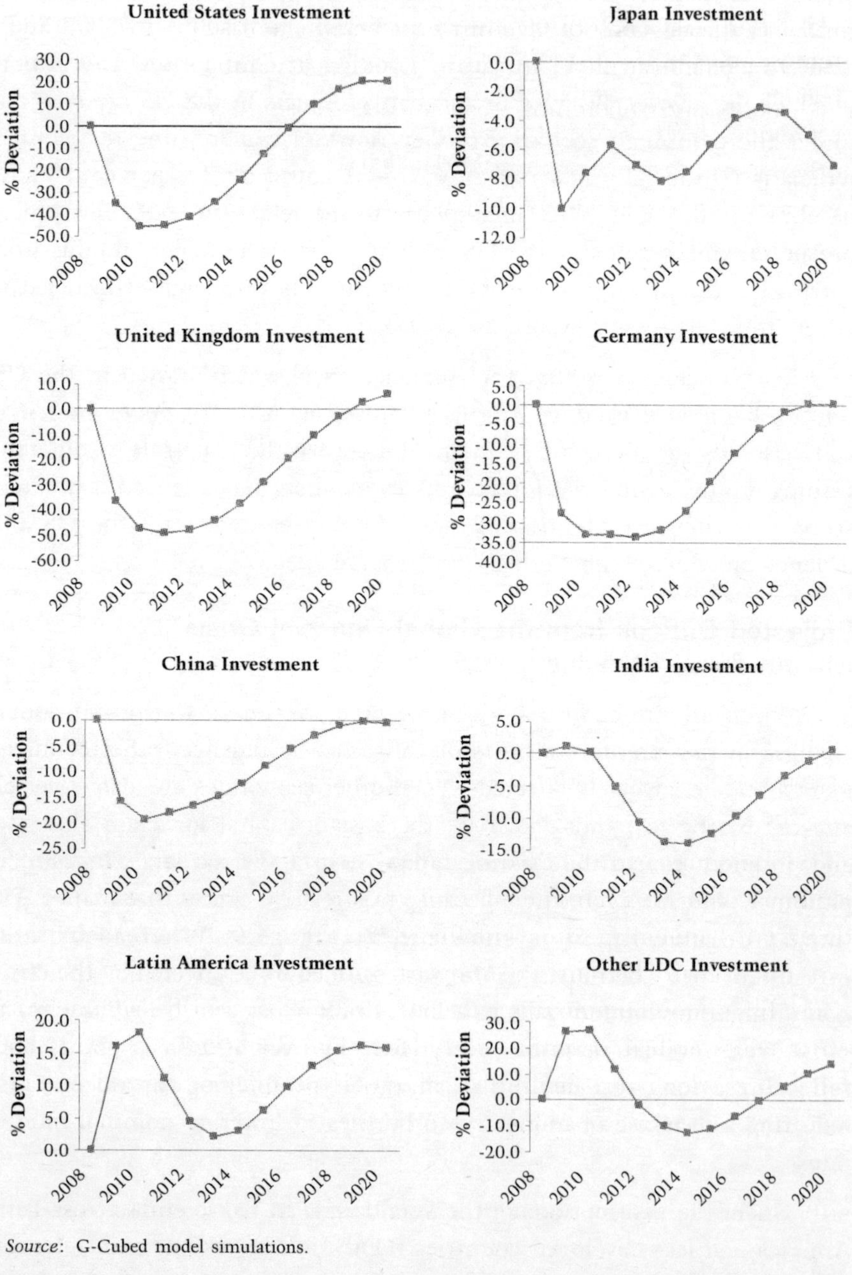

Source: G-Cubed model simulations.

from the global reallocation of investment. Investment in Latin America could be over 15 per cent higher over baseline in 2009 and 2010 and well over 20 per cent for LDCs for the same years. Latin America and other LDCs do not go into recession (see Figure 16.10) as a result of the GFC as represented by the three shocks used in this study. In fact, those two regions experience a slight boost to real GDP. While some Latin American economies such as Argentina are not faring well at the moment, there are other forces at work such as drought and the impact of taxes on their exports. The results in the Appendix Graphs do show that exports from Latin America and LDCs to be hit hard, however. They could be 30 per cent below baseline in both 2009 and 2010.

One of the key features of the crisis is reflected in the results in Figure 16.10. There is a substantially larger contraction in exports relative to the contraction in GDP in all economies. This massive shift in the relationship between trade and GDP is not the result of an assumption about the income elasticity of imports. It reflects some key characteristics of the model. First, imports are modelled on a bilateral basis between countries where imports are partly for final demand by households and government and partly for intermediate inputs across the six sectors. In addition, investment is undertaken by a capital sector that uses domestic and imported goods from domestic production and imported sources. As consumption and investment collapse more than GDP, imports will contract more than GDP. One country's imports are another country's exports, thus exports will contract more than GDP unless there is a change in the trade position of a particular country. The assumption that all risk premia rise and the results that all real interest rates falls everywhere implies small changes in trade balances—a finding consistent with actual outcomes.

Effects of Policy Responses

The results so far have built in a monetary reaction function in the form of a Henderson-McKibbin-Taylor rule for each economy with the short-term nominal interest rate adjusting to a variety of factors in each economy. The rules assumed in the model have generated an endogeneous monetary response which is similar to that observed so far. The assumption of an unchanged fiscal deficit is very different from what has

Figure 16.10

GDP and Trade Effects of GFC

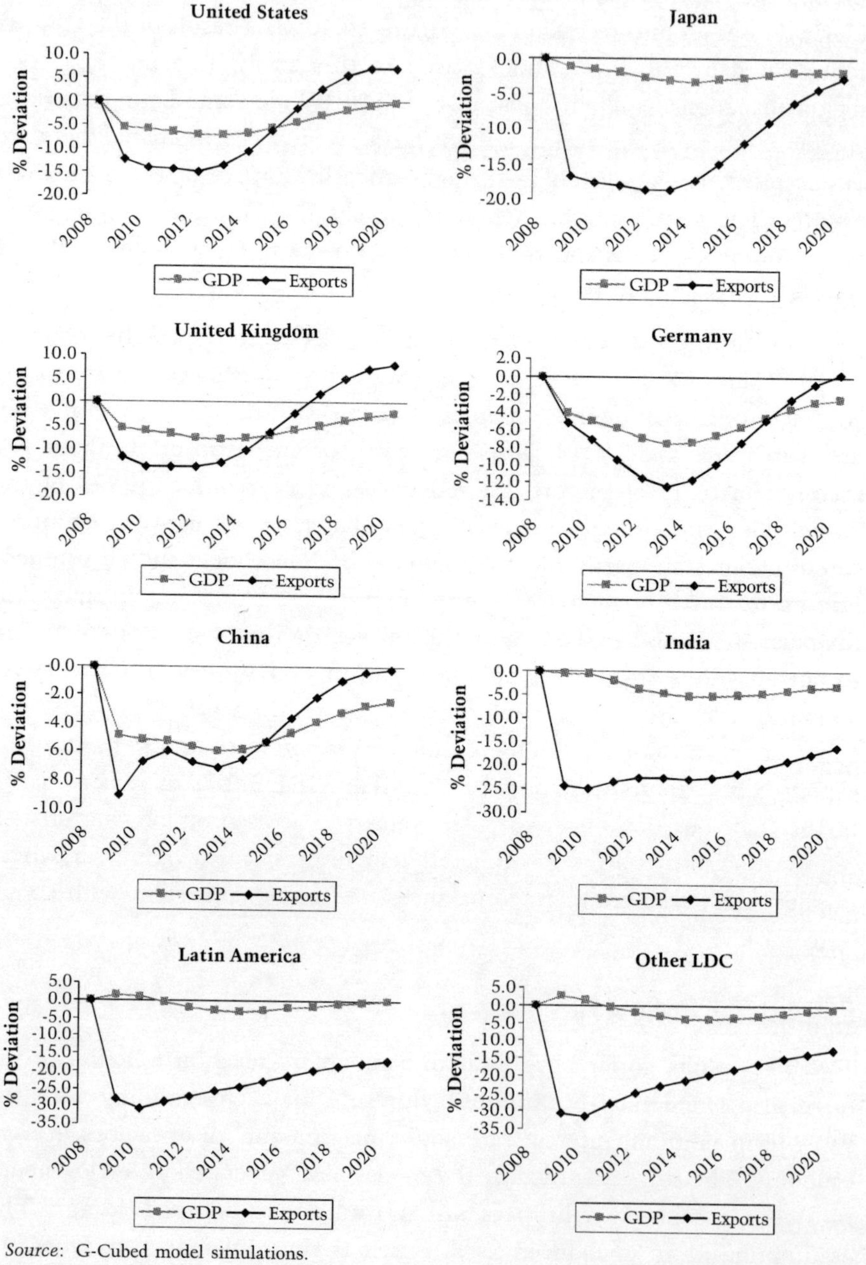

Source: G-Cubed model simulations.

been observed. In this Section we focus on announced fiscal responses. The esimated fiscal policy changes were given earlier in Table 16.5. Note that we do not have infrastructure spending in the model so that the fiscal responses here are assumed to be spending on goods and services and not government investment in physical capital. Expenditure on infrastructure would likely also stimulate medium to long-run supply in the model and, therefore, change the extent to which there is crowding out over time. However, to the extent that even infrastructure spending is a demand stimulus for the first few years before the projects begin to deliver medium-run supply responses, the initial results in this study can be used to understand the short-run impacts of the packages.

Effects of the Fiscal Stimulus Alone

To see the mechanisms at work, the effects of the fiscal stimulus alone are shown in Figure 16.11. These results should be added to the financial crisis results to get a picture of the financial crisis with fiscal response. In discussing these results we will talk about them relative to baseline which can also be interpreted as relative to what would be seen post crisis. It is important to stress that the scenario assumes a reasonably responsive financial sector response to the policy packages. As discussed below other scenarios are possible.

The fiscal stimulus gives a boost to real GDP above baseline for all major economies and China in 2009, the first year of the fiscal packages. The effects are illustrated by referring to China. China's real GDP could be 1.6 per cent above what otherwise would be the case in 2009, but little different from baseline in 2010. Real GDP would be below baseline in 2011 in China as the effects of higher real interest rates kick in. Real interest rates could be over 3 percentage points above baseline in 2009 and 2010 (see Appendix A-16.3) offsetting much of the decline in real interest rates from the global financial shock and monetary policy responses. Real private investment is 9 per cent below baseline in 2010. Considering the massive 11.4 per cent cumulative fiscal stimulus in China, the effect of the fiscal stimulus alone is quite small and transitory.

Note that the fiscal stimulus in the first year raises GDP but for all countries this effect only lasts for a year and is much smaller than many commentators assume (the fiscal multiplier is less than one). Indeed when

Figure 16.11

GDP and Export Effects of Fiscal Response

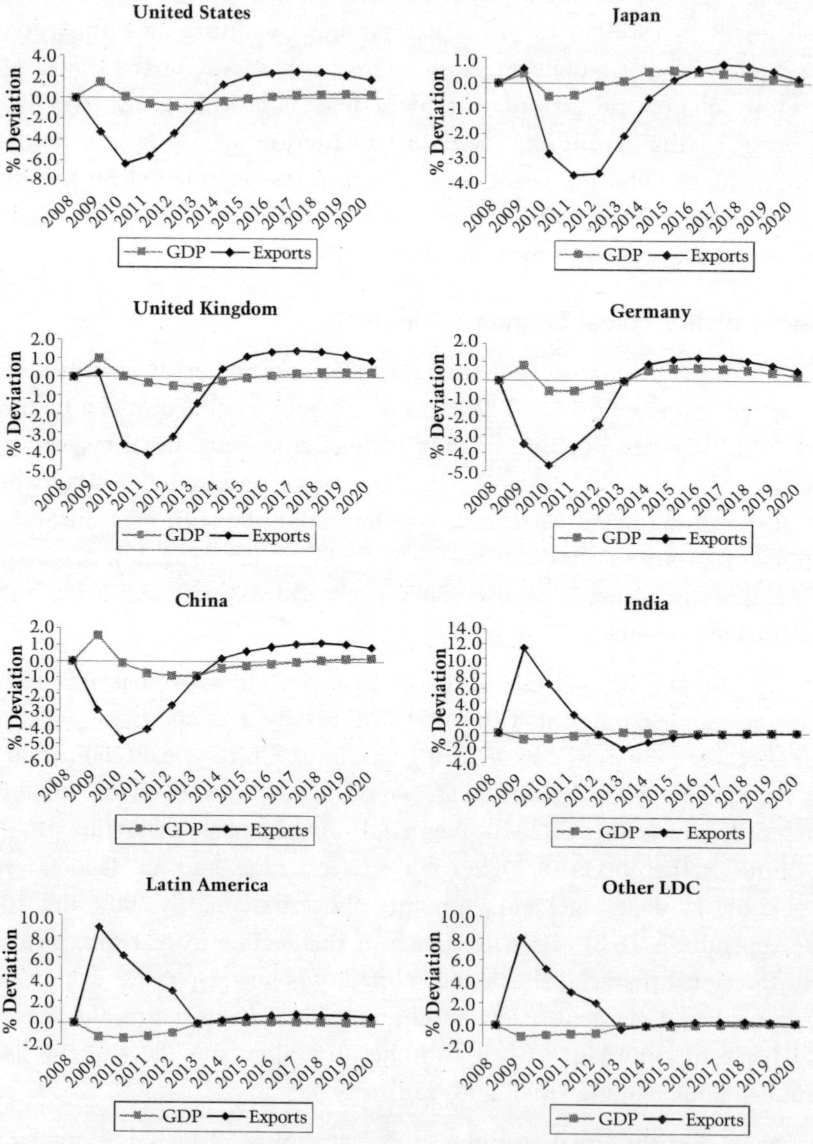

added to the results for the full GFC simulation this fiscal stimulus is not sufficient to completely neutralise the impact of the crisis on GDP. The main reason involves the real interest rate implications of the fiscal stimulus as shown in Appendix A-16.3, Figure 6. The global nature of the stimulus implies an increase in real interest rates which partly offset the spike down in the first year of the shocks. Note, however, that higher real interest rates persist for up to six years after the stimulus. This result points to some serious potential problems to be faced by policymakers during the recovery period from 2010 onwards.

It should be stressed that there might be some delay in the responsiveness of real interest rates in practice, relative to the assumptions in the model. To the extent that central banks hold policy rates at very low levels for a long period because banking systems do not function in a way assumed in the model, there is likely to be less upward pressure of real interest rates and very different story could emerge to the scenario modelled here.[13] With a totally unresponsive private sector, it is possible that the fiscal package might displace private spending in a worst case scenario with no change in real interest rates. In this case, the fiscal spending multiplier may be higher because of a lack of crowding out or it might be lower because the private sector is dormant. Neither case can be completely ruled out.

However, if the major economies respond as modelled in this paper, the fiscal packages also have significant impacts on global trade. In the model the effect of fiscal policy on trade comes in a number of forms operating both through income and relative price effects. If an economy increased government spending, private consumption tends to rise and short-term income increases. However, the increased borrowing tends to increase real interest rates, which reduces private investment.[14] These two responses have opposite effects on trade. In particular, durable good consumption falls because of the rise in real interest rates, while non-durable good consumption rises due to the income increase. The effect is that imports of durable goods fall and non-durables rise. In addition, the higher real interest rate tends to attract foreign capital, which appreciates the real exchange rate and tends to crowd out exports and stimulates income through relative price changes. A country acting alone has a substantial change in the mix of the components of final demand and the real exchange rate dampening on trade tends to dominate the income effect on trade. If there is a global fiscal stimulus, the real exchange rate (or relative price) effects are muted but still present to the extent that the fiscal packages are not symmetric across countries. However, because all countries are acting, the real interest rate effects are accentuated because the call on global savings is much larger than the outcome of any one country acting alone.

Figure 16.11 shows an interesting story where exports of the industrial economies tend to fall as a result of the fiscal package. This occurs for several reasons. Firstly, because the OECD economies have relatively larger fiscal packages (apart from China), their real exchange rate will tend to appreciate relative to the non-OECD economies, crowding out exports. Secondly, these economies tend to export more durable goods whose demand is reduced by a rise in global interest rates. This effect was also present in the GFC simulation where the risk adjusted discount rise rose sharply (even though real interest rates fell) and the demand for durable goods collapsed. Global trade (see Figure 16.13) does not contract in 2009 but falls for several years as growth slows after the fiscal stimulus. By 2014 world trade is above baseline.

Trade Protectionism

The unfortunate tendency to trade protection was noted earlier. So far there has not been an all-out trade war, possibly due to the hard lessons learned during the Great Depression when such a trade war did break out with disastrous consequences. While industrial economies are in theory able to apply tariff rates up to bound tariffs, as they are legally entitled to do under WTO rules, it is possible to go further by invoking special circumstances and by creating no tariff impediments to trade.

To try and capture a plausible change in protection, the actual shock assumed is a rise in all tariff rates by 10 percentage points (i.e., if a tariff was 5 per cent it becomes 15 per cent). The impacts on real GDP from countries increasing tariff rates are shown in Figure 16.12. The overall impacts on global trade are shown in Figure 16.13.

Figure 16.12

GDP Effects of Tariff Rise

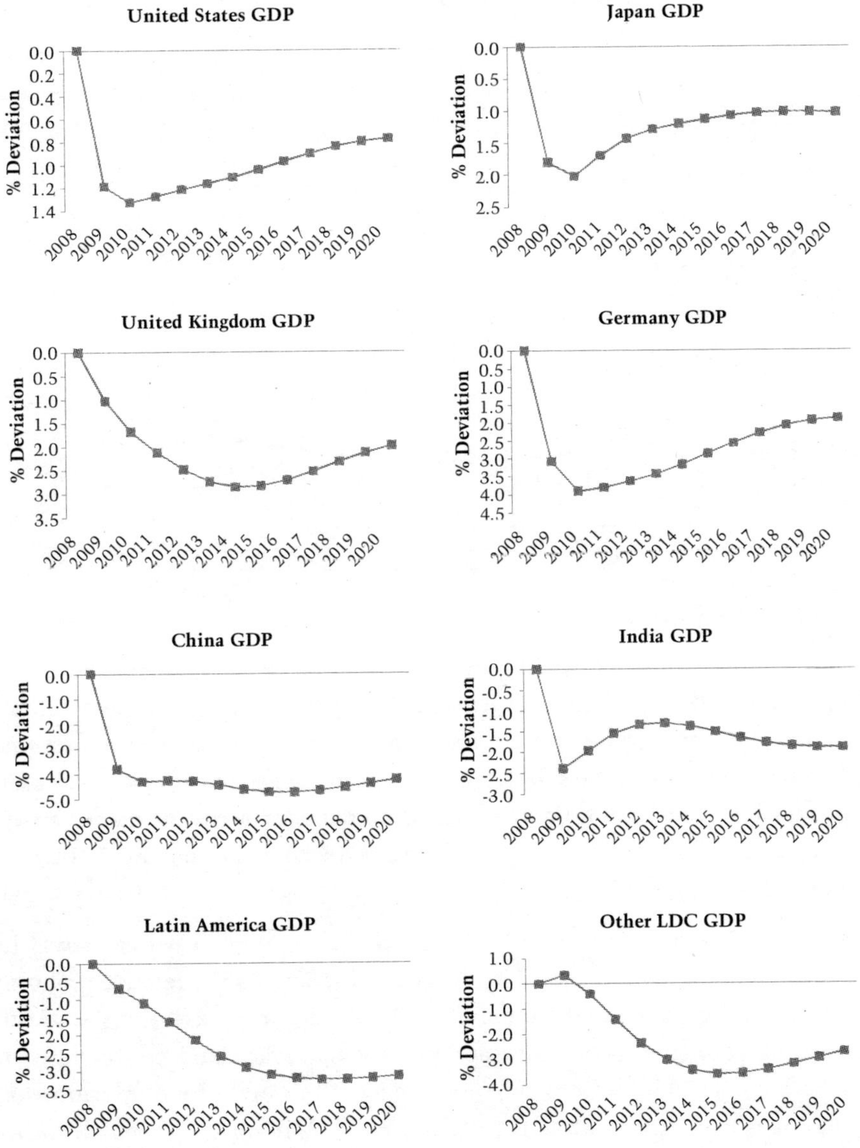

Source: G-Cubed model simulations.

Figure 16.13

Impact of the GFC, Fiscal Response and Trade War on Global Trade

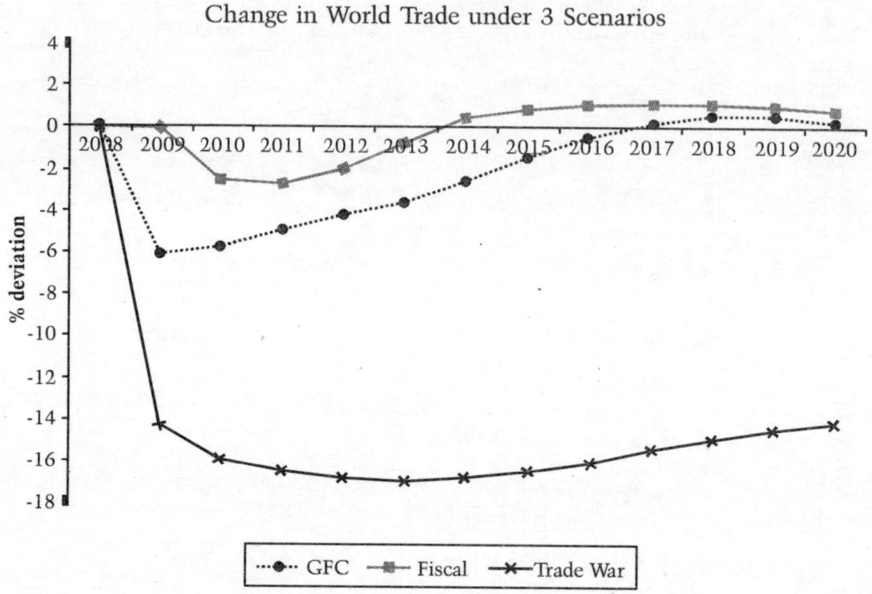

Source: G-Cubed model simulations.

The rise in tariffs by 10 percentage points has a significant negative impact on GDP. The decline in real GDP relative to baseline varies in 2009 between 1.4 per cent for the US and the UK to 4.0 per cent for Germany. The outcomes reflect the relative openness of the economies and the trade linkages between economies. Overall the effects of a rise in tariffs by 10 percentage points, is to reduce trade by nearly 17 per cent by 2012 (see Figure 16.13).

As tariffs rise, the input costs of industries increase which tends to raise costs and reduce demand in the economy. The rise in relative prices of imports also causes import demand to fall which reduces incomes of the exporting countries. This contraction in global trade and contraction in global incomes is self-reinforcing and, hence, the world economy contracts. There is a reallocation of global capital away from sectors in which tariffs have risen because the return to capital in those sectors is expected to fall because demand for those goods that have become more expensive is expected to fall. There is also a rise in the imported price of capital goods which are traded and, therefore, the physical amount of capital created from a constant expenditure on investment is less in all economies. This further contracts potential output.

Table 16.6 decomposes the effects of a change in global tariffs into the effects from the change in tariffs from each country or region listed across the columns on each country. Thus, in 2011 the tariff scenario reduces US GDP by 1.28 per cent below baseline. The impact of the US tariff increase alone on the US is 0.28 per cent in 2011. The US tariff reduces Canadian GDP by 1.76 per cent in 2011 which is the major part of the total loss to Canada of 2.2 per cent of GDP. Most countries are too small to gain from a rise in tariffs although several regions do initially experience a small rise in GDP from their own tariff increased but a fall in GDP on balance when the whole world raises tariffs.

Table 16.6

GDP Consequences of Tariff Changes by 2011: Per cent Deviation from Baseline

	Source of Traiff Change								
	Global	*USA*	*Japan*	*Europe*[1]	*OOECD*[2]	*China*	*India*	*EEFSU*	*ODCs*
United States	-1.28	-0.28	-0.05	-0.25	-0.33	-0.04	-0.01	0.01	-0.33
Japan	-1.69	-0.36	-0.66	-0.15	-0.02	-0.12	0.00	0.02	-0.41
United Kingdom	-2.12	-0.25	-0.02	-1.48	-0.18	-0.02	-0.01	-0.06	-0.09
Germany	-3.80	-0.33	-0.04	-2.64	-0.26	-0.04	-0.01	-0.39	-0.08
Euro Area	-2.93	-0.30	-0.05	-1.84	-0.18	-0.03	-0.01	-0.24	-0.26
Canada	-2.20	-1.76	-0.04	-0.27	-0.21	-0.02	-0.01	0.02	0.08
Australia	-1.36	-0.34	-0.15	-0.32	-0.17	-0.09	-0.02	0.03	-0.30
ROECD	-3.74	-0.37	-0.06	-1.74	-1.21	-0.03	-0.01	-0.19	-0.11
China	-4.26	-0.93	-0.29	-0.29	0.05	-1.12	-0.01	-0.09	-1.58
India	-1.55	-0.20	-0.03	-0.22	0.01	-0.03	-0.61	0.01	-0.47
Other Asia	-3.86	-0.98	-0.18	-0.32	-0.03	-0.42	-0.02	-0.02	-1.88
Latin America	-1.63	-1.32	-0.03	-0.026	0.12	-0.03	-0.01	-0.04	-0.15
Other LDC	-1.43	-0.54	-0.02	-0.60	0.05	-0.04	-0.04	-0.15	-0.09
EEFSU	-3.54	-0.61	-0.05	-2.02	-0.08	-0.07	-0.01	-0.62	-0.08
OPEC	-4.45	-0.90	-0.37	-1.00	-0.20	-0.16	-0.06	-0.12	-1.63

Note: 1. Europe is UK, Germany and Euro Area;
2. OOECD is Canada Australia and ROECD;
3. ODCs is other Asia, Latin America, Other LDC and OPEC.

Source: G-Cubed Model.

For many countries, the effect of a tariff increase alone is to reduce its own GDP. Acting together reduces GDP even more. The favourable demand-side impact of diverting demand from imports to domestic goods is found to be outweighed by the increase in the costs of production. This is a very important result from this paper. Tariff increases are not just beggar-thy-neighbour policies but are beggar-thyself. The reason is because the usual expenditure switching benefits of a rise in tariffs by a country is more than offset by a fall in investment due to rise in the price in imported capital goods and a fall in the return to capital in sectors where protection rises. These two supply contracting effect dominate any demand stimulus in the model. Most simple analytical models take aggregate supply as given and, therefore, the demand switching issue dominates. The supply impact of tariff changes found in the current model is supported by the experience of several decades of substantial expansion in output from countries that unilaterally liberalised trade. In a model with endogeneous capital accumulation and international trade in durable capital goods, aggregate output is not fixed either nationally or globally.

Insights Gained

To represent the effects of the financial crisis on the world economy and trade flows, six elements are needed. For the crisis itself, three shocks are needed to capture the observed drop in asset prices and reduction in demand and trade. It is necessary to simulate the bursting of the housing bubble centred in the US and Europe, but extending elsewhere, rising perceptions of risk by business as reflected in the equity risk premium over bonds and rising perceptions of risk by households.

The policy response has been dramatic. So the analysis has included a monetary easing across the globe and a fiscal stimulus of varying proportions across countries and regions. Also, some trade protectionism has emerged, so far in terms of some tariff increases, some support for industry, such as automobile manufacturers and other effects such as 'buy local' programmes and directives. So a third policy response has been included in the analysis, namely a rise in protectionism. There has also been a rise in financial protectionism, such as directives to banks to lend locally, but minus any estimate of how big this effect is, has not been formally included in this analysis. But financial protection affects capital flows and so would affect trade flows.

Simulating the effect of the crisis itself (that is ignoring the policy responses not already built into the model such as endogeneous monetary policy rule) on the US alone (the 'epicentre' of the crisis) shows several things. Had there not been the contagion across other countries in terms of risk reappraisal, the effects would not have been as dramatic. The adverse trade effects from the US downturn would have been offset to some degree by positive effects from a global reallocation of capital. Were the US alone affected by the crisis, Chinese investment could have actually risen. The world could have escaped recession. When there is a reappraisal of risk everywhere including China, investment falls sharply—in a sense there is nowhere for the capital to go in a global crisis of confidence. The implication is that if markets, forecasters and policymakers misunderstand the effects of the crisis and mechanisms at work, they can inadvertently fuel fears of a 'meltdown' and make matters far worse.

When there is a global reappraisal of risk, there is a large contraction in output and trade. The bursting of the housing bubble has a bigger effect on falling consumption and imports than does the reappraisal of risk, but the re-appraisal of risk has the biggest effect on investment. Rising risk causes several effects. The cost of capital is now higher and leads to a contraction in the desired capital stock. Hence, there is disinvestment by business and this can go on for several years—a deleveraging in the popular business media. The higher perception of risk by households causes them to discount future labour incomes and leads to higher savings and less consumption, fuelling the disinvestment process by business.

The fiscal policy response initially has the desired effect of increasing domestic demand and, hence, real GDP. While the boost to domestic demand on its own boosts trade, there are other effects going on that have an adverse effect on trade. The fiscal stimulus and accompanying borrowing, causes real interest rates to rise over what they would otherwise be. This effect would be diluted if the global economy remained in recession for a long period. However, the natural recovery from the shocks as shown in the results implies that there will be competition by government and the private sector over scarce funds for either private investment or to finance fiscal deficits. The rise in real interest rates (relative to what they would have been) and fall in investment and durable good demand implies that exports fall and do not get back to baseline for several years. For the US, this takes until 2013 and exports are 6 per cent below baseline in 2010. The fiscal stimulus does not apparently help trade largely because of the impact of higher real interest rates on durable goods demand and investment.

So far, cases of rising trade protection have been sporadic as mostly governments have resisted protection to bow to political pressure and protect narrow vested interests. Policymakers are right to be worried about trade protection as a resort to widespread protection would make matters much worse. For example, if countries raise tariffs by 10 percentage points, additional falls of real GDP of between 1 and 4.5 per cent below baseline could occur and exports could variously fall by between 5 and 20 per cent below baseline for major economies. One of the conclusions of this study is that the crisis and trade protection, all work to discourage exports. The asymmetric fiscal expansions redistribute global trade initially with a small impact overall but have a medium-term negative impact on world trade after the first year as the aftermath of the fiscal responses crowd out global demand and slow the recovery.

The need to avoid a rise in protection as a response to the crisis is a key result of this paper. Because the model used has endogeneous capital accumulation and trade in capital goods, a rise in tariffs by one country reduces that country's GDP as well as reducing GDP in other economies. A global tariff war accentuates the losses. Although it is tempting for countries to raise tariffs as a way to switch expenditure from foreign to domestic goods to support domestic demand, this paper finds that the negative supply consequences on investment and more expensive imported durable goods far outweighs any benefit of expenditure switching.

Notes

1. OECD (2009). *http://www.oecd.org/document/12/ 0,3343,en_2649_37431_ 42788172_1 1_1_1_1,00.html*
2. Full details of the model including a list of equations and parameters can be found online at: *www.gcubed.com*
3. These issues include: Reaganomics in the 1980s; German Unification in the early 1990s; fiscal consolidation in Europe in the mid-1990s; the formation of NAFTA; the Asian crisis; and the productivity boom in the US.
4. Federal Housing Finance Agency May 2009, *http://www.fhfa.gov/webfiles/2406/ 1q09hpi.pdf*
5. The sharpest, in fact, since the Volker deflation of the early 1980s.
6. A 10 per cent permanent drop in housing productivity in the United States alone gives a 5.4 per cent drop in housing values one year later. See Mckibbin and Stoeckel (2006).
7. Similarly, the tightening cycle of the mid-1980s was one factor leading to the Savings and Loan crisis.
8. *New York Times*, Thursday, 26 February 2009.
9. Although Russia is not yet a member of the WTO and bound by their laws, they still declared, along with the other G-20 participants, not to increase tariffs.
10. For example see news report in the Financial times. *http://www.ft.com/cms/s/0/ 66454774-5a7c-11de-8c14-00144feabdc0.html*
11. Reported in *International Economics Weekly*, "What's happening to World Trade?" Part II, 24 April 2009.
12. Note that all results are presented as deviations from a baseline projection. A fall in GDP of 4 per cent in year 1, relative to baseline, where the baseline growth rate was 3 per cent is a new growth rate in the first year of negative 1 per cent (i.e., a recession). If the level of GDP remains 4 per cent lower forever, the growth rate of GDP in year 2 is back at baseline growth. Thus in growth rate terms, the crisis is resolved after the first year in many countries although the level of GDP remains below baseline for many years.
13. This argument that monetary authorities may not raise interest rates is made in Christiano et al. (2009).
14. To the extent that there is a substantial supply response through infrastructure, the need for interest rates to rise for a given constrained capacity would be reduced.

References

Auboin, M. (2009). *The Collapse of Global Trade, Murky Protectionism, and the Crisis: Recommendations for the G20*. London: Centre for Economic Policy Research.

Christiano, Eichenbaum and S. Rebelo (2009). "When is the Government Spending Multiplier Large?", *NBER Working Paper* 15394. Cambrdige MA: National Bureau of Economic Research.

Corden, W. Max (2009). *The World Credit Crisis: Understanding It and What to Do. http:// www.melbourneinstitute.com/wp/wp2008n25.pdf*

Greenspan, A. (2007). *The Age of Turbulence: Adventures in a New World*. Sydney: Allen Lane.

Henderson, D.W. and W. McKibbin (1993). "A Comparison of Some Basic Monetary Policy Regimes for Open Economies: Implications of Different Degrees of Instrument Adjustment and Wage Persistence", *Carnegie-Rochester Conference Series on Public Policy* 39: 221-17.

Holmes, J. (2008). Opening remarks by Sir John Holmes, Under-Secretary General for Humanitarian Affairs and Emergency Relief Coordinator at the DIHAD 2008. Conference, 8 April 2008. *http://www.reliefweb.int/rw/RWB.NSF/db900SID/YSAR7DHL88?OpenDocument*

IMF (2009). *Group of Twenty, Meeting of the Ministers and Central Bank Governors,* March 13-14. London, UK. p.4.

McKibbin, W. and A. Stoeckel (2006). "Bursting of the US Housing Bubble", *Economic Scenarios* No. 14. *www.economicscenarios.com*

McKibbin, W.J. and A. Stoeckel (2009a). "The Global Financial Crisis: Causes and Consequences", *Lowy Institute for International Policy Working Paper in International Economics.*

———. (2009b). "Modeling the Global Financial Crisis", Paper prepared for VII Colloquium on Financial Collapse: *How are the Biggest Nations and Organizations Managing the Crisis?*, Jointly organised by the Associazione Luiss-Guido Carli & Fondazione Cesifin "Alberto Predieri" in collaboration with the editors of the Journal of Financial Stability, October 2.

McKibbin, W., D. Pearce and A. Stegman (2007). "Long-term Projections of Carbon Emissions", *International Journal of Forecasting* 23: 637-53.

McKibbin, W.J. and D. Vines (2000). "Modeling Reality: The Need for Both Intertemporal Optimization and Stickiness in Models for Policy-making", *Oxford Review of Economic Policy* 16(4).

McKibbin, W. and P. Wilcoxen (1998). "The Theoretical and Empirical Structure of the G-Cubed Model", *Economic Modelling* 16(1): 123-48, Elsevier, January.

Obstfeld, M. and K. Rogoff (1996). *Foundations of International Macroeconomics.* Cambridge MA: MIT Press.

OECD (2009). *Fiscal Packages across OECD Countries: Overview and Country Details*. Paris, 31 March.

———. (2008). *Main Economic Indicators.* Paris: OECD.

———. (2007a). *OECD-FAO Agricultural Outlook-Database (1970-2016). www.oecd.org/document/53/0,3343,en_2825_494504_39550901_1_1_1_1,00.html.* Accessed May 2008.

———. (2007b). *Producer and Consumer Support Estimates, OECD Database 1986-2005. http://www.oecd.org/agr/support/psecse.* Accessed in May 2008.

Taylor, J.B. (1993). "Discretion Versus Policy Rules in Practice", *Carnegie-Rochester Conference Series on Public Policy* 39(1): 195-214. North Holland, December.

———. (2008). *The Financial Crisis and the Policy Responses: An Empirical Analysis of What Went Wrong.*

———. (2009). "The Financial Crisis and the Policy Responses: An Empirical Analysis of what went wrong", *NBER Working Paper* 14631. Accessed in May 2008.

Wolf, Martin (2008). "How Imbalances led to Credit Crunch and Inflation", *Financial Times*, June 17, 2008.

Appendix A-16.1

Sectoral Growth Rates underlying the Baseline

Following the approach in McKibbin, Pearce and Stegman (2007), the energy sector in the US is assumed to have a rate of productivity growth of 0.1 per cent over the next century. Each non-energy sector has an initial productivity growth rate close to historical experience but gradually converging to 1.8 per cent per year in the long run. We then assume that each equivalent sector in each other country will catch up to the US sector in terms of productivity, closing the gap by 2 per cent per year except for the developing country region which is assumed to close the gap by 1 per cent per year. The initial gaps are, therefore, critical for the subsequent sectoral productivity growth rate. We follow a two step process in determining the initial size of the gap. The first step is to specify the gap between all sectors and the US sectors equal to the gap between aggregate PPP GDP per capita between each country and the US. We cannot easily use sectoral PPP gap measures because these are difficult to get in a consistent manner and with a wide enough coverage for our purposes. Thus, the initial benchmark is based on the same gap for each sector as the initial gap for the economy as a whole. If we then have evidence that a particular sector is likely to be closer to or further away from the US sectors than the aggregate numbers suggest, we adjust the initial sectoral gaps attempting to keep the aggregate gaps consistent with the GDP per capita gaps. We then assume that productivity growth in each sector closes the gap between that sector and the equivalent US sector by 2 per cent per year. The productivity growth is calculated exogenously to the model. We then overlay this productivity growth model with exogeneous assumptions about population growth for each country to generate two of the main sources of economic growth.

Given these exogeneous inputs for sectoral productivity growth and population growth, we then solve the model with the other drivers of growth, capital accumulation, sectoral demand for other inputs of energy and materials, all endogenously determined. Critical to the nature and scale of growth across countries are these assumptions plus the underlying assumptions that financial capital flows to where the return is highest, physical capital is sector specific in the short run, labour can flow freely across sectors within a country but not between countries and that international trade in goods and financial capital is possible subject to existing tax structures and trade restrictions.

Thus, the economic growth of any particular country is not completely determined by the exogeneous inputs in that country since all countries are linked through goods and asset markets. In the analysis in this paper, we start with a projection of the model from 2007 assuming no shocks to relative prices apart from those built into the productivity projections. We then imposed each shock on this baseline to generate results as deviation from the baseline. While the emergence of major developing countries is already partly built into the baseline, we focus on the marginal changes as specified in the scenarios described in the body text.

Appendix A-16.2

Classification of Fiscal Measures for 2009–10[a]

	Fiscal Package[b] (US$b)	*Rescue Package as a Percentage of GDP* (%)	*I. Public Spending on Goods and Services*	*II. Fiscal Stimulus Aimed at Customers*	*III. Fiscal Stimulus Aimed at Firms*
Australia[c]	22.0	1.8	Funding for schools and hospitals, transportation projects (railway and highway) allowance; support for low and middle income families; help to first time home buyers — total spending in this category adds up to approximately $10 billion.	Help to 4 million pensioners, carers and seniors; carer	Supporting car manufacturers; investment allowance
Brazil	3.6	0.2		Extension of Bolsa (CCT programme) to include 5 million more citizens; increase in minimum wage by 12 per cent as of 1 February; tax cuts on consumer loans and personal income to boost car sales	Tax cuts to help auto manufacturers
China	586.0	6.9	Speeding up rural infrastructure construction; accelerating the expansion of railways; airport construction in Western province; upgrading power grids; greater spending on health and education in rural areas; enhancing the construction of sewage and waste treatment facilities (total spending in this category is approximately 3 trillion RMB)	Low rent housing (0.28 trillion RMB); raising minimum grain purchases and farm subsidies; subsidies for low income urban residents; increasing the number of pension funds	Direct tax cuts for nine-industries (steel, telecommunications, automotive, etc.); support and development of high-tech and service industries; remove loan quotas on commercial lenders

contd...

...contd...

	Fiscal Package[b] (US$b)	*Rescue Package as a Percentage of GDP* (%)	*I. Public Spending on Goods and Services*	*II. Fiscal Stimulus Aimed at Customers*	*III. Fiscal Stimulus Aimed at Firms*
France	33.0	1.3	Increasing investments in infrastructure projects	€ 200 payment for 3.8 million impoverished households	Protection for the auto sector; support for business investing in housing and construcion; social tax exemption for employers (with less than 10 workers) who have new employees in 2009
Germany[a]	103.3	1.6	Infrastucture investment (schools and roads) worth €18 billion	Income tax cuts (€ 9 billion); reduction in health insurance contributions (€9 billion taking into account employes as well); €2,500 payment for drivers who buy a low emission car; € 100 cheques per child	Reduction in health insurance contributi-ons
Italy	6.3	0.3	Stepped up public works spending	€2.4 billion cash payments to low income families; mortgage relief; additional welfare spending	Corporate tax breaks

contd...

...contd...

	Fiscal Package[b] (US$b)	*Rescue Package as a Percentage of GDP* (%)	*I. Public Spending on Goods and Services*	*II. Fiscal Stimulus Aimed at Customers*	*III. Fiscal Stimulus Aimed at Firms*
Japan	110.0	2.3	Funds to local goverments to invest in infrastructure projects accelerated introduction of energy saving technologies; tax incentives for energy saving technologies	Aid to unemployed workers; housing assistance; UE insurance extenstion; cash transfers regardless of income	Increased wage subsidies for SME employers; subsidise employers who hire temporary workers as regular employees; inject funds into domestic banks to support small and medium-sized businesses
Russia	20.0	1.1		Tax cuts	Tax cuts
Spain	113.4	8.1	New public work projects; creation of fund for local entities and the special fund for employment and economic reactivation	Tax support measures for families; increase in social welfare; delay in mortgage payments for families with unemployed breadwinners	Tax cuts; increased access to credit for SMEs
United Kingdom	36.4	0.9	Infrastructure spending (£ 3 million)	VAT reduction from 17.5 to 15 per cent (£ 12.5 billion); permanent increase in personal income tax allowance for basic rate taxpayers (£3.19 billion)	Subsidies for employers (upto £ 2,500) who hire workers that have been unemployed for more than six months; other employment measures (£ 1.3 billion)

contd...

...contd...

	Fiscal Package[b] (US$b)	*Rescue Package as a Percentage of GDP* (%)	*I. Public Spending on Goods and Services*	*II. Fiscal Stimulus Aimed at Customers*	*III. Fiscal Stimulus Aimed at Firms*
United States	787.0	5.5	Infastructure spending; production of energy from renewable resources; aid to science facilities and research; broadband service in rural areas; aid to school districts and public colleges; additional aid to schools serving low income areas; increase in the side of Pell grants (education grants)	Tax relief for low wage and middle income workers of roughly US$ 300 billion; extended jobless benefits and retraining; health coverage for the unemployed; temporary increase in food stamps	Help to car makers and other distressed sectors in need of credit
Rest of world	149.2				
Total	1958.2				
World GDP in 2008	62054.1				
Total fiscal package as a percentage of world GDP		3.16			

Note: a- Announced measures by each country. The time period of spending is not clear for most countries.

b- GDP in 2008, IMF.

c- Australia works on a fiscal year basis 2009-10.

d- The timeframe is two years, hence the package was divided by two.

Source: ILS, based on Bloomberg, CNBC and national newspapers.

Appendix A-16.3

Detailed Results

A. Consumption Effects of GFC

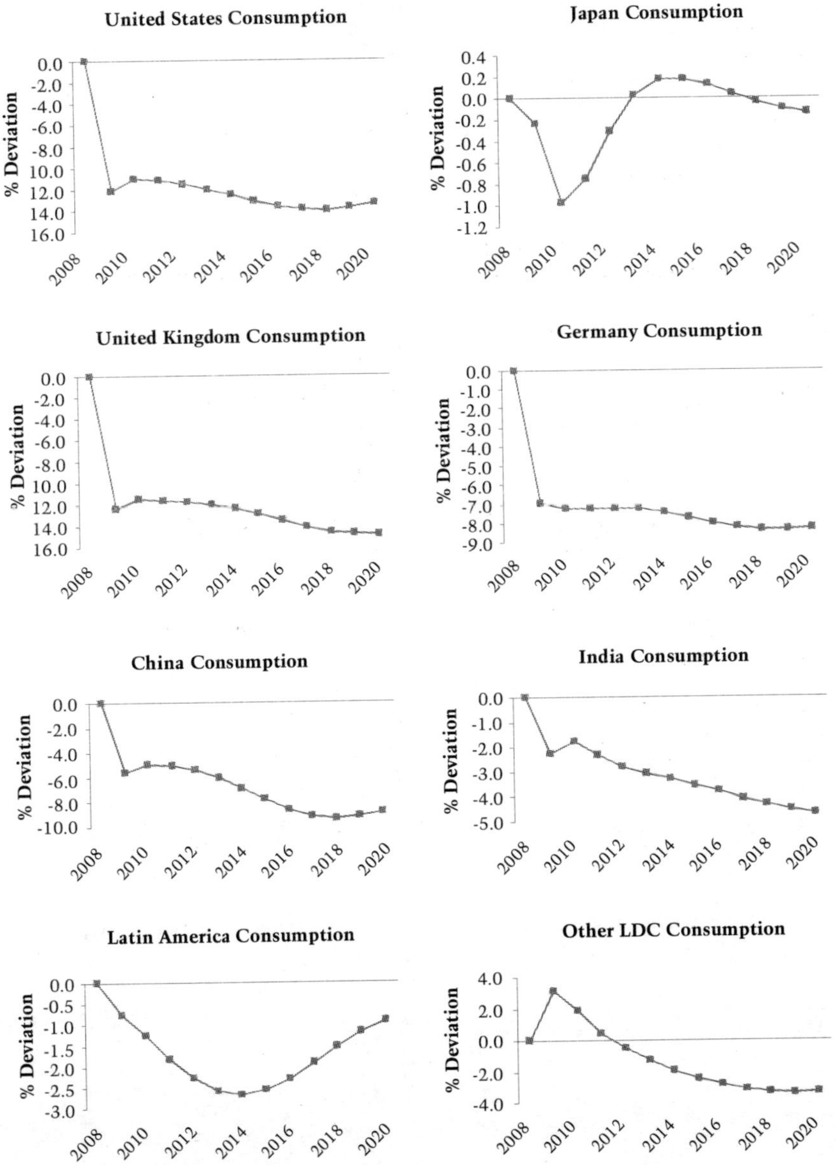

Source: G-Cubed model simulations.

B. Trade Balance Effects of GFC

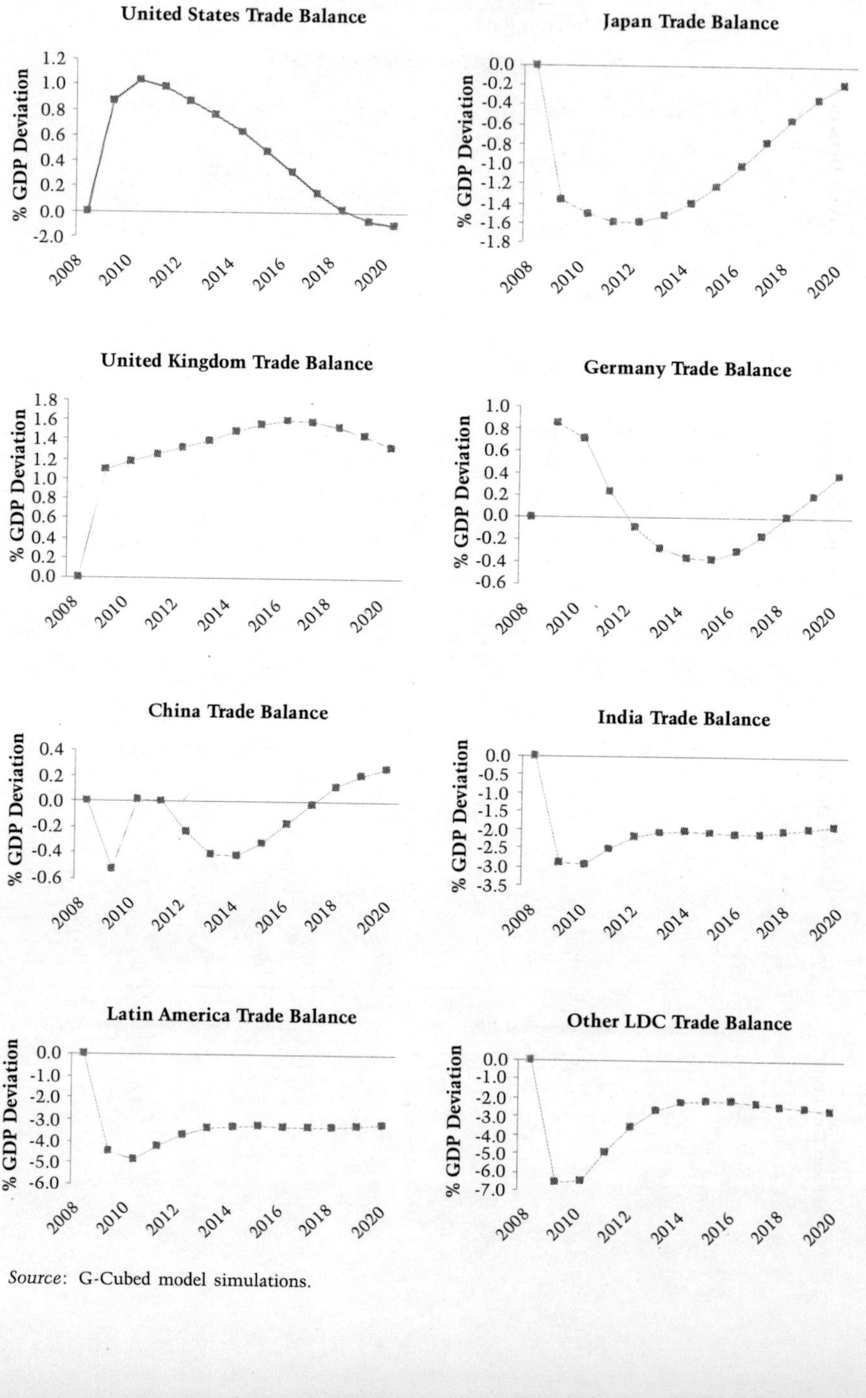

Source: G-Cubed model simulations.

C. Real Interest Rate Effects of GFC

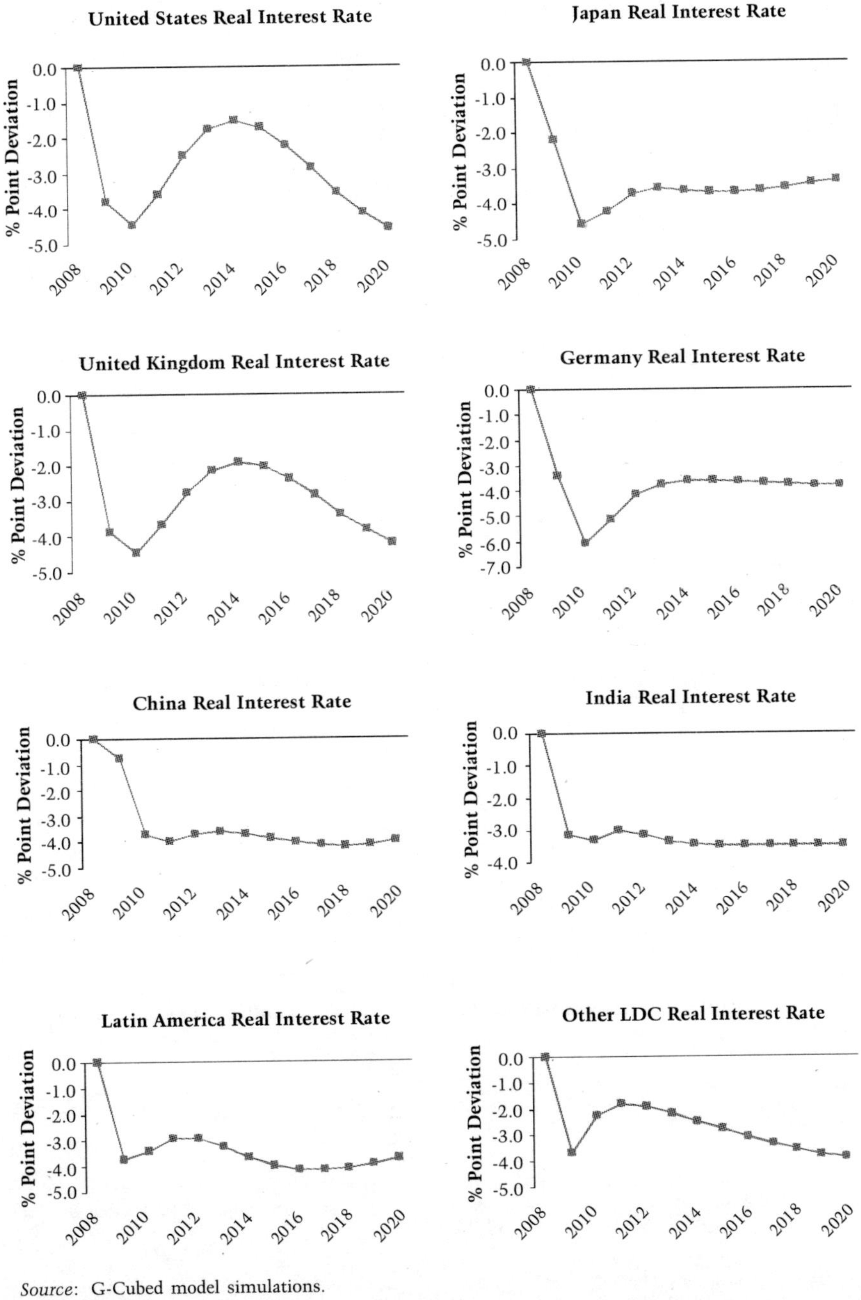

Source: G-Cubed model simulations.

D. Real Effective Exchange Rate Effects of GFC

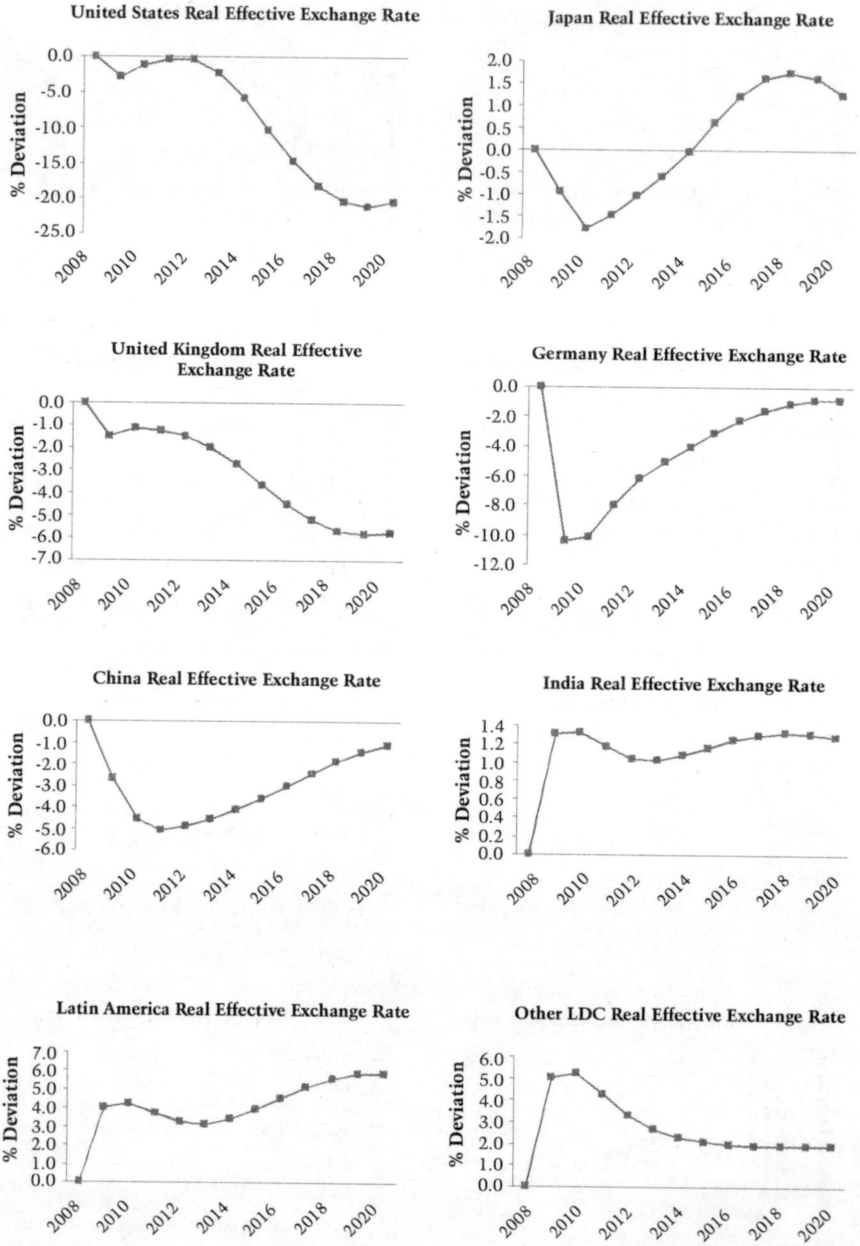

Source: G-Cubed model simulations.

E. Investment Effective of Fiscal Response

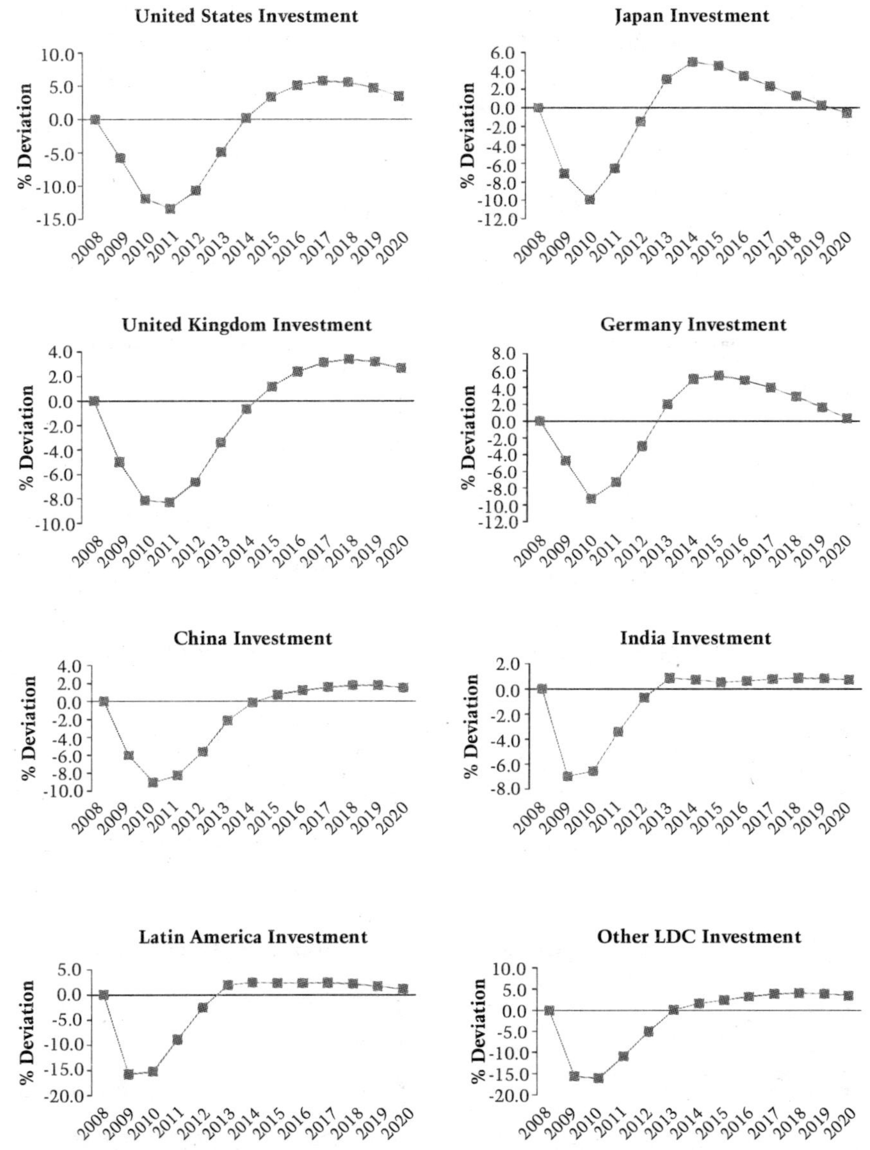

Source: G-Cubed model simulations.

F. Real Interest Rate Effects of Fiscal Response

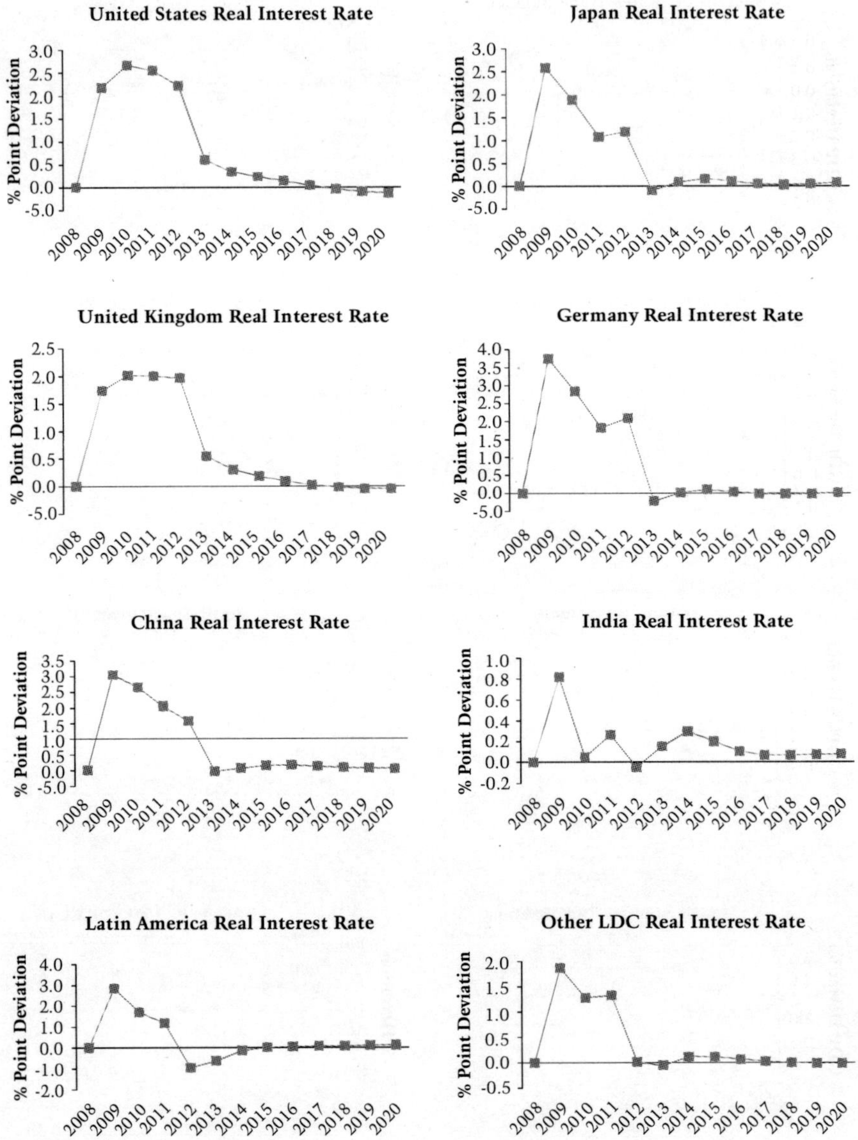

Source: G-Cubed model simulations.

G. Trade Balance Effects of Fiscal Response

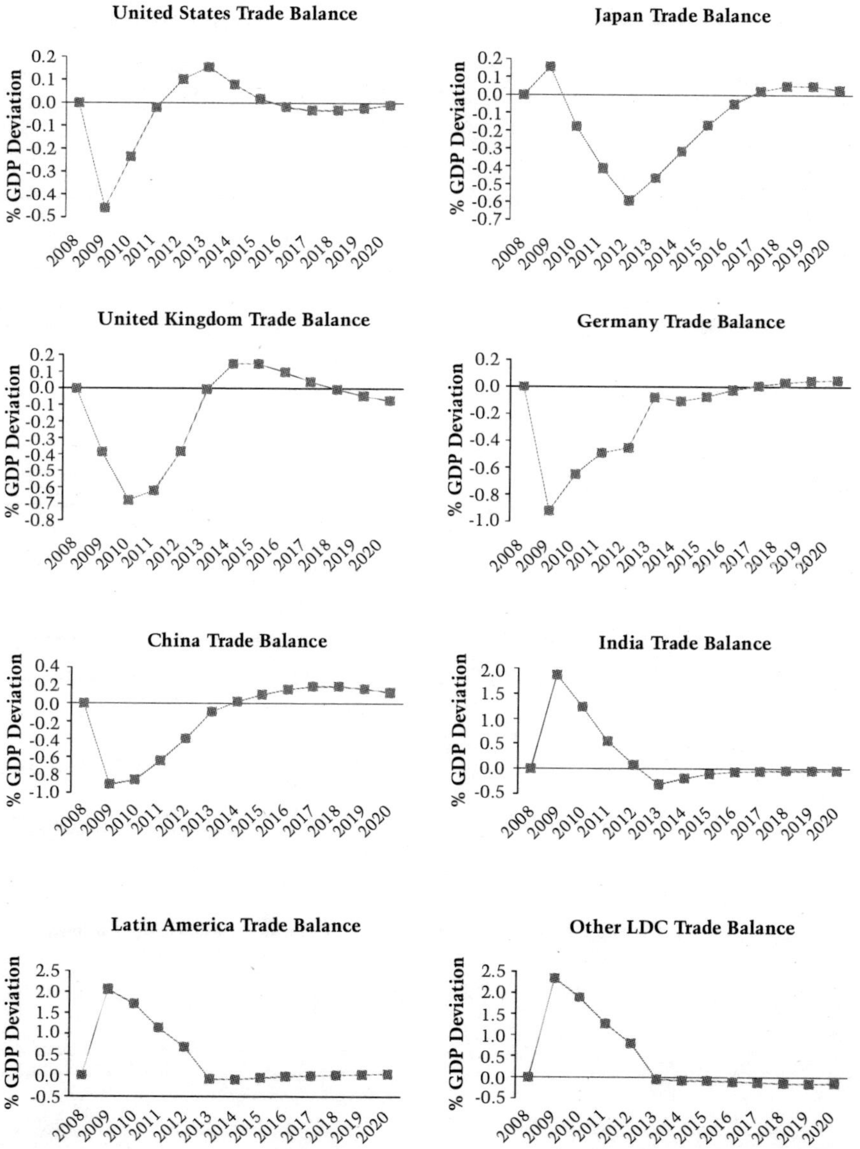

Source: G-Cubed model simulations.

H. Real Effective Exchange Rate Effects of Fiscal Response

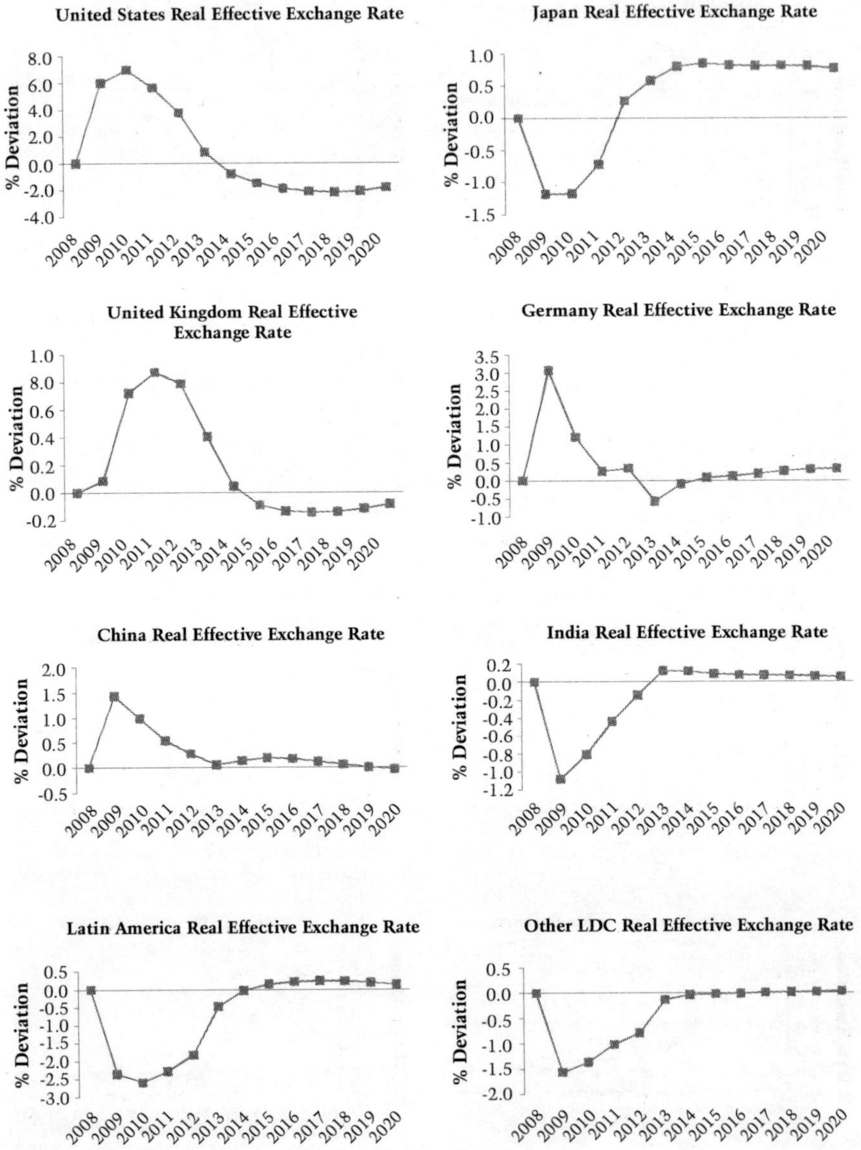

Source: G-Cubed model simulations.

I. Trade Effects of Tariff Rise

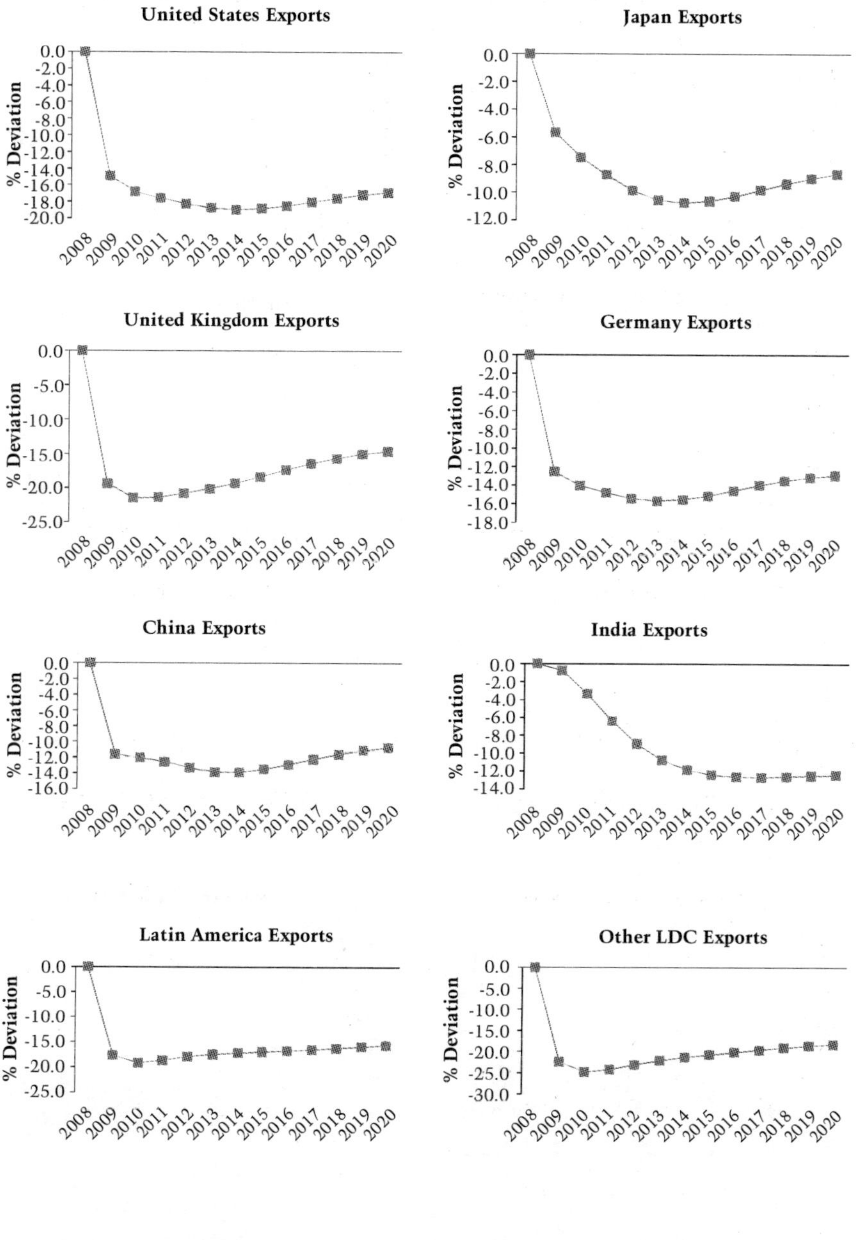

Source: G-Cubed model simulations.

J. Trade Balance Effects of Tariff Rise

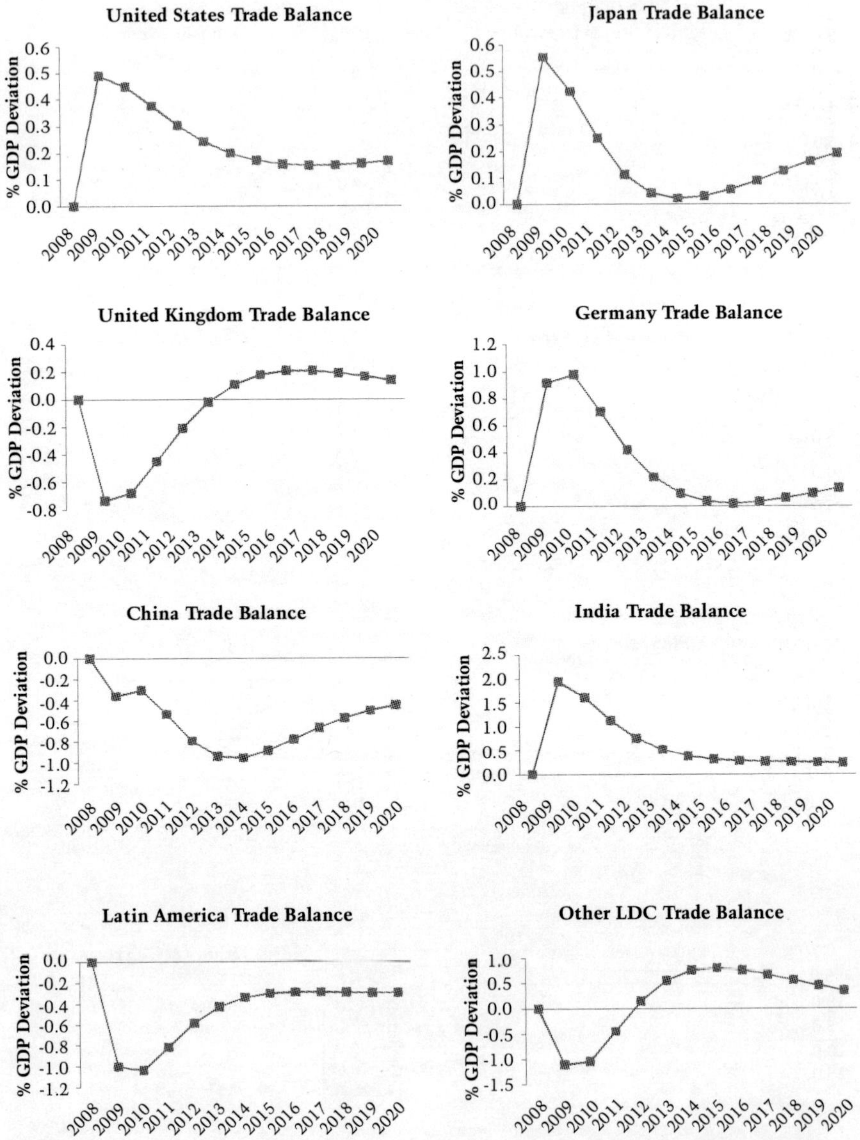

Source: G-Cubed model simulations.

K. Investment Effects of Tariff Rise

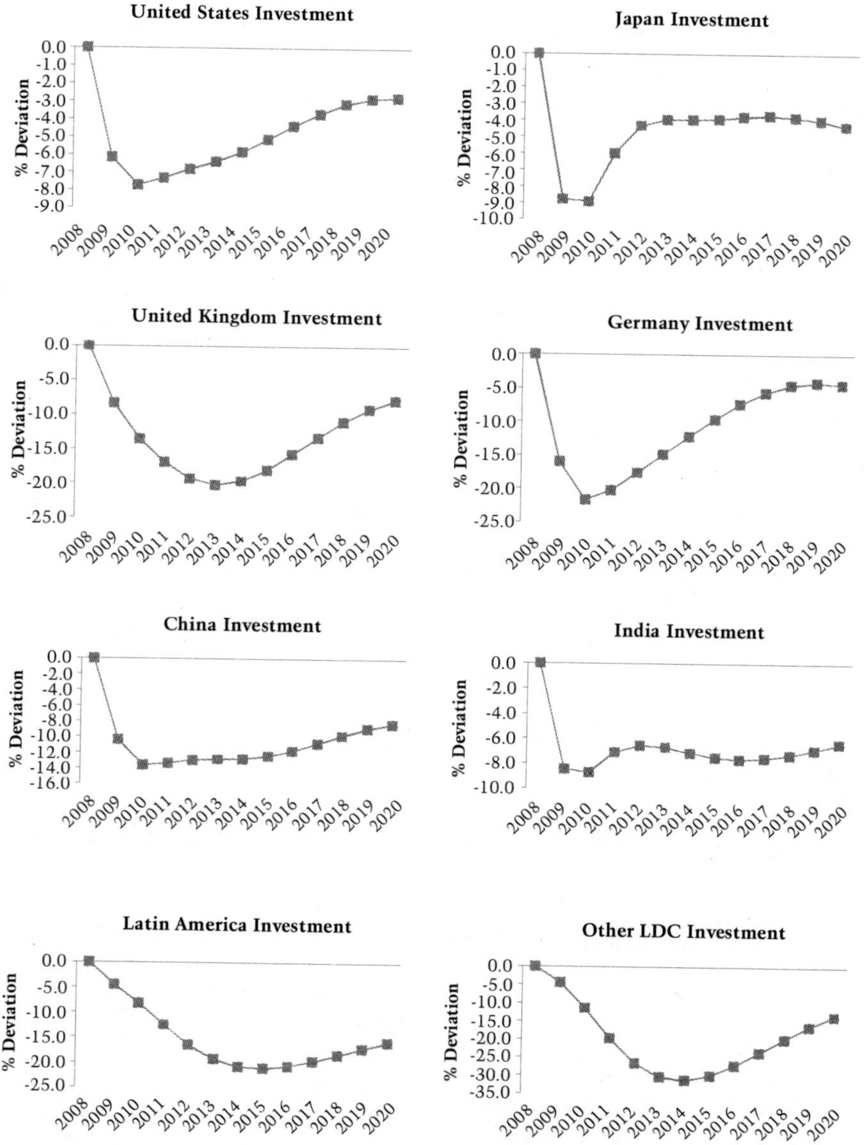

Source: G-Cubed model simulations.

L. Real Interest Rate Effects of Tariff Rise

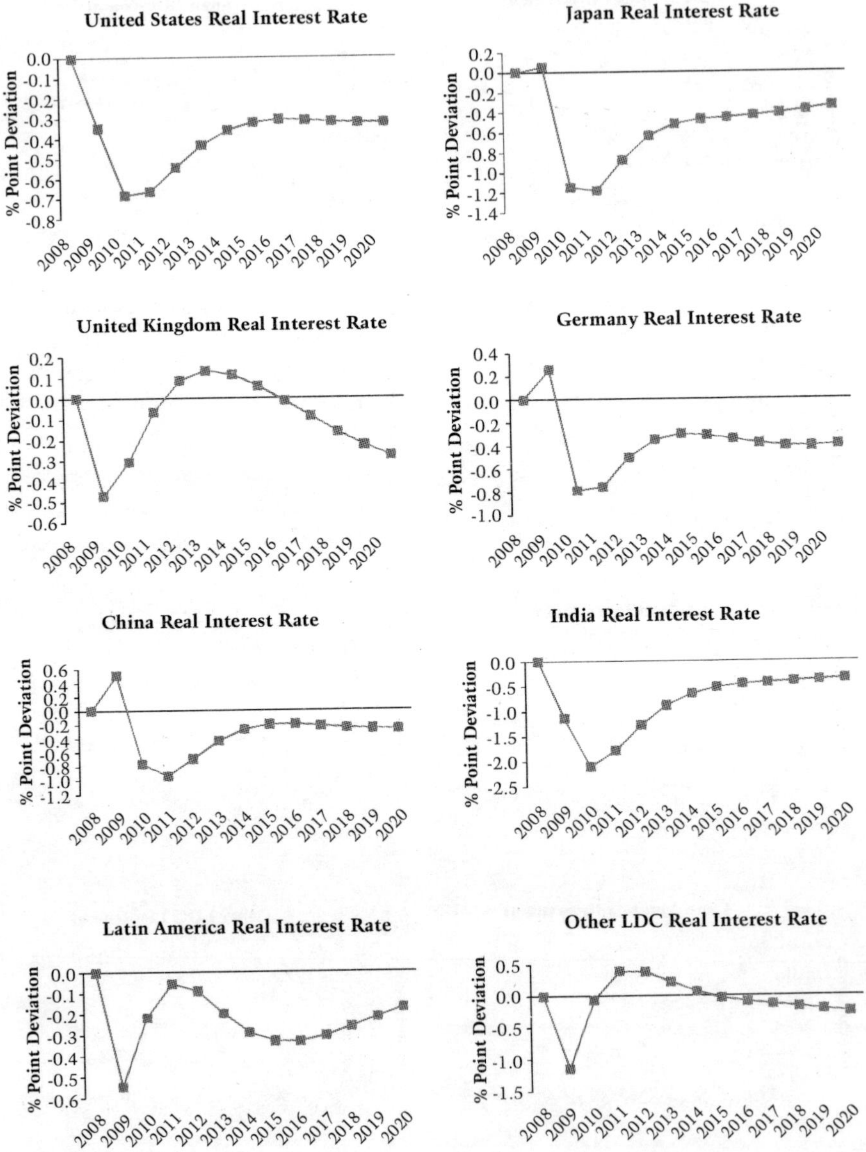

Source: G-Cubed model simulations.

M. Real Effective Exchange Rate Effects of Tariff Rise

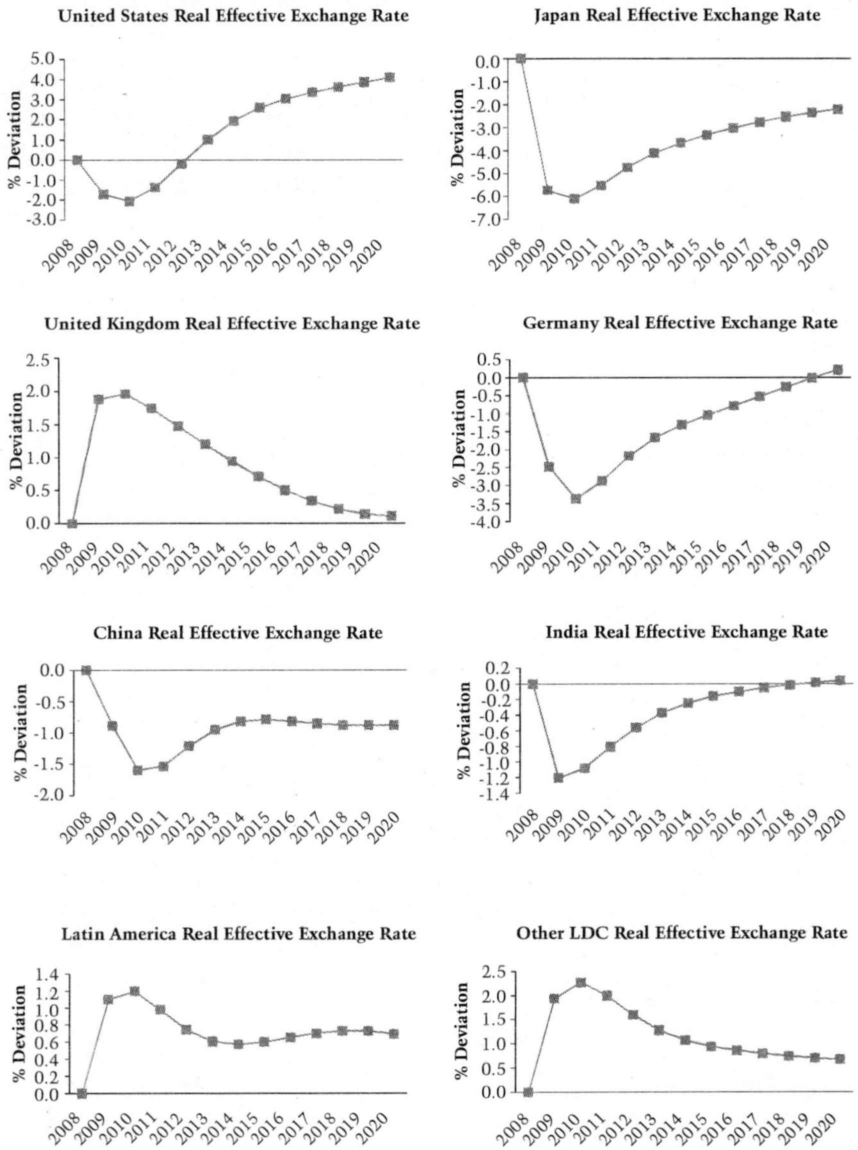

Source: G-Cubed model simulations.

N. Additional Variables for GFC

(% deviation from baseline)	*Gross Domestic Prod*		*Total Employment*	
	2009	*2010*	*2009*	*2010*
United States	-3.51	-3.24	-7.19	-5.64
Japan	-1.63	-1.36	-3.59	-1.56
United Kingdom	-4.02	-3.35	-7.72	-5.41
Germany	-3.71	-2.96	-7.92	-4.16
Euro Area	-3.35	-3.05	-7.20	-5.17
Canada	-2.17	-1.94	-5.23	-3.64
Australia	-0.67	-0.82	-3.70	-2.57
ROECD	-2.87	-2.62	-5.67	-3.67
China	-4.39	-3.50	-9.63	-5.33
India	-1.06	-0.87	-4.64	-2.29
Other Asia	-1.29	-1.22	-5.84	-3.02
Latin America	0.27	-0.34	-2.86	-2.15
Other LDC	1.36	0.36	-0.64	-1.21
EEFSU	-1.75	-1.31	-6.69	-3.20
OPEC	-3.57	-2.37	-11.47	-3.75

O. Additional Sectors Variables

Outut Prices *(% deviation from baseline)*	*Energy*		*Mining*		*Agriculture*		*Durable Manufacture*		*Non-Durable Manufacture*		*Services*	
	2009	*2010*	*2009*	*2010*	*2009*	*2010*	*2009*	*2010*	*2009*	*2010*	*2009*	*2010*
United States	-8.80	-5.30	-8.99	-6.66	-6.51	-4.28	-10.05	-7.46	-5.98	-3.57	-6.45	-3.42
Japan	-3.95	-2.86	-4.49	-3.71	-2.28	-2.71	-5.45	-4.28	-2.42	-2.68	-3.26	-3.14
United Kingdom	-9.66	-6.20	-9.39	-6.79	-5.63	-4.15	-9.38	-7.15	-6.19	-4.25	-7.14	-4.29
Germany	-7.85	-6.33	-7.51	-6.48	-5.79	-5.89	-7.06	-6.83	-6.34	-5.81	-10.97	-7.48
Euro Area	-8.31	-5.52	-7.18	-5.67	-5.38	-4.06	-9.12	-7.26	-6.19	-4.39	-10.02	-6.20
Canada	-5.16	-2.52	-6.58	-4.45	-3.38	-2.37	-7.18	-5.52	-3.32	-2.07	-3.92	-2.23
Australia	-7.28	-3.72	-7.87	-4.89	-3.20	-1.18	-7.62	-5.05	-3.78	-1.48	-3.55	-0.98
ROECD	-7.03	-4.41	-5.84	-4.67	-4.58	-3.62	-6.83	-5.79	-4.07	-3.31	-5.55	-3.96
China	-10.05	-8.55	-9.09	-8.90	-4.93	-6.81	-11.50	-10.07	-6.70	-7.22	-9.93	-8.69
India	-6.68	-4.05	-8.13	-5.88	-3.39	-2.13	-9.06	-6.08	-4.89	-3.08	-6.66	-3.59
Other Asia	-10.45	-7.47	-10.29	-8.26	-5.69	-5.39	-11.77	-9.24	-7.06	-5.93	-8.28	-6.20
Latin America	-6.85	-4.27	-8.51	-6.10	-4.15	-2.86	-10.48	-7.65	-4.58	-3.06	-4.15	-2.61
Other LDC	-7.50	-4.29	-6.76	-4.06	-1.33	0.10	-6.99	-4.58	-3.46	-1.56	-2.13	-0.54
EEFSU	-9.36	-7.21	-9.28	-7.67	-6.54	-6.18	-9.77	-7.98	-7.45	-6.48	-8.33	-6.54
OPEC	-14.34	-10.59	-14.73	-12.20	-10.05	-11.16	-17.53	-13.31	-12.73	-11.00	-17.69	-12.53

cond...

...contd...

Production (% deviation from baseline)	*Energy*		*Mining*		*Agriculture*		*Durable Manufacture*		*Non-Durable Manufacture*		*Services*	
	2009	*2010*	*2009*	*2010*	*2009*	*2010*	*2009*	*2010*	*2009*	*2010*	*2009*	*2010*
United States	-3.25	-3.01	-10.95	-11.16	-6.01	-5.63	-11.74	-12.66	-3.99	-2.74	-3.85	-3.10
Japan	-1.42	-0.65	-5.27	-3.30	-2.33	-1.09	-6.11	-4.56	-2.03	-0.68	-2.16	-1.17
United Kingdom	-4.25	-3.32	-12.12	-12.24	-6.79	-4.99	-12.40	-12.03	-5.21	-3.10	-4.63	-3.34
Germany	-3.46	-1.65	-5.86	-5.19	-5.63	-3.01	-9.85	-8.12	-3.90	-1.59	-2.75	-1.92
Euro Area	-2.51	-1.97	-5.60	-5.65	-4.86	-3.24	-8.69	-9.53	-4.27	-2.61	-3.28	-2.69
Canada	-1.40	-0.98	-8.16	-8.68	-3.71	-3.06	-9.59	-10.21	-2.68	-1.60	-2.88	-1.89
Australia	-1.98	-2.34	-5.60	-6.35	-1.66	-1.17	-5.78	-7.23	-1.27	-0.23	-1.54	-0.82
ROECD	-2.10	-1.43	-5.58	-4.95	-3.62	-2.30	-9.04	-8.75	-3.74	-1.79	-3.34	-2.18
China	-2.79	-1.85	-7.88	-6.45	-3.73	-2.21	-7.90	-6.85	-4.09	-1.98	-4.36	-3.05
India	-1.48	-1.28	-4.89	-5.02	-1.33	-0.32	-3.58	-4.16	-2.36	-1.26	-1.82	-1.35
Other Asia	-1.59	-1.30	-4.84	-4.36	-2.07	-1.00	-6.56	-6.21	-2.44	-1.09	-2.52	-1.55
Latin America	-1.86	-1.74	-7.16	-6.91	-2.03	-1.82	-4.71	-5.60	-0.42	-0.49	-0.80	-0.88
Other LDC	-1.95	-2.43	-2.76	-3.61	2.09	1.09	-1.36	-3.02	0.58	-0.02	0.53	-0.08
EEFSU	-2.87	-1.77	-6.28	-4.91	-2.37	-1.33	-6.85	-5.58	-2.47	-1.17	-2.25	-1.29
OPEC	-1.08	0.20	-7.20	-3.50	-9.54	-3.82	-8.03	-5.38	-7.59	-2.72	-4.53	-2.23

17

Liquidity Risk and Banks' Bidding Behaviour

Evidence from the Global Financial Crisis

Adam Geršl and Zlatuše Komárková*

Introduction

The concept of liquidity has received a renewed attention during the global financial crisis (GFC) that started in summer 2007 in the US sub-prime mortgage market. Before the crisis, economists and policymakers concentrated on causes and consequences of the global excess liquidity, a macroeconomic concept reflecting a sharp rise in credit and the money stock in period: 2003-2007. After the turmoil started, the focus shifted to microeconomic and structural concepts of both market liquidity of relevant financial markets and funding liquidity of financial institutions, mainly banks.

In this paper, we focus on two key dimensions of liquidity: market liquidity and funding liquidity. Markets are liquid if a market participant can trade assets without significantly changing the market price. Funding liquidity denotes a situation where an institution can meet outstanding obligations and is able to raise cash if needed. While conceptually different, the two notions of liquidity are interlinked, a hypothesis corroborated by the evidence from the GFC. Especially, in developed financial markets, such as those in the United States (US), the United Kingdom (UK) and the Euro area, there were occasions when liquidity in certain market segments dried out completely and, simultaneously, some financial institutions experienced problems with settling obligations in timely manner.

* The authors wish to thank two anonymous referees for their helpful comments. The article was supported by the Czech National Bank Research Project No. C6/09. In addition, Adam Geršl acknowledges the support by the Czech Ministry of Education Grant MSMT 0021620841 and Zlatuše Komárková acknowledges the support by the Grant Agency of the Czech Republic GACR 402/08/0067. The findings, interpretations and conclusions expressed in this paper are entirely those of the authors and do not represent the views of any of the above-mentioned institutions.

The aim of this paper is to test whether the link between market and funding liquidity exists also in countries that had no or virtually no relevant exposures to the US sub-prime market and where the banking system had a relatively strong liquidity position. To examine our hypothesis, we select one such country, namely the Czech Republic, and construct separate indices of market and funding liquidity, using daily market data.[1] While this is a common practice for market liquidity indices, funding liquidity is usually measured by indicators based on balance sheet data. To construct a market-based funding liquidity index, we apply a slightly modified version of a strategy suggested by Drehmann and Nikolaou (2009), using data from commercial banks' bidding behaviour in repo operations of the Czech National Bank (CNB). Subsequently, we show that during the peak of the financial crisis (i.e., in the months that followed the collapse of Lehman Brothers in September 2008), indices of market liquidity and funding liquidity exhibited a high degree of comovement.

The main contribution of the paper consists in showing that the Drehmann and Nikolaou (2009) approach can be used to assess funding liquidity risks even in monetary systems where central bank absorbs liquidity from the markets, i.e., in a setting where banks do not bid for liquidity in market operations of the central bank. Further research could replicate this analysis for other countries. This would require detailed data on balance sheets of individual banks and data related to their behaviour in monetary operations, which are not easily available.

The paper is structured as follows: Section II provides definitions of market and funding liquidity and discusses their possible links that can lead to a downward liquidity spiral. Sections III and IV explain, respectively, the construction of the market liquidity index for Czech financial markets and the market-based indicator of funding liquidity of Czech banks. Section V analyses the evolution of both indices during the GFC of 2007-2009. Section VI provides the conclusion.

Market Liquidity *versus* Funding Liquidity

Market liquidity can be defined as the ability of market participants to execute financial transactions in assets of a given volume without causing a significant change in their prices.[2] Market liquidity risk can be then defined as the probability that market transactions cannot occur or can take place only with a significant impact on market clearing prices (Kyle, 1985).

Three basic dimensions of market liquidity are usually differentiated in the literature (Kyle, 1985; Fleming, 2003): tightness, depth and resiliency. Market tightness reflects low costs of unwinding a certain position, meaning that the price at which individual transactions can be undertaken is not very different from the average market prices. Market depth stands for the ability to execute large transactions without excessively affecting the current market prices of an asset. Finally, market resiliency is linked to the speed at which prices recover from a random shock.

Funding liquidity, on the other hand, is a feature of an institution (a bank, usually) rather than a market. There are several definitions of funding liquidity which overlap to some extent. Drehmann and Nikolaou (2009) define funding liquidity as the ability to settle obligations with immediacy. According to the International Monetary Fund (IMF, 2008a), funding liquidity is defined as the ability of a solvent institution to make agreed-upon payments in a timely fashion. Borio (2000) or Brunnermeier and Pedersen (2007) define funding liquidity as the ability to raise cash at short notice either via asset sales or new borrowing. Because the ability of an institution to settle obligations in a timely manner is related to the structure of its balance sheet and is usually applied to banks, funding liquidity is often called banking liquidity or balance sheet liquidity (Praet and Herzberg, 2008; CNB, 2009).

Drehmann and Nikolaou (2009) also define funding liquidity risk as the possibility that over a specific horizon an institution (a bank) will become unable to settle its obligations with immediacy. They emphasise that it is important to differentiate between funding liquidity and funding liquidity risk. They argue that while funding liquidity is a binary concept (a bank can settle obligations or not) and is associated with a particular point in time, funding liquidity risk can in principle reach infinitely many values and is measured over a particular horizon.[3]

Theoretical and practical research has rationalised strong interactions between funding liquidity risk and market liquidity, especially in the periods of crisis (Brunnermeier and Pedersen, 2007; Drehmann and Nikolaou, 2009; Praet and Herzberg, 2008; Frank *et al.*, 2008). Simply put, shocks to funding liquidity can lead to asset sales and may reduce asset prices. Continuous downward pressure on prices can have considerable consequences for market liquidity. This can lead to a feedback loop if lower market liquidity leads to higher margin calls, which in turn increase funding liquidity risk as outflows rise. As banks always try to remain liquid, they launch a new round of asset sales which starts a downward liquidity spiral.

The adverse liquidity spiral can also start from market illiquidity. Impaired market liquidity can hit a bank on both sides of its balance sheet. Assets may become unsaleable in the extreme case of absolute market illiquidity and due to a lack of trading, their value decreases. At the same time, the bank is not able to improve its impaired funding liquidity position through its liability side (by issuing securities or borrowing in the interbank market). When funding liquidity is tight, traders (mostly banks as main market makers start hoarding liquidity) become reluctant to take on positions (especially in high-margin securities). This lowers market liquidity and in turn increases the risk of funding a trade, thus increasing the margins and funding liquidity risk.

The risk of an adverse liquidity spiral increases with stronger linkages between banks and securities markets. Praet and Herzberg (2008) give a number of reasons supporting the existence of strong links between banks and markets. First, banks are the major issuers of securities (both bonds and stocks). Second, interbank funding have become more dependent on market liquidity, as interbank transactions have been increasingly carried out through repurchase agreements. Third, banks have been increasingly mobilising their traditional government and corporate bond portfolios to finance less liquid but higher yielding forms of assets that again can be re-used as collateral. Fourth, profound changes in liquidity management have been implemented with a view to increase efficiency and manage operational risks. Fifth, banks have been increasingly supplying the market with new securitised products, structuring and repackaging in tranches illiquid assets which they redistributed to investors with corresponding risk preferences. Finally, bank lending has taken to new forms, including direct lending to specialised investors such as hedge funds that are very active market participants. All of these aspects have played an important role in the recent financial turmoil and contributed to the observed adverse liquidity spiral that followed in developed financial markets especially after the collapse of the US investment bank Lehman Brothers in September 2008.

Construction of a Market Liquidity Index for the Czech Financial Markets

The construction of a market liquidity index for the Czech financial markets follows the methodology applied by major central banks (e.g., Bank of England, 2007 and European Central Bank, 2007). We first look for variables that would capture the three basic dimensions of market liquidity, i.e., tightness, depth and resiliency and construct sub-indices for four relevant market segments: money market, bond market, foreign exchange (FX) market and stock market. Given that the Czech financial markets are much less developed than for instance those in the UK and the Euro area, the range of possible variables capturing the above mentioned basic dimensions is somewhat limited.

Market tightness is measured by the bid-ask spread, i.e., the difference between the (best) prices at which a financial instrument can be bought and sold. If bid-ask spreads are narrow, market liquidity is high, as the price at which individual transactions can be undertaken is only marginally distinct from the average market prices. On the other hand, if market liquidity is tight, bid-ask spreads are large, as the market maker wants to be compensated for the difficulty of realising a possible prompt sale of an asset. Table 17.1 shows bid-ask spreads across the four selected markets.

As regards market depth, a frequently used indicator is the total volume belonging to all bids in the order book. However, the order book or transaction level data are not easily available, so we approximate this dimension by daily turnover volumes. This is based on the notion that a larger turnover makes it more likely that a sizeable transaction can be performed in a short time without a significant shift in market prices. Total volume data are available for all market segments, except for the FX market. For further calculations, the volume data were detrended by subtracting a linear trend.

Market resiliency can be measured by the price impact indicators, which basically express the extent of the price change caused by a given size of order flow. Similarly to market depth, for the calculation of the price change resulting from order flows microstructural data, such as intra-day transaction and quotation data are needed, but these are not easily available. Thus, we measure market resiliency by the ratio of the return to the transaction volume (the return-to-volume ratio). It is assumed that in illiquid markets, the price will move more for a given trading volume than in liquid conditions, so the ratio should be higher. Similarly to market depth variables, the data are available for all market segments, except for FX markets.

Given that, measuring the individual dimensions of market liquidity involves approximation using relatively aggregate measures in the case of a lack of order book data, supplemental variables that are linked to market liquidity can be used (ECB, 2007). We included a proxy for liquidity premium and the market volatility index. The liquidity premium can be understood as a form of compensation demanded by an investor for the potential risk of having to abandon the position associated with uncertain future market conditions. In calculation of the liquidity premia, we have been limited by the lack of relevant data as the Czech financial system is not so extensive in all its segments. However, for two markets (money and government bond), we gauged two possible indicators of the liquidity premia : for money market, the difference between the two-week interbank rate and two-week CNB repo rate[4] and for government bond market, the difference between bond yields and interest rates swaps (so-called asset swap spread) with the same maturity (Table 17.1). It is expected that the wider the spreads between the rates are, the higher liquidity premia are demanded and the less liquid markets are.[5]

The volatility index is used as a supplementary indicator of market resiliency. Consistent with the theory and practice, highly volatile market prices are likely to reflect low liquidity, as the price reacts too much to every trade given the lack of possible counterparties in the order book prepared to trade for the last price. We include this variable for each market segment (Table 17.1).[6]

Table 17.1

Dimensions and Variables for the Calculation of Market Liquidity Index

Dimension	*Description*	*Money Market*	*FX Market*	*Bond Market*	*Stock Market*
Tightness bid	ask spreads	O/N, 1W, 2W,	1M, 2M, 3M	(spread PRIBOR	*vs* RIBID)
Depth daily turnover* Czeonia volume	All government	Bonds trading on	The Prague stock	Exchange	Index PX
Resiliency Return-to-volume	Ratio	Daily change	in Czeonia	Index/daily	Turnover
Daily changes	of 31 individuals	Government	Bond prices	Daily turnover	Daily changes
of 13 individuals	Stock prices/ daily	Turnover	Liquidity	Premia	Spreads between
Indicator		MM_indicator	FX_indicator	GB_indicator	SM_indicator
		Market liquidity indicator			

Notes: O/N = overnight, W = week, M = month, Y = year, PRIBOR (BID) = Prague Inter-Bank offered (Bid) rate, Index PX = main stock price index of the Prague Stock Exchange, IRS = interest rate swap, CZK = Czech Koruna, USD = United States Dollar, EUR = Euro, GBP = Sterling, CHF = Swiss franc, Czeonia = CZEch Overnight Index Average.

* the daily volume is always de-trended.

Source: Authors.

For each relevant market, all time series entering the calculation were first normalised (using the mean and standard deviation of the whole available time span) and then averaged within each of the five dimensions presented in Table 17.1. Each dimension represents an equal part of the compiled sub-indices for the four individual market segments, which are subsequently smoothed using the Hodrick-Prescott filter (MM_indicator, FX_indicator, GB_indicator and SM_indicator). Finally, the overall market liquidity index is calculated as a simple (unweighted) average of the four (smoothed) sub-indices.[7] Given that the underlying values are normalised, the units in which the index is expressed are standard deviations from historical average. We smoothed the individual sub-indices to more clearly indicate the trend in the market liquidity. The smoothing was applied at the level of the sub-indices (rather than at the level of the overall market liquidity index) to enable clear assessment of liquidity trends in individual market segments (CNB, 2009: 34).

The five dimensions and the four market segments were given equal weights in the composition of the sub-indices and the aggregate index, respectively, as it is *ex-ante* difficult to assess overall relevance of the individual dimensions and segments. For example, for banks, stock market liquidity is probably less relevant than money market liquidity, but this may not hold for other market participants including for example households investing in stock markets through mutual funds.

Clearly, our market liquidity index is only a proxy for overall market liquidity. It is impossible to eliminate from the index certain temporary investors' behaviour that is not necessarily related to market liquidity, such as speculation on changes in monetary policy rates.

For other countries in the Central and Eastern European region, we are aware only of the Hungarian financial market liquidity index compiled by the Hungarian National Bank (Páles and Varga, 2008), which uses a very similar methodology. They calculate sub-indices for the three basic dimensions (across relevant market segments, which exclude the stock market but include the FX swap market), followed by a calculation of an overall index.[8]

Construction of a Market-based Funding Liquidity Indicator for Czech Banks

Funding liquidity is usually measured by indicators based on balance sheet data, such as the ratio of variously defined liquid assets to total or short-term liabilities or the deposit-to-loan ratio. These are available usually at monthly frequency. However, funding liquidity may deteriorate very quickly over a few days, so ideally a more frequent (daily or weekly) indicator of funding liquidity risk would be appropriate to monitor the liquidity situation in financial institutions.

Drehmann and Nikolaou (2009) suggested a way to derive an indicator based on data from banks' bidding behaviour in open market operations of the European Central Bank (ECB). Open market operations conducted by the ECB in weekly frequency serve to provide short-term liquidity (central bank money for a given maturity of one week) to banks in exchange for sufficient collateral.[9] Within the operations, individual banks

Figure 17.1

Deposit-to-Loan Ratios in Selected EU Countries
(% 2008 Resident Loans and Deposits; Non-Bank Institutions)

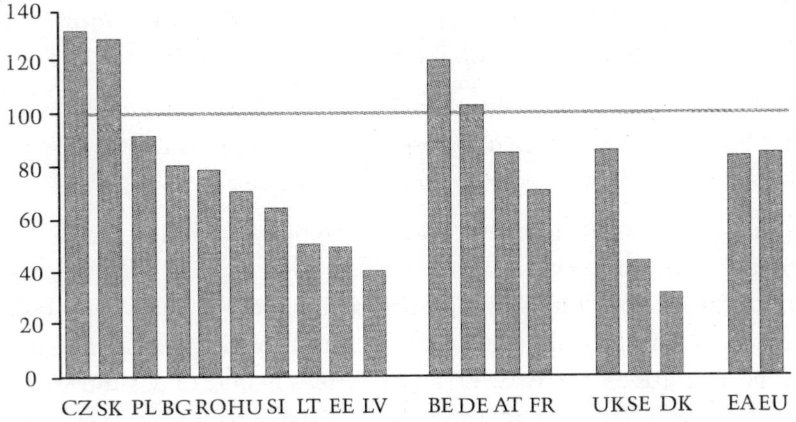

Notes: EA=euro area; EU=average for all EU countries; CZ=Czech Republic; SK=Slovak Republic; PL=Poland; BG=Bulgaria; RO=Romania; HU=Hungary; SI=Slovenia; LT=Lithuania; EE=Estonia; LV=Latvia; BE=Belgium; DE=Germany; AT=Austria; FR=France; UK=United Kingdom; SE=Sweden; DK=Denmark.

Sources: European Central Bank; authors' calculations.

submit bids (volume and price) for the central bank money provided that the bid rate cannot be lower than the minimum bid rate set by the ECB Governing Council. The auction is price-discriminating, i.e., each successful bidder pays for his bid. On the marginal rate, bids may be rationed if the total demand for central bank money is higher than the planned allotment.[10]

Theoretical findings by Nyborg and Strebulaev (2004) suggest that a bank needing to raise cash to settle obligations will bid more aggressively in such an auction, i.e., submit higher bid rate and larger volume, especially if it cannot get liquidity in the interbank market. Using these findings, Drehmann and Nikolaou (2009) build an indicator that is based on the difference between the bid rate and the policy rate (adjusted by the relative share of each bank in the total allotted volume). The higher bid rate and the larger volume demanded by a bank (relative to the total allotment) reflects higher funding liquidity risk of that particular bank.[11]

The Czech banking system features relatively high balance sheet liquidity due to the exceptionally high deposit-to-loan ratio in comparison to both new EU countries as well as other selected EU countries or the Euro area (Figure 17.1). The liquidity surplus of the banking system is absorbed by the CNB via its open market operations in the form of repo tenders. The tenders are harmonised with the ECB tenders.

The only difference is that the CNB tenders have a two-week maturity (rather than one) and are used to absorb rather than provide liquidity to the banking sector and are organised three times a week.[12]

At the first sight, it seems that the liquidity-absorbing nature of the CNB's repo tenders prevent us to apply the Nyborg and Strebulaev (2004) logic to construct a funding liquidity risk indicator out of the bidding behaviour of Czech banks. However, because a bank gives up liquidity in the repo operations for two weeks, it is reasonable to assume that the bank's bidding behaviour will also reflect an assessment of its own liquidity needs and thus the funding liquidity risk. We thus start by assuming that a bank's behaviour in a tender (i.e., both the volume bid and the rate bid) is a function of its balance sheet liquidity.

In systems where banks traditionally demand liquidity from the central bank (e.g., in the Euro area), banks with deteriorating balance sheet liquidity will bid higher amounts more aggressively at an interest rate which is further from (higher than) the set (minimum) limit rate. In the Czech Republic, where the CNB traditionally absorbs liquidity from banks, banks will be less willing to deposit their liquidity with the CNB for two weeks in the case of deteriorating balance sheet liquidity and will do so only at the maximum (limit rate).

The construction of the market index of funding liquidity (MIFL) risk is based on a modification of the approach used by Drehmann and Nikolaou (2009). We first calculate the so-called 'adjusted bid' *(AB)* for each bank i and each day of tender t according to the equation below, which combines information about the spread between the maximum (limit) repo rate and the bid rate and about the relative bid volume to the total liquidity absorbed, i.e.,[13]

$$AB_{it} = \frac{(repo\_rate_t - bid\_rate_{it}).volume_{it}}{total\_volume_t}$$

The bid volume must be weighted by the total volume absorbed to capture factors leading to a change in the bid volume that are not caused by a change in the perceived balance sheet liquidity risk and are common to all banks (e.g. a change in the repo rate or generally lower tender volumes). The main difference to the adjusted bids constructed by Drehmann and Nikolaou (2009) is the opposite interpretation of this variable that arises from the liquidity-absorbing nature of CNB operations, i.e., lower (rather than higher) values of *AB* stand for higher funding liquidity risk. The highest funding liquidity risk corresponds to a situation where a bank is bidding at the maximum (limit) rate, thus the *AB* is equal to zero. This behaviour is interpreted as increased concern about a lack of liquidity on the part of the bank.

One dimension of bidding behaviour that is not captured by the *AB* is a bank's decision not to participate in the CNB tender on a given day at all. This would correspond to an increase in funding liquidity risk as the bank prefers to hold money (for example in the form of an O/N deposit at other banks or at the central bank) and pay the opportunity cost in the form of foregone interest. Thus, we sum the *AB* either across several tender days (for example in a month) for each bank or across banks for each day of the tender.

The last step involves a transformation of the summed *AB* (either for a bank or for a day) to enhance interpretation and presentation. The final MIFL was calculated as a logarithm of the inverse of the summed *ABs* to achieve 'higher MIFL higher risk' relationship. However, as the *AB* often equals zero and so may the sum of *ABs*, before creating the inverse the sum of *ABs* was adjusted by a very small constant ε that is ensuring the existence of an inverse value for any number (including zero). Thus, a bank's MIFL for a given time span (for example a month) was calculated as

$$MIFL_i = \log\left[\frac{1}{\sum_{t=1}^{T} AB_{it} + \varepsilon}\right]$$

while a day's (or tender's) MIFL was calculated as

$$MIFL_t = \log\left[\frac{1}{\sum_{i=1}^{I} AB_{it} + \varepsilon}\right]$$

where I corresponds to the number of participating banks in the given tender.

Higher MIFL indicates a greater risk of an outflow of balance sheet liquidity, while lower MIFL indicates a low funding liquidity risk. We set the constant $\dot{I}$ to 1E-5, so that the resulting MIFL ranges between 0 and 5. It takes the highest value of 5 if a bank (or banks for the day's MIFL) enters repo tenders with the CNB at the limit rate, i.e., the highest possible rate. The data for all 23 participating banks were available for the period May 2007 to March 2009[14] and thus cover the most important period of the GFC for the Czech Republic, including the increased risk aversion towards the Central and Eastern Europe between December 2008 and end of February 2009 (CNB, 2009).

Figure 17.2 shows the banks' monthly MIFL for as a function of the average traditional balance sheet liquidity indicators (the ratios of quick liquid assets to assets, to liabilities and to deposits) lagged by one month to capture the fact that the bidding behaviour is to some extent influenced by the liquidity position in the previous period.[15] The figure suggests that there is a negative correlation between the ratios and the MIFL (of around - 20 per cent; the slope coefficient in Figure 17.2 is - 0.01 and is significant at 1 percentage level) and supports the hypothesis that banks with weaker funding liquidity position tend to bid more aggressively (in the sense of bidding at the maximum limit rate).

Figure 17.2

Relationship between the "Ratio Indicators" of Funding: Liquidity and the Market Index of Funding Liquidity (MIFL)

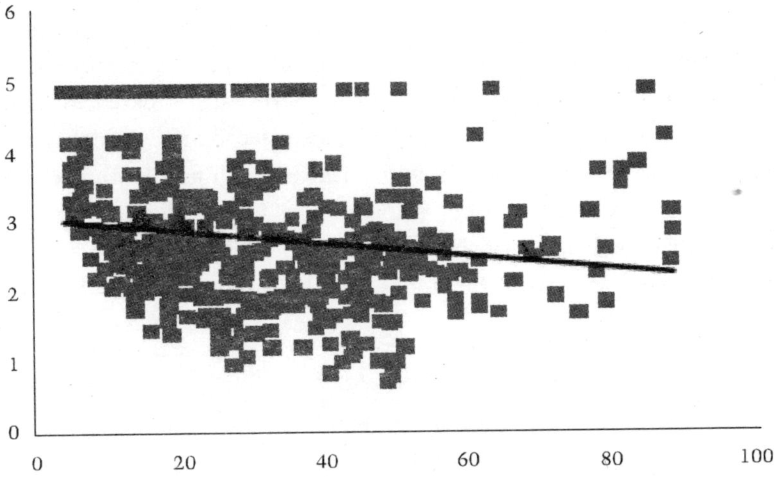

Note: x-axis: average ratios of banks in different months; y-axis: MIFL of banks in the following month.
Source: Czech National Bank; authors' calculations.

The clustering of observations at MIFL = 5 is due to many banks bidding in some months at the maximum limit rate. The visible 'gap' between MIFL values around 4 and 5 is due to selected level of $\dot{I}$ and is kept intentionally to emphasise the 'terminal' value of 5.[16]

Liquidity and the Global Financial Crisis of 2007–2009

The Czech financial system has not been severely affected by the global financial turmoil (CNB, 2008 and 2009). Reflecting mainly their strong focus on retail banking in the as yet unsaturated Czech market, Czech financial institutions had low exposures to toxic assets. The stability of the domestic banking sector in times of financial market turbulence has also been fostered by banks' high balance sheet liquidity and thus minimum dependence on interbank markets, funds from foreign markets or parent companies.

The global financial crisis nonetheless to some extent affected the liquidity in Czech financial markets, as illustrated by the market liquidity index (Figure 17.3). The index signalled declining market liquidity in late 2007 and early 2008, followed by a sharp drop during the peak of the GFC in the months that followed the collapse of Lehman Brothers in September 2008. Nevertheless, when compared to the development of similar indices for the UK financial markets (Figure 17.3),[17] the Euro area (ECB, 2009) or global financial markets (IMF, 2009), liquidity in the Czech financial market was not impaired that much. Hungarian liquidity index followed the same direction as the other indices. The largest decline was evident after the fall of Lehman Brothers and at the beginning of this year. The Hungarian index is currently higher, but below pre-crisis values (MNB, 2009: 32; Chart 2-11).[18]

Figure 17.3

Overall Market Liquidity Indices for the Czech and the U.K. Financial Markets

(in standard deviations from historical average)

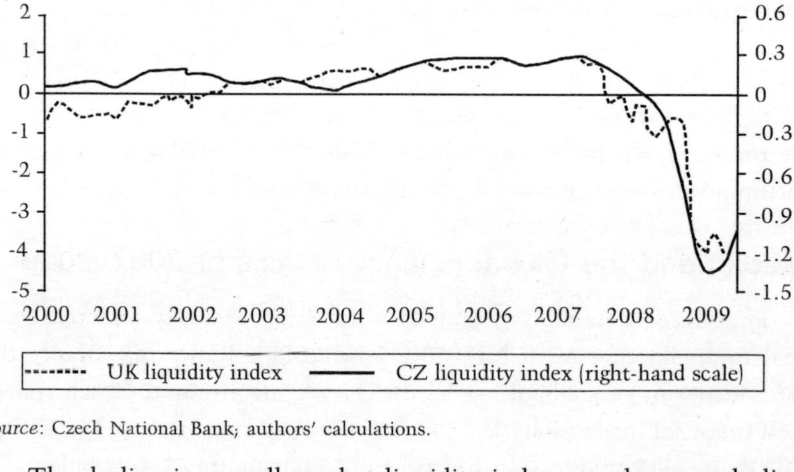

Source: Czech National Bank; authors' calculations.

The decline in overall market liquidity index was due to a decline in all market liquidity sub-indices for individual market segments (Figure 17.4). While in the FX market the decline in liquidity was driven by a combination of wider spreads and a sudden increase in volatility, in the money market it was driven by several simultaneous factors. Bid-offer spreads widened at all maturities from 10 basis points to around 30 basis points, all interbank rates with longer maturities started significantly exceeding the monetary policy rate, trading decreased at maturities longer than one week, and activity was concentrated mostly in the overnight segment. Trading activity decreased and bid-ask spreads widened also in the stock market.

Figure 17.4

Partial Market Liquidity Indices for the Czech Financial Markets

(in standard deviations from historical average)

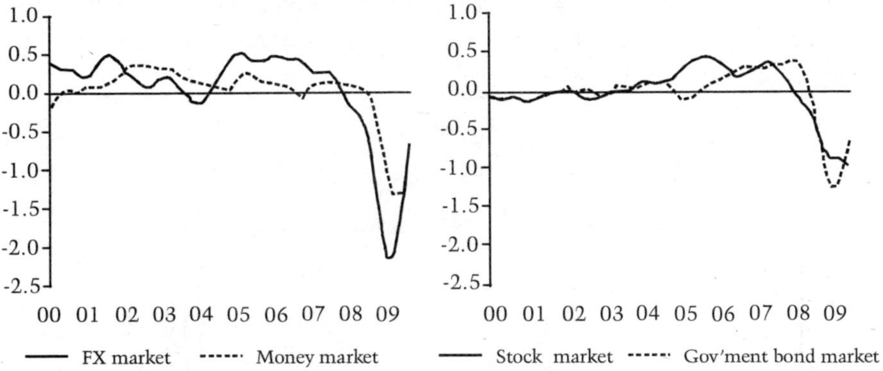

Sources: Czech National Bank; authors' calculations.

Market liquidity problems were also observed in the Czech government bond market. In mid-October 2008, in a situation of excess government bond supply in the market, particularly on the part of foreign institutional investors,[19] market-makers' bid-offer spread widened from the usual 20 basis points to about 300 points. This widespread temporarily almost paralysed trading in this market via market-makers (CNB, 2009).[20]

As a whole, the Czech banking system recorded no major balance sheet liquidity difficulties. There were no bank runs, panics or large withdrawals of liquidity from bank accounts by households and firms.[21] However, the deterioration in market liquidity led to concerns about fund availability and decreased confidence in financial institutions. This stimulated liquidity hoarding, leading to an increased concentration of liquidity in a small group of banks. Thus, as a result of declining market liquidity, the funding liquidity risk increased. This has been reflected in the decrease in the overall liquidity withdrawn in the CNB two-week repo tenders.

The MIFL calculated across all banks for each day of the tender measures the risk of an outflow of balance sheet liquidity for the banking sector as a whole. Figure 17.5 shows that this risk increased primarily in 2008/Q3 and early 2009, when banks' interest in entering tenders with the CNB decreased and if they did enter them, it had to be at a price close to the maximum rate (i.e., the AB equals 0 and thus the MIFL equals 5). The spikes in December 2007 and early 2008 correspond to days where there have been some frictions already in the global markets, the December one partly explained by end-of-year effects.

Figure 17.5

Market Index of Funding Liquidity (MIFL)

(tender's MIFL, Range between 0 and 5)

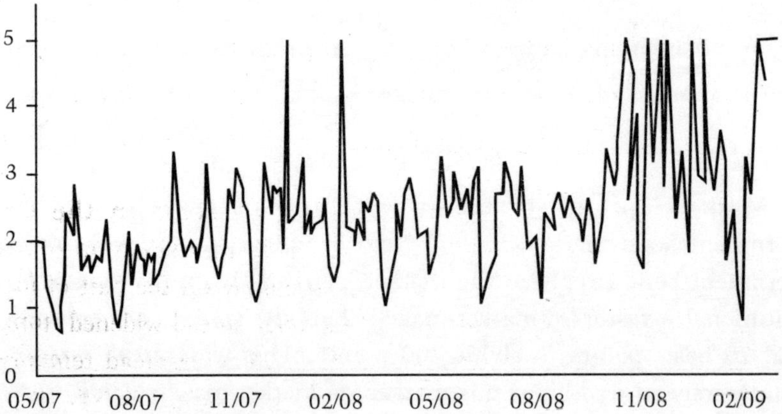

Sources: Czech National Bank; authors' calculations.

The MIFL indicator supports increased concerns regarding a shortage of liquid funds on the market and the hoarding of liquid funds by banks in response to the worsening market situation following the September 2008 events. We can document a downward spiral between funding liquidity risk and market liquidity by juxtaposing the MIFL for each day and the market liquidity index. Figure 17.6 confirms some correlation between market and balance sheet liquidity risk perceived in the whole banking sector (as measured by the MIFL) of around -53 per cent (statistically significant at 1 per cent level) and shows that the risk of an outflow of balance sheet liquidity increased in the Czech Republic after the collapse of Lehman Brothers in September 2008, a period in which the market liquidity declined as well.

Figure 17.6

Relationship between Market Liquidity and the MIFL

(x-axis: market liquidity index; y-axis: tender's MIFL)

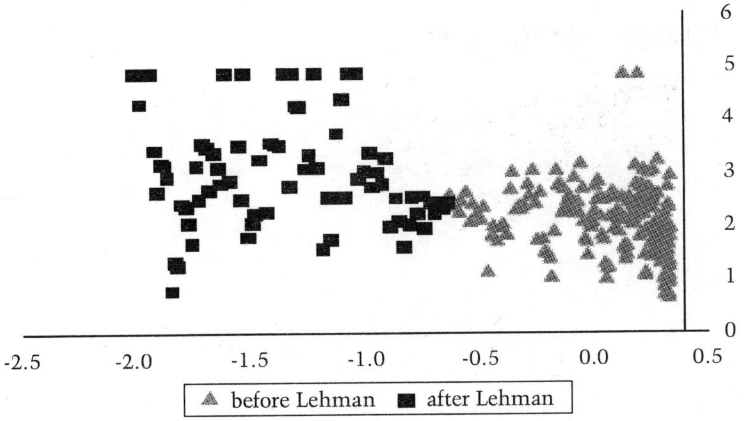

Notes: The individual points are the tender dates (total of 283 points) ranging from 2 May 2007 to 2 March 2009. As the tenders were organized three times a week, the number of the data points is lower than what would correspond to daily frequency.

Sources: Czech National Bank; Bloomberg; authors' calculations.

In October 2008, as a reaction to the evolving adverse liquidity spiral that manifested itself in frictions in the interbank and the government bond market, the CNB introduced a liquidity-providing facility in the form of a fixed rate tender procedure with full allotment at the policy rate plus margin. This new type of operation allowed government bonds to be accepted as collateral (in addition to short-term bills). This helped ease market participants' concerns regarding the potential illiquidity of these securities. This proved useful especially for smaller banks that were lacking liquidity and were unable to find it in the dysfunctional interbank market or secondary government bond market. However, the amounts of the central bank money provided within this facility is much smaller than the volumes that are withdrawn (Figure 17.8). This can be interpreted along two different veins, both positive. First, relatively small amounts of liquidity injections (when compared to liquidity absorbed) were sufficient to improve the liquidity situation. Second, the banking system as a whole was rather resilient to the liquidity problems.

Figure 17.7

Relationship between the "Ratio Indicators" of Funding Liquidity and the MIFL in Two Different Periods of the Crisis

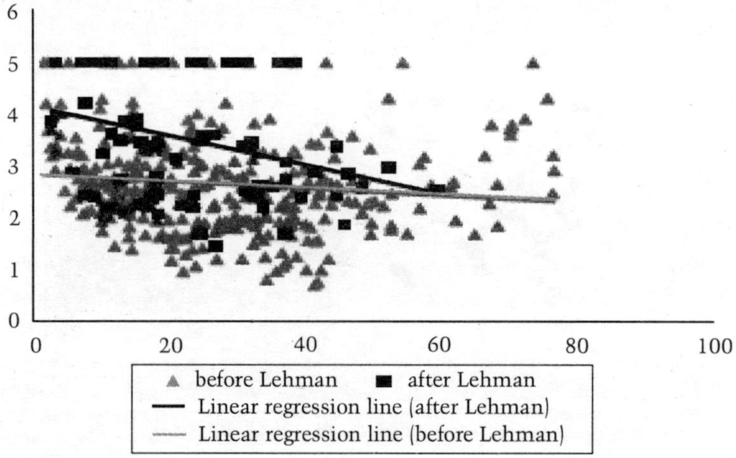

Note: x-axis: average ratios of banks in different months; y-axis: MIFL of banks in the following month.
Sources: Czech National Bank; authors' calculations.

We can also document that those banks that had weaker funding liquidity as measured by the traditional ratio indicators were bidding even more aggressively in the CNB repo tenders after the Lehman Brothers' collapse (Figure 17.7). The linear regression line which shows the relationship between ratio indicators of funding liquidity and the banks' MIFL has steepened in the period between September 2008 and March 2009.[22]

Figure 17.8

CNB: Absorbed versus Provided Liquidity

(in CZK billion, as stock)

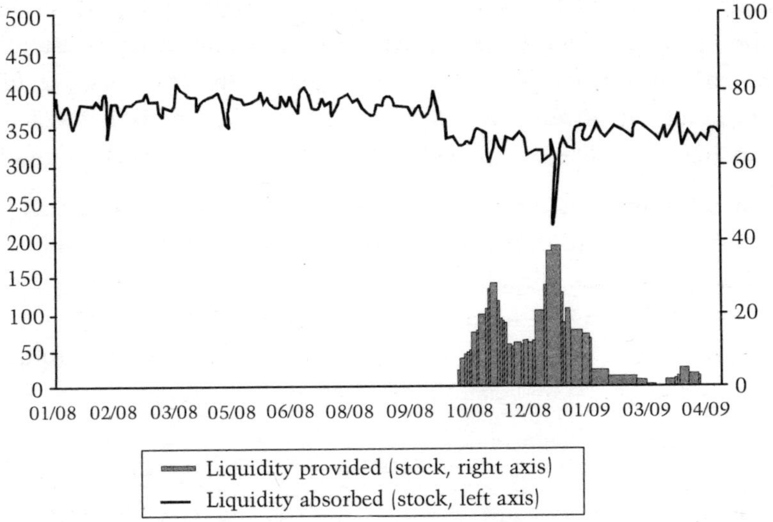

Source: Czech National Bank.

Conclusions

GFC has brought a renewed attention to the liquidity risk and the relationship between market and funding liquidity in banks. The so-called negative liquidity spiral, i.e., situation where declining market liquidity leads to an increase in the risk of funding liquidity outflow, which in turn reinforces the declining trend in market liquidity, emerged to some extent even in countries which were not directly hit by the GFC.

In this paper, we documented the existence of a negative feedback effect between market and funding liquidity in the Czech Republic. We constructed a market-based funding liquidity index using data from banks' bidding behaviour in the repo operations of the Czech National Bank and market liquidity index of Czech financial markets using traditional indicators of market depth, resiliency and tightness. We argue that an assessment of banks' liquidity situation based on selected aggregated ratio indicators should be ideally complemented by some microeconomic analysis that uses individual banks' behavioural data.

The results of the analysis show that in the peak of the financial crisis (i.e., in the two quarters that followed the collapse of Lehman Brothers in September 2008), the indices of market liquidity and funding liquidity showed a significant degree of comovement. However, as the Czech Republic' banking system has a strong balance sheet liquidity position, the magnitude of the adverse liquidity problem was of much lesser extent than in the countries where the crisis originated. To prevent possible further deepening of the adverse liquidity loop, the central bank has reacted by introducing a new liquidity-providing facility which stabilised the markets.

At the same time, it should be emphasised that although there were some signs of adverse liquidity loop, the effect on the banking system was only marginal. The Czech Republic's banking system is one of the strongest in the EU as regards funding liquidity. Czech banks are not dependent on foreign funding and continued to show decent profitability over the whole period of global financial crisis.

Notes

1. For the discussion of relative strengths of the Czech banking system, see CNB (2009).
2. A detailed definition of a liquid market (as applied to the stock market) can be found in Black (1971).
3. Praet and Herzberg (2008) define banking liquidity risk as the inability of a bank to meet outstanding obligations at a reasonable cost. For the discussion on differences between various definitions of funding liquidity and funding liquidity risk, see Drehmann and Nikolaou (2009).
4. The CNB repo rate is the main instrument of Czech monetary policy.
5. The spreads calculated in the above mentioned way include also other risk premia, mainly the credit/counterparty risk premium.
6. We are aware of the fact that higher volatility does not always reflect lower liquidity, but we still see some merit in including it among the variables used to construct the market liquidity index given its relatively high correlation with market liquidity measured by other variables.
7. This index is available from 2000, although until end-2001, it excludes the government bond market, for which data are available only from 2002. (see Section V).
8. Market liquidity indices exist for some emerging markets outside the Central and Eastern European region, usually constructed by the central banks to facilitate their financial stability monitoring. Examples are the stock market liquidity index for China (Lee and Wong, 2009) or market liquidity index for Chile (Banco Central de Chile, 2007: 25).
9. There are also some other less frequent fine-tuning operations and tenders with the maturity of three months.

10. This description was valid only until 7 October 2008, when the ECB changed the operations to a fixed rate tender procedure with full allotment at the policy rate to satisfy any demand for short-term liquidity provided the bank had sufficient collateral. For details, see: *http://www.ecb.int/mopo/implement/omo/html/index.en.html.*

11. To construct an aggregated indicator of funding liquidity risk, Drehmann and Nikolaou (2009), sum the indicator across all banks for each auction.

12. Before May 2006, the CNB repo tenders were conducted daily.

13. If a bank made more than one bid in a single tender or if more than one tender took place in a single day, the bids were averaged.

14. The Czech banking sector consists of 36 banks including branches of foreign banks and specialised savings buildings societies. The 23 banks that participate in the repo operations with the CNB are the most important banks in the country (in terms of both size and activity on the markets), and represent almost 90 per cent of the banking sector assets.

15. We also compared the results using banks' balance sheet ratios and MIFL of the same month and they do not differ.

16. Higher levels of i such as 1E-4 would not produce such a big gap, but there would be a risk of having the same value of MIFL for situations with all banks bidding at marginal rate and situation where, for example, one small bank bids with a positive AB.

17. The UK market liquidity index is constructed as a simple unweighted average of nine liquidity measures, normalised in the period 1999-2004. The series shown is an exponentially weighted moving average (Bank of England, 2007).

18. A comparison with the Euro area, the UK and global market liquidity indices reveals that while the pattern is similar, the global, Euro area and the UK indices increased much more in the 'good' times of low risk aversion and global excess of liquidity in the years 2003-2007 and decreased much more during the global financial crisis 2007-2009 (ECB, 2009: 65, Chart-3.1.; Bank of England, 2009: 5, Chart-1; IMF, 2009: 5, Figure-1.4).

19. Excess market supply of government bonds may have been partly related to a change in the range of collateral accepted by the ECB for operations in the Eurosystem. As the demand for eligible collateral accepted by the ECB increased, the supply of other high quality securities, including Czech government bonds, increased in parallel.

20. The trading volume in the secondary government bond market did not fall, however, trades continued to be carried out through the system of brokers instead of market makers.

21. However, there was a temporary increase in currency in circulation, see CNB (2009).

22. The slope of the relationship changed from -0.006 in the pre-Lehman period to -0.025 in the post-Lehman period. The Chow breakpoint test ($F = 23.9$, prob. $F(2,414)$ =. 0.000) rejects the null hypothesis of no break in the time series in the month of Lehman failure.

References

Banco Central de Chile (2007). *Financial Stability Report.*

Bank of England (2007). *Financial Stability Report.* October.

———. (2009). *Financial Stability Report.* June.

Banque de France (2008). *Financial Stability Review*. Special issue on "Liquidity", No. 11.

Black, F. (1971). "Towards a Fully Automated Stock Exchange", *Financial Analysts Journal* 27(6).

Borio, C. (2000). "Market Liquidity and Stress: Selected Issues and Policy Implications", *BIS Quarterly Review*: 38-51, November.

Brunnermeier, M. and L. Pedersen (2007). "Market Liquidity and Funding Liquidity", *CEPR DP* No. 6179.

Bank for International Settlements (1999). *Market Liquidity: Research Findings and Selected Policy Implications*. Committee on the Global Financial System Publications No. 11.

CNB (2008). *Financial Stability Report 2007*.

———. (2009). *Financial Stability Report 2008/2009*.

Drehmann, M. and K. Nikolaou (2009). "Funding Liquidity Risk: Definition and Measurement", *ECB WP* No. 1024.

ECB (2007). *Financial Stability Review*. December.

———. (2008) *Financial Stability Review*. June.

———. (2009). *Financial Stability Review*. June.

Fleming, Michael J. (2003). "Measuring Treasury Market Liquidity", *Economic Policy Review* 9(3): 83-108.

Frank, N., B. González-Hermosillo and H. Hesse (2008). "Transmission of Liquidity Shocks: Evidence from the 2007 Sub-prime Crisis", *International Monetary Fund Working Paper* No. 08/2008.

IMF (2009). "Global Financial Stability Report: Responding to the Financial Crisis and Measuring Systemic Risks", *World Economic and Financial Surveys*. Washington D.C.:, International Monetary Fund.

International Monetary Fund (2008a). *Global Financial Stability Report*. April.

———. (2008b). *Global Financial Stability Report*. October.

Kyle, A. (1985). "Continuous Auctions and Insider Trading", *Econometrica* 53(6).

Lee, J. and A. Wong (2009). "Impact of Financial Liberalization on Stock Market Liquidity: Experience of China", *Working Paper* No. 03/2009. Hong Kong Monetary Authority.

Magyar Nemzeti Bank (2009). *Financial Stability Review*. November.

Nyborg, K.G. and I.A. Strebulaev (2004). "Multiple Unit Auctions and Short Squeezes", *The Review of Financial Studies* 17(2): 545–80.

Páles, J. and L. Varga (2008). "Trends in the Liquidity of Hungarian Financial Markets: What does the MNB's New Liquidity Index Show?", *MNB Bulletin*. April.

Praet, P. and V. Herzberg (2008). "Market Liquidity and Banking Liquidity: Linkages, Vulnerabilities and the Role of Disclosure", *Financial Stability Review*—Special issue on "liquidity", No. 11. Banque de France

---

Acknowledgement: This chapter has been published as an article in the Czech Journal of Economics and Finance 59(6)/2009 (see the web site *http://journal fsv.cuni.cz/mag/article/show/id/1176)*.